59:1 · · April 2021

T0327109

ENGLISH LANGUAGE NOTES

Transhistoricizing Claude McKay's
Romance in Marseille

GARY EDWARD HOLCOMB AND WILLIAM J. MAXWELL, Special Issue Editors

Of Note: Slavery and the Archive

Transhistoricizing Claude McKay's *Romance in Marseille*

Introduction to the Special Issue

GARY EDWARD HOLCOMB AND WILLIAM J. MAXWELL

Contexts: Gary Edward Holcomb

In February 2020 Penguin Classics published the Harlem Renaissance author Claude McKay's *Romance in Marseille*, a novel that had idled in an archive for nearly ninety years.[1] We believe that the debut of this work of fiction, until recently effectively unknown, may stimulate several critical areas, not only Harlem Renaissance studies but also dialogues across queer, disability, feminist, Marxist, postcolonial, Afro-Orientalist, Black Atlantic, and transatlantic modernist scholarship. As we hope the reader of this special issue will see, McKay's circa 1929–33 text also offers a fecund analytic subject to critics working in Afropessimisim, primitivism, reparations, and surveillance, as well as such emergent approaches as maritime modernism and the politics of pleasure.

As *Romance in Marseille* is a good candidate for an analysis that is not necessarily obliged to a strictly historicist approach, our call for papers welcomed scholarship that explored how McKay's recovered novel offers transhistorical ways of seeing. The novel's near-century-long absence, synthesized with its pertinence to current critical concerns, speaks volumes to a range of past and present moments. The media reception of *Romance in Marseille* proved to be a popular analogue to our interest in welcoming transhistorical readings. Feted for its ability to speak with clarity to the present, not least in its depiction of the persistent crisis of Black bodies under siege, *Romance in Marseille* has shown a considerable suppleness for being read as both an artifact of its historical moment and a work of fiction that acutely resonates with present reading communities.

We first learned of McKay's novel through reading Wayne F. Cooper's indispensable 1987 biography, *Claude McKay: Rebel Sojourner of the Harlem Renaissance*, a text that glosses the obstacles McKay faced while trying to publish it.[2] But *Romance in Marseille*'s adversities ranged even beyond the death of the all-but-forgotten fifty-eight-year-old author in 1948. The final hurdle took the form of the McKay Literary Estate being compelled to prevent a UK university press from publishing the novel, a wrangle that seemed doomed to drag on indefinitely. Over the years, we would

ENGLISH LANGUAGE NOTES

59:1, April 2021 DOI 10.1215/00138282-8814950

check on the legal dispute's status and learn that the UK press had refused to budge. Like a soul on ice, *Romance in Marseille* remained interned in its archival vault at the historic New York Public Library Black studies collection, Harlem's Schomburg Center for Research in Black Culture.

Having all but given up, we were happily amazed five years ago when the estate related to us that the UK press had withdrawn and we had the green light to move forward. The timing was ripe, after all, as a shorter typescript of the novel had surfaced at Yale's Beinecke Rare Book and Manuscript Library. Equally propitious, Jean-Christophe Cloutier, a Columbia PhD student, had uncovered in a Columbia University library archive McKay's lost novel *Amiable with Big Teeth* (2017), a satirical fiction set in Harlem during the Second Italo-Ethiopian War.[3] Cloutier and his research adviser, the Black transnational studies scholar Brent Hayes Edwards, went on to coedit an edition for Penguin Classics. *Amiable with Big Teeth* attracted substantial media enthusiasm, both before and after publication,[4] and Penguin's success with McKay's circa-1941 satire unquestionably paved our way. In the spring of 2018 Penguin Classics signed *Romance*, an artifact known to only a handful of Harlem Renaissance scholars.

Our own research unearthed the unabridged tale of the nightmare of a time McKay had trying to get *Romance in Marseille* into print, not least being objections to placing an African double amputee, brutally cut down at the Ellis Island immigration hospital, at the heart of the narrative. The book's troubles were exacerbated by the inclusion of a motley, intersecting, and, to some, objectionable cast of female and male sex laborers, Black and white radicals, and an array of lesbian and gay characters—despite the title, all deromanticized, including the disabled protagonist, and portrayed in the frankest manner. Correspondence revealed that its various designations, first "The Jungle and the Bottoms," and then "Savage Loving," and finally "Romance in Marseille," came about partly because of McKay's attempts to adapt to publishers', editors', agents', friends', and kibitzers' bemusement over and, in some cases, downright antipathy for the text.

Two busy years later Penguin Classics released the novel as its 2020 Black History Month selection. It's a safe bet that the satirist in McKay would have enjoyed the irony of seeing a major Manhattan publisher take on a tale that the early 1930s New York publishing industry had roundly spurned and then, a still more astounding development, witnessing the once nixed novel become an instant success with the metropolis's mass media. The buzzing began with the *New York Times* preview titled "A Book So Far Ahead of Its Time, It Took Eighty-Seven Years to Find a Publisher." Talya Zax's article introduced a conceit that went viral—that *Romance in Marseille* resonates with present issues.[5] The two-sentence headline of *Washington Post* writer Michael Dirda's February 5 online preview echoes the "ahead of its time" trope: "Claude McKay abandoned 'Romance in Marseille' because it was too daring. He was just ahead of his time." The Pulitzer-winning critic's declaration that McKay's early Great Depression text is "woke" propelled the Penguin Classic into living social and aesthetic discourses: "Today *Romance in Marseille* seems less shocking than strikingly woke, given that its themes include disability, the full spectrum of sexual preference, radical politics and the subtleties of racial identity."[6]

New York magazine writer Molly Young's preview, consummately titled "The Best New Novel Was Written Ninety Years Ago," also articulates the idea of *Romance* finally finding its moment. The "Vulture" section article articulates a kind of post-millennial hipster's genial irony in response to an obscure, near-century-old work of art—so queer, Black, and differently abled—appearing so well into the twenty-first century: "If you skipped the introduction and surrendered access to Google, you could easily mistake it for a novel written last year. It's about bodies, disability, sex, Islam, slavery, and capital. There are lesbians. There is gender-bending. There is socialism."[7] It seems likely, moreover, that McKay would have relished the irony of no less a symbol of American capitalism than the *Wall Street Journal* printing a sensitive, insightful appraisal of his Black anarchist fiction. Proffering lyricism for epic, reviewer Sam Sacks deems *Romance* "as heady and bewitching as the scene of a Vieux Port dance floor."[8]

Nearly ninety years after its composition and rejection, *Romance in Marseille* became a model transhistorical neomodernist text, one that seemed capable of dancing a nimble beguine between temporal breaking points. The novel may claim more than a single past: first it failed to achieve a readership; then for decades both its shorter version and its lengthier revision sat in a state of suspension on New Haven and New York library shelves; and then its indefinite detention, exacerbated by what all thought an irreconcilable legal dispute. And it now lays claim to its *awokened* present, where it speaks to contemporary readers.

Young's insight into the public reception of *Romance in Marseille* imagines two readers. The first has read the prefatory and supplementary matter, and accordingly appreciates as a vital constituent of the text the novel's historical struggle to be born. The other ignores the complementary resources and simply reads the primary text, putting off engaging with the supporting materials until later, if at all, and consequently responding to the text almost as if it were a work of art without a past. But an appreciation of *Romance in Marseille*'s initial extratextual debates and then years of neglect, its former obscurity finally aggravated by its legal quarantine, should disabuse the notion that the current reader may fancy engaging with an untouched artifact. No reader comes to *Romance in Marseille* in a virtuous reading condition because, bearing in mind the struggles the text endured in its passage from the archive into the public sphere and why the obstacles against its realization occurred, no chaste version of the novel exists or ever did. Yet *Romance in Marseille* still qualifies as a contemporary work of art, because this transhistorical classic contains several pasts, none of which may claim it exclusively.

Of all the media responses, the *New York Times* truly fell for *Romance in Marseille*, its motivation consistently having to do with the novel's transhistorical dexterity. In all, the Penguin Classic racked up six *Times* notices, easily the most anomalous being an interview with Joseph Stiglitz on his reading interests. The Nobel Prize–winning Georgist economist admits that he doesn't read much literary writing but mentions that, following a conversation about *Things Fall Apart*, his newly formed reading group will be discussing *Romance in Marseille*.[9] The noteworthy implication is that Achebe's definitive postcolonial classic is being paired with McKay's instant classic for comparative purposes. The most thought-provoking of the newspaper's *Romance* references, however, was an article tackling the topic of defining the classic in multicultural terms. To brand a novel that was never in print a "classic," the very term must undergo a radical reappraisal. As "Penguin Classics and Others Work to Diversify Offerings from the Canon" suggests, a classic in the sense that the Penguin imprint traditionally has used the term is effectively synonymous with *canonical*.[10] Over the past few years, however, Penguin Classics has been expanding the category. Salvaging works by African American, Asian American, Latinx, and other writers—from Nella Larsen to Carlos Bulosan—that were denied a place in the Western or US canon, Penguin Classics has redefined the notion of indispensable literary writing.[11] In publisher Elda Rotor's words: "We're seeing what people are expecting from us, and we want to bring those stories, and a more diverse and inclusive program of stories, into our series."[12]

In view of its capacious, militant cosmopolitanism—composed in Spain and Morocco and set in Manhattan and Marseille—it is fitting that the fascination with *Romance* roamed beyond New York literary culture. *Romance*'s global notice materialized as widely as the United Kingdom, Canada, Greece, Italy, India, Australia, Argentina, and McKay's homeland, Jamaica. Of special pride for us, the *Gleaner*, where McKay published his early vernacular poetry, issued an editorial stating that the novel should stir a national discussion of homophobia in the island nation: "More than seven decades after McKay's death and 91 years after he began writing his novel, the logic of a 156-year-old buggery law, which encroaches on the rights of the individual, diminishes the humanity of a large segment of [Jamaica's] citizens and might have caused him to be jailed, isn't sustainable."[13] In another measure of the novel's queer transhistoricism, the LGBTQ activist site Lambda Literary applauded the novel's vanguard "pansexual" content.[14] And the book's first academic review, praising its internationalist themes, appropriately came out on May Day in the Routledge journal *American Communist History*.[15]

By late March, however, another version of the novel had begun to resonate with reviewers and readers. *Vanity Fair*'s March 25 listing of the Great Depression text as one of its "Great Quarantine Reads" sums up the next phase of *Romance*'s reception.[16] Similarly, in advance of that other day in May, Mother's Day, *New York* magazine's "The Strategist," no doubt inspired by Young's Vulture section review, recommended *Romance* as an online-accessible gift suggestion for offspring who have the sense to observe early hunker-in-place orders.[17] Given the early April date of the *Times* article about Stiglitz's reading list, the mentioned reading group likely turned out to be a Zoom affair, the kind of lockdown exchange that soon would become all too familiar. The *Romance* e-audiobook, vividly read by *Wire* actor Dion Graham, earns a mention in an early April Bookriot.com piece starkly titled "How Audiobooks Are Getting Me through COVID-19." "My eyes," fatigued by "anxiety, sadness, anger," might "have glazed over reading it," confesses Laura Sackton, "but my ears took it in with delight."[18] An October 2020 *Los Angeles Review of Books* interview with the editors of this special issue tackles the grim question of how the narrative's portrayal of Black, disabled, sex laboring, and queer folk, barely existing at the margins of a germinal global capitalism, potentially bespeaks a bleak new existence.[19]

When the virus became our essential social reality, the response to and the character of *Romance in Marseille* adapted to the new exigency, its pansexuality conscripted against the pandemic. As the Penguin Classic took on the dubious celebrity of a plague text, it was as if *Romance* had made its way from the archive to remind us of the transhistorical imperative that the struggles of the oppressed *to be heard* are always in need of committed support and recuperation.

Contents: William J. Maxwell

The eleven academic essays contained in this issue of *ELN*—some of the first ever written on *Romance in Marseille*—treat the novel as an aid to thought rather than a gift to celebrate. Admiration for McKay's condensed lyricism and fertile social imagination isn't always hidden in these essays: that much has been sanctioned by the typically positive affect of literary recovery projects and by the allowances of the recent postcritical turn. But all of the contributions press the novel into service as a tool for thinking anew about McKay's career as a free-range artist-intellectual, and about the many active areas of cultural research that this career predicts and illuminates. Jesse W. Schwartz's essay "'Broken Bits of Color in the Dirt'" leads the way for several reasons: its explicit location in a pandemic present, making common cause with the second wave of *Romance*'s first popular reviews; its equally explicit transhistoricism, assuming that the crises of the past "may not exactly repeat" themselves but that some historical "similarities feel a bit richer than rhyme"; and its status as a kind of theory and anatomy of approaches to situating *Romance* in the intersectional now. "The narrative of *Romance*," concedes Schwartz, "seems to unravel as it approaches various problematics of difference simultaneously." Yet he concludes that in McKay's inability to premaster what we've learned to call intersectionality, "all is not lost." "If the novel and its resonances have returned like a welcoming ghost from an inhospitable machine," McKay also sketches "the outlines of a dialectical 'Black Intersectional International'"—one that reckons with "various differences [in] their entanglement, conjoining without flattening them through the twinned technologies of pleasure and care, and thereby gesturing toward a 'commonism' of the quayside." On Schwartz's version of McKay's Marseille waterfront, erotic and protective attachments to the unmeltable ethnic differences among roving Black populations offer a model for assimilating disparities of culture, gender, sexuality, and political affiliation without blurring all lines of separation.

Schwartz's prelude is followed by a pair of essays that share his interest in the embodied politics of pleasure and care. The first, Agnieszka Tuszynska's "'A Syrup of Passion and Desire,'" roots its queer inquiry in the matrix of postcolonial as well as Black cultural theory. It begins with an enlightening comparison between themes of bodily disintegration in McKay's *Romance* and Frantz Fanon's later essay "The Fact of Blackness" but ironically navigates toward Achille Mbembe's death-haunted necropolitics to clarify McKay's relatively sanguine portrait of sexual desire and fulfillment. For the Black Jamaican–turned–Black world novelist, Tuszynska claims, visions of unshackled sexual expression are not racist obsessions but channels for "legitimizing the selfhood of the socially marginalized characters who populate Marseille's Old Port." The liberating realism of *Romance*'s split focus on the "body-in-pain and body-in-pleasure," Tuszynska determines, is best gauged "by examining the way Mbembe seriously considers the concept of social death yet also pushes against it as a definition of Black ontology." Eric H. Newman's "A Queer Romance" ups the ante of such advocacy of McKay's nonutopian queer positivity. The same-sex romances on the margins of McKay's *Romance*, Newman argues, are the novel's central examples of self-exceeding love and egalitarian social relations. What's more, they outdo the queer likenesses of McKay's earlier, far-better-known novels *Banjo* (1929) and *Home to Harlem* (1928) in both particularity and suggested normalcy. In the last analysis, Newman's abstract submits, *Romance in Marseille* is nothing less than "one of the most sustained [and] nuanced representations of queer life in McKay's archive and in early twentieth-century LGBT literature more generally." If for Newman justice is served, McKay's second Penguin Classic will become his first undisputed queer classic.

The next essay, Laura Ryan's "'A Little Civilization in My Pocket,'" takes up a crucial if implicit element in Tuszynska's and Newman's variations on the theme of McKay's sexology: his engagement with the always racialized and sexualized discourse of primitivism. In particular Ryan complicates the ongoing complication of primitivism most identified with the Australian critic Ben Etherington, who has revisited this long-disreputable modern ism as a productive aesthetic weapon for colonized writers as much as an othering fantasy of the imperial West. Ryan finds value in the spirit of Etherington's revisionism but finds its letter challenged by *Romance in Marseille*. There, she contends, the festive "strategic primitivism" of *Home to Harlem* and *Banjo* is abandoned in favor of a thoroughgoing Depression-era deconstruction of the primitive/civilized opposition—a deconstruction that should also shake McKay's status, reinforced by Etherington, as the New Negro novelist most attracted to primitivism as a double-edged sword to be seized by the racially oppressed. Stephanie J. Brown's essay, "Marseille Exposed," similarly employs *Romance* to advance a reenergized and consequential scholarly debate at the crossroads of race and biopower: in her case, the debate over the racialization of surveillance, or what Simone Browne has labeled the "dark matter" of Black bodies and texts overseen during and after slavery. *Romance in Marseille*, Brown maintains, pleads the case that modern racial surveillance involved "a set of overlapping practices by various agents—the state, the transnational corporation, and a range of other private interests—that constrain[ed] the flourishing of Black migrant lives in the transatlantic world." More unexpectedly, she views McKay's novel as a type of historical diagram tracing how the corporation came to take the leading role in the operation of this complicated panoptical machinery. With its "increasingly global reach into already existing systems of surveillance—from migration checks at national borders to social surveillance among more local interests in Marseille and New York"—the far-seeing international corporation becomes *Romance*'s single most powerful antagonist. Brown's own transhistorical lens, then, reveals McKay's novel as an ingenious, never-tedious history of perhaps the decisive shift in the administration of punitive surveillance in the twentieth century.

The trio of essays following Brown's compose a loosely joined suite exploring the sea, one prime location of the surveillance that troubles Lafala, McKay's cruelly disabled, eventually wealthy, but never-idealized protagonist. Rich Cole's contribution, "Claude McKay's Bad Nationalists," begins with McKay's own boarding of a ship heading from Spain to Morocco and lands on the problem of McKay's self-declared "bad nationalism," a cosmopolitan faith he cultivated just as Black nationalists in the mode of Marcus Garvey set their sights on transatlantic African repatriation. With an eye to the full range of both McKay's imaginative writing and the material history of "transatlantic shipping damages," Cole unveils a *Romance* in which a postcolonized call of the sea inspires Middle Passage–reversing returns to Africa—all the while threatening legal stasis and practically deracializing personal isolation. "The act of litigative justice" that makes the legless Lafala a rich and mobile man, Cole declares, counts at once "as a success consistent with the tenets of liberal individualism" and as a failure consistent with "the realization that there was no longer a recognizable home or community back in Africa for Lafala to return to."

Like Cole's essay, Nissa Ren Cannon's "'No Man's Ocean Ever Did Get the Best of Me'" mines a rich seam of originally nonliterary history to explain *Romance*'s ocean voyages and symbols. Cannon demonstrates that during the same years in which McKay wrote his novel based in part on a Nigerian stowaway's horrific imprisonment on the Fabre Line, Fabre brochures promised paying Euro-American passengers "roomy, airy" cabins and dining rooms complete with "fine French cuisine and pleasing service." *Romance in Marseille*, then, qualifies as an anti-advertisement exposing the barbarism belowdecks that underwrote the conspicuously consumed civilization of the luxury liner. In Cannon's estimation, however, *Romance* is also a handbook to areas of underdevelopment in twenty-first-century maritime and oceanic studies, each of which would do well to apply McKay's text transhistorically to allow for the possibility of "hybrid figures of both labor and leisure." By the time that Lafala's transatlantic tale is through, she observes, he has sailed the ocean not only as a common seaman and frostbitten prisoner but also as "the rare Black man traveling first class." Instructively, however, during all of these journeys, whether sealed in the hold or pampered on an upper deck, the body blows of race are never avoided entirely. Laura Winkiel's "Shoreline Thinking," the final essay in the trio dealing with *Romance* and the sea, breaks from Cannon's in its focus on reification and the limits of fungible liberal subjectivity. Instead of Lafala's incomplete transition from shipboard labor to leisure, Winkiel concentrates on McKay's figures of "flotsam and jetsam" and the transubstantiation of enslaved bodies into the thingified objects they signify. "The social logic and history of racialized disposability alluded to by these terms," she shows, is a core preoccupation of McKay's shoreline text. Paradoxically, so is its proposal that "this long history of expendability contains the seeds of a transformation of Black life via lateral and reciprocal relations with humans and nonhumans alike." When Lafala pictures Aslima, his North African lover, as a "rare tropical garden" during their last meeting, he draws from an old, stereotypical well to link a Black female body with visceral nature. More tellingly, he also assembles "the human and nonhuman in a coterminous and transformative relation," typifying what Winkiel, one of the architects of oceanic studies, dubs the "alluvial" or overflowing quality of *Romance*'s fluidly interpenetrating beings and things.

A pair of essays on McKay's urbane but never landlocked Afro-Orientalism follows the trio on *Romance in Marseille* at sea. Zainab Cheema's "Mooring Aslima" foregrounds the waters of the Mediterranean along with "the Moroccan sex worker whom Lafala loves and leaves over the course of the novel." The "in-between positionality" of Aslima—both courtesan and true lover, Arab and African, faithfully Islamic and constitutionally secular—personifies what Cheema describes as "the trans-Mediterranean diaspora that linked Iberia and North Africa from the eighth-century conquest of Iberia and Provence to the waves of expulsion of Iberian Moors, Jews, conversos, and Moriscos after the 1492 Reconquista." Her essay thus combines a postcolonial feminist take on the most compelling of McKay's many "Orientalized Black women" with deep knowledge of the interreligious Spanish-Moroccan history in which he wrote and partly set his text. The result is a unique account of the implications of *Romance*'s "Maurophilia," the love affair with real and romanticized traces of Moorish forms in Spanish culture first named by Barbara Fuchs. Like Cheema's contribution, David B. Hobbs's "Lyric Commodification in McKay's Morocco" profits from a familiarity with the history of the Maghreb that the editors of *Romance in Marseille* cannot be said to possess. More specifically, Hobbs's essay complements Cheema's in traveling between McKay's novel and his Moroccan-set verse of the 1930s. The publication of *Romance*, Hobbs volunteers, affords "a chance to draw on [McKay's] fiction to help understand his much-neglected late poetry" by fostering "a fuller impression of McKay's years in Africa." McKay's understudied "Cities" sonnets, closely reread in the shadow of *Romance*, place the North African urban spaces of Tétouan and Fez, Marrakech and Tangier, in the position of Aslima, all fated to dream within walled confines and to craft "a cautious but indelible sense of Black liberation within the urban grid." Reworking McKay's novel as a springboard into his late Orientalist verse, Hobbs ultimately interprets the Moroccan city sonnets as a challenge to the usual story of McKay's neat transition from a classically young "poet in the 1910s and early 1920s to a best-selling novelist in the late 1920s and the 1930s." Incongruously enough, in Hobbs's analysis, the publication of another mature McKay novel reminds us that he was a lifelong author of searching, globetrotting lyric poems.

The final essay in the issue appropriately considers what some present-day voices have insisted is the final chapter of the recuperative tradition of Black literary study: Afropessimism. Michael J. Collins's theoretically elaborated "Afropessimism, Liminal Hotspots, and Claude McKay's Aesthetic of Sovereign Rejection in *Romance in Marseille*" plainly flags its major thesis in its first sentence. *Romance*, it reads, is properly regarded as "a novel whose main thematic engagements are not with liberation, freedom, and the transformative potential of desire but with the transtemporal persistence of an anti-Blackness that inflicts on the Black subject a condition of 'endless kinetic movement' and rejection from sovereignty." Collins understands McKay's fiction as a precocious illustration of what Afropessimists from Jared Sexton to Frank B. Wilderson regard as the permanent, ontologically fixed nature of Western Afrophobia. He couches Lafala's costly acceptance of personal reparations after his amputation as a departure from McKay's early Marxism, a memorable symbolic lesson that "anti-Black racism operates as something more than a consequence of economic inequality." Collins himself departs from something like the main line of Afropessimistic thought in fusing its logic with the anthropological category of the "liminal hotspot," defined by Monica Greco and Paul Stenner in 2017 as a space and occasion "characterised by the experience of being trapped in the interstitial dimension between different forms-of-process."[20] Put more directly in relation to *Romance*, Collins resolves that McKay's novel is shot through with an always pressing but always arrested longing for existential development, a state of petrified mobility in which "Black children are on the cusp of a new being but are kept from that final status by being subjected to endless motion." To Collins's mind, the extended liminal hotspot that opens between *Romance*'s covers finally implies that "anti-Blackness operates within colonialism by suspending the imaginary of precolonial Black sovereignty" without ever allowing "Black being fully into the fold of modern power." In this McKay novel, at least, the Black colonial condition hangs precariously between equally tempting, equally unreachable pre- and postcolonial objectives.

Which is not to say that Collins denies the general interpretive value of transhistoricism—among other things, a concept that reserves the possibility of escaping suspension within a single, stationary, and securely bounded historical frame. When considering *Romance* as evidence of changes in McKay's thought, Collins proposes that the novel bookmarks "a distinctive, specifically pessimistic, phase of McKay's career in which 'Home,'" in Harlem or elsewhere, "is dwelled on as a philosophical impossibility." Such a phase indeed chimes transtemporally with Afropessmism and other intellectual artifacts of our age "of Trump, the new Right, and the supposed failures of the Obama era." In this, like the articles before it, Collins's essay imagines *Romance in Marseille* as a text simultaneously of, after, and somewhat against its own time, a transtemporal key in novelistic form unlocking previously hidden moments in both McKay's writing life and the evolving life of the paradigms, disciplines, and crises through which we currently read it. Taken together, the ingredients of this special issue—eleven distinct but mutually illuminating ways of looking at *Romance*—testify that McKay was a bad historicist in the same ironic and honorific sense in which he was a bad nationalist. Much as his commitment to violating the national stemmed from his brilliant observation of its inescapable effects, his firm grasp of the shaping pressure of historical immediacy sparked a desire to break tired laws of the historical imagination—above all, those laws that would restrict *Romance in Marseille* and similar historical fictions to summoning just one isolated moment at a time. To paraphrase the moral of McKay's sonnet "To the Intrenched Classes," written in modernism's very good year of 1922, history's past-beset "power is legion, but it cannot crush," because "mine is the future grinding down today" (lines 1, 9).[21]

GARY EDWARD HOLCOMB is professor of African American literature and studies at Ohio University. He is author of *Claude McKay, Code Name Sasha: Queer Black Marxism and the Harlem Renaissance* (2007), coeditor of *Hemingway and the Black Renaissance* (2012), and editor of *Teaching Hemingway and Race* (2018). With William J. Maxwell he coedited McKay's circa 1929–33 novel *Romance in Marseille* (2020), and with Brooks Hefner he is coediting the McKay letters.

WILLIAM J. MAXWELL is professor of English and African and African American studies at Washington University in St. Louis, where he teaches modern American and African American literatures. He is author of *F.B. Eyes: How J. Edgar Hoover's Ghostreaders Framed African American Literature* (2015), which won an American Book Award in 2016, and *New Negro, Old Left: African American Writing and Communism between the Wars* (1999). He is editor of the collection *James Baldwin: The FBI File* (2017); of Claude McKay's *Complete Poems* (2004, 2008, 2013); and, along with Gary Edward Holcomb, of McKay's previously unpublished novel *Romance in Marseille* (2020).

Notes

1   McKay, *Romance in Marseille*.
2   Cooper, *Claude McKay*.
3   McKay, *Amiable with Big Teeth*.
4   See Lee, "New Novel of Harlem Renaissance Is Found."
5   Zax, "A Book So Far Ahead of Its Time." The print version came out two days later: Zax, "Far Ahead of Its Time, and Finally Published."
6   Dirda, "Claude McKay Abandoned 'Romance in Marseille.'"
7   Young, "The Best New Novel."
8   Sacks, review.
9   *New York Times*, "The Nobel-Winning Economist."
10 de León, "Penguin Classics and Others."
11 Larsen, *Passing*; Bulosan, *America Is in the Heart*.
12 de León, "Penguin Classics and Others."
13 See James, *Holding Aloft the Banner of Ethiopia*, 27–28.
14 Kaler, "Claude McKay's *Romance in Marseille*."
15 Levin, review.
16 *Vanity Fair*, "Thirty-One Great Quarantine Reads."
17 *New York*, "Seventy-Nine Gifts for Every Type of Mom."
18 Sackton, "How Audiobooks Are Getting Me through COVID-19."
19 Holcomb and Maxwell, "Claude McKay in Our Time."
20 Greco and Stenner, "From Paradox to Pattern Shift."
21 McKay, "To the Intrenched Classes."

Works Cited

Bulosan, Carlos. *America Is in the Heart*. New York: Penguin, 2019.
Cooper, Wayne F. *Claude McKay: Rebel Sojourner in the Harlem Renaissance; A Biography*. Baton Rouge: Louisiana State University Press, 1987.
de León, Concepción. "Penguin Classics and Others Work to Diversify Offerings from the Canon." *New York Times*, March 30, 2020. www.nytimes.com/2020/03/30/books/diverse-canon-penguin-classics.html.
Dirda, Michael. "Claude McKay Abandoned 'Romance in Marseille' Because It Was Too Daring. He Was Just Ahead of His Time." *Washington Post*, February 5, 2020. www.washingtonpost.com/entertainment/books/claude-mckay-abandoned-romance-in-marseille-because-it-was-too-daring-he-was-just-ahead-of-his-time/2020/02/05/1c215cc4-46a1-11ea-ab15-b5df3261b710_story.html.
Gleaner. "Claude McKay's New Relevance to Jamaica." February 13, 2020. jamaica-gleaner.com/article/commentary/20200213/editorial-claude-mckays-new-relevance-jamaica.
Greco, Monica, and Paul Stenner. "From Paradox to Pattern Shift: Conceptualizing Liminal Hotspots and Their Affective Dynamics." *Theory and Psychology* 27, no. 2 (2017): 147–66.
Holcomb, Gary Edward, and William J. Maxwell. "Claude McKay in Our Time: A Conversation with Gary Holcomb and William J. Maxwell on 'Romance in Marseille.'" Interview. *Los Angeles Review of Books*, October 23, 2020. lareviewofbooks.org/article/claude-mckay-time-gary-holcomb-william-j-maxwell-romance-marseille.
James, Winston. *Holding Aloft the Banner of Ethiopia: Caribbean Radicalism in Early Twentieth-Century America*. New York: Verso, 1998.
Kaler, Michael. "Claude McKay's *Romance in Marseille* Charts the Misadventures of an Eclectic Bunch of Social Outcasts." *Lambda Literary*, March 15, 2020. www.lambdaliterary.org/2020/03/romance-in-marseille.
Larsen, Nella. *Passing*, edited by Thadious M. Davis. New York: Penguin, 2003.
Lee, Felicia R. "New Novel of Harlem Renaissance Is Found." *New York Times*, September 14, 2012. www.nytimes.com/2012/09/15/books/harlem-renaissance-novel-by-claude-mckay-is-discovered.html.

Levin, Meredith. Review of Claude McKay's
  Romance in Marseille. *American Communist
  History*, May 1, 2020. www.tandfonline.com
  /doi/abs/10.1080/14743892.2020.1758523.
McKay, Claude. *Amiable with Big Teeth: A Novel of
  the Love Affair between the Communists and the
  Poor Black Sheep of Harlem*, edited by Jean-
  Christophe Cloutier and Brent Hayes Edwards.
  New York: Penguin, 2017.
McKay, Claude. *Romance in Marseille*, edited by Gary
  Edward Holcomb and William J. Maxwell.
  New York: Penguin, 2020.
McKay, Claude. "To the Intrenched Classes." In
  Complete Poems, edited by William J. Maxwell,
  149. Urbana: University of Illinois Press,
  2004.
New York. "Seventy-Nine Gifts for Every Type of
  Mom." April 29, 2020. nymag.com/strategist
  /article/best-gifts-for-mom.html.
New York Times. "The Nobel-Winning Economist
  Who Wants You to Read More Fiction."
  Interview with Joseph E. Stiglitz. April 9,
  2020. www.nytimes.com/2020/04/09/books
  /review/joseph-e-stiglitz-by-the-book-interview
  .html.

Sacks, Sam. Review of *Romance in Marseille*. *Wall
  Street Journal*, February 21, 2020. www.wsj
  .com/articles/fiction-mother-son-and-bottle
  -11582303046.
Sackton, Laura. "How Audiobooks Are Getting Me
  through COVID-19." *Bookriot.com*, April 7,
  2020. bookriot.com/how-audiobooks-are
  -getting-me-through-covid-19.
Vanity Fair. "Thirty-One Great Quarantine Reads,
  Chosen by the *Vanity Fair* Staff." March 25,
  2020. www.vanityfair.com/style/2020/03/31
  -great-quarantine-reads-chosen-by-the-vanity
  -fair-staff.
Young, Molly. "The Best New Novel Was Written
  Ninety Years Ago." *New York*, February 6,
  2020. www.vulture.com/2020/02/romance
  -in-marseille-claude-mckay.html.
Zax, Talya. "A Book So Far Ahead of Its Time, It
  Took Eighty-Seven Years to Find a Publisher."
  New York Times, February 5, 2020. www
  .nytimes.com/2020/02/05/books/claude
  -mckay-romance-marseille-harlem-renaissance
  .html.
Zax, Talya. "Far Ahead of Its Time, and Finally
  Published." *New York Times*, February 7, 2020.

"Broken Bits of Color in the Dirt"

The Afterlives of Slavery and the Futures Past
of a Black Intersectional International
in *Romance in Marseille*

JESSE W. SCHWARTZ

Abstract This essay examines the numerous critical claims of "timeliness" around the recently recovered novel *Romance in Marseille* as well as Claude McKay's own numerous commitments and challenges as they emerge therein: the multiple and enduring afterlives of slavery, the Bolshevik Revolution and the burgeoning of its stiflingly bureaucratic Thermidor under Stalin, the various theoretical and programmatic complications that issues of race and gender posed for international socialism alongside the promises and disappointments of emancipatory politics writ large. However, in attempting to adjudicate such problematics of difference, McKay also provides the outlines of a dialectical "Black Intersectional International," thereby gesturing toward a "commonism" of the quayside.
Keywords racial capitalism, Claude McKay, intersectionality, Black radical tradition, socialism

> The body is transformed by love.
> —Jordy Rosenberg, *Confessions of the Fox*

In 1919 a specter haunting Europe for decades had finally sloughed off its shadow to emerge as the Communist International in a newly Bolshevik Russia, a global flu pandemic was still killing tens of millions, and the optimistically appointed "war to end all wars" was asked at Versailles to take a few decades off from turning large swaths of the world into a human abattoir. At the same time, Francisco Franco had already been a brigadier general for three years (the youngest in all of Europe), Mussolini founded the Fasci Italiani di Combattimento, and Hitler officially joined the German Workers' Party (which would change its name to the National Socialists in a few short months). Meanwhile, in New York City, a twenty-something Claude McKay would publish his most famous poem, "If We Must Die," in response to a very long, very hot, and very Red Summer in which a spectacular series of brutal anti-Black riots in more than two dozen communities were joined with the fierce antiradicalism of the nation's first formal "Red Scare."

ENGLISH LANGUAGE NOTES

59:1, April 2021 DOI 10.1215/00138282-8814961
© 2021 Regents of the University of Colorado

A century later, in the spring of 2020, to be exact, the silence or the sirens in Brooklyn are broken mostly by the cheers erupting from apartment windows each night at 7:00 to celebrate those workers deemed "essential." The borough's previously rowdy and raucous Myrtle Avenue—declared "a be-be itching of a place" by the inimitably named Strawberry Lips nine decades earlier in McKay's *Home to Harlem*—is now quiet (quiet, that is, for Brooklyn).[1] All of this as a new global depression looms, a quarter million worldwide are already dead from COVID-19 (and counting), and fascist epigones from India to Brazil to Hungary expand their power under various banners of purity, patriotism, and pride (several now using the pandemic as cover for near-martial law). In the United States alone, unemployment nears 15 million, a self-described Jewish democratic socialist came within a few primary victories of fighting barbarism head on, and George Floyd is murdered by a Minnesota cop whose camera-ready nonchalance sparks the largest protest movement in US history.[2] All of this as the richest nation on earth is led by a sycophantic cabal whose cruelty is matched only by its cupidity, the world's dumbest gangster at the helm. History may not exactly repeat itself, but some similarities feel a bit richer than rhyme.

And then, tempest-tossed until lobbed like a bomb, McKay's novel, *Romance in Marseille* (1929–33), suddenly lands in our own time to remind those of us fortunate enough to forget that there is never not a crisis. Rather, never not *crises*. Or, as Walter Benjamin famously suggested about the Angel of History, "Where we perceive a chain of events, he sees one single catastrophe which keeps piling wreckage upon wreckage and hurls it in front of his feet."[3] Finally added to the pile is a "new" novel by a canonical author more lauded than read, a text whose existence was known for decades, that was written about from the archives, yet was abandoned like a Dickensian foundling and then strangled by bureaucratic legalese for decades until its current emergence as a lost jewel of the Harlem Renaissance. *Romance*, it seems, was always ready for *us*.[4]

Thoroughly unloved by agents and presses in its own time, the novel's contemporary reviewers now seem locked in dubious battle over who can best declare *Romance*'s timeliness, as if it had been dropped upon the world in rescue, a skeleton key with which to make sense of the supposedly straight line between the last century and our own. The *New York Times* insists that *Romance* is "a book so far ahead of its time, it took eighty-seven years to find a publisher."[5] The *Washington Post* declares the novel "less shocking than strikingly woke" and its author (again) "ahead of his time."[6] Even the self-appointed socialist mouthpiece of record, *Jacobin*, declares the book "a recognizable portrait of precarious living" while the arch doyens at *Vulture* declare that the "best new novel was written ninety years ago" and is so "out of time" that "if you skipped the introduction and surrendered access to Google, you could easily mistake it for a novel written last year."[7] English-language newspapers from New York to Australia to McKay's native Jamaica hail *Romance*'s provocative nowness in its tender treatment of the many marginalized figures that inhabit its pages: the lumpen-precariat, unapologetically queer lovers, practiced and practical thieves, migrants and refugees, colonial subjects, sex workers, members of the Black diaspora, political radicals of numerous stripes—it seems nearly everyone has found a roomy and sympathetic home in McKay's slim little book.[8]

The adulation is grand, of course, though little good it does McKay now, who died sick, penniless, and mostly alone in Chicago in 1948. But it's definitely been a good few years for an author who's been gone more than seven decades: 2017 saw the release of his actually lost critique of white and Black radicals in Harlem, *Amiable with Big Teeth*. Yet this much longer and arguably more polished novel received far fewer declarations of timely relevance than *Romance* despite the fact that the books share a number of related themes, and even though *Amiable* was begun just a few years after *Romance* was left behind in Tangier. In fact, by comparison, *Amiable* was largely hailed as a novel precisely *of* its time. Henry Louis Gates called it a "major discovery" that "dramatically expands the canon of novels written by Harlem Renaissance writers."[9] Brent Hayes Edwards, one of the book's two editors, proclaimed it "the key political novel of black intellectual life in New York in the late 1930s."[10] And its enthusiastic reviewer in the *Atlantic* nonetheless relegated it to the status of a "historical document" whose import is the "unparalleled insight into this relatively understudied moment in black American history."[11] Significant, to be sure, but in a register many of us might more readily describe as "academic."

We might ask, then, what it means that all these reviewers so comfortably declare *Romance*'s contemporaneity, as if the book had always been umbilically linked to our different and distant present. Do these easy, one-to-one assessments absolve us of more rigorous analyses, defanging some of the novel's political bearing by applying it so unquestionably to our own? Are we at risk of instrumentalizing *Romance*, with nearly everyone so certain that the text is teeming with salvageable materials for our own needy present as if in useful warning from a time traveler in reverse?

Speaking about both risk and instrumentalization, Theodore Martin has recently argued that "surprisingly little thought has been given to the meanings and implications of the contemporary as a critical category,"[12] but that

> one way to begin to answer this question is to consider the contemporary not so much an index of immediacy but as a *strategy of mediation*: a means of negotiating between experience and retrospection, immersion and explanation, closeness and distance. Put simply, the contemporary is a critical concept. It must be imagined before it can be perceived; it is not just a moment that contains us but a moment that we must first conceive *as* a moment. The contemporary compels us to think, above all, about the politics of how we think about the present. The contours and currents of our current moment—its temporal boundaries, its historical significance, its deeper social logics—are inseparable from the historically determined and politically motivated ways we choose to divide the present from the past.[13]

Romance, then, might be contemporary simply because we have collectively willed it to be so, because readers find some kind of resonance in "its deeper social logics," locate a sense of closeness to its distance, and feel contained by a moment that they have first brought into being *as a moment*. Perhaps in this time of what many euphemistically call "heightened political sensitivities," *Romance*'s reception at the collapse of this past/present border is best understood by what Lisa Lowe calls a "past conditional temporality," the "what could have been" in which "it is possible to conceive the past, not as fixed or settled" but as "a space of reckoning that allows us to revisit times of historical contingency and possibility to consider alternatives that may have been *unthought* in those times."[14] McKay himself intuited this sense of collapse and conflation due to the great deforming machineries of modernity in his own era, linking coloniality, race, and temporality in typically poetic phrasing: "For I was born, far from my native clime, / Under the white man's menace, out of time."[15] Indeed, the author's itinerant life often reads like a *Zelig* of early twentieth-century racial and political marginalization: the story of a British imperial subject, perpetual migrant, erstwhile communist, and Black queer radical emigrating from the Jamaican periphery to globalizing ports and world-financial capitals. Here's McKay in London talking imperialism with Ho Chi Minh. Now he's off to New York to debate radical politics with Max Eastman and play literary big brother to Langston Hughes. Next it's on to Moscow to discuss literature with Trotsky and openly chide the Third International about racism in the CPUSA.[16]

Something like its author's biography, *Romance* largely follows the drifting misadventures of Lafala, an African immigrant in Europe who loses his legs to frostbite after being imprisoned as a stowaway on a freighter bound for New York. But his physical loss soon becomes a windfall thanks to the help of a shrewd lawyer, a twist that catalyzes much of the action to follow in the glorious squalor of Marseille's Quayside. Yet while the ensuing tangles of cash, love, drinking, and jealousy crowd much of the plot, the frames for many of these misadventures—migrations, holds, ships, (dis)abilities, littorality, and the raced and gendered commodification of bodies—shape the tale in ways that rehearse Saidiya Hartman's contention that the signals and symptoms of the "afterlife of slavery" remain very much *in* our lives after all.[17] McKay wastes little time forging these connections between present and past, beginning his novel with the main character bemoaning his amputation in a large Manhattan hospital, lying "like a sawed-off stump" and pondering "the loss of his legs" in dramatic medias res.[18] This abjection performs the double labor of being at once deeply personal to the character as well as inexorably linked to his lineage. In this case, his missing limbs become liminal, a threshold between his own body and the histories of the Black diaspora writ large. Or, in the words of Darieck Scott, "abjection is a way of describing an experience, an inherited (psychically introjected) historical legacy, and a social condition defined and underlined by a defeat."[19] It is not surprising, then, that the first time Lafala manages to forget his seemingly new abject form is during a Fanonian dream sequence, in which the same slumbering fantasy that returns his legs also magically allows him to shed his skin because "in heaven . . . [t]here were no black things there. . . . Lafala was transfigured beyond remembering what complexion he was, but his legs were all right there, prancing to the lascivious music of heavenly jazz" (*RM*, 6).

Lafala's dream parodies the linkage between the Black body and abjection, imagining that his legs can only return when that body also loses the Blackness that all but ensured their loss in the first place. But his white wholeness is maintained only for a moment, as the African American character that greets Lafala in the hospital upon awakening not only returns the Black body firmly to Lafala's consciousness but also showcases the opposite of White Heaven in vivid stereotype, with his "huge black face, yellow teeth in a badly molded mouth" (*RM*, 7). Lafala's new friend has learned a thing or two during a life spent entirely in the New World, however, and is therefore the first to explain a far less dreamy and far more American way to have Lafala's legs reimbursed: suing for lots of cash. The ironically named Black Angel thus helps him find the right "go-get-'im-skin-and-scalp-him" lawyer (*RM*, 9) who charges the shipping line for imprisoning Lafala belowdecks, winning a fortune for them all in court. Payout in hand and cork prostheses on foot, Lafala triumphantly heads back to Marseille.

From here, *Romance* remarks on a number of the pressing social concerns of its time that continue to reverberate into our own: the multiple and enduring afterlives of slavery; the Bolshevik Revolution and the burgeoning of its stiflingly ideological and bureaucratic Thermidor under Stalin; the theoretical and programmatic complications that issues of race posed for international socialism alongside the often more rigid contours of these movements around questions of gender; and even the unspoken wake of McKay's sexual desires, whose parameters in this text were finally, if only partially, named. The narrative of *Romance* in fact seems to unravel as it approaches various problematics of difference simultaneously, echoing a number of contemporary demands to engage these categories within an intersectional frame. Yet in the failure of *Romance*'s romance, I argue, all is not lost. If the novel and its resonances have returned like a welcoming ghost from an inhospitable machine, McKay's novella also provides, *avant la lettre*, the outlines of a dialectical "Black Intersectional International"—one that attempts to reckon with the various differences appraised in service of their entanglement, conjoining without flattening them through the twinned technologies of pleasure and care, and thereby gesturing toward a "commonism" of the quayside.[20]

The Intoxication of Fellowship

Like McKay's groundbreaking 1928 novel *Home to Harlem*, *Romance* certainly knows its way around a bar. That first best seller of the Harlem Renaissance famously infuriated W. E. B. Du Bois, who found its direct and unflinching scenes of proletarian Black life to be so far beneath those who might lead the race back into the sun that he quipped "after the dirtier parts of its filth I feel distinctly like taking a bath."[21] *Romance* finds McKay *enfant terrible*-ing further still, doubling down on a rich social cosmology rooted almost entirely in the bacchanalia that left Du Bois feeling so debauched. Yet McKay's bar scenes resonate not only with filial rebellion but also the more sober contention that pleasure *as such* might also represent a politics of strategic, if admittedly temporary, fellowship—and therefore ironically contribute to the robust propaganda Du Bois averred to be the whole point of art in the first place.[22] As Samuel R. Delany concordantly noted about communal gratification in pre-Giuliani Times Square porn theaters (in a text we can also imagine Du Bois loudly disavowing), "Beyond pleasure, these were people you had little in common with. Yet what greater field and force than pleasure can human beings share?"[23]

For such a slim book, *Romance* is thick with the grit, glory, and grime of wine-fueled late nights in dark bars, when bodies press against strangers, assignations are planned (and most likely carried out), and the possibilities of encounter expand beyond the boundaries of Black bourgeois propriety. Or, as McKay impolitically explained to Arturo Schomburg, "I make my Negro characters yarn and backbite and fuck like people the world over" (*CM*, 218). During our first visit to the Tout-va-Bien, Lafala's favorite of the louche boîtes that populate the Quayside, we are quickly greeted by untrammeled binge drinking, numerous puns about the nether regions of anatomy, and a fluidity of desire and democracy of demographic so robust that any participant might head for a Du Boisian bath the morning after. Amid this carnal oblivion, however, the patrons also take part in a literary experiment that simultaneously welcomes, protects, and celebrates difference while pricking wide open the supposedly inviolable borders of individual subjectivity. Put differently, McKay produces a network of affiliation through intermingled technologies of inebriated and inebriating affect.

In the Spinozist terms of Brian Massumi, the transmission of affect occurs through "a prepersonal intensity corresponding to the passage from one experiential state of the body to another and implying an augmentation or diminution in that body's capacity to act."[24] And it is this prepersonal but necessarily relational state of encounter that McKay seems to find potentially political, at least within the subjective blending over wine at the Tout-va-Bien. While the narration of the novel relies primarily on typically realist distinctions between characters, these delineated individuals begin to blend into one another in the barrooms through shared affects linked by pleasure (dancing, music, desire, intemperance). In one instance, for example, a comparative discussion of Lafala's misfortune between named speakers devolves into a shared hilarity in which the "café resounded with a bellyful of laughter, ebony-smooth-and-shining laughter, bronze-sounding laughter, tawny-throated laughter, sweet-money laughter over Lafala and his luck" (*RM*, 37). Loosing Du Bois's chains, McKay offers a provisional and polychromous community brought about by collective pleasure and a little too much wine, what Gary Edward Holcomb refers to as "a kind of postcolonial phenomenological conditioning of becoming, an emergence beyond race to culture built on the potential for revolutionary mergings."[25] This single-bellied, hyphen-heavy variegation of dark flesh carries other political valences as well. It links Black peoples from across the diaspora, functions as a leveling rebuke against the colorism of McKay's native Jamaica, and perhaps takes another swipe at Du Bois—whose office staff at the *Crisis* were all apparently so light-skinned that, after one visit, Marcus Garvey quipped he was "unable to tell whether he was in a white office or that of the NAACP."[26] What's more, the focus on flesh without bodies recalls Hortense Spillers's distinction between the two as the "central" division "between captive and liberated subject-positions," in which the flesh is "that zero degree of social conceptualization that does not escape concealment under the brush of discourse."[27] McKay, however, attempts to liberate all this flesh from its previously embodied subject-positions through his own literary discourse: the narration traverses the range of nonwhite skin without distinction, connecting as it colors, passing from grinning body to body without qualification or comment, and collapsing all conversationalists into a mass of laughter, an ad hoc network created by their discussion of Lafala's windfall and no doubt augmented by his endless purchasing of rounds.

Yet McKay never allows this blended sameness to come at the cost of eliding difference altogether, avoiding what Aimé Césaire, whose own formulation of "Negritude" was deeply indebted to McKay's work, dismissed as "emaciated universalism." As Césaire warned, "There are two ways to lose oneself: walled segregation in the particular or dilution in the 'universal.'"[28] McKay makes sure to dance up to and around this line carefully. During his scenes of amalgamated intoxication, the only policing that occurs involves the protection and promotion of difference itself. As Aslima—a popular Marseille sex worker and reason for Lafala's return— enters the bar, she demands a French song so that she might "dance the jolly pig" (*RM*, 39). While everyone else "let loose a salvo of applause," one "little Arab" cries "Halouf!" in her direction, a "French word, extracted from an Arabic source, meaning pork, and emphasizing the uncleanliness of this meat" (*RM*, 149n9). Yet rather than be cowed by either the religious sensitivities she's offended or the insult aimed at a woman dancing for the entertainment of men, Aslima doubles down: "I dance it and you eat it." This only catalyzes her antagonist's desire for violence: "Me eat pig? You dirty slut!" Inflamed by her dismissal of both culinary prohibitions and gendered restrictions on behavior, the aggrieved Arab tries to attack Aslima, "but the Negroes at the bar barred his way," protecting her virtue to be and do whatever she pleases in this permissive space. Even the assailant's own difference is quickly reenshrined once his desire to police others is quelled. In the end, Aslima "shrugged, dabbing her face with a handkerchief. The Arab didn't mean to do any harm anyway, but as a good Quaysider he had to show his mettle" (*RM*, 39).

McKay's use of free indirect discourse here and at several other moments in the text returns us to embodied differences dissolved through transient relational forces. Or rather, while the pursuit of pleasure connects the characters at the level of scene, free indirect discourse links them—and the reader—at the level of technique. As Gérard Genette explains, "style indirect libre" is a narrative strategy in which "the narrator takes on the speech of the character, or, if one prefers, the character speaks through the voice of the narrator, and the two instances are then merged."[29] Such definitional ambiguity from a notably systematic thinker highlights the profound narrative instability within free indirect discourse, a style that forces the reader to navigate a complex account unmoored from either the narrator or a specific character, creating a "merged" point of view that is simultaneously neither and both (or whichever the reader "prefers"), thereby co-opting readers themselves into flattening and merging apparently distinct subjectivities by asking them to choose.

The historical arrival of this narrative style was recently contextualized by Fredric Jameson in a schema also reminiscent of McKay's revolutionary desires for intoxicated community. For Jameson, the invention of realist fiction by its mid-century European practitioners was contemporaneous with two intimately linked social developments: the "historic emergence of the bourgeois body" and "the rise of affect with the emergence of the phenomenological body in language and representation."[30] Even as a maker of the famously modern Harlem Renaissance, McKay was far more hip in his themes than his resolutely realist prose. In the words of his biographer, Wayne F. Cooper, "If his style was in most respects anachronistic . . . his essential message of alienation, anger, and rebellion was thoroughly modern" (*CM*, 166). Inspired early by classic British poetry, he eschewed most of the formal innovations of modernism and supported Max Eastman's "attacks on the modernists in art and literature" (*CM*, 95). So if, as Jameson argues, the birth of affect was contemporaneous with the emergence of the bourgeois body and its fantasies of individual agency, and if realist literature was the most vigorous representational fable of its personal sovereignties (possessive individualism, self-determination, and, in this case, the unquestioned existence of a singular "self" at all), then free indirect discourse directs the reader's attention to the artifice of these insides and outsides by illuminating the promiscuous merging of supposedly discrete bodies through the very affects that brought them into being. McKay's barroom techniques become a kind of literary showcase for the tensions inherent in Jameson's double and contradictory conceptual emergence of realism in which the same affective phenomena that give rise to the possibility of "individual subjects" in the first place also undermine their putative autonomy. Late nights at the Tout-va-Bien, then, render the supposedly inviolate realist subject a fiction, preserving these characters' staggering alterity while also enabling the formation of provisional communities during their dissolute dissolutions.

The Uses of Abjection beyond the Human

McKay may have unsettled the limits of discrete bodies in *Romance*'s bar scenes, but he takes flight from the human entirely in his frequent animal imagery. And what timing: the novel coronavirus has reminded the world that many of the supposed distinctions between the human and animal worlds are far more ideological than material. Birds, bats, pangolins, monkeys, pigs: all have returned to the forefront of media consciousness as possible "vectors" of infection, transmission, and disease. Pigs in particular have long been "regarded as potential intermediaries in the process by which a bird disease became a human disease, since pig cells share features of both human and bird cells," a threshold that reaches across and thereby connects biological classes.[31] Though perhaps comical to imagine now, after leaving Tuskegee, McKay pursued his college career as an agriculture major at Kansas State University, where he studied hog farming and pork production alongside "general geology, and insects and spraying."[32] One could even argue that he rose to literary fame with the help of figurative pigs. These animals were deployed in his most famous poem, "If We Must Die," as well as in "A Roman Holiday," published together in the July 1919 issue of the *Liberator*, and it was these two pig poems that "signaled the beginning of his life as a professional writer" and enshrined his status as a voice of African America.[33]

But McKay had a very different liminality in mind in *Romance*, where pigs are invoked forty-nine times, and never once literally.[34] A totem animal of sorts, the figure of the pig joyously grounds the novel in the many mucks of desire, an imagined escape from all propriety and prepossession attached to the Black characters at which it is aimed. For example, one typical exchange between Lafala and Aslima runs this way:

"Let's finish chatting and be living pigs," said Aslima.

"I can't be as piggish as in my able-bodied days," said Lafala.

"Pigskin!" Aslima exclaimed. "Forget about your feet now and thank God it wasn't something worse that was cut off."

"Alright, piggy."

"I've been a pig all my life," said Aslima. "But with you I don't feel that it's just a mud bath. I feel like we're clean pigs." (*RM*, 41)

In this exchange, piggishness serves a number of distinct but interrelated functions that take us both beneath and beyond the human, all of them playfully ensconced in the simple pleasure of bodies wallowing together. If the novel begins with the trauma of abjection that functions simultaneously at the level of the individual and an entire race, McKay's pig imagery attempts to move beyond the violence undergirding the human/animal distinction entirely. To revel in the porcine abject is to renovate what Mel Chen calls the "racial politics of animality," which reminds us that the history of various racisms "are themselves built upon many complex animal hierarchies . . . each of which can potentially implicate directly the charge of racial abjection without reference to race itself."[35] To be "living pigs," then, is not to simply disavow the abjections that infuse Blackness, animality, and their many malignant historical intersections. It is instead to recover what is lost within those strictly circumscribed bodies of knowledge that demand such severe demarcations and enforcement between definitions of "the human" in the first place, what Sylvia Wynter calls the "differing facets of the central ethnoclass Man vs. Human struggle."[36]

Aslima's subjunctive demand to "stop talking and be living pigs" also echoes the process of becoming-animal theorized by Deleuze and Guattari. In consonance with McKay's characters, becoming-animal also constitutes "an entire politics" that "express[es] minoritarian groups, or groups that are oppressed, prohibited, in revolt, or always on the fringe of recognized institutions," a state of deterritorialization wherein the concept of the human, and, ostensibly, its limits both real and perceived, are deracinated and thereby transformed.[37] This idea of a movement beyond the body, transcending its abjection, can also help explain why, for Aslima, Lafala's absent legs are no obstacle. We might even read her arch aside about not losing "something worse" as a multiple entendre signaling, in addition to his intact genitalia, that Lafala also hasn't lost his ability to play these very language games that allow him to exceed his (dis)ability as well as the delimiting subjectivities of the human, reminding us that "becoming pig" concerns self-effacing pleasures rather than specific acts, parts, and fantasies of bodily integrity. While Aslima's phrase "pig all my life" seems to make reference to both her marginalized birth and her source of income, her supposedly unyielding abjection can be converted through the intimacy that she and Lafala now share. They become clean pigs who, through the mutual fulfillment of desire, slip off the markers of subjectivity that historically defined them, and, at least for a moment, thus rise above the mud.

As Freud reminds us in one of his reflections on the creative artist, "The opposite of play is not what is serious but what is real."[38] In this spirit, we might ask what exactly McKay is playing at in all his piggish seriousness. The fact that McKay began *Romance in Marseille* in Spain (a country also rightly famous for its pigs) is less surprising if we consider what Maria DeGuzmán argues is the "long shadow" of Iberia on the racial imaginary of the Anglo-American world. Noting that the figure of the Spaniard became "over the course of the nineteenth century . . . a figure of dangerous, implosive 'racial' mixture," DeGuzmán contends that between the more common Black/white binary lies "a critically unacknowledged third position or figure, that of the not-right-white or the off-white, the figure of 'the Spaniard.'"[39] And it is through this "off-white" figure that an imaginary of Spain emerges, one in which the racial borders among bodies are far less inflexible and therefore more suspect.

Yet while these suspicions of racial slippage no doubt discomfited many of the white writers and intellectuals DeGuzmán engages with in her book, a number of Black artists and thinkers unsurprisingly found this racial porosity inspiring. Robert Reid-Pharr's *Archives of Flesh* extends DeGuzmán's analysis in this generative register and offers some purchase on the possible linkages between McKay's language of porcine possibility, erotic attachments, and the many histories of the "human" that otherwise seem impertinently unconnected. Naming a vast "African American Spanish archive," Reid-Pharr insists on "the centrality of the Iberian Peninsula in the development of what eventually came to be known as globalization and humanism," the latter's construction built "upon the indissoluble distinction between 'Man' and animal," a distinction which "reaches its highest—and most bizarre—level of clarity at those many moments in which some human animals are understood to be more human than others."[40]

At the same time, however, Iberia also "signaled for African American intellectuals a species of Spanish promise and possibility, an opening by which the vulgar fiction of white superiority might be mitigated."[41] McKay explicitly recognized the fungible racial borders of Spain as he began writing *Romance* there, asserting in his autobiography that he "had lingered long enough . . . to become aware of the strong African streak in [Spain's] character."[42] Considering McKay's Jamaican pedigree, we might enlarge Reid-Pharr's archival frame into an African *Americas* Spanish archive, one that allowed McKay to think through linkages between race, region, and animality thanks in part to "the peninsula's strategic position at the crossroads of Europe, Africa, and the Middle East."[43] The "African streak" McKay felt in Spain was also apparently strong enough to prod him in the direction of Africa itself, and he soon landed in Morocco to continue his ill-fated novel. There, the "vulgar fiction of white superiority" frayed immediately as he learned that his Black Martinican host was considered "a French citizen, was rated as a European worker," was paid "about six times what the native doing the same work got," and therefore "the black sailor was really living 'white' in Africa" (*LW*, 298). These already troubled Western codes of race and nation faded further as McKay left the "overwhelming European atmosphere of Casablanca" for Fez, where he "got into the inside of Morocco" and "went completely native" (*LW*, 298, 299). In Fez, claims McKay's autobiography, the distance between differences muddle in full-throated harmonic hybridity, as the sounds of "native musicians playing African variations of the Oriental melodies in the Moroccan cafés" lift him like Lafala's heavenly dream in the hospital. Suddenly, McKay avers, "For the first time in my life I felt myself singularly free of color-consciousness. I experienced a feeling that must be akin to the physical well-being of a dumb animal among kindred animals, who lives instinctively and by sensations only, without thinking" (*LW*, 300).

McKay's reverie in Fez was soon interrupted by overzealous French and British officials who tried to expel him. And even though these particular "pigs" were unsuccessful in kicking him out of Morocco, the "incident spoiled my native holiday" and McKay was forced to realize that "even in Africa I was confronted by the specter, the white terror always pursuing the black. There was no escape anywhere from the white hound of Civilization" (*LW*, 303, 304). Even if ultimately unsuccessful, however, by drawing on his experiences in Spain and Morocco and, in his own words, "going native," McKay was able to imagine a voyage beyond the remit of colonial consciousness and the restrictions, elisions, and silences enmeshed in its narrow definition of "the human." Or, in Aslima's words, spoken as she frames the collapse and conflation of the human/animal boundary, "we'll be happy pigs together as often as I am free. I want to convince you that I am human at bottom" (*RM*, 41). McKay's *figura* of the pig, then, reclaims a sense of the "mess" around this boundary and enjoins that we "listen," that we pay attention to those humans at bottom and at the bottoms. As an animal most commonly raised for meat, used for turning over the soil, or purchased as a pet, McKay's prosodic pig underlines the shared space between human and animal, master and slave, by demanding that we justify why a few get coddled and some go till, while most simply get killed.

On the Uses and Disadvantages of Theory against Life

McKay had been involved with international socialism long before he wrote the first words of *Romance* in 1929. And from the very start, his enthusiasm for the revolution in Russia had been tempered by his skepticism about the Comintern's ability to assess the crucial analytical linkages between race and class—never mind the hierarchies, local nuances, and profound differences within and between various races and peoples that would also need suturing in the service of global revolution. Even more troubling, McKay "found that far too many communists and socialists were themselves afflicted with the racist phobias common to the age." Early on, therefore, he came "to doubt the wisdom of an international Communist movement based so firmly upon a Russian leadership whose interests could not always be identical with those of Communists in other countries" (*CM*, 162, 129).

Despite these misgivings, McKay, alongside a number of other transnational radicals of color, also recognized that Moscow remained by far the most popular and powerful revolutionary force around. With the machinery of an entire nation-state behind them, the Bolsheviks' unprecedented transnational reach opened up numerous routes through which Black radicals could more easily travel. This is why, in the succinct phrasing of Minkah Makalani, "organized Marxism represented less the source and more the moment of [Black radical] politics."[44] Even if Black radicals found a party leadership "that repeatedly proved either indifferent to questions of race or openly hostile to black radicals' organizing initiatives and ideas," they also "realized a global network with other black radicals through the

Comintern's networks and international meetings."[45] Russia-aligned diasporic Black radicals, then, understandably made pragmatic use of Russia's structures and institutions to "renovate and make critical already existing activity," hoping that a somewhat less white world communist movement might "shade or complete a good many of the doctrine's points."[46] This hope, of course, would become a central question in many analyses of Black radicals' relationships with Moscow—and never more so than during the 1920s and 1930s, the period of McKay's strongest engagement. As William J. Maxwell asks, "Was the Soviet-sponsored Marxian theory of the Negro Question underpinning the exchanges between New Negro and Old Left a clueless, domineering Russian import, innocent of or hostile to independent black thought?" Or "did the meeting of black American life and the theory imperfectly transmitted from the Comintern to the U.S. party transfigure both?" And if the latter, what was the role played by "the black voice McKay brought to Moscow in the early 1920s, the voice of Harlem Renaissance bolshevism?"[47]

The possibility of a theoretical dialectic between the Black radical tradition and organized Marxism is in part the flipside of Cedric Robinson's field-defining contention that Black Marxism cannot be a mere "variant of Western radicalism whose proponents happen to be Black," but must qualify as "a specifically African response to an oppression emergent from the immediate determinants of European development in the modern era."[48] As a result, Black Marxism foregrounds the absolute necessity of thinking the terms *Black* and *Marxist* together dialectically, and in particular of applying the pressure of the first term on the latter. In Robinson's view, Marx committed a fundamental double oversight—or, rather, the same omission from two different vantage points. As Robin D. G. Kelley explains, Robinson "takes Karl Marx to task for failing to comprehend radical movements outside of Europe" while at the same time illustrating how "Marxism also failed to account for the *racial* character of capitalism."[49] In *Freedom Dreams*, however, Kelley demonstrates that the Black radical tradition also generates far more than critique by fostering a "revolution of the mind, . . . not merely a refusal of victim status . . . , an unleashing of the mind's most creative capacities, catalyzed by participation in struggles for change."[50] For example, while Moscow may have hoped to spread socialism by helping disparate peoples recognize their related exploitation through the language of class, Black people in the Americas alone had already spent centuries forming alliances with lower classes of whites, Native Americans, and others in maroon communities and other structures of collective living. These Indigenous traditions of affinity and cohabitation, brought together through shared struggle, creatively imagined new modes of survival adequate to the demands of the early twentieth century. For his part, McKay also sympathized with the position of Cyril Briggs, the cofounder of the African Blood Brotherhood, who feared that these traditions of resistance might at times slip into a too-facile Black nationalism like that advocated by Marcus Garvey, and so McKay viewed such movements primarily as incremental tools of consciousness-raising, where, "for subject people, at least, Nationalism is the open door to Communism" (*CM*, 117).

In 1922 McKay traveled to the Fourth Congress of the Third International, where he met such Bolshevik luminaries as Leon Trotsky and Nikolai Bukharin, and where his dark skin made him an instant celebrity. The speech he delivered before the gathered body of Communist luminaries made his concerns about Soviet racial theory plain. He championed the Bolsheviks for a "Third International [that] stands for the emancipation of all the workers of the world, regardless of race or color, and . . . not merely on paper like the Fifteenth Amendment of the Constitution of the United States of America." But he also emphasized that the question of race affected the revolutionary potential of Bolshevik Communism—not only because this issue was used as a wedge against white labor to prevent class solidarity, but also because "there is a great element of prejudice among the Socialists and Communists of America."[51] One of the main sticking points for McKay, then, was Moscow's reluctance to address the racism within its own international cadres, particularly those party affiliates in the US Left, which, if allowed to fester, would render the Russian Revolution as useful for nonwhite peoples around the world as "formal" equality was for Black Americans under Jim Crow.

McKay's other major concern, however, was harder to articulate within the genre of a party address, and may be why it emerges so readily in his fiction: the arid and dogmatic application of Marxism, mixed with an inert and mechanistic view of humanity, which seemed to surface more frequently the farther Russia moved past its revolution. As McKay quipped about the would-be revolutionaries hanging around London's International Club, "They have no idea of what constitutes practical socialism. They talk, but they never try to live" (*CM*, 131). The deadening mission-creep he saw emerging from Stalinism left McKay at times so skeptical about the movement that he complained to Max Eastman, "Wherever I look in the Communist International I see nothing but dry rot" (*CM*, 219).

McKay was thus dismayed by what he saw as the blanket application of an airless and reifying Marxism in the party's engagement with non-European peoples. As Aimé Césaire would similarly conclude in his resignation letter to the French Communist Party a few decades later, "It is neither Marxism nor Communism that I am renouncing . . . [;] it is the usage some have made of Marxism and Communism that I condemn. That what I want is that Marxism and Communism be placed in the service of black peoples, and not black people into the service of Marxism and Communism. That the doctrine and the movement would be made to fit men, not men to fit the doctrine or the movement."[52] In the face of what McKay often viewed as inexorable prophecy rather than nuanced materialist analyses, he too searched for a Marxism a little more vulgar than what Russia had to offer.

Yet while the tangle of humanity might be a substantial obstacle for social theory, it lands squarely within the ambit of imaginative literature. McKay's conception of a theory against life in *Romance* provides us with a fertile middle ground between his less overtly political novels—*Home to Harlem* and *Banjo*—and his trenchantly fatalistic and aggressively anticommunist final novel, *Amiable with Big Teeth*. In fact, when *Romance* introduces us to the "Seaman's and Worker's Club," one of many such institutions that had been "springing up in the principal European ports" "in the decade following the era of the Russian Revolution," its theoretically advanced lifelessness and clumsy misunderstandings of the desires of actual proletarians are the first details presented, standing in stark relief to the distant port area's lively entertainments. Even if the club's "atmosphere was right," it was "situated—God knows why—in the drabbest and least interesting proletarian and factory quarter of Marseille" so that "not many seamen could be persuaded to go up there," compared to "Quayside where all the drifters and bums, the outcasts and outlaws of civilizations, congregated like wasps together in hate and love feeding and buzzing over the scum" because, though "stinking, there were broken bits of color in the dirt" (*RM*, 73). For the McKay of *Romance*, Soviet-affiliated Marxism may have had the right atmosphere, but what did it matter if so few made it through the door?

Even worse were the proselytizers that lay in wait for any would-be converts. Étienne St. Dominique is the first scholastic Communist we meet in the novel, his name invoking both the colonial name of prerevolutionary Haiti, the first Black republic, and its most famous liberation leader, François Dominique Toussaint-Louverture.[53] With acid sharpness, McKay cruelly conjures up radical ghosts representing perhaps the greatest successes of the Black radical tradition while also describing the sterile parlor room of a dusty Communist club on the edge of town. Far from inspiring any revolutionary ardor, this St. Dominique is better known as "something of a philanderer" with a "cultivated accent" and "refined manners"—in short, a bourgeois-mannered would-be organizer who might have more in common with the French merchant class than with Toussaint. Dominique's friend, the president of the club, only reinforces this disappointment: he is "a very polite person from the middle class" who had "been a professor in his earlier life" and "was in no way ambitious," just wanting "a place where he could help serve the cause of the ignorant workers as conscientiously as he had once instructed young students" (*RM*, 76). His gentle but pedantic top-down approach, at odds with the revolutionary negotiations of Cedric Robinson and nearly as far off from Maxwell's hopes of a dialogue between Harlem and Moscow, unsurprisingly frames proper revolutionary movement as a one-way ticket from Russia to the rest of the world. The professor even goes so far as to assure Lafala, with all the tact of a white racist uncle, that he is merely "trying to help your people here in Marseilles" (*RM*, 76). This unconvincing doctrinal focus, about as far from the vibrant delights of Quayside as a civics class, leaves little doubt why Lafala remains unmoved by "the new social truth" (*RM*, 77, 76). As "a child of black bush Africa," a victim of both colonialism and the ship's frigid and disfiguring hold, Lafala underlies McKay's exposure of the implausible abstraction of international socialism when removed from living contact with the Black diaspora. If, as Robinson asserted, "Black radicalism is a negation of Western civilization," it is no radicalism at all if it follows European manners in a setting so tedious that the guests can't help but nod off.[54]

McKay's political and literary engagement with revolutionary Russia and the multitude of peoples gathered beneath the mantle of the International demanded that he grapple with forms of difference he believed Soviet Marxism was unequipped—or unwilling—to truly engage. This may be one of the reasons why Lafala ultimately imagines the amelioration of his poverty only in incremental and personal terms, a thing of "more comfort, more spaciousness and cleanliness," rather than systemic change (*RM*, 77). St. Dominique tries to explain to Lafala that returning as a rich man to the bush will only import these impoverished social relations along with him, predicting the defeatist climax of the novel: "We can't go back to Africa. *You* can as an individual. But we can't as a people" (*RM*, 77). McKay collapses the impossibility of Garvey's dream into Lafala's lack of interest in Russian diktats, no matter how brightly colored the stacks of pamphlets in the Seaman's Club. Dull in comparison to the delights of Quayside and without more robust explanatory power for someone with Lafala's pedigree, that particular ship, like the final voyage of the bankrupt Black Star Line, has long since sailed.

The Future History of a Black Intersectional International

McKay's main thrusts against Moscow involved its limited commitment to issues of race and the impoverishing rigidity of Communist theory. But *Romance* points to at least one more analytical omission that propels the novel into our own moment most of all. Unfortunately for her, Aslima is the character who functions as the cipher for our contemporary problematics. Though her nightmarish end is decried as a vagary of fate, we might denaturalize her death by picking at the many tangled reasons why she is the only truly tragic character in the text: a figure born into slavery, stolen from her tiny family, trafficked in sexual servitude, and eventually made to bear the full weight of the plot as it collapses upon her through the twin niceties of heartbreak and murder. In fact, her centrality to the novel seemed to take even McKay by surprise, explaining to his literary agent, "The Arab girl is growing bigger than I ever dreamed and running away with the book and me" (*RM*, xxvi). But where might Aslima be running the book *to*? And why, after an already captive life at the peripheral extremes, is it necessary for McKay to erase her with such spectacular suffering and harm? While McKay explored Black abjection in any number of his works, most of his sympathetic main characters are either substantially untroubled by their material situations or able to navigate successfully around them (think of Banjo in his titular novel, or Jake in *Home to Harlem*). Aslima, by contrast, seems fully captured by her biography, propelled through a dizzying array of "scenes of subjection" grounded in entanglements between her gender, race, heritage, religion, and "debased" employments.[55] She is not only the intersectional figure par excellence in the novel; she also offers McKay an opportunity to recognize where his own blindness might resound by way of the aporiae he located within international socialism, while also offering contemporary readers an opportunity to rethink intersectionality's promise and limits through what still remains, as it were, on the margins.

Aslima's narrative is a slave narrative. And though, in this case, the body of water she travels around is the Mediterranean, her life recalls what Stephanie Smallwood explains as "the transformation of African captives into Atlantic commodities."[56] Born in Marrakech as the daughter of a Sudanese slave sold by the Moors, Aslima's very hometown stands as a porous boundary between peoples, cultures, and regions, "that city of the plain where savagery emerging from the jungle meets civilization" (*RM*, 42). Aslima is stolen for resale from her mother and then sold hand to hand, her early life an investment for someone else's eventual return because she "was worth a little prize and someday a nice little sum could be realized on her virgin beauty" (*RM*, 45). Once, in language linking both bonds and bondage, she is said to reach "maturity," Aslima is then circulated around networks as transnational and ethnically varied as that of the Fourth Congress. Her "first personal adventure" is having her virginity sold to a "colored sub-officer from one of the French West Indies" who takes her to Casablanca and leaves her there. After that, she "carried on transient love affairs with native and white" until she was sold "into a house of love" in Marseille by a young Corsican: "Many were the African and Oriental seamen who stopped to look in at the open door at the little savage curled up on the mattress regarding them with mischievous half-closed eyes" (*RM*, 45–46). Mixed-race, Caribbean, Black, white, "native," European, "Oriental," African: Aslima's transactional encounters link the world of the global proletariat and the routes of empire with more comprehension than the Red tracts handed out at the Seaman's Club. Slavery for her is indeed no *after* life at all. And in a novel full of manifold takes on rutting love—hookups, marriage, clear dealings, true lifelong desire, and everything in between, queer and straight alike—all of her "adventures" are mediated explicitly by exchange until her final affair with Lafala. While his feet were, in a sense, reimbursed once and in total by the shipping company, Aslima's body continually produces value for any number of pockets but her own. Momentarily, however, and despite their complicated pasts, the two lovers court each other much like other modern European couples: They attend movies and hold hands in the darkened theater; they dine al fresco while sharing bottles of wine; and they roam the city's lurid streets with dedicated flânerie. Though these scenes afford Aslima some sense of freedom, her biography and business consistently push back against any possibility of liberation. Whether as "a burning brown mixed of Arab and Negro and other wanton bloods perhaps that had created her a barbaric creature," or even more comprehensively commodified as "a near-native thing," her past haunts her possibilities for other futures, the "realization" of value for herself and by herself perpetually withheld (*RM*, 4, 5).

Despite *Romance's* much-touted "contemporary" feel, McKay obviously had no recourse to recent intersectional theories, methods, or approaches. Famously named in Kimberlé Crenshaw's two landmark articles, published in 1989 and 1991, respectively, "the intersectional experience is greater than the sum of racism and sexism, [and] any analysis that does not take intersectionality into account cannot sufficiently address the particular manner in which Black women are subordinated."[57] This "greater than" position frames intersectional analysis as both procedural and dialectic, combining the subject-positions of race and gender to produce experiences both different from and in excess of any single axis of stratification. In the three decades since Crenshaw's definition, the concepts and methods of intersectionality have complemented, expanded, challenged, critiqued, and often superseded a number of other heuristic approaches in large swaths of the social sciences and humanities that engage with "difference" writ large. Yet, as Jennifer C. Nash argues in *Black Feminism Reimagined*, such primacy also carries substantial challenges and costs. Providing a vivid gloss on the interwoven histories of the concepts collected under the rubric of intersectionality, Nash details how the adoption of the term has at times reinscribed some of the very elisions and silences the method was designed to foreground. In particular, while numerous women's and gender studies programs loudly tout the centrality of intersectional approaches on departmental websites as their "signature analytic," Nash locates several problems that arise from such academic prominence.[58] On the one hand, she argues, if "nothing is more damning than the accusation of 'white feminism'" and intersectionality now "stands as the field's primary corrective," then Black feminist theory's "demand for inclusion" is over and "the labor of the field is complete" (*BF*, 15). On the other hand, at the institutional level "intersectionality has been rhetorically mobilized as an ethic of diversity, . . . in part because naming intersectionality is often imagined to stand in for performing a kind of intellectual and political work" (*BF*, 25). Both critiques function in related ways, whereby to claim that one's school or department "does intersectionality" can obviate some of the material political demands and insights arising from the analytic itself.

Looking to disaggregate intersectionality from formal reification or any single moment of inauguration, Nash's account sees it "as part of a cohort of terms that black feminists created in order to analyze the interconnectedness of structures of domination" (*BF*, 6). But she also finds that "the peculiarly contentious battles" around the term are significantly instructive because they "implicate the body that haunts the analytic—black woman—even if she is not explicitly named as such" (*BF*, 2). In the words of Avery F. Gordon, this rhetoric of haunting returns us to "the meeting of force and meaning, because haunting is one way in which abusive systems of power make themselves known."[59] With this formulation in mind, we might say that the haunting figure of the "black woman" emerges at the site where the meaning of intersectionality runs into the disciplining force of the institution. And I would suggest as well that the Black woman represented by Aslima haunts *Romance* in ways that resonate vibrantly with this intersectional specter. If McKay felt that organized Marxism would be hopelessly European without deeper links to the Black radical tradition and, conversely, that the tradition itself might collapse into various nationalisms without the global class-based analysis of Marx, Aslima's treatment in the text indicts all sides of this argument by remaining firmly exorcised from both. Yet, by reading her vision and fate through an intersectional frame, we might attempt to redress this durable absence and therefore aid a theoretical revenant in her long-deferred escape.

Even without the rhetoric of intersectionality at hand, McKay understood that "the Negro question is inseparably connected with the question of women's liberation," and his engagement with revolutionary Russia only solidified these associations.[60] As Kate Baldwin observes, "McKay's Soviet work demonstrated how thinking through the question of an alternative socialist future necessitated rethinking the relationships among gender, race, and nation."[61] However, though much of his writing engaged sympathetically with the day-to-day difficulties specific to life as a Black woman—the influential "triple oppression" formulated by Claudia Jones and effectively rendered in the title of Angela Davis's *Women, Race, and Class*—McKay's fiction also at times walked a fine line between critique and reproduction of this imbricated subjection.[62] In *Romance*, for example, while nearly all the main characters have landed in Marseille either by chance or choice, Aslima arrives only after being sold into sexual servitude. What's more, while the men in the novel mostly come, go, labor, and frolic on their own terms, Aslima must dutifully report to Titin, an abusive pimp who always complains she's either not earning enough or, worse, holding out.

McKay also, it seems, had little patience for metaphysics. He even poked fun at Jean Toomer's genuflection at the altar of G. I. Gurdjieff, a fashionable mystic of his time, writing to Walter White that "Toomer could accomplish more in fiction if he would not let his tendency toward mysticism interfere with his sense of reality" (*CM*, 214). Yet, while Lafala's White Heaven was clearly marked out as a dream, Aslima's subsequent "vision" is named exactly that (twice), goes on for several pages, and allows her to quite literally save Lafala's life while also setting in motion the imminent conclusion of her own. After yet another dressing-down by her pimp, with Titin screaming at her about wanting "to go naked again" in the "jungle," "wear a banana leaf," and live as "a good and naked squaw to [Lafala] in a hut in the bush" rather than continue to sell herself for his profit, Aslima finds herself on "a terrace which overlooked the beautiful bay" and is so moved by a sunset tableau that she becomes "lost in it," as "children played in the sand. Loving couples sat spaced apart with their backs to the sea" and, moving offshore, "the little fishing boats huddled together coloring the slightly moving waves. Farther off the big ships loomed upon the horizon in shadow and gloom" (*RM*, 60). Considering Marseille's *longue durée* as the principal port for French empire—linking the colonies, peoples, and commodities of Morocco, Algeria, and Tunisia with the interior of France—as well as its place as an important node in the French slave trade, it's no accident that the view of the bay is what conjures Aslima's vision. Her gaze reproduces a form of civilizational stagism from the shore on out, from little kids to loving bonded pairs to small and human-scaled labors and finally to the "shadowy" and "gloomy" large vessels that once held pairs in bondage.[63] The ocean reverie becomes hypnotic "after a long strange interval" as she and the reader find themselves suddenly transported to "the heart of an antique white-washed city" recalling her Moroccan childhood, complete with "loud mounting music . . . [,] as if a thousand golden-throated muezzins were calling in one mighty chorus" (*RM*, 60). St. Dominique may have warned Lafala that he could not return to a precolonial Africa, but Aslima's vision allows her to do exactly that, where she finds a "stamping and dancing to barbaric music" "as if in evocation of the first gods who emerged out of the ancient unfathomed womb of Africa to procreate and spread over the vast surface of the land" (*RM*, 61). However, Aslima's arrival in this prehistorical deep time does not seem to offer a retreat to some facile argument about humanity's originary sameness. Rather, returning to Lisa Lowe, we might view the scene as the ultimate recourse to a kind of past conditional temporality, of all the roads humanly possible, taken, and denied, and of all the potentials of the past that remain to be activated by the present.

Beginning with a calm collectivity built on "kindred people" enjoying "a loving feast," Aslima's vision unspools into "a gorgeous gorging" followed by dancing to "the belly-moving beat of the drum" and then blooms into a ritualistic celebration of difference, "reflecting all the colors of life" (*RM*, 61). But as soon as differentiation by color is introduced, Aslima is "repelled, fascinated, and awed by a flaming sword" that narratively cleaves this fundamental human unity further: "All the people of the earth were assembled under that dome and worshipping that sword [of life]. Some were slaves and some were free; some were wanton and some were happy. Some were strange and some were sad; some were lighthearted and some were heavy-burdened. But all were worshippers, subject creatures, making sacrifices to it" (*RM*, 61). Here is McKay's most comprehensive theory of subjectification, at least as presented in *Romance*: its differential processes emerge from varied material histories, the immense multiplicity of differences—of type, of feeling, of disposition, of existence itself—all chained together by the awe and terror and beauty of "The Sword of Life!" So far, so good, if not blithely romantic about a few million bygone nightmares. But even within a field of difference as large as humanity itself, Aslima is still marked out as distinct, for "among the multitude was one group apart that was offering up body and soul as a sacrifice. And in the midst of that group was Aslima divided and struggling against herself. She did not want to surrender all of her, but she could not detach herself" (*RM*, 62).

Division, detachment, struggle, surrender: Aslima's accretion of difference makes worshipping the sword impossible due to the excessive burden she's made to bear, body and soul, flesh and self, unable to "detach" any particularity from her whole, and always one group apart. While we're never told who else is in this group, we do know who's not: Aslima "saw Lafala among the free and cried out fearfully to him. But he could not go to her" (*RM*, 62). As the unfree Black woman at the center of her own vision, Aslima is asked to sacrifice all so that everyone else might more comfortably worship at the altar. If, in the often-quoted words of Audre Lorde, "There is no such thing as a single-issue struggle because we do not live single-issue lives," Aslima's aggregated issues as a Black woman in the human crowd make her own struggle comparatively impossible to bear.[64]

This figure of the "black woman"—whose sacrifice is at once both required and silenced—isn't only haunting intersectionality in *Romance*, however, and it makes sense that she appears in a novel appraising, among other concerns, the complications that questions of race posed for international socialism. Since Mary Helen Washington defined the formation "black left feminism" almost twenty years ago, a number of studies have emphasized "a path-breaking brand of feminist politics that centers working-class women by combining black nationalist and American Communist Party positions on race, gender, and class with black women radicals' own lived experiences."[65] Scholars such as Erik S. McDuffie, Cheryl Higashida, and Carol Boyce Davies have recovered "the radical black female subject" so often "disappeared from major consideration in a range of histories."[66] Intersectional by design, these rescued histories showcase the range, centrality, and importance of Black women activists as they drew strength, strategies, and solace from a number of overlapping and entangled radical traditions, showcasing what H. L. T. Quan, riffing on Cedric Robinson, calls "geniuses of resistance."[67]

Why, then, might McKay place what seems like a consonant Black left feminist insight within the one metaphysical moment of the novel that overtakes Aslima and remains largely unrelated to the rest of the plot? Why have this momentary fugue recall an ancient "out-of-Africa" mythos clad in the language and iconography of a religion that begins truly at "the beginning"—or at least in McKay's imagination of it? In short, why all the drama? In *Becoming Human* Zakkiyah Iman Jackson offers one possible explanation, arguing "that black female flesh persistently functions as the limit case of 'the human' and is its matrix-figure" due to the fact that "Eurocentric humanism needs blackness as a prop in order to erect whiteness."[68] In Jackson's framing, Black women become both the *ur*-space around which definitions of "the human" metastasize as well as the foundational object that supports and structures those meanings upon their emergence. Challenging previous attempts to read Blackness in Western imaginaries as fixedly other than, below, or nonhuman, she offers the useful concept of "plasticity" as a corrective that allows for all fungible possibilities through "a mode of transmogrification whereby the fleshy being of blackness is experimented with as if it were infinitely malleable lexical and biological matter, such that blackness is produced as sub/super/human at once, a form where form shall not hold: potentially 'everything and nothing' at the register of ontology."[69] Defying demarcations that attempt to codify Black abjection, plasticity resists any final verdict on a withheld humanity, therefore remaining able to assist with potentially any anti-Black ideological expediency.

Through a play on the link between matter, mater, and maternal, Jackson affirms that if Black female flesh is "an enabling condition of an imperial Western humanist conception of *the* world *as such*," then "the specter of black mater—that is, nonrepresentability—haunts the terms and operations tasked with adjudicating the thought-world correlate" in ways that illuminate both Nash's Black woman haunting the halls of intersectionality and Aslima's attempts to run away with McKay's text.[70] By reading Aslima's vision through these dual lenses of haunting and suspended humanity, the scene becomes legible not as simple analogy or didactic parable but as an alternative mode of political meaning-making that demands we overcome "the continued blindness to black feminism *as an autonomous intellectual and political tradition*" in and on its own terms (*BF*, 16). Much as Cheryl Higashida refers to the subjects of her book as "Black Internationalist Feminists," we might imagine Aslima running McKay's novel *toward* a dialectical imbrication of all these terms in the service of outlining a Black Intersectional International, one that approaches the work and thought of Black women not as a supplement to (white) feminism nor as an extension of a Black radical tradition, but as an epistemology on its own terms, for which any mere grafting is either crude distortion or simply impossible.[71] Arising from the foundational insights flowing from the "triple oppression," Aslima's dreamtime struggle suggests a generative combination and compromise among intellectual traditions—Black radicalism, Marxism, Black left feminism, and intersectionality—all energized by a central dialectic that necessarily exceeds the sum of its terms, while preserving their distinct clarities, objects, and approaches; and activated by materialist praxes that would necessarily recur back onto the traditions themselves. As Marx argued, "theory becomes a material force when it grips the masses."[72] And by combining these approaches intersectionally, these masses might finally become truly *massive* as well. Inexhaustibly comprised of new differences like the crowds around the Sword of Life, the engine of this dialectic would ideally insure against any fantasies of comprehensive fullness or mere inclusion, remaining instead, as Lenin demanded, a "*living*, many-sided knowledge (with the number of sides eternally increasing), with an infinite number of shades of every approach and approximation to reality (with a philosophical system growing into a whole out of each shade)"[73]—in short, a necessarily unfinished knowledge, system, and praxis to which anyone wandering around Quayside might finally respond, thereby aiding this movement endlessly toward an impossibly exhaustive and inclusive completion.

But it is already too late for Aslima. Faithful to the end, she believes that Lafala will take her to Africa so they can live as "two loving pigs going away together to hide in the jungle" (*RM*, 123). Instead, she finds out secondhand that he has left for Africa without her, and she returns to Titin, who is furious to see such a golden meal ticket take flight. Understandably desperate and despondent, Aslima rushes toward him in attack and the pimp empties his pistol into her body, calling "upon hell to swallow her soul." Even so, we might draw the iciest solace from her sacrifice, body and soul, a group apart: if Lafala's dream opens the novel in a jazzy White Heaven where there are no Black things and ends with a fortune in exchange for his feet, Aslima's closing vision—because "women were always suffering for men" (*RM*, 68)—attempts small compensation for her intolerable triple burden with a dialectical draft of "immeasurably rich content," one forever building upon itself in the service of emancipation for good.[74]

All Workers Are Essential

To return to the contemporary one last time: by agreeing with Martin that "the political demands placed on us by our present depend on how we first decide what belongs to the present," then we have already decided that *Romance* is a ninety-year-old new book finally added to the catastrophic pile of our own time.[75] But instead of hunting for its "answers," we might, as Elizabeth Freeman suggests in another context, make use of the novel's strange, old newness to begin "mining the present for signs of undetonated energy from past revolutions."[76] And not a minute too soon: it is now midsummer 2020. The death toll from COVID-19 stands at over 650,000 worldwide, 150,000 in the United States alone (and still very much counting). No one cheers anymore at 7:00 p.m. and the Jewish socialist now sends out emails asking for money a few times a week, but the streets have exploded with a fury far less manageable than a Democratic primary. Federal troops have been deployed to bloody photo ops in Portland and other cities, where they disappear protestors into unmarked vehicles. Nancy Pelosi, no great tribune of the left, calls them Trump's "stormtroopers" (by tweet, of course).[77] Representative Jim Clyburn compares them to the Gestapo. In New York, the NYPD throws eighteen-year-old trans activist Nikki Stone into a white minivan for the outrageous crime of "making graffiti." Witnesses call it "a kidnapping."[78] Myrtle Avenue is be-be itching all over again, but this time with marchers chanting slogans behind masks.

Earlier this year a narrow strip of land in North Brooklyn was renamed Marsha P. Johnson State Park.[79] Since her memorial was unveiled, at least twenty-seven trans or gender-nonconforming people in the United States have been murdered.[80] Most are Black women. Peppermint, a Black trans activist, explains to the *New York Times* that she thinks "the notion of intersectionality is becoming more readily available for people to understand that a win for one group or one identity doesn't necessarily equal an automatic win for the other." At the same time, unemployment is down to "only" 11.1 percent and 43 million Americans are at risk of losing their homes over the next few months. Breonna Taylor's killers still walk free, still wear badges, still carry guns. Among the many objects thrown at cops during the protests: a pig's head. "True pigs for life," Aslima might say (*RM*, 123). But she's already gone, disappeared into what Harney and Moten call "the *undercommons of enlightenment*, where the work gets done, where the work gets subverted, where the revolution is still black, still strong."[81] And where, despite the news—ominous, monstrous, relentless—there are still, like Aslima's beloved Quayside, endless bits of color in the dirt.

JESSE W. SCHWARTZ is associate professor of English at LaGuardia Community College, City University of New York. He has held fellowships with the Deutscher Akademischer Austauschdienst in Osnabrück, Germany, as well as the National Endowment for the Humanities. His current project traces the intersections between racialization and anticapitalism in the late nineteenth and early twentieth centuries, with a focus on representations of the Russian Revolution in US print cultures. A board member of the journal *Radical Teacher*, he has been published there as well as in *Nineteenth-Century Literature*.

Acknowledgments

I would first like to thank the anonymous reader who provided a number of very generous and generative suggestions. I would also like to thank William J. Maxwell and Gary Edward Holcomb for their patience, editorial guidance, and general bonhomie throughout this process. Sari Altschuler and Chris Carpenter deserve immense gratitude for their *very* last-minute comments, but mostly for assuring me that an essay drafted almost entirely during lockdown did not end up reading quite as unhinged as its conditions of composition. Finally, Yvette Grant warrants endless praise for her eleventh-hour edits, but even more so for sharing a small apartment with me throughout a global pandemic.

Notes

1   McKay, *Home to Harlem*, 64.
2   Buchanan, Bui, and Patel, "Black Lives Matter."
3   Benjamin, *Illuminations*, 269.
4   The real reason, of course, that *Romance* has finally found us is thanks to the ceaseless yeoman efforts of its editors. With gratitude, a toast to you both!
5   Zax, "A Book So Far Ahead of Its Time."
6   Dirda, "Claude McKay."
7   Landin, "When Harlem Renaissance Novelist Claude McKay"; Young, "The Best New Novel."
8   *Gleaner*, "Claude McKay's New Relevance to Jamaica"; Woodhead, "Fiction Reviews."
9   Lee, "New Novel."
10   Lee, "New Novel."
11   Wilson, "A Forgotten Novel."
12   Martin, *Contemporary Drift*, 1.
13   Martin, *Contemporary Drift*, 5.
14   Lowe, *Intimacies*, 175.
15   McKay, *Complete Poems*, 174.
16   All of this can be found in the only full biography of McKay: Cooper, *Claude McKay* (hereafter cited as *CM*).
17   For more on littorality, see King, "Off Littorality." The phrase *afterlife of slavery* is from Hartman, *Scenes of Subjection*, 6.
18   McKay, *Romance in Marseille*, 3 (hereafter cited as *RM*).
19   Scott, *Extravagant Abjection*, 17.
20   For a helpful history and definition of commonism, see Haines and Hitchcock, "Introduction."
21   Du Bois, review, 202.

22   Whatever the limitations of his view, Du Bois could certainly not be accused of equivocation. The full quote is: "All art is propaganda and ever must be, despite the wailing of the purists. I stand in utter shamelessness and say that whatever art I have for writing has been used always for propaganda for gaining the right of black folk to love and enjoy. I do not care a damn for any art that is not used for propaganda" ("Criteria," 295).

23   Delany, *Times Square*, 56.

24   Massumi, "Notes," xvi.

25   Holcomb, *Claude McKay*, 172.

26   Lewis, *W. E. B. Du Bois*, 51. For more on colorism, see Kerr, *The Paper Bag Principle*.

27   Spillers, "Mama's Baby," 67.

28   Césaire, *Discourse*, 152.

29   Genette, *Narrative Discourse*, 174.

30   Jameson, *The Antinomies of Realism*, 42, 32, 42, 4, 181.

31   Spinney, *Pale Rider*, 18.

32   For more on his higher education, see *CM*, 69–71.

33   McKay, "Sonnets and Songs"; *CM*, 103, 101.

34   This does not include the several mentions in the introduction as well as the notes.

35   Chen, *Animacies*, 34–35.

36   Wynter, "Unsettling the Coloniality," 261.

37   Deleuze and Guattari, *A Thousand Plateaus*, 247.

38   Freud, "Creative Writing and Day Dreaming," 437.

39   DeGuzmán, *Spain's Long Shadow*, xxvii.

40   Reid-Pharr, *Archives of Flesh*, 12–13.

41   Reid-Pharr, *Archives of Flesh*, 11.

42   McKay, *A Long Way from Home*, 296 (hereafter cited as *LW*).

43   Reid-Pharr, *Archives of Flesh*, 11.

44   Makalani, *In the Cause of Freedom*, 12.

45   Makalani, *In the Cause of Freedom*, 12.

46   Gramsci, *Selections*, 331; Makalani, *In the Cause of Freedom*, 12.

47   Maxwell, *New Negro, Old Left*, 68, 72.

48   Robinson, *Black Marxism*, 73.

49   Kelley, "What Did Cedric Robinson Mean?"

50   Kelley, *Freedom Dreams*, 191.

51   McKay, "Report on the Negro Question," 16.

52   Césaire, "Letter to Maurice Thorez," 150.

53   The significance of his name is discussed at length in Holcomb and Maxwell's introduction to *Romance*.

54   Robinson, *Black Marxism*, 73.

55   Obviously, this phrase is indebted both to Saidaya Hartman's book of the same title and to the concept therein. See Hartman, *Scenes of Subjection*, 22.

56   Smallwood, *Saltwater Slavery*, 36.

57   Crenshaw, "Demarginalizing the Intersection of Race and Sex," 140.

58   Nash, *Black Feminism*, 26 (hereafter cited as *BF*).

59   Gordon, *Ghostly Matters*, xvi.

60   McKay, *The Negroes in America*, 77.

61   Baldwin, *Beyond the Color Line*, 27–28.

62   For more on Claudia Jones, see Davies, *Left of Karl Marx*; and Davis, *Women, Race, and Class*.

63   For more on France's slave trade, see Geggus, "The French Slave Trade." For more on Marseille's connection to French imperialism and its slave trade, see Hewitt, *Wicked City*.

64   Lorde, *Sister Outsider*, 130.

65   Washington, "Alice Childress, Lorraine Hansberry, and Claudia Jones," 185, 193–98; McDuffie, *Sojourning for Freedom*, 3.

66   Davies, *Left of Karl Marx*, 1.

67   Quan, "Geniuses of Resistance," 39.

68   Jackson, *Becoming Human*, 4.

69   Jackson, *Becoming Human*, 3.

70   Jackson, *Becoming Human*, 39.

71   Higashida, *Black Internationalist Feminism*.

72   Marx, introduction.

73   Lenin, "On the Question of Dialectics," 360.

74   Lenin, "On the Question of Dialectics," 360.

75   Martin, *Contemporary Drift*, 5.

76   Freeman, *Time Binds*, xvi.

77   Pelosi, "Unidentified stormtroopers."

78   Spectrum News Staff and Tuchman, "Mayor: Protester's Arrest."

79   Parks, Recreation and Historic Preservation, New York State, "Marsha P. Johnson State Park."

80   Human Rights Campaign, "Violence."

81   Harney and Moten, *The Undercommons*, 26.

Works Cited

Baldwin, Kate. *Beyond the Color Line: Reading Encounters between Black and Red*. Durham, NC: Duke University Press, 2002.

Benjamin, Walter. *Illuminations*, translated by Harry Zohn. Durham, NC: Duke University Press, 2008.

Buchanan, Larry, Quoctrong Bui, and Jugal K. Patel. "Black Lives Matter May Be the Largest Movement in U.S. History." *New York Times*, July 3, 2020. www.nytimes.com/interactive /2020/07/03/us/george-floyd-protests-crowd -size.html.

Césaire, Aimé. *Discourse on Colonialism*. New Delhi: Aakar, 2010.

Césaire, Aimé. "Letter to Maurice Thorez." *Social Text*, no. 103 (2010): 145–52.

Chen, Mel. *Animacies: Biopolitics, Racial Mattering, and Queer Affect*. Durham, NC: Duke University Press, 2012.

Cooper, William F. *Claude McKay: Rebel Sojourner in the Harlem Renaissance*. Baton Rouge: Louisiana State University Press, 1987.

Crenshaw, Kimberlé. "Demarginalizing the Intersection of Race and Sex: A Black Feminist Critique of Antidiscrimination Doctrine, Feminist Theory, and Antiracist Politics." *University of Chicago Legal Forum*, no. 1 (1989): 139–67.

Davies, Carol Boyce. *Left of Karl Marx: The Political Life of Black Communist Claudia Jones.* Durham, NC: Duke University Press, 2007.

Davis, Angela Y. *Women, Race, and Class.* New York: Vintage, 1983.

DeGuzmán, Maria. *Spain's Long Shadow: The Black Legend, Off-Whiteness, and Anglo-American Empire.* Minneapolis: University of Minnesota Press, 2005.

Delany, Samuel R. *Times Square Red, Times Square Blue.* New York: New York University Press, 2019.

Deleuze, Gilles, and Félix Guattari. *A Thousand Plateaus: Capitalism and Schizophrenia,* translated by Brian Massumi. Minneapolis: University of Minnesota Press, 1987.

Dirda, Michael. "Claude McKay Abandoned 'Romance in Marseille' Because It Was Too Daring. He Was Just Ahead of His Time." *Washington Post,* February 5, 2020. www .washingtonpost.com/entertainment/books /claude-mckay-abandoned-romance-in -marseille-because-it-was-too-daring-he-was -just-ahead-of-his-time/2020/02/05/1c215cc4 -46a1-11ea-ab15-b5df3261b710_story.html.

Du Bois, W. E. B. "Criteria of Negro Art." *Crisis,* no. 32 (1926): 290–97.

Du Bois, W. E. B. Review of *Home to Harlem* and *Quicksand. Crisis,* no. 35 (1928): 202.

Freeman, Elizabeth. *Time Binds: Queer Temporalities, Queer Histories.* Durham, NC: Duke University Press, 2010.

Freud, Sigmund. "Creative Writing and Day Dreaming." In *The Freud Reader,* edited by Peter Gay, 436–42. New York: Norton, 1995.

Geggus, David. "The French Slave Trade: An Overview." *William and Mary Quarterly* 58, no. 1 (2001): 119–38.

Genette, Gerárd. *Narrative Discourse: An Essay on Method,* translated by Jane E. Lewin. Ithaca, NY: Cornell University Press, 1983.

Gleaner. "Claude McKay's New Relevance to Jamaica." February 13, 2020. jamaica-gleaner .com/article/commentary/20200213/editorial -claude-mckays-new-relevance-jamaica.

Gordon, Avery F. *Ghostly Matters: Haunting and the Sociological Imagination.* Minneapolis: University of Minnesota Press, 2008.

Gramsci, Antonio. *Selections from the Prison Notebooks,* edited by Quintin Hoare and Geoffrey Nowell Smith. New York: International, 1971.

Haines, Christian P., and Peter Hitchcock. "Introduction: No Place for the Commons." *minnesota review,* no. 93 (2019): 55–61.

Harney, Stefano, and Fred Moten. *The Undercommons: Fugitive Planning and Black Study.* New York: Minor Compositions, 2013.

Hartman, Saidiya. *Scenes of Subjection: Terror, Slavery, and Self-Making in Nineteenth-Century America.* Oxford: Oxford University Press, 1997.

Hewitt, Nicholas. *Wicked City: The Many Cultures of Marseille.* London: Hurst, 2019.

Higashida, Cheryl. *Black Internationalist Feminism.* Champaign: University of Illinois Press, 2011.

Holcomb, Gary Edward. *Claude McKay, Code Name Sasha: Queer Black Marxism and the Harlem Renaissance.* Gainesville: University Press of Florida, 2007.

Human Rights Campaign. "Violence against the Transgender and Gender Non-conforming Community in 2020." *Human Rights Campaign.* hrc.org/resources/violence-against -the-trans-and-gender-non-conforming -community-in-2020 (accessed August 2, 2020).

Jackson, Zakiyyah Iman. *Becoming Human: Matter and Meaning in an Antiblack World.* New York: New York University Press, 2020.

Jameson, Fredric. *The Antinomies of Realism.* New York: Verso, 2015.

Kelley, Robin D. G. *Freedom Dreams: The Black Radical Imagination.* Boston: Beacon, 2002.

Kelley, Robin D. G. "What Did Cedric Robinson Mean by Racial Capitalism?" *Boston Review,* December 13, 2019. bostonreview.net/race /robin-d-g-kelley-what-did-cedric-robinson -mean-racial-capitalism.

Kerr, Audrey Elisa. *The Paper Bag Principle: Class, Colorism, and Rumor and the Case of Black Washington, D.C.* Knoxville: University of Tennessee Press, 2006.

King, Tiffany Lethabo. "Off Littorality (Shoal 1.0): Black Study off the Shores of 'the Black Body.'" *Propter Nos* 3 (2019): 40–50.

Landin, Conrad. "When Harlem Renaissance Novelist Claude McKay Decamped for the Port of Marseille." *Jacobin,* July 2, 2020. jacobinmag.com/2020/07/claude-mckay -marseille-review-literature.

Lee, Felicia R. "New Novel of Harlem Renaissance Is Found." *New York Times,* September 14, 2012. www.nytimes.com/2012/09/15/books/harlem -renaissance-novel-by-claude-mckay-is -discovered.html.

Lenin, V. I. "On the Question of Dialectics," edited by Stewart Smith, translated by Clemence

Dutt. In vol. 38 of *Collected Works*, 357–61. 4th ed. Moscow: Progress, 1976.

Lewis, David Levering. *W. E. B. Du Bois, 1919–1963: The Fight for Equality and the American Century*. New York: Holt, 2001.

Lorde, Audre. *Sister Outsider: Essays and Speeches*. New York: Penguin, 2020.

Lowe, Lisa. *The Intimacies of Four Continents*. Durham, NC: Duke University Press, 2015.

Makalani, Minkah. *In the Cause of Freedom: Radical Black Internationalism from Harlem to London, 1917–1939*. Chapel Hill: University of North Carolina Press, 2011.

Martin, Theodore. *Contemporary Drift*. New York: Columbia University Press, 2017.

Marx, Karl. Introduction to *A Contribution to the Critique of Hegel's Philosophy of Right*. 1844. www.marxists.org/archive/marx/works/1843 /critique-hpr/intro.htm.

Massumi, Brian. "Notes on the Translation and Acknowledgments." In Deleuze and Guattari, *A Thousand Plateaus*, xvi–xix.

Maxwell, William J. *New Negro, Old Left: African-American Writing and Communism between the Wars*. New York: Columbia University Press, 1999.

McDuffie, Erik S. *Sojourning for Freedom: Black Women, American Communism, and the Making of Black Left Feminism*. Durham, NC: Duke University Press, 2011.

McKay, Claude. *Complete Poems*, edited by William J. Maxwell. Champaign: University of Illinois Press, 2008.

McKay, Claude. *Home to Harlem*. Boston: Northeastern University Press, 1987.

McKay, Claude. *A Long Way from Home*. New York: Furman, 1937.

McKay, Claude. *The Negroes in America*, translated by Robert J. Winter. Port Washington, NY: Kennikat, 1977.

McKay, Claude. "Report on the Negro Question: Speech to the Fourth Congress of the Comintern, Nov. 1922." *International Press Correspondence* 3 (1923): 16–17.

McKay, Claude. *Romance in Marseille*, edited by Gary Edward Holcomb and William J. Maxwell. New York: Penguin, 2020.

McKay, Claude. "Sonnets and Songs." *Liberator* 2, no. 7 (1919): 20–21.

Nash, Jennifer C. *Black Feminism Reimagined: After Intersectionality*. Durham, NC: Duke University Press, 2019.

Parks, Recreation and Historic Preservation, New York State. "Marsha P. Johnson State Park (East River State Park)." parks.ny.gov/ parks/155/details.aspx (accessed August 9, 2020).

Pelosi, Nancy (@SpeakerPelosi). "Unidentified stormtroopers. Unmarked cars. Kidnapping protesters and causing severe injuries in response to graffiti." Twitter, July 17, 2020, 9:10 p.m. twitter.com/speakerpelosi/status /1284294427654197248.

Quan, H. L. T. "Geniuses of Resistance: Feminist Consciousness and the Black Radical Tradition." *Race and Class* 47, no. 2 (2005): 39–53.

Reid-Pharr, Robert. *Archives of Flesh: African America, Spain, and Post-humanist Critique*. New York: New York University Press, 2016.

Robinson, Cedric. *Black Marxism: The Making of the Black Radical Tradition*. Chapel Hill: University of North Carolina Press, 2000.

Scott, Darieck. *Extravagant Abjection: Blackness, Power, and Sexuality in the African American Literary Imagination*. New York: New York University Press, 2010.

Smallwood, Stephanie E. *Saltwater Slavery: A Middle Passage from Africa to American Diaspora*. Cambridge, MA: Harvard University Press, 2008.

Spectrum News Staff and Lindsay Tuchman. "Mayor: Protester's Arrest in Unmarked NYPD Van Troubling, but Is No Portland." *NY1*, July 28, 2020; updated July 29, 2020. www.ny1.com/nyc/all-boroughs/news/2020 /07/29/video-shows-protester-being-pulled -into-unmarked-van-by-nypd.

Spillers, Hortense J. "Mama's Baby, Papa's Maybe: An American Grammar Book." *Diacritics* 17, no. 2 (1987): 64–81.

Spinney, Laura. *Pale Rider: The Spanish Flu of 1918 and How It Changed the World*. London: Vintage, 2017.

Washington, Mary Helen. "Alice Childress, Lorraine Hansberry, and Claudia Jones: Black Women Write the Popular Front." In *Left of the Color Line: Race, Radicalism, and Twentieth-Century Literature of the United States*, edited by Bill Mullen and James Edward Smethurst, 183–204. Chapel Hill: University of North Carolina Press, 2003.

Wilson, Jennifer. "A Forgotten Novel Explores How Communism Tried to Win Over Harlem." *Atlantic*, March 9, 2017. www.theatlantic.com /entertainment/archive/2017/03/a-forgotten -novel-reveals-a-forgotten-harlem/518364.

Woodhead, Cameron. "Fiction Reviews: *Romance in Marseille* and Three Other Titles." *Sydney Morning Herald*, June 5, 2020. www.smh.com .au/culture/books/fiction-reviews-romance-in -marseille-and-three-other-titles-20200601 -p54yho.html.

Wynter, Sylvia. "Unsettling the Coloniality of
    Being/Power/Truth/Freedom: Towards the
    Human, after Man, Its Overrepresentation—
    An Argument." *CR: The New Centennial
    Review*, no. 3 (2003): 257–337.
Young, Molly. "The Best New Novel Was Written
    Ninety Years Ago." *New York*, February 6,
    2020. www.vulture.com/2020/02/romance
    -in-marseille-claude-mckay.html.
Zax, Talya. "A Book So Far Ahead of Its Time, It
    Took Eighty-Seven Years to Find a Publisher."
    New York Times, February 5, 2020. www
    .nytimes.com/2020/02/05/books/claude
    -mckay-romance-marseille-harlem-renaissance
    .html.

"A Syrup of Passion and Desire"

Transgressive Politics of Pleasure in Claude McKay's *Romance in Marseille*

AGNIESZKA TUSZYNSKA

Abstract   This article examines the politics of transgressive pleasure and desire in Claude McKay's novel *Romance in Marseille*, as a response to what Achille Mbembe, departing from Foucault's notion of biopower, has termed necropolitics. In the novel, the interlocking hegemonic systems of racism and capitalism function as mechanisms of necropower—the power of determining whose lives are deemed worthy and whose bodies are deemed disposable—which is executed through the procedures of mutilation, surveillance, poverty, and sexual exploitation. Foregrounding the titular "romance," McKay's novel features characters who engage in romantic and sexual relationships that subvert the expectations of heteronormativity, sexual economy, and the color line. Anticipating the twenty-first-century theories that locate sovereign power in the body, McKay politicizes and radicalizes desire as a response to the racialization, criminalization, and dehumanization of his novel's lumpen characters.
Keywords   Claude McKay, African American literature, transgressive pleasure, necropower, Achille Mbembe

Romance, Social Death, and Black Pleasure

A reader of Claude McKay's *Romance in Marseille* also familiar with Frantz Fanon's "The Fact of Blackness" (1952) may find the parallels between McKay's posthumously—and only recently—published novel's initial chapters and Fanon's famous essay nothing short of stunning. In a striking opening image, McKay starts the novel with his West African protagonist, Lafala, lying in a New York City hospital "like a sawed-off stump" contemplating "the loss of his legs" and feeling like "[a] block of blackness in a hospital shirt."[1] As *Romance* begins, following Lafala's capture on a New World–bound ship on which he illegally embarked in Marseille, and then his imprisonment in a freezing deck toilet, his lower legs have just been amputated due to frostbite. This actual amputation and the acute racial self-awareness that Lafala experiences in its wake foreshadow the metaphorical amputation of subjectivity experienced by Fanon's narrator in confrontation with a white person's exclamation: "Look, a Negro!"[2] Yet, despite the undeniable correspondence between both

ENGLISH LANGUAGE NOTES
59:1, April 2021   DOI 10.1215/00138282-8814972
© 2021 Regents of the University of Colorado

texts' colonial subjects' sense of bodily disintegration combined with agential loss, *Romance in Marseille* and "The Fact of Blackness" diverge in important ways. Fanon closes his essay with his narrator struggling "to rise" and regain his sense of self, yet, under the weight of "paralyzed" "wings," feeling ultimately defeated (FB, 140). McKay, by contrast, fills the remainder of his novel with occasions for not just Lafala, who returns to Marseille later in the novel, but also for other abject characters living in the "dream port" to find respite and even self-actualization in intimate and erotic bonds, or the titular "romance." Desire and sexual fulfillment—unavailable to the Black man in Fanon's world—become not only a refuge but also a way of legitimizing the selfhood of the socially marginalized characters who populate Marseille's Old Port in McKay's novel.

McKay's centering of the bodily experience of his characters in this newly published novel will not surprise anyone who considers the author's oeuvre. Fascination with the somatic dimension of experience in its full range—from the body as a source of exploitation to its role as a source of pleasure—is ubiquitous in McKay's works. On the one hand, there is the writer's commitment to the embodied pain of those who struggle, such as the speaker of his proletarian poem, "The Tired Worker," a line from which, "Peace, O my rebel heart!," is engraved on McKay's tombstone:

> O whisper, O my soul! The afternoon
> Is waning into evening, whisper soft!
> Peace, O my rebel heart! for soon the moon
> From out its misty veil will swing aloft!
> Be patient, weary body, soon the night
> Will wrap thee gently in her sable sheet,
> And with a leaden sigh thou wilt invite
> To rest thy tired hands and aching feet.
> The wretched day was theirs, the night is mine;
> Come tender sleep, and fold me to thy breast.
> But what steals out the gray clouds red like wine?
> O dawn! O dreaded dawn! O let me rest
> Weary my veins, my brain, my life! Have pity!
> No! Once again the hard, the ugly city.[3]

The poem's speaker is an exploited worker whose desperate need for relief from the daily toil drives him to appease his revolutionary spirit ("rebel heart") and prioritize the "weary body" (line 5), the "tired hands," and "aching feet" (line 8). The primary focus, then, falls on the corporeal torment of the worker, the body's toil and exhaustion and its longing for ever-elusive rest, the "tender sleep" (line 10) disturbed by "dreaded dawn" (line 12). The speaker's body appears suspended in the state of seemingly never-ending and nightmarish wakefulness. McKay's anatomical detailing of the body parts affected by relentless exhaustion in the poem evidences the author's usual attentiveness to the body with all its sensory complexity. On the other end of McKay's somatic spectrum of experience is the body's ability to feel satisfaction, such as one described in this scene from McKay's novel *Home to Harlem*: "In the middle of the floor, a young railroad porter had his hand flattened straight down the slim, cérise-chiffoned back of a brown girl. Her head was thrown back and her eyes held his gleaming eyes. Her lips were parted with pleasure and they stood and rocked in an ecstasy. Their feet were not moving. Only their bodies rocked, rocked to the 'blues.'"[4] The scene's eroticism, while relatively subdued compared to other parts of the novel, offers a glimpse of McKay's portrayal of the body as *also* a source of sensual gratification, the prominence of which famously led W. E. B. Du Bois to wish for a bath after reading *Home to Harlem*.

Yet, despite the prevalence of corporeality in McKay's work, in *Romance in Marseille* the writer's career-long meditation on the multifaceted role of the bodily experience in the lives of the dispossessed comes full circle. Here, the body in its suffering and the body in its bliss are two sides of the same coin. The narrative's "romance" refers not only to the novel's central affair between Lafala and his lover, Moroccan sex worker Aslima, but also to a range of relationships and intimate encounters within the diverse group of characters populating Marseille's dock district. The title's collective dimension allows for a better understanding of how passion and pleasure challenge the rules of sex economy, the color line, and heteronormativity in the text.

McKay's portrayal of multiracial, queer, and disabled bodies navigating, bending, and breaking the boundaries of permissible pleasure anticipates the work of twentieth- and twenty-first-century scholars who locate sovereign power in the body and who advocate for expanding the definition of resistance beyond the realm of the political. Of particular interest here are thinkers who have looked for a new understanding of Black oppositional practices in the embodied lived experience of Black people, from Audre Lorde's Black feminist application of this idea in "The Uses of the Erotic: The Erotic as Power" (1984) and Paul Gilroy's reading of Black cultural expression as the "politics of transfiguration" in *The Black Atlantic* (1993) to the more recent theories testing the limits of Afropessimism.[5] Among the latter, the work of Cameroonian philosopher and historian Achille Mbembe stands out as an especially helpful frame for a discussion of McKay's novel. More specifically, I believe that the novel's focus on the body-in-pain and body-in-pleasure can be productively framed by examining the way Mbembe seriously considers the concept of social death yet also pushes against it as a definition of Black ontology.

In his 2003 essay "Necropolitics," Mbembe explores the place given to "life, death, and the human body (in particular the wounded or slain body) . . . in the order of power." Building on Michel Foucault's critique of sovereignty and its relation to biopower, Mbembe writes, "The ultimate expression of sovereignty resides, to a large degree, in the power and the capacity to dictate who may live and who must die."[6] It is important to note that death here doesn't always mean a literal loss of life but may also refer to "the creation of death-worlds" and subjecting people to "conditions of life conferring upon them the status of living dead."[7] Those death-worlds, in other words, are the conditions of social death discussed by Orlando Patterson, Saidiya Hartman, Frank Wilderson, Jared Sexton, and others.[8]

According to Mbembe, necropower stands for the power to determine whose lives and bodies are worthy and whose are disposable. Characters in *Romance in*

Marseille—most notably the novel's central character, Lafala—experience the workings of this "politics of death" in myriad ways. On three different occasions, Lafala is imprisoned, two of which involve institutionalization: in an immigration hospital and in jail. The third instance of Lafala's captivity involves the time when he is locked up in a toilet by the crew of the ship on which he stowed away. Later, when he is held patient/prisoner in an American hospital awaiting deportation to Marseille, his fellow patient, an African American by the name of Black Angel, comments on the dehumanizing implication of that gesture: the gesture of placing a person in a confined space meant to contain excrement and cold enough to give Lafala frostbite. Black Angel says: "But that ain't possible in Gawd's kingdom. They wouldn't do that to a hog" (*RM*, 8). The place of Lafala's confinement on the ship—a palimpsest of the Middle Passage—functions as an example of what Mbembe names the topographies of cruelty (such as the colony or the plantation during slavery), a place where "normal" societal rules do not apply and where those subjected to this system are reduced to the condition of nonhumans. As Lafala cries out during his final incarceration in the book, in the "abominable" Marseille jail (*RM*, 105), having collectively spent so much time in captivity makes him feel he "just can't bear it anymore" and like he will "go crazy" (*RM*, 104). Lafala's experiences and sentiments are representative of the novel's portrayals of the characters' physical entrapment and the psychological experience of losing their sense of self.

But Mbembe's scrutiny of the dehumanizing effects of necropolitics also leads him to the conclusion that "the argument about the turning of human beings into things or about social death has its limits."[9] Like the world of McKay's *Romance*, Mbembe's ruminations about both the conditions of abjection and resilience occupy the triangular space outlined by (African) America, France, and Africa. Perhaps it is partly his engagement with the Francophone postcolonial archive, to which "the kind of absolutization of blackness one finds in some variants of Afro-pessimism is foreign" that leads him to emphasize the "paradoxical element" of agency in the context of death-worlds.[10] Moreover, he argues that for those whose oppression is profoundly bodily, the agential possibilities are also located in the body. Even as he devotes his famous essay to necropower, Mbembe observes in his discussion of chattel slavery that "breaking with uprootedness and the pure world of things of which he or she is but a fragment, the slave is able to demonstrate the protean capabilities of the human bond through music and *the very body* that was supposedly possessed by another."[11] Elsewhere, Mbembe continues his reflections on the liberatory function of bodily and even sensual practices in his detailed analysis of Congolese music and dance.[12] Mbembe describes the music of the Congo as a multisensory experience "evoked in the body by what might be called 'sound forces,' and . . . experienced at different levels of intensity and through different organs," and he sees the dancing that often accompanies it as "a way of journeying outside the self."[13]

Mbembe's emphasis on the importance of music and dance in the (post)colonial context also brings to mind McKay's other Marseille-based novel, *Banjo: A Story without a Plot* (1929), with its own array of abject characters who seek respite from the hardships of their vagabond life in one another's companionship and communion over food, drink, and—most notably—music and dance. McKay's first novel-istic tackling of the necropolitical framing of Black lives in the Old Port lends itself well to an Afropessimist reading. The threat of police violence and incarceration is omnipresent in *Banjo*, and direct commentary on racism and colonialism, primar-ily from the novel's Haitian intellectual protagonist Ray, takes up a much more sig-nificant portion of the novel than it does in *Romance*. Drawing a correlation between Black social death and Black sociality, toward the novel's end, Ray reflects on the tit-ular character's carefree, life-affirming attitude as a response to the lynching of Banjo's brother back in his native United States: "no mechanical-pale graveside face, but a luxuriant living up from it."[14] However, despite surface similarities, Black social life in *Banjo* differs from its depiction in *Romance* in significant ways that make the latter more boldly celebratory of identities and bodies deemed as dis-posable. The sensual potential of music-infused sexuality never becomes realized as true intimacy in *Banjo*. Here, sex enters the characters' daily lives primarily as a commodity and the novel's primary emphasis is on extrasexual male intimacy, which evolves throughout the book's many scenes portraying eating, "sweet booz-ing," "swapping stories," and playing or listening to music (*B*, 33, 78).[15] As a response to necropower's grip, *Banjo*'s music provides a soundtrack to a more masculinist and less radical vision of resistant sociality than the one offered by McKay's second Marseille novel's transgressive "romance."

Importantly, Mbembe ties the need for the somatic expression in dance to the struggle experienced by generations of Congolese people: "With ugliness and abjec-tion all about, the goal of the noise is to compel the body to escape from itself."[16] If such an escape is another word for freedom, which, to Mbembe, is "a key element for individual autonomy," then this is precisely how McKay affords a taste of it to his characters in *Romance*: via bodily, and more specifically erotic, sensation.[17] Necro-power, which manifests in the novel through the mechanisms of mutilation, incar-ceration, and sexual exploitation, finds its counterforces in pleasure and desire, which allow the characters to maintain or regain a sense of wholeness and self.

Marseille the Alluring, Marseille the Repelling

"Marseille is the world's wickedest port," writes a British-born travel writer, Basil Woon, in *From Deauville to Monte Carlo: A Guide to the Gay World of France* (1929),[18] a book published the same year McKay started working on *Romance in Marseille*.[19] Yet, despite their impressions of Marseille being formed around the same time, Woon's and McKay's responses to the city's "wickedness" contrast sharply. Clearly addressing an audience belonging to the leisure class, Woon advises his readers to only peek at "how the other side of the world lives" "by daylight," as "it is not wise to venture into this district at night unless dressed like a stevedore and well armed." A nighttime stroll may expose a visitor to "thieves, cut-throats and other undesirables" who "throng the narrow alleys" and to "sisters of scarlet . . . in the doorways of their places of business, catching you by the sleeve as you pass by." Mar-seille does not "fail to thrill," Woon writes, but "the dregs of the world are here unsifted."[20]

Woon's advice regarding Marseille is that of one outsider to another. He sug-gests that the city is worth a glance to those with a taste for slumming, yet, despite his voyeuristic fascination with it, Marseille also inspires in him fear and disgust. Not so in McKay or his characters. Although Marseille is not just the "port of seamen's dreams" but also "their nightmares" in *Romance* (*RM*, 29), the gritty reality of France's second city does not stop the novel's protagonist, Lafala, from feeling "crazy to see Marseille again" while he lies incapacitated in the New York City hospital "hankering all along for the caves and dens of Marseille" (*RM*, 105, 28). Lafala is not the only character who cannot bear being away from Marseille and especially from Quayside, the novel's name for the harborside neighborhood where McKay's international, multiracial cast of characters—doubtless "the dregs of the world" Woon referred to—build a home for themselves. Lafala's West Indian friend, Babel, who stowed away on the same ship and, having avoided capture and detention, unlike Lafala, nevertheless faces a degree of obstacles in his efforts to return to Marseille, also feels the city's pull. Stranded in Genoa, Babel feels that "Quayside was big in his body, singing in his head and calling, insistently calling him" (*RM*, 85). His visceral response—he experiences the emotional longing for Marseille as a bodily one—shows how deeply the Old Port anchors itself in the hearts of McKay's characters. Quayside summons them with a siren's call, and, like Odysseus, they follow the beckoning, notwithstanding the risks.

Despite all major characters in *Romance* being transplants from elsewhere, Marseille in the novel is home. McKay's view of the city is filled with affection for the familiar. Unlike, for example, Walter Benjamin's sympathetic yet voyeuristic account of Marseille in his 1928 hashish protocols, the novel presents the city as a participatory experience for the initiated, not a place to visit. In stark contrast to McKay's characters' immersion in "the pleasures of Quayside" (*RM*, 86), flâneur Benjamin describes himself wandering around Marseille in a drug-induced haze and appreciatively taking in the sights—with a self-aware ethnographic distance and "free of all desire."[21] No wonder, then, that the description of the city, as Lafala beholds it on his return from America, paints an erotic image of a feminized Marseille: "Wide open in the shape of an enormous fan splashed with violent colors, Marseille lay bare to the glory of the meridian sun, like a fever consuming the senses, alluring and repelling" (*RM*, 29). The city appears here as a nude, inviting and seductive, though also "repelling." In *Romance*, then, Marseille is a wicked city still, but to those who know it intimately it is also like a lover's body: open and welcoming.

McKay's Marseille bursts with the energetic hustle and bustle of "innumerable ships, blowing out, booming in, riding the docks, blessing the town with sweaty activity" (*RM*, 29) and is peopled with a mix of working- and underclass characters of different races, nationalities, and from various walks of life. It is the "port of bums' delight" that gives "sustenance to worker and boss, peddler and prostitute, pimp and panhandler" (*RM*, 29). Home to "a colored colony" (*RM*, 29), the novel's Quayside is where the characters spend most of their time. Importantly, apart from Lafala's hotel room and Aslima's "lair" (*RM*, 45), the narrative highlights places of social gatherings and entertainment as important elements of the setting. Those spaces, much like the "interzones" discussed by Kevin Mumford in his foundational study of sex districts in early twentieth-century Chicago and New York, are sites of "intricate, intimate encounters between people designated as different."[22]

Among them, the most prominent is Café Tout-va-Bien, "the rendezvous of the colored colony . . . owned by a mulatto" (*RM*, 31), which serves as the stage for many of the novel's focal interactions among the characters. La Créole, "one of the most popular of the loving houses of Quayside," is another neighborhood staple, "much frequented and touted by the colored Quaysiders" and "recommended . . . to colored newcomers" (*RM*, 95). Finally, located away from Quayside but frequented by its inhabitants—in particular, by two of the novel's gay characters—there is Petit Pain. The atmosphere of this "little café bar" "located . . . in a narrow and somber alley" combines "something a little sinister and something very alluring" suggesting an enigmatic ambience that is "difficult to define" (*RM*, 116). These establishments, where the novel's characters engage in interracial and nonheteronormative intimate encounters, allow those who otherwise occupy societal periphery to exercise agency through what I call carnal sociality. Like for Mumford, for McKay "the margin is at the center," and the erotic exchanges therein can be seen as oppositional practices.[23]

Adding to the image of Quayside as an interzone is the specter of surveillance that is never too far from the narrative's surface. Mary Dewhurst Lewis's fascinating study of policing of migrants in interwar Marseille offers a helpful frame for McKay's depiction of his characters' relationship with the city's authorities. Lewis notes that in the 1920s and 1930s, although most of Marseille's population lived in the villages on the city's periphery, the port districts were the most heavily policed.[24] As McKay's Quayside faithfully illustrates, Marseille's port districts were peopled with "floating populations," including "stevedores, sailors, migrants for whom Marseille was simply a way station en route to a final destination," and people whose unstable earnings did not allow for an annual apartment lease (*RM*, 70). The increasing French anxiety over the question of nationhood at that time had led the French police to develop "a set of entrenched practices and regulations by virtue of which so-called rootless persons were classified as inherently dangerous to society." They therefore targeted foreigners "who fit into their preconceived ideas of social instability and danger" (*RM*, 68). Additionally, while colonial migrants made up only about 4 percent of the port districts' population (*RM*, 72), a paternalistic racist "notion that mainland French society offered more freedom than colonial migrants could handle, making their uprooting both more pronounced and more destabilizing than that faced by other migrants" (*RM*, 75), exposed migrants like many of the Quaysiders to close surveillance and risk of arrest, which often led to their expulsion (*RM*, 72).

If protecting his respectable readers from the Old Port's underclass is Woon's concern, it is the dangers that the latter themselves face—from the police—that McKay's novel highlights. In part 3 Lafala and Babel are both arrested and jailed "for the misdemeanor of stowing away." The punishment is frightening in its implied open-endedness: "They could be imprisoned for about six months; besides, they might be held for an indefinite length of time before being brought to trial" (*RM*, 99). A whole new level of cruelty is added by the difficulty of "see[ing] a prisoner in jail unless one was a relative" (*RM*, 97), making uprooted single migrants such as Lafala and Babel vulnerable to the possibility of lonely imprisonment with no visitations for an undetermined length of time. The novel's other characters are also no strangers to arrests. The narrative's introduction of the character of Big Blonde, who is revealed to be gay in the following paragraph, includes a mention, as if in passing, of his frequent "trouble with the police." The subsequent passage, "Sometimes he was jailed for a short term; sometimes he went into hiding," withholds the reasons for Big Blonde's "trouble with the police," yet it implies that the novel's queer characters are also not safe from surveillance (*RM*, 95). Finally, a scene in which Big Blonde and Babel dance with each other at the Petit Pain, an establishment without a dancing license, and hope that the police will not "interfere" (*RM*, 119) suggests an ever-present possibility of raids and surveillance in Quaysiders' lives. Lafala likely voices the sentiment of many when he declares, "Political or criminal, the police is all the same to me" (*RM*, 79).

McKay's portrayal of his characters' spaces of leisure and their tense relationship with the local authorities is a key narrative maneuver that sets the stage for the reading of pleasure in *Romance* as both a survival strategy and a transgression. Despite its sympathetic tone, the depiction of Marseille's pleasure "dens" (*RM*, 28) and the characters' run-ins with the police underscores the perception of this dockside community of transients as deviant by those outside it, especially those in power. Their sexuality becomes a symptom of deviation from the middle-class, heterosexual, family-oriented norm. At the same time, this deviant pleasure, juxtaposed to the characters' experiences with policing and loss of (bodily) sovereignty, becomes the novel's language of autonomy.

Deviant Desire as Agential Possibility
The kinds of liaisons formed by McKay's characters are what Cathy Cohen considers as a possible locus of radical resistance, which she calls *the politics of deviance*. Like Robin Kelley and James Scott before her, Cohen, a political scientist, is interested in how "individuals with little power in society engage in counter normative behaviors."[25] What makes Cohen's analysis so interesting in the context of McKay's novel is her focus on sexual and relationship practices of the most marginalized and their perceived deviance. Cohen speculates about whether, by "situating their lives in direct contrast to dominant normalized understandings of family, desire, and sex," those who have been rejected by the norms of the dominant order could "secure small levels of autonomy in their lives" and therefore be seen as engaging in "a radical politics of the personal."[26] As a hypothesis born out of Cohen's bringing together of queer theory and African American studies, this question could very well be applied to the fictional world of McKay's novel, where multiracial lumpen characters find themselves forming erotic bonds well outside the boundaries of white middle- and upper-class heteronormative parameters.

While the novel's first part focuses on the tragic circumstances of Lafala's disability, parts 2 and 3 paint a vibrant image of the Old Port's community that welcomes the protagonist on his return. Throughout these two parts of the novel, the narrative circles back into Quayside's bars and cafés, emphasizing two characteristics of the harbor district: the heterogeneous status of its lumpen crowd and the role of erotic play in their social life. A scene depicting a party at the Tout-va-Bien, thrown for Lafala on his release from jail later in the novel, shows Quaysiders as a motley crew: "All the old habitués were there, the low-down gangs of old-and-hard youth, girls and men, white and brown and black, mingled colors and odors." The emphasis falls not only on the diversity of the celebrants, however, but also on the sensual dimension of their fellowship as they "come together drinking, gossiping, dancing and perspiring to the sound of international jazz" (*RM*, 106). A subsequent description of the "dancing and perspiring" bodies takes on an increasingly sensuous tone: "Everybody was close together in a thick juice melted by wine and music. There was little room for foot play. Just all together, two in one swaying, shuffling around, bumping and bumping up and down belly to belly and breast to breast" (*RM*, 107). The image of bodies fusing with one another in a bacchanalian metaphor of "a thick juice," followed by an enumeration of body parts engaged in repeated "bumping" "up and down," creates a strongly sexual innuendo, enhanced by the abandonment of punctuation in the final, seemingly rushed and breathless part of the sentence. Beyond just crossing the color line, McKay's "white and brown and black" characters melt into one another in an erotic trance, as if becoming one body.

Given the preoccupation of McKay's other Marseille novel with music and his interest in exploring the transgressive capacity of pleasure, one might expect scenes like the one described above to fill the pages of *Banjo*. The closest *Banjo* comes to the sort of erotic play that drives the dance in *Romance* is a scene depicting "black bodies in a close atmosphere," dancing to the tune of the titular character's banjo playing, "generating sweat and waves of heat" (*B*, 50). But the novel's arguably most sensual relationship is one not between any set of dancers or lovers but between Banjo and his musical instrument, which, as he explains in the novel's early pages, "is moh than a gal, moh than a pal" (*B*, 6). While Banjo's legal name, Lincoln Agrippa Daily, signals a hedonistic philosophy of seizing the day in response to life's cruelties, his nickname makes clear that his vision of pleasure seeking centers music and a masculine community built around it, as his dream of forming an orchestra indicates. While music and dance in *Romance* occasion the novel's central transgressive sensuality, in *Banjo* they are primarily vehicles for less norm-bending notions of community.

Racial divisions are not the only ones Quaysiders in *Romance* transgress in their carnal communions. The novel features a wide array of sexual practices and preferences that resist heteronormativity. Frequent references to Quayside's sexual economy involving relations among transient sailors and both female and male sex workers help frame the novel's depiction of pleasure as unbound by the hegemony of social acceptability. More important, among the characters who help shape the novel's central conflicts, several occupy a spectrum from involvement in same-sex relationships to a display of queer desire and sexual fluidity. La Fleur Noire, described as a "big-mouthed brown orchid," who is Aslima's greatest rival in the battle for "dominion" over Quayside's robust sex-work business, does not actually "go crazy over men" (*RM*, 30, 29, 41). In fact, she "goes with them only to make money," while sharing nonmercantile erotic affections with a "Greek girl" (*RM*, 41). The gay "white Quaysider" Big Blonde's typographically feminine name does not in any way render this "big, firm-footed, broad-shouldered" dock laborer effeminate; instead, it emphasizes his hypermasculine exterior, resembling that of proletarian heroes featured in sociorealist art (*RM*, 94). Big Blonde's unclear past makes him "an outstanding enigma of Quayside," but his relationship with a younger man, Petit Frère, employed as "the boy of the house" by the brothel La Créole, is a known fact in the port district (*RM*, 94–95). Not only are La Fleur's and Big Blonde's choices of intimate companions known to the novel's other characters, but they also have no bearing on the perception of their respective femininity and masculinity, speaking to the text resisting common gender stereotypes associated with same-sex-oriented people.

Finally, perhaps the most telling commentary on the ubiquity and relative acceptance of same-sex desire comes in the novel's scene depicting Babel, whose own affair with a woman earlier in the novel suggests that he is heterosexual, warmheartedly joking about the fluidity of desire with Big Blonde. The scene takes place at Petit Pain, "Big Blonde's favorite place when he was in a sentimental mood and wanted to spend a quiet evening with his little friend," Petit Frère (*RM*, 116). Having joined Big Blonde and his young boyfriend at the café, along with Lafala and two other characters, Babel is led by a playful conversation to good-naturedly pretend to "steal" Petit Frère from Big Blonde (*RM*, 118–19). Then, in a continuation of friendly merrymaking, Babel, described earlier in the novel as "huge" (*RM*, 83), begins to dance with the equally big-framed Big Blonde while singing "a little song" about a man "stricken" by "the fairy moon," as a result of which he goes "far away from my loving wife" (*RM*, 119), leaving her to pursue a union with another man. In combination with other portrayals of nonheteronormative behavior and desire, this scene underlines the novel's insistence on normalizing intimacy that falls outside the prescribed rules of romance.

The underscoring of nonnormative sexuality recurs throughout the novel in myriad forms, reminding the reader that no matter how marginal their status, the characters partake freely in carnal pleasure. In addition to emphasizing interracial and nonheterosexual bonds, the narrative stresses other ways that the characters exercise their right to erotic fulfillment outside the confines of middle-class respectability. For example, the novel depicts the personal lives and intimate relationships based on desire and affection of sex workers, both male and female, outside the sexual economy governing their labor. Aslima, Le Fleur, and Petit Frère are all involved in romantic and sexual affairs based on passion and fondness; their capacity for genuine desire adds dimension to them as characters and humanizes them. The novel also resists tipping its hat to notions of sexuality as propagating the goals of a traditional heterosexual family. On two rare occasions when marriage is mentioned at all, it is discussed not as a matter of legitimizing a relationship or as a "natural step" toward fulfilling the goal of a union between lovers but as a strategic move to protect the woman (in both cases, Aslima) by either facilitating her international mobility or ensuring her financial security (*RM*, 72, 90). Moreover, the novel's uninhibited sex talk is never accompanied by any reference to reproduction or traditional family structure. Not a single child character or even a mention of children appears in the pages of *Romance*, apart from brief flashbacks of Lafala's and Aslima's own childhoods. Sexual pleasure, the novel insists, is the one domain that cannot be fully co-opted by the exclusionary systems of capitalism, racism, and heteronormativity and is the one form of agency that even the most marginalized can access.

Granted, financial security goes a long way in taking off the pressure of survival and freeing the mind to enjoy romantic pursuits, as Lafala notes. In a scene showing Lafala planning a rendezvous with Aslima, he walks by the docks at dawn, seeing workers "in the waiting line for the day's work." Lafala ponders the difference the insurance money from the shipping company has made in his life: "He was free now to think about love instead of the depressing possibility of whether or not he would have today's daily bread." He reflects on the days when he, too, like the "tired worker" of McKay's poem, "went with the early rising stream to take his place" in that same line of dock laborers. Lafala notes in particular that Western capitalism exacerbates the pain of the have-nots: "In the primitive life such as he had lived as a boy, civilized necessities were superfluous. But how depressing it had been to exist in the heart of civilization and be too poverty-stricken to afford them" (*RM*, 71). Yet, despite Lafala's musings on his altered financial status, the scene does not suggest that exclusion from the pleasures of consumerism prevents those at the margins from enjoying bodily pleasure. The novel supplies plentiful evidence that many other characters who do not share Lafala's newly acquired wealth—and even Lafala himself, before stowing away—find respite and joy in erotic play.

But, as Cathy Cohen has asked, can such respite and joy be seen as resistance? She ultimately concludes that intent and tangible change in the distribution of power should be the measure of whether or not seemingly defiant acts can be seen as radically oppositional. Thus, she argues, those behaviors and practices that do not stem from an actual political impulse or that do not bring about actual change are no more than "attempts to create greater autonomy over one's life, to pursue desire, or to make the best of very limited life options."[27] This set of criteria would eliminate McKay's characters' carnal sociality from consideration as an anti-hegemonic practice. The novel does not feature the characters mobilizing their sexual energies toward any politically conscious goals. In fact, the only major character who is politically minded, Étienne St. Dominique, a Marxist "mulatto from Martinique" (*RM*, 73), finds Quaysiders' fondness for socializing at brothels "depressing," and, despite his assurance to Lafala that "he liked Quayside and Tour-va-Bien," he is clearly perceived as an outsider to Marseille's "interzones," as Lafala feels "a little ashamed" of his status as a regular in Quayside while talking to St. Dominique (*RM*, 75). Thus the world of radical politics and the world of carnal pleasures do not appear to mix well in *Romance*. In light of Cohen's conclusions, that would cast McKay's "passion and desire" as devoid of oppositional potential (*RM*, 36).

But I want to suggest another line of argument, one leaning on the lessons of both Black feminism and the tension between Afropessimism and Black optimism, which point to the need for acknowledging the survivalist role of sociality in the lives of the dispossessed, and of pleasure as a particularly agential function of the social. Fred Moten's interrogation of the limits of Black social death—or necropower, to use Mbembe's term—leads him to ask, "How can we fathom a social life that tends towards death, that enacts a kind of being-toward-death, and which, *because of* such tendency and enactment, maintains a terribly beautiful vitality?"[28] Moten encompasses the answer within the question itself: by claiming that the vibrancy of Black sociality exists not *despite* but *because of* the condition of social death that has marked Black life since slavery. Like Mbembe, he emphasizes the dialectic between the politics of death and the sociopolitical, or the rich expressions of quintessentially subversive Black social life. That social life, Moten argues, is infused with the quality of "fugitivity": "a desire for and a spirit of escape and transgression of the proper and the proposed. It's a desire for the outside, for a playing or being outside."[29] The rejection of imposed restrictions and limitations that Moten describes here is precisely what drives not only Lafala's literal illicit escape on a New York–bound ship but also the characters' carnal practices that allow "the body to escape from itself," in Mbembe's terms.

Moten's and Mbembe's Black-optimist ideas about Black social life find their antecedent in the work of Audre Lorde. For Lorde, social death is a fact of Black life. "We were never meant to survive," she writes in "A Litany for Survival" (line 24).[30] Yet, rather than inspire resignation, the inevitability of necropower's hold on Black lives calls for opposition—"it is better to speak" (line 32)—and for survivalist celebration of Black social life, including carnal sociality, as evidenced in Lorde's declaration that "our erotic knowledge empowers us" (UE, 57). In her famous essay Lorde argues that the erotic "heightens and sensitizes and strengthens all my experience," thus implying that agency rooted in the erotic can radiate its influence into other areas of experience (UE, 58). As a counterforce to all that which dehumanizes, Lorde notes that the erotic serves as her connection to her own "capacity for joy" and "a reminder of my capacity for feeling" (UE, 56–57). Lorde's emphasis on the ability of the erotic to help restore a sense of humanity to those who have been denied it has reverberated through Black feminist discourse, even giving rise to what the activist and writer Adrienne Maree Brown calls "pleasure activism." Brown advocates for reclaiming one's right to pleasure as a liberatory practice for both Black people and others who have experienced oppression: "It's not an accident that on this land, Black people have been told, 'You're 3/5 of a person.' If you don't feel like you're fully human, then where in that are you supposed to believe you have access [to pleasure]?"[31] In invoking the lasting symbolism of—and the psychic damage caused by—the Three-Fifths Compromise of 1787, Brown suggests that desire and its fulfillment can be seen as acts of taking back, or reclaiming, the right to the full range of human experience. Lorde writes, "In touch with the erotic, I become less willing to accept powerlessness." This is precisely the sort of shield against "resignation, despair, self-effacement, depression, self-denial" (UE, 58) with which desire and pleasure equip McKay's characters, none of them more so than the novel's protagonist.

Blackness and Amputation as Agential Loss

The narrative arc of the novel does not allow the book's central pair of lovers, Lafala and Aslima, to reunite until the novel's second part. Having stowed away after Aslima robs him, making him Quayside's laughingstock, Lafala returns from his ultimately tragic trip to America with a hefty sum of insurance money and a yearning to see the Moroccan beauty again, if without his lower legs. Setting the stage for the titular romance takes up the novel's first part, which centers on the physical and psychic wounds Lafala suffers as a result of his unsuccessful illicit journey and his amputation. By means of a contrast, the focus on Lafala's loss of subjectivity in part 1 helps highlight his reignited relationship with Aslima in parts 2 and 3 as the ultimate realization of the novel's theme of pleasure as an agential force.

Lafala's stay in the immigration hospital after his lower legs are amputated is marked by layers of incapacitating experiences. The loss of his legs deprives him of what he considers "his greatest asset" (*RM*, 6). To a large extent, Lafala's body before the amputation defined his identity. Back in West Africa, "the older tribesmen appraised the worth of the young by the shape of their limbs. Long legs and slender made good swimmers. Stout legs and thick, good carriers" (*RM*, 3). One's body and its performative functions, Lafala learned, are gateways to becoming an agent in the world. Unsurprisingly, then, in referring to his lost limbs as his "dependable feet," Lafala ascribes to the amputated body parts agency-bestowing qualities (*RM*, 6).

The devastating effect the surgery has on Lafala resembles the crushing impact of a racist reaction to his presence that Frantz Fanon's narrator in "The Fact of Blackness" hears from a white person: "'Dirty nigger! Or simply, 'Look, a Negro!'" (FB, 109). Fanon continues:

> I came into the world imbued with the will to find a meaning in things, my spirit filled with the desire to attain to the source of the world, and then I found that I was an object in the midst of other objects.
>
> Sealed into that crushing objecthood, I turned beseechingly to others. Their attention was a liberation, running over my body suddenly abraded into nonbeing, endowing me once more with an agility that I had thought lost, and by taking me out of the world, restoring me to it. But just as I reached the other side, I stumbled, and the movements, the attitudes, the glances of the other fixed me there, in the sense in which a chemical solution is fixed by a dye. I was indignant; I demanded an explanation. Nothing happened. I burst apart.
> (FB, 109)

His mutilation functioning as the equivalent of Fanon's jarring exclamation, Lafala finds himself trying to reconcile his present condition with the memories of a more hopeful time. Like Fanon's narrator, who "came into the world" with "the will" and "desire" for greater things and then "found that I was an object in the midst of other objects," Lafala recalls the "glory and joy of having a handsome pair of legs" and the "worth" they bestowed on him as a young man with potential for greatness, as "he lay helpless" in his hospital bed (*RM*, 3–4).

Lafala's "agility" literally "lost" with the removal of his greatest physical attribute (FB, 109), he is left feeling emasculated, his "sawed-off stump" (*RM*, 3) of a body a grim match to Fanon's "body suddenly abraded into nonbeing." Lafala, too, turns "beseechingly to others" for affirmation (FB, 109). Being "really handsome" (*RM*, 7) and used to enjoying "the passionate chamber music of life" with lovers, legs intertwined "like a quartette of players" (*RM*, 4), he now hopes for a "feminine word of encouragement" from the nurses, but they "could not grant him" any (*RM*, 9). In fact, he feels further humiliated by the nurses' responses to him: "In their eyes, in their silence about his future, he saw only pity, that terrible dumb pity that can sweep the fibers of feeling for a fine man or beast that has fallen from self-sufficiency into a hopeless case" (*RM*, 9). Lafala's feeling of shame is only exacerbated by the "sympathetic glances" of other hospital staff toward him, a "terrible attention" (*RM*, 9, 6) instead of what brings "liberation" (FB, 109). Worse still, "'Poor boy!' a doctor would ejaculate passing his cot" (*RM*, 9). The paternalistic, racist connotation of *boy* coupled with the double entendre of *ejaculate* insinuates white masculinity's assertion of its power over an incapacitated Black man whose sexuality may otherwise be perceived as a threat and a menace.

Feeling stripped of his sense of self, Lafala responds to the white onlookers in a manner strikingly parallel to that of Fanon's narrator, who feels "indignant" when confronted with the objectifying white gaze. For Fanon, the feeling that "the glances of the other fixed me there" describes the moment when the Black man's subjectivity becomes lost and his selfhood becomes nothing more than "a thousand details, anecdotes, stories" out of which "the white man . . . had woven me" (FB, 111). The process of becoming Black is psychological but is felt viscerally. Under the white man's gaze, Fanon writes, "consciousness of the body" becomes "a third-person consciousness" (FB, 110). In other words, it is a hyperawareness of seeing oneself being seen by another and remade—or "fixed"—by the beholder's narrative of one. Fanon's process of becoming Black, then, captures the essence of dehumanization.

As a close examination of Lafala's grappling with the aftermath of the amputation reveals, the maiming becomes to him an extension of his generally marginal status, one more loss in a line of them: "In a strange land, without home, without friends, without resources, without his greatest asset—his faithful feet" (*RM*, 6). His missing legs stand for a physical manifestation of his marginalization: as a poor Black colonial subject, and now also "an amputated man" (*RM*, 24). In fact, Lafala's experience with corporal mutilation occasions his own process of becoming Black, or becoming abject. It is first signaled when, having suffered a bout of despair over his newly disfigured body, Lafala has a dream about being in heaven. The first thing the reader learns about this heavenly place, even before finding out that Lafala's "legs were all right there," is that "there were no black things there." The erasure of Blackness from Lafala's vision of heaven renders him "transfigured beyond remembering what complexion he was" (*RM*, 6).

If it is telling that Lafala's fantasy escape from his disability is simultaneously an escape from Blackness, the moment of Lafala's waking proves even more revelatory: "[He] opened his eyes and saw a huge black face, yellow teeth, and a badly-molded mouth, bending over him" (*RM*, 7). The first image Lafala sees on returning from his world of raceless fancy is that of Blackness, ascribing a race to the harshness of his reality. Importantly, it is not just any Black face. His Black hospital roommate's actual appearance aside, Lafala's mind, still suspended between dream and reality, conjures up an image of a racist caricature with exaggerated and distorted features, bringing to mind the white-generated "details, anecdotes, stories" that Fanon's narrator sees as stereotypes replacing his personhood (FB, 111). At first still unaware that he is awake, Lafala muses, "Black things in heaven! Good God!" (*RM*, 7), as if shocked by the very possibility of Blackness entering his dreamed-up paradise. Then the reality of his wakefulness dawns on him suddenly—"and he was black in hell" (*RM*, 7), just like Fanon equating the acute awareness of his racial identity with being "locked into the infernal circle" (FB, 116).

At this juncture, Fanon's narrator and Lafala become almost indistinguishable. Where McKay's limited omniscient narration cries out on Lafala's behalf, "A block of blackness in a hospital shirt. Why was he dumped down so violently upon the fact of himself . . . ?" (*RM*, 7), Fanon echoes with "My blackness was there, dark and unarguable. And it tormented me, pursued me, disturbed me, angered me" (FB, 117). Generating an even closer correspondence between the two, Fanon uses the metaphor of amputation to describe the loss of subjectivity in the process of becoming Black: "What else could it be for me but an amputation, an excision, a hemorrhage that spattered my whole body with black blood?" (FB, 112). He continues, "My body was given back to me sprawled out, distorted, recolored, clad in mourning" (FB, 113), conjuring the image of none other than McKay's Lafala in the mind of a reader familiar with both texts.

In her analysis of the Fanonian becoming-Black, Amber Musser notes that the "biologization of the Negro" involved in this process can be seen as "a mode of becoming-flesh" and is therefore "particularly dehumanizing because it reinforces the status of the body as flesh at the cost of personhood."[32] Like Musser, I draw on Hortense Spillers's crucial "distinction . . . between 'body' and 'flesh'" as one differentiating "between captive and liberated subject-positions" to underscore the focus on *body as flesh* in the novel's early scenes of Lafala's psychological and physical torment.[33] Perhaps the most arresting example of this appears in a scene where Lafala reflects on his institutionalization in the hospital—where "he was not a patient only, but technically also a prisoner held for deportation"—and remembers having been told in the past that "hospitals were the final passage to the grave for poor and unknown persons. The black drifters were superstitiously afraid of hospitals. They said the doctors never had enough corpses for laboratory work and would not worry about the life of a poor unknown beggar when a body was wanted for dissection" (*RM*, 15, 6). Lafala realizes that to those in charge of the institutions that now control his life, his existence boils down to the usefulness of his flesh. This prompts his macabre musings about the disposability of his disabled Black body and the possibility of its further mutilation as a cadaver.

McKay's rhetorical maneuvers ensure that we see Lafala as entirely stripped of agency, emphasizing what Spillers calls a "captive subject-position." For example, the use of passive voice in descriptions of what is done to Lafala, or what happens to his body, as in, "was lifted into a waiting taxi-cab and whisked away," suggests utter loss of subjectivity. When Lafala's lawyer arrives to prevent his deportation before the resolution of the legal case concerning his compensation for the loss of his feet, the lawyer "finally found the helpless black on the company's pier." The lawyer says to Lafala: "I'll see that you don't go back to the port you stowed away from, for you never can tell what they might do to you there" (*RM*, 15–16). Both the characterization of Lafala as "helpless" and the expression "what they might do to you" further mark Lafala as not the one in charge of his own existence. In addition to both the institutional handling and the disability, Lafala is aware of his status as a West African under colonialism: "He belonged to one of the parceled regions and was therefore either a colonial subject or a protected person" (*RM*, 20). The word *belonged* marks Lafala as unfree and—as a possession—less than human. Yet it is Lafala's own definition of himself that is the most telling. He tells Black Angel: "I'm an amputated man" (*RM*, 24). Lafala's use of *amputated* as a modifier to describe himself rather than his lower legs shows that he sees himself through the prism of his injured flesh, as a lack or an absence. That which is amputated no longer is. Unsurprisingly, Lafala feels that "life was now behind him" (*RM*, 6). He has not died, yet he does not feel alive, either. His is a death-world.

"Passion and Desire" as Repair

While the initial pages of *Romance in Marseille* and "The Fact of Blackness" show startling parallels in the portrayal of their Black colonial subjects' struggle with agential loss and its bodily implications, the comparison between the two texts finds its limitations at the end of part 1. In fact, the likeness between Fanon's narrator and Lafala ends where desire in *Romance* begins. Fanon's essay ends on a somber note, with a "crippled veteran of the Pacific war," an amputee like Lafala, making a comparison between Blackness and disabling bodily mutilation: "Resign yourself to your color the way I got used to my stump"; "we're both victims," he tells his fellow train passenger, to whom the narrator refers as "my brother" (FB, 140). At first, the narrator resolves to "refuse to accept that amputation," suggesting that he wishes to push against the loss of his autonomy and the subsequent dehumanization, both implied as inevitable under the conditions of racism. He even declares that his "chest has the power to expand without limit" and that he intends to "rise." But before he can fulfill this promise to himself, he gives in to a feeling of paralysis and "[begins] to weep" (FB, 140).

By contrast, Lafala returns to Marseille and regains his lost appetite for life and sense of self. The crucial difference that allows for McKay's devastated protagonist's renewed self-affirmation lies in the place afforded to desire and pleasure in the novel. As Musser points out about Fanon, "Nowhere . . . does he describe sexual desire on the part of the Negro." Musser shows that this lack of "recognizable" Black desire in Fanon means that sexuality can only contribute to the objectification of the Black man, since his sexuality "produces pleasure for [white] others," making him a sex object.[34] McKay, on the other hand, uses desire to equip his characters, and especially Lafala, with a weapon against objectification. It is the erotic that facilitates access to reclaiming subjectivity in *Romance*.

Given how damaged Lafala is by the novel's opening events, Mbembe's reflections on the dialectic between necropower and vitality prove helpful yet again. Pleasure as a mending mechanism that helps a broken man like Lafala restore his sense of agency can be productively theorized along the lines of Mbembe's ideas about the notion of repair. Recalling his travels around the African continent in an interview, Mbembe observes that everywhere he has gone, "the most striking thing is the number of people busy repairing something—whether a car, . . . a tire, a house, a pair of shoes, a piece of dress, every single little thing." Sometimes, he notes, they start a new project from scratch, like building a house, "run out of money, then live for years in an unfinished structure, take a long time to save again and then they pick it up where they left off" and continue, even if the job "might never be completely done in their lifetime."[35] Mbembe's point is that people whose world has been destroyed—subjected to the mechanisms of necropower—such as those inhabiting the postcolony, feel the need to engage in practices of gathering the pieces of what is left and putting them back together. "Something significant must be going on in these practices of the everyday," Mbembe says. "To repair is to be alive."[36]

Noting its "liberatory" quality, Mbembe stresses that "reparation is the opposite of destruction."[37] While seemingly self-evident, that statement is nothing to take for granted when looking into the lives—real or imagined—of those who experienced devastating levels of injury. Corresponding to the bodily experience of the harm he has suffered, as even his psychical struggle manifests in bodily ways, McKay's protagonist's reclamation of his agency takes on a corporeal form. Somatic pleasure becomes a counterforce against Lafala's experience of abjection. Even before his return to Marseille, the narrative places Lafala in a scenario where his "amputated" sense of self is given a chance of repair. In the scene Lafala takes a trip to Harlem with Black Angel. It is no accident that the first time that desire and carnal sociality enter the novel's plot, the setting is the Mecca of the New Negro and New York's very own version of "Quayside," which McKay painted so vividly in *Home to Harlem*. Here Lafala has a sexual encounter with two women who seem undisturbed by what he sees as his body's incompleteness and inadequacy. In fact, in a welcome challenge to his self-perception, the women turn his legs into objects of desire and sources of pleasure: "He was pitied and praised and beamed upon and his stumps of legs were fondled and caressed as if they were honeysticks" (*RM*, 17). This phallic image signifies the newly begun process of restoring not only Lafala's masculinity but also his sense of wholeness and sovereignty.

Soon after returning to Marseille, Lafala resumes his "romance" with Aslima. Although at first nostalgic about the "infectious and tantalizing . . . jigging of his feet" and disturbed by his "shrunken stumps"—which she sees herself as having caused—Aslima ends up spending the night with Lafala and "reveal[ing] herself to him as she had never done before nor to anybody in Marseille" (*RM*, 33–34). In this context these words suggest extrasexual eroticism, a willingness to be vulnerable and give in fully to the experience. The encounter ends with Aslima refusing to accept a payment from Lafala and thus redefining the value of the sex that took place as measured in pleasure rather than money. During a future encounter between the two, when Lafala alludes to his self-perceived diminished sexual prowess by saying, "I can't be as piggish as in my able-bodied days," she responds with a reassuring innuendo: "Forget about your feet now and thank God it wasn't something worse that was cut off" (*RM*, 41). She dismisses the notion of his incompleteness and hints at the pleasure-granting qualities of his body.

Lafala's taking and giving of pleasure becomes a transformative force as the novel's bodily centered descriptions of the character indicate. From the focus on

Lafala's mutilated and pained body and emotional turmoil, the novel moves to sensuous characterizations of his responses to Aslima's charms. When watching her dance, for example, Lafala feels his blood become "warm with carnal sweetness" (*RM*, 39). When he recalls her dance later, "his ears were humming with the music of her honey-dripping words" and "[a] sweet shiver shocked his whole body" (*RM*, 40). While Lafala's body serves as an important barometer of necropower's effect on the marginalized in the first part of the narrative, in the later sections devoted to his affair with Aslima, the focus shifts to Lafala's senses and the ways he experiences pleasure: "Of all the ways of loving he had experienced, none had ever wrought such delicious havoc on his senses as Aslima" (*RM*, 46). "Wrought . . . havoc" suggests an all-encompassing sensation, a wholeness of sorts. From "an amputated man," who is defined by the missing parts of himself, Lafala has been transformed into a man whose "capacity for feeling," to use Lorde's phrase, has expanded so vastly that he experiences existence itself with heightened intensity.

If *Home to Harlem* made Du Bois want to take a bath, a reader of *Romance in Marseille* might relish a vision of how the esteemed author of *The Souls of Black Folk* (1903) would have reacted to it, had he had a chance to read the manuscript. Likely, no amount of lather would be a match for McKay's "forbidding and tumultuous Quayside against which the thick scum of life foams and bubbles and breaks in a syrup of passion and desire" (*RM*, 29). But if tempted to discard the novel as "sex hash" as its early critics did,[38] Du Bois would have been missing the point of *Romance*. In its sensual relations among characters, the novel engages some of modernism's greatest obsessions about the body—its social and economic value; its efficiency, completeness, and fitness; and its relation to mobility and performativity—while simultaneously answering how those whose bodies have been deemed disposable and exploitable survive their own objectification. In a gesture of literary near prophesy, McKay's novel anticipates Fanon's tackling of the Black agential loss and foreshadows the response offered to it by Fanon's disciple, Mbembe, who theorizes that "the Black Man . . . is the only human in the modern order whose skin has been transformed into the form and spirit of merchandise. . . . But there is also a manifest dualism to Blackness. In a spectacular reversal, it becomes the symbol of a conscious desire for life, a force spring forth, buoyant and plastic."[39] Beyond underscoring the survivalist quality of Black social life's buoyancy, as Mbembe and other theorists would do decades later, *Romance* also expands the condition of social death and its carnal counterweight to non-Black abject identities, as if foreshadowing Mbembe's discussion of "a Becoming-Black-of-the-World," or ever-multiplying forms of violence and marginalization present in today's world.[40] Like Mbembe, McKay's "novel out of time" offers a Black tradition of pleasure-affirming sociality as a form of resistance against dehumanization.[41]

In his poem "The Tired Worker," McKay's speaker can find no relief; his toil and turmoil never stop, and there will be no "peace" for this "rebel heart" (line 3) and "weary body" (line 5) until, it seems, death brings it. Meanwhile, in *Romance in Marseille*, the characters' experiences oscillate between abjection and pleasure, making the description of the Petit Pain café's atmosphere an apt account to Quaysiders' lives as "strangely balancing between the emotions of laughter and tears, ribaldry and bitter-sweetness" (*RM*, 116). Instead of placating their hearts and imploring their bodies to be patient, they boldly reach toward their desires and claim their pleasures freely and, in the process, assert their agency and humanity.

AGNIESZKA TUSZYNSKA is associate professor of English at Queensborough Community College–City University of New York, where she teaches African American literature and writing. She also volunteers as an educator in prisons and jails with College Justice Program, teaching college-prep workshops and facilitating book discussion groups. Her research focuses on African American literature of the Jim Crow era and the Harlem Renaissance and prison literature. Among other publications, her work has previously appeared in *MELUS* and *Dialogues in Social Justice: An Adult Educational Journal*, and her essay on Willard Motley is forthcoming in the *College Language Association Journal*.

Notes

1   McKay, *Romance in Marseille*, 4, 7 (hereafter cited as *RM*).
2   Fanon, "The Fact of Blackness," 109 (hereafter cited as FB).
3   McKay, "The Tired Worker."
4   McKay, *Home to Harlem*, 194–95.
5   Lorde, "The Uses of the Erotic" (hereafter cited as UE); Gilroy, *Black Atlantic*, 37–38.
6   Mbembe, "Necropolitics," 12, 11.
7   Mbembe, "Necropolitics," 40.
8   See Patterson's *Slavery and Social Death*; Spillers, "Mama's Baby, Papa's Maybe"; Hartman, "The Burdened Individuality of Freedom"; Hartman, *Lose Your Mother*; Sexton, "The Social Life of Social Death"; Wilderson, "The Prison Slave as Hegemony's (Silent) Scandal"; and Wilderson, "Afropessimism and the End of Redemption."
9   Mbembe, "Conversation."
10   Mbembe, "Conversation"; Mbembe, "Necropolitics," 22.
11   Mbembe, "Necropolitics," 22; emphasis added.
12   The following sources offer more information about the role of music in the sociopolitical African-diasporic tradition: Gilroy, *The Black Atlantic*, for a discussion of the potential of Black folk expression, and especially Black music, "to conjure up and enact the new modes of friendship, happiness, and solidarity that are consequent on the overcoming of the racial oppression" (38); Kelley, *Race Rebels*, for a discussion of the use of Black folk expression in African American labor activism; and Camp, "The Pleasures of Resistance," for an analysis of enslaved women's use of clothing, style, and dance during outlaw slave gatherings as a form of resistant pleasure.

13   Mbembe, "Variations," 73, 86.
14   McKay, *Banjo*, 322 (hereafter cited as *B*).
15   For more on the portrayal of Black men's bonding as identity- and community-forging in *Banjo*, see Brown, "Shadow of Intimacy."
16   Mbembe, "Variations," 85.
17   Mbembe, "Necropolitics," 13.
18   Dregni, *Gypsy Jazz*, loc. 2959. Although *gay* was already used to mean "homosexual" in same-sex communities, Woon appears blissfully oblivious to that fact, making the title of his guide appear naive, especially when read in the context of McKay's overtly queer narrative.
19   Holcomb and Maxwell, introduction, vii.
20   Dregni, *Gypsy Jazz*, loc. 2959.
21   Benjamin, "Hashish in Marseilles," 143.
22   Mumford, *Interzones*, xvii.
23   Mumford, *Interzones*, xii.
24   Lewis, "Strangeness of Foreigners," 71.
25   Cohen, "Deviance as Resistance," 30.
26   Cohen, "Deviance as Resistance," 30.
27   Cohen, "Deviance as Resistance," 40.
28   Moten, "Case of Blackness," 188; emphasis added.
29   Moten, *Stolen Life*, loc. 2867.
30   Lorde, "Litany for Survival."
31   Brown, interview.
32   Musser, *Sensational Flesh*, 108.
33   Spillers, "Mama's Baby, Papa's Maybe," 67.
34   Musser, *Sensational Flesh*, 93.
35   Mbembe, "Conversation."
36   Mbembe, "Conversation."
37   Mbembe, "Conversation."
38   Holcomb and Maxwell, introduction, xxxv.
39   Mbembe, *Critique*, 6.
40   Mbembe, *Critique*, 7.
41   Young, "Best New Novel."

Works Cited

Benjamin, Walter. "Hashish in Marseilles." In *Reflections: Essays, Aphorisms, Autobiographical Writings*, edited by Peter Demetz, 137–45. New York: Schocken, 1986.

Brown, Adrienne Maree. Interview with Catherine Lizette Gonzalez. *Colorlines*, February 26, 2019. www.colorlines.com/articles/pleasure-activism-adrienne-maree-brown-dares-us-get-touch-our-needs.

Brown, Jarrett H. "The Shadow of Intimacy: Male Bonding and Improvised Masculinity in Claude McKay's *Banjo: A Story without a Plot*." *Journal of West Indian Literature* 21, nos. 1–2 (2012–13): 1–22.

Camp, Stephanie M. H. "The Pleasures of Resistance: Enslaved Women and Body Politics in the Plantation South, 1830–1861." *Journal of Southern History* 68, no. 3 (2002): 533–72.

Cohen, Cathy. "Deviance as Resistance: A New Research Agenda for the Study of Black Politics." *Du Bois Review Social Science Research on Race* 1, no. 1 (2004): 27–45.

Dregni, Michael. *Gypsy Jazz: In Search of Django Reinhardt and the Soul of Gypsy Swing*. New York: Oxford University Press, 2008. Kindle.

Du Bois, W. E. B. "Review of *Home to Harlem* and *Quicksand*." *Crisis*, no. 35 (1928): 202.

Fanon, Frantz. "The Fact of Blackness." In *Black Skin, White Masks*, translated by Charles Lam Markmann, 109–40. New York: Grove, 1967.

Gilroy, Paul. *The Black Atlantic: Modernity and Double Consciousness*. London: Verso, 1993.

Hartman, Saidiya V. "The Burdened Individuality of Freedom." In *Scenes of Subjection: Terror, Slavery, and Self-Making in Nineteenth-Century America*, 115–24. New York: Oxford University Press, 1997.

Hartman, Saidiya V. *Lose Your Mother: A Journey along the Atlantic Slave Route*. New York: Farrar, Straus and Giroux, 2008.

Holcomb, Gary Edward, and William J. Maxwell. Introduction to McKay, *Romance in Marseille*, vii–xxxix.

Kelley, Robin D. G. *Race Rebels: Culture, Politics, and the Black Working Class*. New York: Free Press, 1994.

Lewis, Mary Dewhurst. "The Strangeness of Foreigners: Policing Migration and Nation in Interwar Marseille." *French Politics, Culture and Society* 20, no. 3 (2002): 65–96.

Lorde, Audre. "A Litany for Survival." In *The Collected Poems of Audre Lorde*, 255. New York: Norton, 1997.

Lorde, Audre. "The Uses of the Erotic: The Erotic as Power." In *Sister Outsider: Essays and Speeches by Audre Lorde*, 53–59. Freedom, CA: Crossing Press, 1984.

Mbembe, Achille. "Conversation: Achille Mbembe and David Theo Goldberg on *Critique of Black Reason*." *Theory, Culture and Society*, July 3, 2018. www.theoryculturesociety.org/conversation-achille-mbembe-and-david-theo-goldberg-on-critique-of-black-reason.

Mbembe, Achille. *Critique of Black Reason*. Durham, NC: Duke University Press, 2017.

Mbembe, Achille. "Necropolitics." *Public Culture* 15, no. 1 (2003): 11–40.

Mbembe, Achille. "Variations on the Beautiful in the Congolese World of Sounds." *Politique africaine* 100, no. 4 (2005): 69–91.

McKay, Claude. *Banjo: A Story without a Plot*. New York: Harper and Brothers, 1929.

McKay, Claude. *Home to Harlem*. Boston: Northeastern University Press, 1987.

McKay, Claude. *Romance in Marseille*, edited by Gary Edward Holcomb and William J. Maxwell. New York: Penguin, 2020.

McKay, Claude. "The Tired Worker." In *Selected Poems*, edited by Joan R. Sherman, 40. Mineola, NY: Dover, 1999.

Moten, Fred. "The Case of Blackness." *Criticism* 50, no. 2 (2008): 177–218.

Moten, Fred. *Stolen Life*. Durham, NC: Duke University Press, 2018. Kindle.

Mumford, Kevin J. *Interzones: Black/White Sex Districts in Chicago and New York in the Early Twentieth Century*. New York: Columbia University Press, 1997.

Musser, Amber Jamilla. *Sensational Flesh: Race, Power, and Masochism*. New York: New York University Press, 2014.

Patterson, Orlando. *Slavery and Social Death: A Comparative Study*. Cambridge, MA: Harvard University Press, 1982.

Sexton, Jared. "The Social Life of Social Death: On Afro-pessimism and Black Optimism." *Tensions*, no. 5 (2011): 1–47.

Spillers, Hortense J. "Mama's Baby, Papa's Maybe: An American Grammar Book." *Diacritics* 17, no. 2 (1987): 64–81.

Wilderson, Frank B. "Afropessimism and the End of Redemption." *Occupied Times*, March 30, 2016. theoccupiedtimes.org/?p=14236.

Wilderson, Frank B. "The Prison Slave as Hegemony's (Silent) Scandal." *Social Justice* 30, no. 2 (2003): 18–27.

Young, Molly. "The Best New Novel Was Written Ninety Years Ago." *New York*, February 6, 2020. www.vulture.com/2020/02/romance-in-marseille-claude-mckay.html.

A Queer Romance

Centering the Margins in Claude McKay's *Romance in Marseille*

ERIC H. NEWMAN

Abstract This essay argues that the queer romances at the margins of Claude McKay's *Romance in Marseille* operate as sites of possibility for a happy, egalitarian social relation that is longed for but not otherwise accessible in the novel. The essay contends that this novel, read against *Home to Harlem* (1928) and *Banjo* (1929), offers one of the most sustained, nuanced representations of queer life in McKay's archive and in early twentieth-century LGBT literature more generally, one in which same-sex-oriented characters are rendered as normal, integral figures in urban life rather than as outré characters whose primary function is to add spice to the narrative. As the novel demonstrates the continuing appeal of queerness as a site for imagining a more liberated, loving form of social organization—one that relishes the pleasure-in-difference that is a hallmark of McKay's writing—it also anticipates formations within the queer liberationist politics of the decades that followed.
Keywords Claude McKay, LGBTQ studies, queer modernism, Harlem Renaissance, romance

I n the early 1930s, as Claude McKay began revising the rough manuscript for a new novel titled *The Jungle and the Bottoms* (published in 2020 as *Romance in Marseille*), the once-celebrated writer was at a grim turning point in his career. Financially on the ropes and battling a number of health issues as a result of treatment for sexually transmitted diseases,[1] McKay was scrambling to produce a novel that could rival the runaway success of *Home to Harlem* (1928). Meanwhile the outside world was loping toward another major war, convulsed by the Great Depression and its ripple effects on the developing global economy. In the United States, the erosion of popular support (and governmental tolerance) for the sexual exploration and gin-fueled bohemias that had defined the Roaring Twenties ushered in a cultural conservatism and broken idealism that had begun to percolate through McKay's literary world.[2] In the 1920s McKay and contemporaries including Langston Hughes, Richard Bruce Nugent, and Nella Larsen had forged new pathways in African American and modernist literature with their representation of how race,

ENGLISH LANGUAGE NOTES
59:1, April 2021 DOI 10.1215/00138282-8814983
© 2021 Regents of the University of Colorado

sexuality, and gender were lived and understood in the still-young twentieth century. Yet the dawn of the 1930s saw the publication of Wallace Thurman's *Infants of the Spring* (1932), a satire that proclaimed the self-immolating end of the Harlem Renaissance's dreams of racial and sexual utopias. Thurman's bitterly funereal novel also marked a departure from the sentimental toward a grittier, hard-edged realism that was in keeping with the transition from early to midcentury American literature. This is all to say that the early 1930s was a rather odd time for McKay to be at work on a romance, especially one that features one of the period's most strikingly nuanced representations of homosexuality, one in which same-sex desire appears not as the decadent aberration of a modern age but as a social, erotic relation possessed of all the honor, depth, and egalitarianism that McKay so often found lacking in heterosexual romance.

As both a novel and a window onto its historical moment, *Romance in Marseille* marks at once a steadfast fidelity to and departure from McKay's prior work and the literature of what we have come to call "queer modernism." The novel centers on the tale of Lafala, a young African who opens the story having lost both legs to frostbite after stowing away on a merchant vessel. Brought to the port city of Marseille—the scene of McKay's earlier novel *Banjo* (1929)—Lafala finds himself engaged in a legal battle that promises transformative wealth in the form of insurance damages to be paid out by the shipping company. Armed with this windfall-in-waiting, Lafala picks back up with Aslima, a local prostitute who had conned him on his last visit to Marseille, determined to show her up but also to win her back. As the characters negotiate a pas de deux of love complicated by distrust, readers take in a kaleidoscopic view of the port city's denizens: prostitutes, laborers, political organizers, revelers, queers, entertainers, proprietors, and legal authorities. If romance is the central plot of the novel, what *should* be its central love story fails in the end, and Lafala returns to Africa without Aslima. In this way, *Romance* recalls the anxieties around heterosexual unions in both *Home to Harlem* and *Banjo*, anxieties that proceed from the way that capitalism shapes a misogynist view of relations between the sexes: women conniving to get money from men, and men desiring sexual gratification but also freedom from the constrictive (often financial) bonds of the couple. As the central relationship fails, McKay keeps a hold on the utopian possibility of romance as the journey toward egalitarian relation in the queer relationships that migrate toward the center of the text. Through two such couplings—between the burly laborer Big Blonde and the young hustler Petit Frère, and between the queenly prostitute La Fleur Noire and her unnamed Greek girlfriend—McKay maintains the optimism his work has for interclass contact and new possibilities of the social while investing them with a durability, even a *fidelity*, that is markedly at odds with the lauded vagabondage and itineracy of *Home to Harlem* and *Banjo*.

In these queer couplings McKay forges new ground while returning to old themes, such as the prostitute romance, the critique of capital, the loving representation of the underclass, and the celebration of homosocial camaraderie. Yet, as the strident political debates (about Black internationalism and diasporic identity) of earlier novels appear to retreat from view, a call for queer dignity emerges as an auxiliary politics of *Romance*. That new politics may well have taken its lead from

McKay's experience living in Morocco, which his biographer, Wayne Cooper, explains was a place where sexual fluidity invited not only new experiences but also contact with queer writers, including Paul Bowles and Charles Henri Ford.[3] The latter's *The Young and Evil* (1933), cowritten with the film critic Parker Tyler, includes a nested series of reflections on gay male subjectivity and strident appeals for freedom of expression that resemble the articulation of male homosexuality in *Romance*, which Cooper commends for its "frank" and "sympathetic" exploration of "the plight of homosexuals in Western society."[4] In a distinct turn from his earlier work, McKay's *Romance* eschews the more sensationalist representation of queer characters—both in McKay's writing and in early twentieth-century depictions of homosexuality more generally—in order to represent starkly modern, matter-of-fact gay and lesbian relationships that challenge the sad-queer affect that is such a hallmark of LGBTQ fiction from the early twentieth century.

In this essay I argue that *Romance in Marseille* makes important interventions in the representation of homosexuality in McKay's writing and thought as well as in early twentieth-century American literature more generally (with the understanding that McKay explodes such national boundaries). In the figure of Big Blonde, I argue, McKay offers readers a matter-of-fact portrait of a heroic, chivalrous gay male subject who revises the then-dominant view of male homosexuals as effeminate and given to vice or weakness. In his representation of gay and lesbian couples, I claim, McKay articulates a social order at the margins that is more felicitous, egalitarian, and liberated than its dominant, heterosexual counterpart, a position that circulates in his earlier fiction but is more full-throatedly claimed in *Romance*. Finally, I argue that in a scene of homophobic attack near the end of the novel McKay at once stakes a claim for the dignity of the much-maligned homosexual *and* evinces a political stridency and self-confidence in the young hustler Petit Frère. As I read the difference in Big Blonde and Petit Frère's responses to that attack, I locate an anticipation both of the movements for queer liberation that would define LGBTQ politics and identity and of that identity's formations in the second half of the twentieth century. Taken together, these extraordinary achievements, in the context of early twentieth-century American literature more generally and as a development within McKay's writing, at once explain why *Romance in Marseille* was not published in its own time and the value that it offers us as readers in the present.

Big Blonde: Recasting Queer Identity after the Pansy Craze

Readers familiar with the canons of early twentieth-century and modernist queer literature will find themselves struck by Big Blonde, the butch working-class queer who appears in the last third of the novel as a chivalrous, heroic character. It is worth examining in detail the opening description of Big Blonde not only for its novelty within queer literature of the period but also for its similarity to and departure from McKay's representation of queer subjects in prior novels.

> Big Blonde was like a hero straight out of Joseph Conrad, an outstanding
> enigma of Quayside. A big, firm-footed, broad-shouldered man, splendidly
> built with the haunting eyes of a lost child. He worked on the docks, a happy

worker, active like a madman reckless with his strength, making it hard for his fellow workers to keep up the pace. But he had no interest in the workers' unions and in spite of his natural roughness there was a singular and foreign air of refinement about him.[5]

Big Blonde shifts fluidly across gender norms in several ways. As a "big, firm-footed, broad-shouldered man," he is rendered as the athletic "hero" type that is celebrated in heterosexual culture and that would, as a result, become the centerpiece of gay male-oriented physique magazines in America and Europe by midcentury. Yet Big Blonde also bears the "haunting eyes of a lost child" that mark him as a queer in their literalization of what Christopher Nealon identifies as the lost, "foundling" character of early twentieth-century queer identity,[6] and in their identification of an adult male with an earlier stage of development (the "child") that signals his deviation from the chrononormative[7] rhythms of maturation and development idealized in heterosexual culture. A similarly asymmetrical dyad can be located in the idealization of Big Blonde's "natural roughness" as a superior laborer who is the envy of his fellow dockworkers, a trait that sits strangely with his alienating possession of a "singular and foreign air of refinement." While his prowess as a worker imbues Big Blonde's character with the trappings of a normative masculinity, his foreignness and "refinement" are qualities that connote the effeminacy and effeteness that typify queer characters in McKay's previous novels. Recall, for example, how Ray, the Haitian intellectual and autobiographical stand-in from *Home to Harlem* and *Banjo*, is alienated—is marked as *queer*—from the Black and working-class communities of those novels precisely because of his refinement and difference.[8] Finally, Big Blonde's name slides from the masculine register of bigness, where *Big* is a referent for his large and "splendidly built" male body, to the feminized form of *Blonde*. In this way, Big Blonde's name suggests a queer doubleness by which he flouts gender norms as neither the typical portrait of an effete homosexual nor a purely heterosexual masculine ideal through which he is rendered as "a hero straight out of Joseph Conrad." McKay's literary allusion in *Romance in Marseille* to Conrad's heroes—and, as Gary Holcomb and William Maxwell imply, perhaps also to the male heroes of Ernest Hemingway, a central writer of American masculinity between the wars[9]—casts Big Blonde as a distinctly different homosexual character for a period in which homosexuals were primarily identified through their gender nonconformity.[10]

Before turning to the unique representation of Big Blonde's relationship with his lover, Petit Frère, I want to reflect on McKay's political positioning of Big Blonde as a queer outlaw. As noted in the passage above, despite the character's representation as a hulking embodiment of working-class masculinity and his status as an exceptional laborer, Big Blonde has no interest in the politics that saturate his trade, indeed has "no interest in the workers' unions" (*RM*, 95). This does not mean, however, that Big Blonde does not enact a politics of his own. In the place of an affinity for labor or racial politics (and Big Blonde is, pointedly, white), McKay endows this character with the spirit of the radical queer outlaw that would become more prominent in LGBTQ literature in the post–World War II era: "It was gossiped that [Big Blonde] had once held a respectable position in the merchant service, but he never talked about his past life. Because of his quixotic habit of getting into difficulties, he was often in trouble with the police. Sometimes he was jailed for a short term; sometimes he went into hiding" (*RM*, 95). Though the narrator leaves us little of substance here to explain Big Blonde's falling out with the merchant service, the adjective *respectable*, combined with Big Blonde's open homosexuality, suggests that he may have been dismissed for buggery/sodomy or some other crime of "indecency" associated with homosexuality. The idea that queerness may be the source of the character's "quixotic habit of getting into difficulties" is evidenced by the example of Big Blonde's having "broke[n] up the furniture in the saloon of the loving house of La Creole, because a boy companion of his was insulted there" (*RM*, 95). In the aftermath of the incident, the narrator tells us that Big Blonde became "a good friend of . . . the proprietress, and the boy of the house, Petit Frère," securing not only a new lover but also a camaraderie with the demimonde milieu of this particular loving house, noted for being "much frequented and touted by the colored Quaysiders" (*RM*, 95). The inclusion of this detail also makes clear that Big Blonde's difficulties are a result of what would be considered a traditionally chivalrous act: the defense of a beloved's honor. In this way, McKay makes Big Blonde a heroic outlaw, a significant departure from queer representation in his time and, to a great extent, in the later twentieth century.

In such moments, we glimpse in Big Blonde the emergence of a more fully realized radical queer subject in McKay's writing, though with significant limitations I will discuss further at the end of this essay. Big Blonde's queerness puts him in a confrontational relationship to legal authority and the norms of bourgeois respectability, but it also invites the building of supportive networks with sex workers and people of color, suturing a community among the underclass that readers today might see as productively intersectional or at least one that finds value and solidarity across race, gender, and class. Of course, this Whitmanesque inclusivity that flouts the norms of any organized community—Big Blonde runs from the law, yes, but he does not embrace the unions or other forms of imagining collective resistance[11]—is central to McKay's political vision, where the hybrid forms of life to which diaspora and queer desire give shape are the utopian foundations of a better world we might strive to bring into being. Yet Big Blonde appears to represent something different, or perhaps something in excess of this goal, a sort of surplus to the outsider figures who populate McKay's earlier writing. While he may anticipate, in ways that are striking for their shared setting and disposition, the figure of the queer outlaw celebrated in the work of Jean Genet—whose 1947 novel *Querelle de Brest* dilates on the passions and betrayals of a bisexual sailor in another French port city more than a decade after McKay wrote *Romance*—Big Blonde achieves such status without being a villain, a malcontent, or even a threat to the public, even if he may be a threat to the order desired by the heterosexual police state. A jovial outsider, Big Blonde thwarts bourgeois norms: he is open about his same-sex attraction, he is a capable and "happy" worker who nonetheless has no investment in employment, and he is a lovable fugitive from the law. As such, he manages a unique thing: to be an outsider without being alienated. In Big Blonde, McKay gives us a character who exceeds the norms of queer literary representation in his time, a queer subject whose model of the social not only challenges gender and sexual norms but also creates new ones.

Romance at the Margins: McKay's Queer Couplings

The two queer couples in *Romance in Marseille*—La Fleur Noire and her "Greek girl," and Big Blonde and Petit Frère—mark a tremendous departure in the representation of same-sex love in McKay's writing while continuing to preserve a familiar space of idealized relation that escapes the restrictive relations organized by capital. The distinction can be seen at once in these marginal characters' migration toward the center of the narrative, especially the novel's peculiar dilation over the male homosexual couple's relationship, and in their apparent durability. In McKay's earlier work, queer figures are typically lone wolves who fleetingly appear to add sensationalist spice to club interiors and encounters on the street—those "dark dandies . . . loving up their pansies" in *Home to Harlem*'s The Congo or the Senegalese "boys" who "dance better male with male or individually, than with girls" at the Café African in *Banjo*.[12] By contrast, queer characters in *Romance in Marseille* appear exclusively in couples and are more fully realized characters. These relationships are idealized above that of the main heterosexual pairing between Aslima and Lafala in large part because they lack the suspicion and economic gamesmanship that McKay frequently identifies at the center of heterosexual relationships. That these queer couples take shape amid, and often in contrast to, the circuits of ephemeral pleasure that marked the representation of queer desire in the earlier novels signals a shift away from the idealization of vagabondage toward a longing for a more stable, one dares to say *domestic*, life in *Romance*. This change is articulated late in the novel when Babel, one of Big Blonde's closest companions, observes that "the vagabond life was all right for a man without property or position, but responsibility and vagabondage could not go together" (*RM*, 109). The fact that McKay's queer characters never appear to attain "property or position" in the novel—those being the burdens of Lafala's struggle as someone who has suddenly come into money and must vie with others willing to play him for it—presents their relationships as social formations in which McKay sees the possibility of a world-securing stability that would not require giving in to the demands of the bourgeois good life.

These unique features of queer representation in *Romance* are evidenced quite clearly in the lesbian character La Fleur Noire, who marks out a place for herself at the top of the Quayside hierarchy specifically because she does not desire men. When Lafala cannot understand how La Fleur is so successful in her trade even though she is not attached to a male lover or protector (as Aslima is to Titin), Aslima explains: "Because [La Fleur's] different from most of us. She doesn't go crazy over men. She hates men and goes with them only to make money. Her Titin is that Greek girl. . . . She attracts lots of men . . . because they think she's got something hidden in her to give up, when she really has nothing at all. Nothing for men" (*RM*, 41). The separation of romance from her work in the sex trade enables La Fleur an autonomy that none of the other girls, including Aslima, possesses in the demimonde economy of the Quayside. La Fleur sleeps with men only for money, exempting her from the complicated entanglements faced by Aslima and Latnah, Aslima's counterpart from *Banjo*, or by their mutual predecessor from *Home to Harlem*, Felice. As a result, La Fleur takes the unnamed "Greek girl" as her lover—that national distinction playing on associations between Greece and homosexuality[13]—and does so in a way that does not mirror the protector/lover relationship but rather transforms it. La Fleur is her own protector, an independent businesswoman for whom the Greek girl is a companion and lover rather than a pimp. La Fleur may in fact be the only truly autonomous woman in all three novels.

That more egalitarian relationship is borne out by an exchange later in the book between the two women, when Lafala proposes to buy La Fleur's services and her love for the evening, however high the price.

> La Fleur whispered to her girlfriend: "I think it's going to be black tea tonight."
> "Save the sugar for us," her friend whispered back.
> "That goes without saying," said La Fleur. (*RM*, 52)

The metaphor of having "black tea," a reference to Lafala's Blackness, enables the expression of a lesbian love that is more authentic and "sweet" than heterosexual sex. The Greek girl implies that La Fleur should spend all her sexual energy not on this new client but rather on her "girlfriend" back home. What is interesting about these exchanges is that La Fleur is represented neither purely as a titillating example of urban sexual decadence nor in the often-misogynist light in which women appear in McKay's writing; rather, she is a woman in control of herself, her economic situation, and her romantic relationships. While McKay clearly uses the metaphor of "black tea" and "sugar" to humorous effect, he does so not to make fun of La Fleur but to make fun of Lafala, the straight male who believes that his wealth can buy him any pleasure and the love of any woman. La Fleur's aside to the Greek girl makes it clear that she saves the very best, the dearest part of her love and body, for a woman to whom she gives it freely. When Lafala rebuffs La Fleur after she makes fun of him, the narrator notes that "[La Fleur] did not want to walk all the way down to Quayside [for] she had no money. She hated to go back to her Greek friend like that. Soured and empty-handed after she had left the Tout-va-Bien so triumphantly with Lafala" (*RM*, 55). Unlike the relationship between Aslima and Titin, where failing to provide money from sex work puts the former at risk of the latter's violence because their relationship is one of economic dependence, La Fleur does not want to go back "empty-handed" to her lover out of a sense of wounded pride.

The most fully realized queer relationship in *Romance* is between Big Blonde and his lover, Petit Frère. Despite their brief appearance toward the end of the novel, they represent one of the happiest, most untroubled relationships in all of McKay's writing. The love between the young male hustler and the butch laborer is free of the mutual suspicion, double-dealing, and temptations of the urban demimonde that so often provide plot-moving conflict and strain in the heterosexual relationships centered in the rough trilogy formed by *Home to Harlem*, *Banjo*, and *Romance in Marseille*. In these tales, prostitutes and their lovers must always weigh whether or not they can trust each other, whether one is merely out for money or the other is ready to leave at the first sign of a new adventure, and thus are always somewhat at odds with each other. In a world of ephemeral attachments, the relationship between Big Blonde and Petit Frère is remarkably *durable*, a feature that may suggest McKay's increasing comfort with representing homosexual desire in his writing and his idealization of more permanent, stable relationships that serve as alternatives to the soured utopia of vagabondage but that still provide freedom and security without compromise.

The exceptional quality of homosexual love in general and the relationship between these two men specifically can be seen in an exchange between Big Blonde and Babel as *Romance in Marseille* reaches its climax. Worried that Titin will kill Lafala because of the latter's relationship with Aslima, Babel attempts to enlist Big Blonde's help, calling on him to save this heterosexual gone astray. Yet, for Big Blonde, the drama is nonsensical:

> Big Blonde said it was common knowledge that the protectors were well
> organized and he couldn't believe that Lafala would easily allow himself to fall
> into a trap. Babel replied that it wouldn't be so hard to believe if Big Blonde was
> less interested in petit frères and more in petites filles. Big Blonde guffawed
> and excused himself from joining Lafala and the others that night for just that
> reason. He and Petit Frère were going to dine together and afterward resort to
> a certain little café. . . . (*RM*, 112; ellipsis in original)

Here McKay suggests that sexual desire orients one's reading of social relations, their meaning, and determines the action to be taken in response. While the skeptical reader might argue that one who loves male hustlers could just as easily get into trouble with the proprietors of the brothels where they work as his straight counterpart, Babel proposes that male homosexual love renders the subject immune to the illogical tendencies inspired by heterosexual passion. To parse the words above, Big Blonde would understand how Lafala could get into such a dangerous situation if he were sexually attracted to women rather than to men. The logical conclusion of Babel's point, we may understand, is that heterosexual love leads men to make foolish decisions, whereas the love of "petit frères" does not blind the subjects to reason, enabling them to read the facts of the world as they are.

This point is emphasized in the Big Blonde's decision to defer getting entangled in Lafala's affairs "for just that reason"—because he sexually prefers boys over girls—and announces that he is off for a date with Petit Frère. The language with which the narrator describes Big Blonde's mood in anticipation of the date at once emphasizes the giddy exhilaration of going to see a lover and marks that experience as superior to the heterosexual romance:

> Big Blonde replied that he was engaged for the night with Petit Frère and he
> became quite lyrical about it. Nothing could make him break the engagement.
> Not for the love of a drinking party which always delighted him, nor the
> bouquets of the rarest wines, nor the music of hymen though sweet with the
> honey of the queen bee and glorious like the songs of Solomon's loves, no not
> for the virgin stars of the sky nor a brighter shining moon. (*RM*, 111–12)

So great is Big Blonde's desire for a date night with Petit Frère that he would give up all partygoing pleasures, including the pleasures of women signified in "the music of hymen," "the honey of the queen bee," and "the virgin stars of the sky." The invocation of "the songs of Solomon's loves"—a reference to the biblical verses in which a young woman, her lover, and a removed chorus describe the ecstasy of heterosexual desire—is a pointed example of what appears here as a belief in queer superiority. If Big Blonde's desire to see Petit Frère surpasses even this ancient example of "glorious" romance, it makes the other pleasures of the Quayside or even—following the invocation of the moon and stars—of the cosmos itself pale in comparison. Growing "quite lyrical about it," Big Blonde offers a queer "Song of Solomon," his amorous frenzy blending into the narrator's articulation of a great and unmatched romantic feeling. That this love, here and elsewhere, is never derided as simply about sex, in direct distinction from, say, the language of "pigs" that is often used in Aslima and Lafala's descriptions of their love for one another, also suggests that McKay locates something purer, better, more refined in homosexual love than its heterosexual counterpart.

"In Another Quarter": *Romance*'s Queer Time and Place

While these queer characters offer a starkly utopian version of coupling possibilities in *Romance in Marseille*, they are not free of the harsh realities that assailed queer people during a period when laws and cultural scrutiny forced much queer life underground, even in the urban centers where it had so recently thrived. The location and sudden eruption of violence into the scene of Big Blonde and Petit Frère's date not only demonstrate how queer life is oddly cordoned off from the novel's main social spaces but also suggest a divergence in attitudes about queerness between the two men, one that appears to hinge on the question of queer shame. At the same time, the odd inclusion of this episode, which has no real bearing on the action of an otherwise straightforwardly plotted novel, implies an unresolved tension in McKay's queer expression, caught between the desire for a world in which queers might not be cowed by shame but faced with a present in which they are. This may explain why *Romance* at once embraces what Cooper marks as the novel's sympathetic "discuss[ion] of the plight of homosexual in Western society" and its apparent retreat from engaging that question too boldly. As I explore this material in the following section, I want to weave these concerns together as a way of demonstrating the unique place of *Romance in Marseille* not only within McKay's work and queer modernism more generally but also with regard to the way that the tension between Big Blonde and Petit Frère's reactions mirrors an ongoing struggle with queer shame that the politics of pride attempts to scuttle in the present. In other words, the tension between a revolutionary new pride and the shame with which society attempts to shape and control queer life is still unresolved in our time, even if it looks different than it did in McKay's.

After dinner at a Chinese restaurant, where Petit Frère scarfs down "chopped pork and celery, chopped chicken, fish with thick sauce, rice and tea" (*RM*, 115), not only a sort of advertisement for the big appetite of a *petit* lover but also a way of aligning queerness with the Orient that connects McKay's writing to other strains of queer modernism,[14] Big Blonde and Petit Frère head to the Petit Pain, a bar described as distinct in both location and mood from the bars that inflect McKay's Marseille in both *Romance* and in *Banjo*:

> The bar was in another quarter of Marseille far removed from Quayside and its hectic atmosphere. It was located in the vicinity of the principal railroad station in a narrow and somber alley. Like the street there was something a little sinister and something very alluring in this café, but difficult to define. It was a quality strangely balancing between the emotions of laughter and tears, ribaldry and bittersweetness. (*RM*, 116)

The Petit Pain is quite literally on the other side of the tracks from the bars and clubs that are the usual haunts of Quaysiders, in a world of its own that offers an escape both peaceful and "somber" to its queer clientele. Underscored here is the duality of queer life as McKay captures it. The café is "a little sinister" yet also "very alluring," and its affective charge is drawn from its "balancing between the emotions of laughter and tears, ribaldry and bittersweetness." That movement between pleasure and sadness, acceptance and dejection, is characteristic of much queer representation during the period, as has been well documented,[15] and informs the affective tension in much twentieth-century LGBTQ literature[16] as queer people grappled with an emergent sense of social and historical identity that encouraged their self-acceptance *as queer people* against mainstream culture's efforts to keep shame and alienation in place as modes of controlling queer subjects and their desires.[17]

While the Petit Pain balances between happiness and sadness, it is also a place where various social worlds collide under the umbrella of queer desire, a hybrid community in keeping with McKay's utopian embrace of a Whitmanesque erotics of heterogeneity. As the narrator surveys the bar, his eye catches "two men of middle-class respectability" playing dice with "three lads evidently of the slum proletariat," "two fine and handsome sailors" sharing drinks with "a young man slickly dressed in black like a professional dancer," and a lone soldier nursing a beer (*RM*, 116). The encounters between economic and professional classes at the bar offer queerness as a category that cuts across the dividing lines that keep a repressive, normative society in place while also witnessing the loneliness that can attend queer community, seen in the figure of the soldier. Added to this mix is the asymmetrical pairing of Big Blonde and Petit Frère: one an easygoing and hypermasculine laborer; the other a sleeker, younger, effeminate male prostitute, described as "a simple kid" with a "pale prettiness and [an] insolent mouth" (*RM*, 117, 112). As a hybrid space, the bar invites forms of unexpected contact, as when a group of young female prostitutes stops by to see Petit Frère and when St. Dominique, who has come to the bar with Babel and Lafala to find Big Blonde, marvels that the girls are "so affectionate" with him, given that their "little brothers steal business away from them" (*RM*, 118). Babel dismisses this idea, explaining that these queer and straight youths "are all young and jolly and working together at the same trade" (*RM*, 118). While the emphasis appears to be on the all-encompassing sex trade of Marseille, it also points to the fungibility of sexual object choice, namely, that a pretty, young boy may be just as appealing to a male customer as a pretty, young girl. The interchange-ability of the sexual object without, as is clear in this context, calling into question the sexuality of the male customer corresponds to the early twentieth-century atti-tudes about sexuality as social identity; in other words, the binary between hetero-sexuality and homosexuality was defined by the difference between active and pas-sive sex roles.[18] This flexibility is playfully suggested when Babel makes a pass at Petit Frère and, rebuffed by Big Blonde, starts dancing with his friend, "swaying to the music of the moon," adding in a note that demonstrates awareness of police surveillance of queer spaces that "the police can't interfere for this ain't no dancing" (*RM*, 119). When Lafala warns Babel to "look out the moon madness don't get you too," Babel replies, "I'm crazy all ways bar none"—that is, just like the male custom-ers who frequent prostitutes, he too may go with a man as easily as he goes with a woman. In such moments, McKay articulates queerness's circulation in Marseille as a roving desire, a flexible possibility that can take shape not merely in the remote space of the Petit Pain but potentially anywhere sex is to be had. In this manner, queer admixture garners its utopian social gloss once again in McKay's writing, as a mode of relation through and across difference, as a new model of the social that might emerge from the circuits of erotic desire.

As the bar scene closes, a sudden moment of violence disturbs the action and prompts a remarkable split in the reactions of Petit Frère and Big Blonde. A woman selling dolls and knickknacks enters the bar to peddle her goods to the group. When Petit Frère rejects her, calling her an "old cow," "old and ugly," and a "jealous has-been" (*RM*, 120), she leaves the bar as the men gather around the boy in laughter. In a few moments, she returns to slap Petit Frère in the face with a paper "full of filth"—likely feces or some other unsanitary dirt from the street—and shouts at him: "There! That is your life" (*RM*, 120). The suggestion here is clearly that Petit Frère, as a male prostitute and habitué of a queer-friendly bar like the Petit Pain, is filth, excrement, trash. As he has done in the past, Big Blonde rushes to defend his lover and "knocked [the woman] sprawling to the floor and flung the basket through the door of the café, scattering its contents" (*RM*, 120). When Petit Frère returns from washing himself up in the bathroom, he is defiant rather than defeated: "If I ever run across that old sow again I'll cut her twat out and give it to the dogs" (*RM*, 121). Meanwhile Babel tries to rouse the despondent Big Blonde, only to find that his burly friend is "crying softly" at his table. Petit Frère goes to comfort him, and Babel and the rest of the Quayside gang exit the bar, leaving the couple alone.

A strange turn of events in an already strange chapter, this homophobic encounter provokes very different reactions in the two gay characters: Big Blonde crying in shame, Petit Frère vowing vengeance. For the younger Petit Frère, shame is not part of his reactive calculus, nor, apparently, is any recognition that perhaps he was wrong to insult the old woman. Rather, he cleans himself up and emerges from the confrontation ready to attack this woman who has maligned his life and his love. While Big Blonde's immediate reaction is violence, what follows is shame and sadness, indicating that the woman's rebuke of queer life touches him much more deeply than it does Petit Frère. This shame is forecast earlier in the scene, when the narrator explains that Big Blonde is sometimes nervous about so openly *being homosexual* with his heterosexual friends, even if his same-sex desire is no secret: "Now that the lads had invaded his retreat, [Big Blonde] gave himself will-ingly to the enjoyment of the party. He didn't want to impose Petit Frère upon them when he was invited. But it was alright to have him in the crowd since they had come themselves to find him. And Petit Frère was pleased" (*RM*, 118). This moment of exposition reveals Big Blonde's mixed feelings about his sexual differ-ence, suggesting that there are limits (real or imagined) to how he experiences what has heretofore read as a surprisingly matter-of-fact (for its time) acceptance of his homosexuality.[19] Just as the Petit Pain is far removed from the main thor-oughfares of the Quayside, so too is queerness far removed from those sites of public, visible sociality; Big Blonde must find a "retreat" where he is free to express himself as a homosexual. While his friends' female lovers pose no threat to their easygoing camaraderie, Big Blonde clearly worries that to introduce Petit Frère would "impose" on those friends, perhaps because Petit Frère is more effeminate and, by trade, marked as a homosexual in ways that Big Blonde is not.

The scene speaks at once to a fiery new spirit of rebellious pride within this gay community (Petit Frère) as well as to the shame and social isolation that limited the lives of gay men throughout the twentieth century (Big Blonde). In this sense, while I have argued that the figure of Big Blonde emerges as a radical queer subject in McKay's fiction, one that anticipates the queer outlaw character of later fiction, he is not necessarily ready to take any direct political action, to stand up for him-self on account of his queerness. That task falls to Petit Frère's generation and those to come after, even as critics like Heather Love have argued, the stigma and experience of shame clings to queer communities in the present in ways that the politics of pride and a belief in the march of progress would have us deny.[20]

Judging from the cultural currents of the time and what I have attempted to lay out above as the novel's unapologetic representation of queerness, it is hard to dispute that *Romance in Marseille* failed to appear in McKay's lifetime because it was ahead of its moment. In Gary Holcomb's reading of *Romance's* failed publica-tion history, the novel's "sexual frankness" is complemented by McKay's personal resistance to push the novel into publication. Holcomb recounts a letter from editor Clifton Fadiman to Max Eastman in which Fadiman rejects *Romance* as "sex hash," unpublishable in a time when printing "racy novels"—those that dealt unguardedly with subject of sex, especially queer sex—could invite pornography charges. Hol-comb also notes, however, that McKay "almost certainly could have eventually pub-lished his novel . . . with a more liberally disposed [publishing] house."[21] Was McKay trapped in the same way as Big Blonde, living a queer life but, in the mode of his generation, wary of the ills queer publicity could bring? Does the figure of Petit Frère, unashamed and ready to fight, operate in the novel as a kind of wish fulfillment? These questions cannot be answered, of course, yet the existence of the novel in the present is some testament to McKay's willingness to keep the dream of *Romance* alive, its queer characters moving into the present just as they migrated from the margins of the text, staking a claim for themselves against the harsh realities of their day. The interventions that Big Blonde, Petit Frère, La Fleur Noire, and the Greek girl make in the novel call out for a freer future and find them-selves, as last, in our time as a reminder of what was possible to think in the past and what remains to be thought in our present.

ERIC H. NEWMAN is a scholar and critic based in Santa Monica, California. He received his PhD in English from the University of California, Los Angeles, in 2018. He is the Gender and Sexuality editor of the *Los Angeles Review of Books*.

Notes

1   Cooper, *Claude McKay*, 267.

2   George Chauncey has marked this period as one in which "gay men and lesbians began to seem less amusing than dangerous," no longer a titillating ornament for urban nightlife but a threat to the stability of a nation already on the brink of collapse. Campaigns to close queer bars and other nightlife spaces resulted in the sudden erasure of queer representation and being from their prior centrality to the development of a distinct urban culture. For his full account of this dramatic shift, see Chauncey, "The Exclusion of Homosexuality."

3   Cooper, *Claude McKay*, 277–78.

4   Cooper, *Claude McKay*, 268.

5   McKay, *Romance in Marseille* (hereafter cited as *RM*), 94.

6   For Nealon, early twentieth-century homosexual subjects understood themselves as being from another place, longing for reunion with a culture and people from whom they had been separated, thrown as they were into a heterosexual culture that did not, and could not, accept them and whose cultural sanctions they could not win (*Foundlings*).

7   I borrow this term from Elizabeth Freeman, who identifies the chrononormative as the rhythm of life's unfolding in a manner supporting the reproduction of citizens fit for a heteropatriarchal order (*Time Binds*). By falling outside the moments that mark one's development in heterosexual life—birth, marriage, reproduction, and death—the queer subject remains arrested, unable to participate in marriage and social reproduction, ever a child.

8   For a reading of Ray as a queer figure in *Home to Harlem* and *Banjo*, see Holcomb, "'Dark Desire All Over the Pages'"; Holcomb, "The 'Rude Anarchy' of 'Black Boys' in *Banjo*"; and Newman, "Ephemeral Utopias."

9   Holcomb and Maxwell, introduction, viii.

10   There are, of course, important outliers to this trend, including Edward Prime-Stevenson's *Imre: A Memorandum*, a 1906 novel whose main character, Oswald, a somewhat feminized queer fleeing persecution in England to settle in Hungary, falls in love with a strapping soldier whose butch masculinity provides at once the promise of a new life for Oswald and a masculine ideal with which he combats the derision of same-sex-oriented men as effeminate, weak, and undeserving of praise. His soldier/lover provides Oswald with a view of homosexuality as a surplus rather than deficit of masculinity, a socially recuperable form of same-sex desire. In a sociohistorical vein, I am reminded again of Chauncey's argument that homosexuality as an identity in the early twentieth century was primarily the product of one's sexual performance and position. Terms like *fairy* were applied only to men who were not gender conforming in their presentation, much as homosexual identity was primarily ascribed to men who played the passive role in homosexual sex. Men who presented as normatively masculine and who played the active role in sex were not generally understood to be homosexual. See Chauncey, "Christian Brotherhood."

11   Holcomb identifies Big Blonde as the "queer *inconnu*—unaffiliated, persecuted by the authorities—and because of this he is dedicated to the socialist revolution if carnally incapable, like McKay, of being a disciplined follower" (*Claude McKay, Code Name Sasha*, 201). My reading of Big Blonde as a queer outlaw joins this interpretation along the axis of the character's rebellious, uncontrollable spirit.

12   McKay, *Home to Harlem*, 30–31; McKay, *Banjo*, 48.

13   This association may be particular to lesbian identity in McKay's writing, as readers may recall that Ray identifies Sappho as a "great Greek poet" whose stories "gave two lovely words to modern language . . . Sapphic and Lesbian" (*Home to Harlem*, 128–29).

14   Fiona Ngô beautifully traces how references to the Orient proliferate in modernist literature specifically around the site of queerness's expression. In her reading of Thurman's *Infants of the Spring*, Nugent's *Gentleman Jigger*, and other works, Ngô demonstrates how locating the "ontological and epistemological schemas of imperial logic" and the desire to "confound [that imperial logic's] authoritative classifications" helps these authors articulate queer Black identity in and through Orientalist tropes (*Imperial Blues*, 82). In this sense, Ngo claims that this writing doubles on the figure of the Orient as both "outside of the West as a

fantasy of the exotic" and "inside the West as a badge of distinction for those who can know the Orient" (90–92).

15 See Boone, *Libidinal Currents*; Love, *Feeling Backward*; and Nealon, *Foundlings*.

16 I am thinking here of such examples as Barnes's *Nightwood*, Prime-Stevenson's *Imre: A Memorandum*, and Ford and Tyler's *The Young and Evil*. These are representative of queer novels from the period in which characters' jubilation around queer sex or romance is often paired with anxiety and sadness as a result of the impossibility of living openly and its impact on potential relationships, the prejudice of mainstream society and the police force, or generalized feelings of shame.

17 I use the term *queer people* here to emphasize what scholars of queer modernism have come to understand as the rise of an ethnic account of homosexuality—one thinks, for example, of the narrator's describing gay men in Prime-Stevenson's *Imre* as "a race with hearts never to be kindled by a woman" and wondering, "Was our race of gold or excrement? As rubies or as carrion?"—against the medical account of homosexuality that gave shape to the typology of the invert. Nealon describes this emergence as the outgrowth of a queer "foundling" identification that marked the homosexual of the early twentieth century as "an exile from sanctioned experience" who anticipated "a reunion with some 'people' or sodality who [might] redeem this exile and surpass the painful limitations of the original 'home'" (*Foundlings*, 2). It is important to note here that such "foundling" identification, particularly in its articulation of homosexuality as an altogether different *race* in the ways that Prime-Stevenson's quoted material suggests, is primarily characteristic of white queer literature.

18 Chauncey, "Christian Brotherhood," 189–93.

19 Holcomb describes this condition as being between "two spheres," a position from which Big Blonde "perceives when it is possible for such worlds—the orbit of the proletariat and the place of the queer—to intersect and when such a convergence is not so favorable" (*Claude McKay, Code Name Sasha*, 215–16).

20 Love documents the persistent appeal of the melancholic, tragic, and shameful in queer literature and culture as a counter to the politics of pride that would relegate those feelings to the past. Thus attempts to account for and return to narratives of "damage" in queer studies are often confronted with the urge "to resist damage and affirm queer existence" (*Feeling Backward*, 3). In Love's account, only by facing

the damage of the past and recognizing "the persistence of the past in the present" (19) can we truly do the work of queer liberation.

21 Holcomb, *Claude McKay, Code Name Sasha*, 175–76.

Works Cited

Barnes, Djuna. *Nightwood/Ladies Almanack*. New York: Quality Paperback Book Club, 2000.

Boone, Joseph Allen. *Libidinal Currents: Sexuality and the Shaping of Modernism*. Chicago: University of Chicago Press, 1998.

Chauncey, George. "Christian Brotherhood or Religious Perversion? Homosexual Identities and the Construction of Sexual Boundaries in the World War I Era." *Journal of Social History* 19, no. 2 (1985): 189–211.

Chauncey, George. "The Exclusion of Homosexuality from the Public Sphere in the 1980s." In *Gay New York: Gender, Urban Culture, and the Makings of the Gay Male World, 1890–1940*, 331–54. New York: Basic, 1995.

Cooper, Wayne F. *Claude McKay: Rebel Sojourner in the Harlem Renaissance*. Baton Rouge: Louisiana State University Press, 1987.

Ford, Charles Henri, and Parker Tyler. *The Young and Evil*. Gay Men's Press, 1989.

Freeman, Elizabeth. *Time Binds: Queer Temporalities, Queer Histories*. Durham, NC: Duke University Press, 2010.

Holcomb, Gary Edward. *Claude McKay, Code Name Sasha: Queer Black Marxism and the Harlem Renaissance*. Gainesville: University Press of Florida, 2007.

Holcomb, Gary Edward. "'Dark Desire All Over the Pages': Race, Nation, and Sex in *Home to Harlem*." In Holcomb, *Claude McKay, Code Name Sasha*, 91–138.

Holcomb, Gary Edward. "The 'Rude Anarchy' of 'Black Boys' in *Banjo*." In Holcomb, *Claude McKay, Code Name Sasha*, 139–70.

Holcomb, Gary Edward, and William J. Maxwell. Introduction to *Romance in Marseille*, by Claude McKay, vii–xxxix. New York: Penguin, 2020.

Love, Heather. *Feeling Backward: Loss and the Politics of Queer History*. Cambridge, MA: Harvard University Press, 2009.

McKay, Claude. *Banjo: A Story without a Plot*. New York: Harcourt, Brace, Jovanovich, 1929.

McKay, Claude. *Home to Harlem*. Boston: Northeastern University Press, 1987.

McKay, Claude. *Romance in Marseille*, edited by Gary Edward Holcomb and William J. Maxwell. New York: Penguin, 2020.

Nealon, Christopher. *Foundlings: Gay and Lesbian Historical Emotion before Stonewall*. Durham, NC: Duke University Press, 2001.

Newman, Eric H. "Ephemeral Utopias: Queer
    Cruising, Literary Form, and Diasporic
    Imagination in Claude McKay's *Home to
    Harlem* and *Banjo*." *Callaloo* 38, no. 1 (2015):
    167–85.
Ngô, Fiona I. B. *Imperial Blues: Geographies of Race
    and Sex in Jazz Age New York*. Durham, NC:
    Duke University Press, 2013.
Nugent, Richard Bruce. *Gentleman Jigger: A Novel of
    the Harlem Renaissance*. Cambridge, MA:
    Da Capo, 2008.
Prime-Stevenson, Edward. *Imre: A Memorandum*.
    Peterborough, ON: Broadview, 2003.
Thurman, Wallace. *Infants of the Spring*. New York:
    Modern Library, 1999.

"A Little Civilization in My Pocket"

Complicating Primitivism in *Romance in Marseille*

LAURA RYAN

Abstract   This article argues that *Romance in Marseille* marks a significant shift in Claude McKay's approach to primitivism, one that necessitates a reconsideration of his reputation—based on his two novels of the late 1920s—as perhaps the Harlem Renaissance's foremost proponent of "strategic primitivism." Tracing the development of McKay's primitivism from *Home to Harlem* (1928) and *Banjo* (1929) to his most recently published novel, this essay suggests an evolution along philosophical, political, and stylistic lines. *Romance in Marseille* deconstructs the primitive/civilized binary, forgoing the antiracist potentialities of primitivism for the utopian possibilities of international Marxism, interracial collaboration and queer love.

Keywords   primitivism, Claude McKay, Harlem Renaissance, strategic primitivism

In a lighthearted and seemingly unremarkable exchange, La Fleur Noire, a well-known prostitute of Marseille's Quayside, jokes with Lafala, the protagonist of Claude McKay's *Romance in Marseille* (ca. 1933; 2020), about the cats "amusing themselves noisily on the roofs" outside his hotel room: "'The cats are carrying on terribly on the roofs,' she said. 'And the two-footed ones are just as bad under the roofs,' said Lafala. 'It's the same life everywhere,' La Fleur giggled."[1] La Fleur's quip, "'It's the same life everywhere,'" recalls a similar declaration by Jake Brown in the earlier McKay novel, *Home to Harlem* (1928). On the eve of his friend Ray's departure to sea, Jake warns him not to expect a different life on the other side: "'The sea is hell and when you hits shore it's the same life all ovah.'"[2] Both statements suggest the simultaneity of lived experience at different locations within the capitalist world-system and the impossibility of any true escape to a different life. Ray, the Caribbean intellectual, cannot leave behind his education and its associated civilization to live more spontaneously and instinctively, to fully experience the "primitive joy of Harlem" and the "romance of being black" that Jake embodies (*HH*, 109, 154). Lafala, on the other hand, seems suspended between two modes of being and two systems of value. Alternately indifferent to and obsessed by money, largely cut off from the culture and traditions of his childhood (but equally unable to

ENGLISH LANGUAGE NOTES

59:1, April 2021   DOI 10.1215/00138282-8814994
© 2021 Regents of the University of Colorado

comprehend the political and cultural mores of Europe and America), his years of drifting have left him "half-civilized in a Quayside way" (*RM*, 46).

What sets *Romance in Marseille* and its characters apart from *Home to Harlem* and *Banjo: A Story without a Plot* (1929) and theirs, this essay argues, is at base a shift in McKay's representation of the primitive/civilized binary. It is a shift that necessitates a reconsideration of McKay's primitivism more widely and that raises larger questions about the ways we think about primitivism today. McKay has long been perceived and characterized as one of the Harlem Renaissance's foremost proponents of what is sometimes known as "strategic primitivism." Nathan Huggins, in his seminal 1971 *Harlem Renaissance*, indeed avers that "of all the Harlem writers and artists none grasped the lure of Negro primitivism more eagerly than Claude McKay. . . . Again and again, the message: the human and vital black man is alien in the sterile, mechanized European civilization."[3] More recently, Ben Etherington's *Literary Primitivism* (2017) casts McKay as the archetypal naive, earnest literary primitivist; in the companion novels *Home to Harlem* and *Banjo*, Etherington argues, there is "an abiding sense that authentic primitive experience is still within reach."[4] Such interpretations of McKay's primitivist credentials have not (and could not have) taken into account the publication of two of his novels in recent years: *Amiable with Big Teeth* (2017) and *Romance in Marseille*.

This essay argues that the latest of these, *Romance in Marseille*, marks a significant philosophical, political, and stylistic shift in McKay's attitude toward primitivism. In particular, the essay tracks the evolution of primitivism in what Gary Edward Holcomb calls his "queer black anarchist trilogy": *Home to Harlem, Banjo,* and *Romance in Marseille*.[5] This shift in McKay's primitivism, I contend, is congruent with wider political and cultural developments of the 1930s. As many Harlem Renaissance artists became disillusioned with the New Negro philosophy and turned instead to Marxism in the midst of the Great Depression, so the primitivism of earlier years was largely abandoned and critiqued as a symptom of the New Negro's overreliance on white patrons and its desire to cater to white audiences. The post-Renaissance period called for new ways of thinking and new modes of critique; the realization, heightened by the Depression, that oppression on the basis of race was intimately connected to class oppression prompted a shift of emphasis for many Black writers. Where in the earlier two novels primitive and proletarian are depicted as almost one and the same—the character of Jake is both a model worker and an embodiment of "primitive joy"—in *Romance in Marseille* this equation is troubled, and McKay effectively deconstructs the (already unstable) primitive/civilized binary constructed in *Home to Harlem* and *Banjo*.

Primitivism today remains a fraught topic. Since the 1980s it has been widely recognized as an idealization of non-Western cultures grounded in the unequal power relations of imperialism and entailing the reproduction of racist stereotypes. In recent years, this narrative has been complicated. Etherington, for example, sees literary primitivism as a reaction to a particular moment in history and a project pursued most enthusiastically by those "most violently torn from previous forms of social organization": the colonized subjects on whom the expansion of the capitalist world-system exercised the greatest impact.[6] Literary primitivism is pursued through language and form (what Etherington calls an "aesthetics of immediacy"); it is an "aesthetic project" characterized by "a movement through the mediate toward the immediate" that looks to generate "a process of transformation toward the primitive."[7] This essay uses and adapts some of Etherington's key concepts in order to trace the nature of McKay's evolving primitivism across his "queer black anarchist trilogy." It engages with *Literary Primitivism*'s thesis that primitivist literature, when written by "the Other," can be read as an act of anticolonial resistance. It argues, however, that the resistance of *Romance in Marseille* is founded not on a prizing of "the primitive" as antithetical to the evils of "civilization" and the associated desire to generate "a process of transformation toward the primitive" but on the interrogation and deconstruction of these very categories.[8]

Romance in Marseille registers McKay's belief, relayed in "A Negro Writer to His Critics" (1932), that "Negro life in its pure state" does not exist, that "modern civilization has touched and stirred the remote corners" of the world.[9] The novel reveals the extent to which McKay by the 1930s could not believe that truly primitive life existed or that a physical return to the "jungle" would mean a psychological or spiritual return to instinctive living. Lafala's return to Africa at the end of the novel is in no way a return to "primitive" life; it is in some ways a symptom of his rejection of the primitive (and of his lover Aslima) and his commitment to money and to his (still somewhat precarious) place in the patriarchal capitalist world-system. If *Home to Harlem* and *Banjo* can be read (in simple terms) as novels in which McKay overtly celebrates and prizes the primitive (embodied in the virile Black male characters of Jake and Banjo) above the civilized (represented in both novels by the inhibited Caribbean intellectual Ray and by the occasional roughly drawn white character), *Romance in Marseille* offers a far more obviously complex and nuanced vision of the primitive/civilized binary.

It is also a vision, I suggest, that is far more radical than the primitivist model of which critics like Etherington have deemed McKay's work to be representative. The primitivism of *Home to Harlem* and *Banjo* had pitted Black against white, lauding Black instinctiveness and spontaneity and denigrating the unnatural, constrained ways of "civilized" white people, all while glorifying virile, masculine Black characters and excluding women almost entirely. Such a dynamic precluded the possibility of real interracial solidarity and denied the importance of women, but in *Romance in Marseille* action across lines of race, gender, and sexuality is posited as a potential (indeed, perhaps the only feasible) way forward.

The first part of this essay reviews the strategic primitivism that characterized much work of the Harlem Renaissance, especially McKay's *Home to Harlem* and *Banjo*. The following section explores the ways in which *Romance in Marseille* can be seen to deconstruct primitive/civilized binaries, tracing the stylistic differences that echo this wider shift in McKay's thinking and using Etherington's concept of the "nonsynchronous primitive remnant" to examine a series of objects, characters, and moments that blur the lines between "the primitive" and "the civilized."[10] Finally, this essay considers how the ending of *Romance in Marseille* in particular reflects on the politics of primitivism and ultimately posits the interracial solidarity of international Marxism as a far more inclusive and hopeful way forward.

Primitivism Revisited: The Strategic Primitivism of the Harlem Renaissance

In the early twentieth century, many white modernists displayed a fascination with all things "primitive." The popularization of Freudian theory that blamed civilization for modern man's neurosis, a new appreciation of African art among post-impressionist artists, and a general postwar disenchantment with Western civilization fueled the modernist penchant for the primitive. In the aftermath of the Great War, white American writers like Gertrude Stein, Waldo Frank, and Carl Van Vechten turned for inspiration to African Americans, in whom they identified a certain vitality and a vibrant, creative force lost to America's white inhabitants. Consequently, as Wayne F. Cooper notes, "blacks became the repository of an elemental health that Europeans no longer possessed."[11]

While white American and European modernists were engaging with notions of the primitive as a potential wellspring of creative energy and rejuvenation, Black writers were also interested in the power of primitivism (if for rather different reasons and to different ends). So-called strategic primitivism offered African American artists a powerful mode of cultural critique whereby long-established binaries that negatively yoked Blackness to uncivilized savagery and positively associated whiteness with civilization and modernity could be recalibrated and hierarchies overturned.[12] For Edward Marx, primitivism in this context "may be seen as the beginnings of a cultural critique aimed at 'modernity,' which sought to overturn the value-laden hierarchy of civilized and modern over savage and primitive, a preliminary stage to the eventual breakdown of the distinction itself."[13] Many older Harlem Renaissance figures, however, saw primitivism as inherently demeaning and false. For those like W. E. B. Du Bois, who famously scorned McKay's first novel for its evocations of the primitive, depictions of African Americans as closer to nature and sexually liberated only pandered to the expectations of white audiences; for racial advancement, they were thoroughly counterproductive.

Primitivism thus assumed a contested position in the Harlem Renaissance. Black artists were subject to what Marx calls "an artistic double bind," caught between the demand to cater for an educated Black audience and a (potentially much larger, more lucrative) white audience.[14] McKay was certainly not immune to the whims of the literary market; *Home to Harlem* appeared at the height of the 1920s fascination with Black culture, when Harlem was a magnet for white Americans eager to discover the secrets of its jazz bars and dance clubs. Appearing on the heels of Van Vechten's controversial *Nigger Heaven* (1926), his portrayal of Harlem life (whether intentionally or not) played to the desires of a white readership seeking exoticism and escapism. Yet primitivism for McKay was, most important, a vehicle for critique; at the height of the Harlem Renaissance, he was perhaps the foremost proponent of primitivism as a means of celebrating Black identity and upending the damaging binaries elucidated above.

McKay felt deeply that the key to the success of the New Negro movement lay in extolling a specific Black identity rather than conforming to white cultural and social standards. As Ray declares in *Banjo*: "'If this Renaissance we're talking about is going to be more than a sporadic or scabby thing, we'll have to get down to our racial roots and create it.'"[15] "Get[ting] down to our racial roots" for McKay meant reappropriating and recalibrating primitivism for antiracist ends. If European art had long figured the primitive as the feminized product of a culture geographically and temporally remote from Western modernity, McKay's primitivism in *Home to Harlem* and *Banjo* was decidedly masculine, metropolitan, and modern.

The two novels of the late 1920s establish a clear distinction between "primitive" and "civilized." Instinctive, uninhibited Black characters like Jake and Banjo embody the modern primitive; they live spontaneously and (generally) joyfully, experiencing and delighting in all that the nightlife of Harlem and Marseille has to offer. In both novels, Ray, a Haitian intellectual and McKay's clearest alter ego, serves as a counterpoint. Ray is largely an outsider to the primitive ways of his friends; inhibited and self-conscious, he intellectualizes his feelings rather than simply acting on them, as Jake or Banjo would. Thus, when in *Home to Harlem* Ray and Jake find themselves at a brothel in Philadelphia, Jake "fall[s] naturally into its rhythm," while Ray wishes he could be "touched by the spirit of that atmosphere" (*HH*, 194) but cannot bring himself to enter into it. In this character, McKay demonstrates the pernicious and deadening effects of civilization and of a white education.

McKay thus engages with the traditional primitivist inversion of hierarchies that explicitly prizes the primitive above the civilized. In *Home to Harlem* this entails a clear prizing of Blackness over whiteness. Excluded from the true "primitive joy of Harlem" (*HH*, 109), the white urban population can only observe the "mad riotous joy" of the jazz club: "The white visitors laugh. . . . Here are none of the well-patterned, well-made emotions of the respectable world" (*HH*, 337). The "well-made emotions" of the white world contrast with those "simple, raw emotions and real" of the Black jazzers that "may frighten and repel refined souls" (*HH*, 338). This white deficit of real emotion extends to an implied sexual deficiency. In *Banjo* Ray conjectures that "white people had developed sex complexes that Negroes had not" because "the white man considered sex a nasty, irritating thing, while the Negro accepted it with primitive joy" (*B*, 262). McKay thus inverts the racist discourse which figured Black sexuality as wild, threatening, and aberrant by rendering white sexual inadequacy and inhibition as unnatural and abnormal.

These efforts to overturn prevailing racist discourses and attribute value to Jake's instinct and natural spontaneity are subverted at the end of *Home to Harlem*, however, in McKay's description of Ray as "a reservoir of that intense emotional energy so peculiar to his race" and "a touchstone of the general emotions of his race" (*HH*, 265–66). "Life," McKay's narrator cautiously suggests, "burned in Ray perhaps more intensely than in Jake" (*HH*, 265). Ultimately, McKay prizes the life of the educated, inhibited Ray above that of the working-class everyman, Jake. Having inverted racial hierarchies by prizing Blackness over whiteness, McKay reinforces class hierarchies. He thus challenges the positioning of groups within binaries without contravening the binaries themselves, effectively failing to dismantle racist discourse. Also problematic in this regard is McKay's exclusion of women from his conception of the primitive; Congo Rose is described as "a wonderful tissue of throbbing flesh" (*HH*, 42), but Jake feels sometimes that she has "no spirit at all—

that strange, elusive something that he felt in himself" (*HH*, 41). As Tracy McCabe notes, "anti-racist primitivism" in this context "works within, not outside of, the realm of dominant ideology."[16]

In these novels McKay sought to depict his Black characters as embodying simultaneously a kind of primordial health and a radical modern insurrection; "the Negro," Holcomb notes, here represents both "a figure of Lawrentian 'blood-knowledge'" and "paradoxically . . . a signifier for modern change, for insurgency— . . . a counterhegemonic agent that immanently cannot cede to modern capitalist and nationalist dominion."[17] Such depictions not only paradoxically reinforce the hierarchies they looked to overturn but come finally to undermine the very concept of the primitive. How can these characters be both primitive, existing outside capitalism, and modern, radical insurgents fighting against it?

Romance in Marseille confronts this issue directly. The subtle discrepancies and ambivalences that characterize the primitivism of *Home to Harlem* and *Banjo* are made manifest in the later novel. In much the same way that *Romance in Marseille* makes central and important the queer characters and same-sex relationships that had been only marginal or implied in earlier novels, McKay here presents the contradictions and complications of primitivism writ large. *Romance in Marseille*, then, represents not a complete departure but a heightening of and a reckoning with several themes and strands of thought that are only underlying or implicit in the earlier works. As the final part of this essay will argue, McKay's altered attitude toward primitivism must be understood as part of a larger shift in emphasis. The complex, much-altered primitivism of *Romance in Marseille* allows for a far more inclusive and expansive politics than the rootless, masculine, homosocial primitivism of the earlier novels.

McKay had already begun to move away from the male-only model of *Home to Harlem* and *Banjo*; his 1933 novel, *Banana Bottom*, marked a stark departure in several senses. Not only was it set in rural Jamaica rather than in a metropolitan hub, but it centered on a female protagonist and followed a far more traditional, linear plot than his previous novels. Writing in Morocco in the early 1930s, though certainly keen to repeat the commercial success of *Home to Harlem*, McKay had evidently tired of producing the picaresque narratives that had made his name as a novelist. Coupled with this formal evolution, he moved away from the celebratory images of Black male vitality and the prizing of male friendship above heterosexual romance. *Banana Bottom*'s traditional ending sees the union of Bita, an educated, worldly young woman, and Jubban, an uneducated peasant farmer. Their marriage seems at least in part to settle the tension between civilized and primitive left unresolved in the earlier novels, but this was also an enduring personal tension for the author himself.

Since the publication of his earliest Jamaican poetry collection, edited and with introductions by his English mentor, Walter Jekyll, McKay had often been cast as primitive, as a voice of peasant Jamaica and later of Black America. Responding in "A Negro Writer to His Critics" (1932) to those "discriminating critics" who (still) approach his work "as if [he] were a primitive savage and altogether a stranger to society," McKay declares:

> Whatever may be the criticism implied in my writing of Western Civilization I do not regard myself as a stranger but as a child of it, even though I may have become so by the comparatively recent process of grafting. I am as conscious of my new-world birthright as my African origin, being aware of the one and its significance in my development as much as I feel the other emotionally.
>
> One of my most considerate critics suggested that I might make a trip to Africa and there write about Negro life in its pure state. But I don't believe that any such place exists anywhere upon the earth today, since modern civilization has touched and stirred the remote corners. I cherish no Utopian illusions about any state of human society. Poets may dream, but dreams are ferment of the stuff of experience. The poet of a subject people may sing for the day of deliverance without being afflicted by fanciful visions of any society of people in which the eternal problems of existence would not still exist.[18]

He then affirms that he can see no reason for an African American intellectual to "go to any part of Africa to undertake an experiment in living unless he [feels] irresistibly forced to do so."[19] McKay carries no illusion that an ideal form of primitive life untouched by "modern civilization" exists. There is no sense, he recognizes, in "going back" to Africa in search of "Negro life in its pure state"; this is not the object of his primitivism, and this is made evident in *Romance in Marseille*. The sketch that Lafala makes from memory of his native village, featuring "a road cutting through the bush and a European house dominating the huts" (*RM*, 71), perfectly illustrates McKay's feeling that the capitalist world-system has touched even the most seemingly far-flung corners of the globe.

"A Negro Writer to His Critics" does not necessarily suggest a transformation in McKay's beliefs regarding the primitive since the publication of his novels of 1928 and 1929. Rather, it suggests a change in his methods moving forward. The essay is in large part an expression of the frustrations he faced as a Black writer, of the double bind that confronted the New Negro artist compelled to tread an almost impossible line between pleasing African American audiences and intellectuals and appealing to white cultural consumers. McKay's attempts at strategic primitivism had evidently been misunderstood and proved ineffectual (if profitable, in the case of *Home to Harlem*). In *Romance in Marseille*, then, he takes a very different approach. Here the primitive/civilized binary is pushed to its limits in a move that impels it beyond the scope of the debates and disagreements that had characterized the reception of *Home to Harlem* and divided two generations of African American writers, leaders, and intellectuals. Du Bois might well have reacted as negatively to *Romance in Marseille* as he had to the 1928 novel, but perhaps for quite different reasons.

Primitivism Revised: *Romance in Marseille*

If *Home to Harlem* and *Banjo* had used strategic primitivism in a bid to overturn pernicious racial stereotypes and hierarchies, then in *Romance in Marseille* McKay challenges and breaks down the discrete categories of civilized and primitive. The shift in focus is not immediately obvious, however; in a mode comparable to that of the earlier novels, the opening pages of *Romance in Marseille* figure the Black male body—its legs in particular—as the ultimate embodiment of Bergsonian élan vital. In Lafala's native village, "the sight of fine bodies supported by strong gleaming legs" provided a "rare delight" to the members of the tribe (*RM*, 3). Not only this, but an individual's value and function within tribal society would be determined by the form of their legs: "The older tribesmen appraised the worth of the young by the shape of their limbs. Long legs and slender made good swimmers. Stout legs and thick, good carriers. Lithe and sinewy were runners' legs. And long swinging monkey arms marked expert climbers of palms and jungle trees" (*RM*, 3). One's legs, in this context, are essential facets of one's identity.

Almost all of Lafala's memories of childhood, pursuits of adulthood, and enjoyment of life have been dependent on his legs. From "childhood's leg play, running and climbing and jumping, and dancing in the moonlight in the village yard" and his playmates tracing his naked form, to "the new delight of legs" he learns after missionaries take him "from the bush to the town" and put his legs in pants (*RM*, 3–4):

> Legs like a quartette of players performing the passionate chamber music of life. Loud notes and soft, notes whispering like a warm breath, a long and noiseless kiss, flutes and harps joined in enchanting adventures, in ritual unison, trembling and climbing together in the high song of life and leaving unforgettable sensations in the blood, in the brain.
>
> Legs of ebony, legs of copper, legs of ivory moving pell-mell in columns against his imagination. . . . Dancing on the toes, dancing on the heels, dancing flat-footed. Lafala's dancing legs had carried him from Africa to Europe, from Europe to America.
>
> Legs. . . . Feet that were accustomed to dig themselves into the native soil, into lovely heaps of leaves, and affectionate tufts of grass, were now introduced to luxuries of socks and shoes and beds of iron.
>
> Lafala had gone on wandering impressionably from change to change like a heedless young pilgrim with nothing but his staff in his hand and playing variations on the march of legs. Come trouble, come worry, blue days without a job, without food, without love. . . . Dance away. . . . Think not of age, of accident, the festering and mortification of youth and poisoned worms corroding through the firm young flesh to the sepulchral skeleton. His dancing legs would carry him over all.
>
> Suddenly they were jerked off and there he lay helpless. (*RM*, 4)

The above passage narrates through Lafala's legs a trajectory from Africa to America, from connection to nature to the "luxuries" of civilization and from a life lived joyfully and itinerantly to one suddenly halted when his legs are unceremoniously "jerked off." Lafala's legs are not only the means by which he overcomes "trouble," "worry," lack of employment, food or love; they are his means of navigating the world and even, McKay suggests, of eluding fears of death and aging. In losing his lower limbs, then, Lafala is effectively removed from both the bodily system of value into which he was born and the vagabond way of life he embraced as an adult.

Much literature of the Harlem Renaissance had depicted the physical strength, vigor, and general vitality of Black characters as a counter to the pernicious stereotypes and medical racism that had often cast African Americans as physically and mentally unfit and inferior to their white counterparts. As Holcomb and William J. Maxwell observe in their introduction to *Romance in Marseille*, "McKay was among the New Negro authors most identified with black male vitality, his early fiction elevating a still-primal black manhood above an emasculating West to overturn the venerable racist opposition between the civilized and the primitive."[20] These images of Black male vitality, Holcomb and Maxwell note, were inspiring for Négritude writers like Aimé Césaire and Léopold Senghor, for whom *Banjo* in particular became a canonical text. That in *Romance in Marseille*, then, McKay chooses as his protagonist a man first introduced to the reader as "a sawed-off stump" (*RM*, 3)—a fragmented Black body from the outset—already appears to mark a distinct and important shift away from the strategic primitivism of *Home to Harlem* and *Banjo*.

To a large extent, it would seem, the primitivism of the Harlem Renaissance and of McKay's earlier novels had been incompatible with disability. Yet losing his legs does not diminish Lafala's thirst for life or dampen his sexual appetites. Indeed, his newfound wealth affords him an elevated status that allows him to indulge all the more freely in such pleasures. Lafala's disability thus seems an ironic manifestation of what McKay saw as the "especial handicaps" faced by "the colored man . . . under the worldwide domination of occidental civilization."[21] When these "especial handicaps" are translated into physical disability, the financial gains that accompany them in fact render Lafala far better equipped to thrive under "occidental civilization": a culture in which money is prized above almost all else.

The removal of Lafala's legs is a watershed moment both in the character's life and in the narrative and formal trajectory of the novel; it constitutes a stylistic cutoff point as well as a physical amputation. In the passage above, for example, the cumulative and repetitive lists and descriptions of legs of all colors, punctuated by ellipses and gaining momentum, are halted by a single unpunctuated sentence: "Suddenly they were jerked off and there he lay helpless." The primitivism of *Home to Harlem* and *Banjo* had been conveyed through luxuriant, overflowing prose and epistrophe. The scenes that most exemplify this style see large groups congregating in the clubs and bars of Harlem and Marseille, with music and dancing. The "Jelly Roll" chapter of *Banjo* is a salient example; it culminates with Banjo and his friends playing "Shake That Thing" to a riotous dancing crowd: "Jungle jazzing, Orient wriggling, civilized stepping. Shake that thing! Sweet dancing thing of primitive joy, perverse pleasure, prostitute ways, many-colored variations of the rhythm, savage, barbaric, refined—eternal rhythm of the mysterious, magical, magnificent—the dance divine of life. . . . Oh, Shake That Thing!" (*B*, 60). Alliterative lists are interspersed with song lyrics, melding music and prose, and the diversity of the dances and rhythms is emphasized: alternately "savage, barbaric, refined." This is exactly the "aesthetics of immediacy" that Etherington sees as central to literary primitivism: the "jazz style" that "wants to be the immediate manifestation of that ancestral force that otherwise is consumed by white 'civilization.'"[22]

There are glimpses of these techniques of immediacy in *Romance in Marseille*, as in one scene in which characters gather at the Tout-va-Bien to celebrate Lafala's release from prison:

> Everybody was close together in a thick juice melted by wine and music. There was little room for foot play. Just all together, two in one swaying to swaying, shuffling around, bumping and bumping up and down belly to belly and breast to breast. . . .
>
> Aslima also felt the beguine for Lafala and was swaying and swaying her arm around his shoulder, both of them swaying warmly together. Lafala wanted to dance. He had never felt the desire so strongly since his accident. The beguine rhythm caught him by the middle, drop to drop. The music swelled up and down with a sweep and rushed him off his feet. (*RM*, 107–8)

This passage is structured by repetition and captures a mood similar to that of the end of *Home to Harlem*, in which the "jazzers" at the Baltimore are "all drawn together in one united mass, wriggling around to the same primitive, voluptuous rhythm" (*HH*, 337). In both cases, one can imagine a group of dancers so tightly packed that they seem to merge into one in a hedonistic haze of music and alcohol. Yet in the scene from *Romance in Marseille*, the language is far more pared down, more constrained, than the climactic linguistic overflow of the "Jelly Roll" chapter. Music is described, but it does not penetrate the rhythm of the prose.

Such a stylistic turn suggests that in *Romance in Marseille* the primitive has ceased to be the everyday, modern reality that it had been in the two novels of the 1920s. In those works, the primitive had thrived in contemporary Harlem and Marseille, but in the later novel, "immediacy" seems, somewhat paradoxically, to be accessible only in the distant past or in the realm of fantasy. In *Romance in Marseille*, instances of the "jazz style" most reminiscent of *Home to Harlem* and *Banjo* are reserved in large part for flashbacks and dreams, like Lafala's memories of his earlier (preamputation) life or Aslima's later vision of "an antique white-washed city" (*RM*, 60). Following an argument with her pimp, Titin, Aslima sits alone at night on a bench overlooking the bay, when she is suddenly transported to a very different scene in which she discovers "a great procession of loose-robed men and women and children marching as to a midnight ritual, stamping and dancing to barbaric music" (*RM*, 60–61). A "loving feast" follows, with the gatherers "kneeling and squatting upon magic-like carpets and piles of rainbow cushions under lights like variegated flowers and shrouded in clouds of rarest incense" and "a gorgeous gorging" (*RM*, 61). Dancing then ensues:

> When the feasting was finished the belly-moving beat of the drum roused the people again after an interval of rest to dancing and chanting over and over again repeating and reiterating from pattern to pattern unraveling the threads of life from the most intricate to the simplest to the naked bottom as if in evocation of the first gods who emerged out of the ancient unfathomed womb of Africa to procreate and spread over the vast surface of the land. (*RM*, 61)

The ritualistic, repetitive chanting and dancing here, relayed in one long, unpunc-tuated sentence, sees human life stripping down to its essentials, going back to what is surely the ultimate "primitive" source: "the ancient unfathomed womb of Africa." Aslima, "repelled, fascinated and awed" by what she is witnessing, finds herself in the midst of "one group apart that was offering up body and soul as a sacrifice"; she is "divided and struggling against herself. She did not want to surrender all of her, but she could not detach herself" (*RM*, 62). Aslima's vision—recalling in some ways Ray's drug-filled dream of *Home to Harlem*, in which he hallucinates a sexual-ized "blue paradise" (*HH*, 158)—expresses her horror at the prospect of primitive experience. Not only are evocations of the primitive confined in large part to mem-ories, visions, and dreams, but they are at times, as in this example, traumatic.

The stylistic shift between *Home to Harlem* and *Banjo* and *Romance in Mar-seille* is also registered at the semantic level. Etherington notes that "the word *prim-itive* is used nineteen times in *Banjo*, sometimes positively, sometimes neutrally, but never negatively."[23] In *Romance in Marseille*, rather tellingly, the word is used on only four occasions: Lafala accepts his sizable financial settlement with "primitive dignity that appeared like indifference"; his boyhood is described as a "primitive life"; Aslima dances a "primitive flamenco"; and Falope, a West African clerk, tells St. Dominique, "a mulatto from Martinique," that "'you can't be primitive and pro-letarian at the same time'" (*RM*, 17, 71, 108, 73, 114). None of these usages appears particularly negative, but neither are they celebratory or joyful. Indeed, McKay's use of the word in *Romance in Marseille* suggests a sensitivity to its connotations that had not always been present in earlier works. The first and second titles McKay attributed to the text that would become *Romance in Marseille* are interesting in this regard; "Savage Loving" and "The Jungle and the Bottoms" suggest a sensa-tional mode of primitivism that the novel in its final published form does not deliver. These titles allude to the mood of the late 1920s and the "strategic" primi-tivism discussed above, but *Romance in Marseille* is clearly the product of a very different mood and moment.

The novel's opening closely connects Lafala's legs with his early life in his native village. It is unsurprising, then, that once cruelly parted from his legs, McKay's protagonist should look to connect in other ways with his roots. Seized by a desire for activity during his convalescence and the nervous wait for the results of his legal case, Lafala decides to fashion tribal girdles from "hemp and varicolored wool" (*RM*, 13). His ability to make the girdles—based on "the only clothing that his tribeswomen used to wear" (*RM*, 13)—is portrayed as his only remaining con-nection to the women of his tribe. They appear in some ways a perfect example of what Etherington calls the "non-synchronous primitive remnant." Primitive remnants, according to Etherington, are "objective reminders of previous social realities"—souvenirs of a precolonial era and mementos of a precapitalist world—capable of triggering the reanimation of "primitive experience" even at the center of the capitalist world-system.[24]

Lafala's Jewish lawyer, to whom he presents as a gift one of the girdles, indeed seems to evoke the power of the primitive remnant to bring about an experience of nonsynchronicity: "It carried me back to very ancient times . . . the times when my people were also divided into tribes and wore girdles just as your people do today" (*RM*, 14). The lawyer's comment is an attempt at cross-cultural sympathy, but the equation here of modern-day Africa with ancient Israel is a clear indication that he sees Lafala's "people" as less developed than his own. The comparison here speaks clearly to Ernst Bloch's concept of "the simultaneity of the non-simultaneous."[25] Modernity, McKay reminds us, encompasses both the skyscrapers of New York City and the jungles of Africa.

Lafala's makeshift girdles are perhaps the foremost symbol of *Romance in Marseille*'s complex primitivism. Made with multicolored wool instead of the dyed straw used by his tribeswomen, they are not primitive or ancient at all. They are false, or at least hybrid, remnants, at once emblematic of what remains of Lafala's native culture and of the impossibility of reproducing it in the United States. The making of the girdles can be seen as Lafala's attempt to engage once more with a cultural heritage slipping from his grasp, but producing them does not set off the kind of reactivation of primitive experience that Etherington describes. Rather, the girdles are the first in a series of tropes that indicate the blurring of the lines between primitive and civilized, ancient and modern, African and Western.

Aslima's bedroom is described as "a poor little affair but cleverly arranged to suggest the exotic": "The water pitcher was made in Spain and the bowl in France but nevertheless the atmosphere they created was effectively African" (*RM*, 45, 46). The contents of the room are of European origin, but they are posed in such a way as to produce the effect of an "exotic" space. In another scene, Aslima's "primitive flamenco" (*RM*, 108) again suggests a melding of African and European. Indeed, Aslima—described as "a child of North Africa out of Marrakesh, that city of the plain where savagery emerging from the jungle meets civilization" (*RM*, 44)—is herself a kind of hybrid.[26] In her character, as in Lafala's, the primitive/civilized binary is questioned and pushed. Aslima is described early in the novel as "a burning brown mixed of Arab and Negro and other wanton bloods," "a barbaric creature" (*RM*, 4), "full of an abundance of earthly sap" (*RM*, 29) and "a near-native thing" in whom Lafala sees "a way to go back . . . , if he could ever wrench free from the fascinating new idols native to go again" (*RM*, 5). Certainly, his romantic and sexual relationship with Aslima, in which they are repeatedly figured as "loving pigs" (*RM*, 123), seems to offer at least some sense of consolation and healing following the loss of his legs. It is tempting, then, to read her as the potential antidote to the corrupting and crippling (both literally and metaphorically) effects of civilization on Lafala. But Aslima is also, of course, partly responsible for the loss of Lafala's legs; he stowed away after being hurt and humiliated when she stole from him. Thus, while Aslima may be seen to represent Lafala's best chance at a return to the primitive—to the fulfilled, vital, happy mode of being described in the novel's opening pages— she is also the root cause of the event that propels him into a very different, more "civilized" phase of life.

As a prostitute, Aslima is enmeshed in a system that monetizes sex and commodifies both female and male bodies (though, significantly, she refuses Lafala's offers of payment for sex). Lafala's fine legs, once amputated, also become party to a system of value very different from that upheld in his childhood village. At the prospect of receiving a payout for his lost limbs, he marvels at the idea that "a pair of black feet on the shelf" might be worth a thousand dollars (*RM*, 9). In the transition from dancing, itinerant, sustaining legs to the prosthetic cork legs he is granted as part of his settlement, Lafala assumes a new position in the world. His new position and his shifting values are indicated in his prizing of "a large, important-looking envelope" that he flaunts at a Quayside bar, "conspicuously displaying the foreign stamps" (*RM*, 35). Though the letter itself has no monetary value, the correspondence from "a solid established banking house" regarding the transference of his funds offers him "a luxurious feeling of importance," and he feels "fine to be a little on the inside of great big firm things and being addressed as 'Mister' and 'Esquire.' That was so different from the vagabond black troubadour days" (*RM*, 35). The letter for Lafala represents his status as one at least "a little on the inside" of a global economic system in which he previously, as a "vagabond black troubadour," had very little involvement.

Lafala's relationship to money throughout the novel seems to be constantly in flux, however. It is not simply that after losing his legs he suddenly values money above all else. Indeed, his complex and changing attitude toward money is only one aspect of his generally uneven and fluctuating character. When Black Angel first mentions the prospect of a financial settlement to Lafala, he is incredulous at the idea that he could be paid "'for getting cold feet'" after stowing away "'on a white man's boat'" (*RM*, 8). When word reaches the hospital that he has been awarded a large settlement, Lafala seems largely unmoved: "But although it was really a big sum, exceeding anything his imagination was capable of, he was less excited than the nurses and his fellow patients. He accepted the godsend with a primitive dignity that appeared like indifference" (*RM*, 18). At this point, he is far more interested in the cork legs that should allow him to walk and even dance again. Yet only a few pages later, when an official informs him that he is "'entitled to more money'" (*RM*, 20), Lafala wants it, in spite of his earlier agreement with his lawyer: "Lafala's mind was fully occupied with the official statement 'entitled to more money.' . . . More money. That was the slogan of life. Everybody and all the world wanted more money. Those who had none wanted some. And those who had some wanted more. And the more many had the more they wanted" (*RM*, 21). This passage suggests the extent to which Lafala has absorbed the Western obsession with "more money." He is even critical of those who are foolish with their money: "'Negroes spend too much. Always showing off and spreading themselves big on nothing'" (*RM*, 37). Yet in other moments he acts almost disdainfully and irresponsibly in his spending, placing the prospect of carnal pleasure above money-sense. When Aslima's archrival La Fleur suggests that her services might be "'dearer after Champagne,'" Lafala replies: "'Don't think about the price. Money is nothing to me'" (*RM*, 52).

McKay's protagonist is alternately seduced by the status and the options that money affords him and unmoved by his newly found financial freedom. At times generous, even careless, with his spending and at others tightfisted and cautious, Lafala's shifting attitude to money matters seems indicative of his unstable relation to "civilization" in a wider sense. Though perceived and (whether jokingly or disparagingly) characterized by those around him as a "jungle kid" and a "half-helpless savage" (*RM*, 35, 129), Lafala is in fact, as McKay said of himself, as much a product of "Western Civilization" as he is of the African bush. He is a "jungle kid" who carries a cane and enjoys many of the trappings and comforts of Western life. Indeed, he comes in some ways to embody the simultaneity of the nonsimultaneous in the novel and the blurring of primitive and civilized.

Lafala is in many ways at odds with the protagonists of *Home to Harlem* and *Banjo*. He is in some sense an inversion of Ray. Where the Haitian intellectual decries the rottenness of civilization (despite—or perhaps because of—his own enmeshment in it), wishing that he could rid himself of his "little education" and lose himself "in some savage culture in the jungles of Africa" (*HH*, 274), Lafala at times appears to dread the idea of returning to Africa and "the thought of the thousands who lacked the barest civilized necessities" (*RM*, 71); he relishes the idea of being a part of civilization, of having money and a sense of social standing. In the two earlier novels, Ray is the character most committed to the project of celebrating the primitive aspects of Black life; he strives to "bring intellect to the aid of instinct" (*B*, 172) in an effort he hopes will improve the lives of those he encounters in Harlem and Marseille. Lafala, by contrast, seems concerned only with his own interests.

Ray's absence in *Romance in Marseille* is an important indicator of a change in McKay's thinking around the utility of the kind of "strategic" primitivism that had been so in vogue and so divisive at the height of the Harlem Renaissance a few years earlier. It was a conscious decision for McKay not to include Ray in either *Romance in Marseille* or any of the novel's earlier incarnations. He explained this decision in a letter to his agent, W. A. Bradley, averring that there would be no Ray character because he had "realized that the form was very awkward and that some of [his] best scenes, the love ones for instance, would be stifled by it."[27] The novels featuring Ray had been characterized by long, debate-like dialogues considering issues around race relations and Black life in Harlem and Marseille; especially in *Banjo*, any plotlines involving or even suggesting romantic entanglements had been distinctly secondary to this discourse.

The Communist recruiter Étienne St. Dominique is perhaps the closest equivalent to a Ray/McKay character in *Romance in Marseille* (though, as Holcomb and Maxwell note, he was likely based at least in part on the Senegalese Communist Lamine Senghor).[28] Like Ray, he is an intellectual (a former student) and a sometime writer—he impresses Lafala with his "cultivated accent and his refined manners" (*RM*, 74)—and both men are intent on changing and improving the lives of the vagabond inhabitants of Marseille, but St. Dominique's aims and means of making change are quite different from Ray's. In using his connections in the white world and his literary credentials to free Lafala, he does mirror Ray's desire to "bring intellect to the aid of instinct," yet St. Dominique urges interracial collaboration and the "new social ideal" (*RM*, 76) rather than pitting Black and white in opposition. For St. Dominique, himself of mixed race, the real issues are not racial but economic; Lafala's case, he feels, is "proletarian," with "little race to it" (*RM*, 103). *Romance in Marseille* then demonstrates the impossibility and indeed the ultimate undesirability of Ray's project and the need for a more inclusive and radical way forward at the novel's ending.

Primitive or Proletarian: A New Alternative?

Early on in *Romance in Marseille*, Lafala hears tell of the Back-to-Africa movement in "the land of the missionaries" (*RM*, 4): "Lafala heard the other Negroes discussing the Back-to-Africa news and wondering what would become of it. Lafala listened and was stirred too. Return. . . . Return. . . . Turn away from strange scenes and false gods to find salvation in native things" (*RM*, 5). The tone here is somewhat mocking, suggesting the naïveté of those inclined to believe and to follow the calls of Marcus Garvey's Universal Negro Improvement Association (UNIA). This is perhaps unsurprising given McKay's comments in "A Negro Writer to His Critics." That the novel *does* end with Lafala returning to Africa might thus seem an odd conclusion. It may be that McKay was contemplating his own imminent return— not to his native Jamaica, but to the United States, where he arrived in early 1934, likely only a few months after the completion of *Romance in Marseille*—with mixed feelings. Yet this conclusion can also be read as a statement on primitivism and its utility (or, indeed, its current inutility).

It is worth returning at this point to an important exchange that received only cursory attention earlier in this essay. It sees Lafala, St. Dominique, Babel, and Falope—another character who blurs binaries with his European features and claims to be of "Arab and Portuguese blood" (*RM*, 75)—discussing love. More specifically, they are discussing Lafala's desire to marry Aslima and take her back to Africa with him. Falope struggles to understand the plan; he suggests that Lafala "'must be spoiled by civilization'": "'What you're planning to do isn't right at all. It isn't African. It's a loving white way'" (*RM*, 114). Lafala refutes this accusation: "'Oh, no, I've passed all through that already. . . . I went crazy once, black fool that I was, but I got over it'" (*RM*, 114). This exchange is fascinating and puzzling for several reasons. Falope's objections are in large part class based; returning to Africa with Aslima as his wife would, he feels, be a betrayal of Lafala's "proper position" as a "better man, a bigger man" now of some wealth and standing (*RM*, 113). Of course, it is "civilization" that has granted him this very position. Falope's argument and Lafala's responses here negatively associate "civilization" and "a loving white way" with the passion and spontaneity that would see Lafala and Aslima sail off together. A passionate love affair between two African characters is cast as the product of a corrupting civilization, again demonstrating the extent to which the primitive/ civilized binary has been confounded by this juncture in the novel.

The discussion of love continues. Having made the point that *love* is a four-letter word in English and five in French, St. Dominique declares: "'I prefer to think of love without letters'" (*RM*, 114). About this, his West African friend is again skeptical: "'Like the time when it was naked and we were too, before we went to school to learn our letters,' said Falope. 'No, Dominique. You can't be primitive and proletarian at the same time. We can't go back again. We have studied our figures and learned our letters. Now we are civilized'" (*RM*, 114). The interruption of a boy with La Fleur's troubling letter for Lafala gives St. Dominique no room to respond and Falope has the last word in the discussion. That McKay's primary mouthpiece is silenced on this crucial point suggests the validity of Falope's logic.

The premise of McKay's primitivism in *Home to Harlem* and *Banjo*, broadly stated, had suggested that primitive and proletarian in these contexts are practically one and the same thing. However, as Falope advises, this idea seems inherently flawed. One cannot be both primitive—beyond the reach of the capitalist system—and a "proletarian," oppressed by it. There is a decision to be made here between two opposing paths. Lafala chooses neither. His seemingly inexplicable change of heart after a night spent with Aslima sees him privilege "the practical side of his nature . . . over the sensual" and do "as his agent wished" (*RM*, 127). In following the orders of his official agent and leaving Aslima with only one hundred dollars "to return home" (*RM*, 128), Lafala discounts the authenticity of their relationship (by finally rendering it transactional) and cements his alliance to the system that broke him physically and rewarded him financially. Aslima, with no "home" to return to, is left to die.

Romance in Marseille thus ends on a far more unsettling and pessimistic note than McKay's other novels. Where *Home to Harlem* and *Banjo* both end hopefully with their protagonists poised for further adventures, and *Banana Bottom* concludes more conventionally in marriage, *Romance*'s denouement sees Lafala leaving for Africa alone and Aslima being killed by Titin in dramatic fashion. In returning to Africa without Aslima but with "[a] little civilization in [his] pocket," Lafala chooses money over love and the comforts of civilization over the possibilities of primitive life reactivated. There is no suggestion in this ending that a new location might hold the answers, that Lafala's return to Africa might bring about a true reconnection with his roots or a return to instinctive living. As Falope explains to St. Dominique, there is no going back; it's the same life everywhere.

Where *Home to Harlem* and *Banjo*, as Leah Reade Rosenberg observes, "envisioned an international black homosocial and subaltern political community that existed largely outside of and against modern capitalism," in *Romance in Marseille* there is no sense in which these characters can feasibly exist outside the capitalist world-system.[29] No journey "back to Africa" will constitute a real escape from "the steam-roller of progress" (*HH*, 155). *Romance in Marseille* does not refute Ray's claim that "'civilization is rotten'" (*HH*, 243), but it does suggest that one must accept its inescapability; efforts to run from the civilized world or to defy capitalism, whether through primitive living or romantic vagabondage, are ultimately futile.

Lafala boards the ship to Africa (offstage and without great fanfare) with a little civilization in his pocket and cork legs attached to his body; he has become an embodiment of the broken-down primitive/civilized binary. The question at the end of the novel, then, is where such a breakdown leaves one. The narrative ends on such an abrupt and unsatisfying note that we cannot be entirely sure. If *Romance in Marseille*, as Holcomb and Maxwell affirm, offers "a warning of the tragedy that haunts male-only strategies for universal Negro improvement," then it seems also to anticipate much later scholarly critiques that deconstructed the very categories of primitive and civilized.[30] With this long-unpublished novel, McKay offered a vision of the primitive/civilized binary that was not straightforward. It could not be easily dismissed as "primitive" propaganda, because McKay by this time no longer believed in the efficacy of such "strategic" primitivism.

Of course, McKay was not the only New Negro writer to lose faith in the power of primitivism; the shift identified above between *Romance in Marseille* and the two earlier novels, *Home to Harlem* and *Banjo*, needs to be understood within the wider cultural and political contexts of the 1930s. With the onset of the Great Depression, the 1920s vogue for all things "Negro" and "primitive" was largely forgotten. For many New Negro writers, this meant a move toward more practical thinking and often, more specifically, toward Communism. Langston Hughes had also dabbled in primitivism during the 1920s, but by the early 1930s, as Anthony Dawahare notes, "he clearly was moving away from his nationalist perspective as a Harlem Renaissance writer and . . . toward a view of class rather than race as the basis for both economic racism and collective struggle."[31] His revolutionary poetry of this time indeed suggests that Hughes took seriously the idea that Black and white might be united under a red banner; in the 1934 poem "One More 'S' in the USA" he writes: "Come together, fellow workers / Black and white can all be red."[32] In the same period, he was mercilessly satirizing the primitivism of the previous decade in stories like "Rejuvenation through Joy." He would later, in *The Big Sea* (1940), employ a Marxist critique of the Harlem Renaissance, averring that "the ordinary Negroes hadn't heard of the Negro Renaissance. And if they had, it hadn't raised their wages any."[33]

The post-Renaissance turn also, in some cases at least, granted women a greater role. In Hughes's work this is evident in *The Ways of White Folks*, a 1934 collection begun in Moscow and inspired in part by his travels across the Soviet Union in 1932 and 1933.[34] Here strong, Black women—like Cora of "Cora Unashamed" and Oceola of "The Blues I'm Playing"—are depicted as central to the fight for racial liberation as they had rarely been in literature of the preceding decade. Though the Harlem Renaissance, as Cheryl A. Wall affirms, was not "a male phenomenon," it was very often, as in Alain Locke's 1925 introduction to *The New Negro*, coded as masculine and characterized by masculinist rhetoric.[35] In *Banjo* and *Home to Harlem*, then, the female characters are consistently excluded from McKay's celebratory primitivism and associated with fixity, boredom, and death and largely depicted as agents of capitalism intent on keeping men immobile, domesticated, tied down as either exploited wage slaves or emasculated "sweet men." The choice presented at the end of both novels is between the freedom and possibility of transnational, homosocial friendship and the stifling fixity of heterosexual union (having chosen the latter at the end of *Home to Harlem*, Jake appears at *Banjo's* close complaining of "'too much home stuff'" [*B*, 303]). Women are dispensable and unnecessary; as Banjo assures Ray at *Banjo's* end, they do not need women to forge forward: "'A woman is a conjunction. . . . Wese got enough between us to beat it a long ways from here'" (*B*, 336). In *Romance in Marseille*, by contrast, women are fundamental to the action and portrayed as full and complex characters rather than mere "throbbing flesh"; Aslima and La Fleur in particular are crucial to *Romance's* multiple plots.

The novel's end reveals that La Fleur's rivalry with Aslima is fueled in part by the former's romantic feelings for the latter. Same-sex desire is intimately intertwined with the move toward interracial collaboration, the greater involvement of women, and ultimately with the alternative to strategic primitivism posed at the end of the novel. In McKay's work, queer love, radical politics, and racial liberation very often go hand in hand; as Holcomb avers, "McKay's black Marxism cannot be disentangled from his queer resistance."[36] In *Home to Harlem* and *Banjo*, queerness is almost always either only implicit or marginal, but in *Romance in Marseille* queer characters are made central. The need for queer and interracial solidarity is embodied perhaps most clearly in the character of Big Blonde. A late addition to the novel, Big Blonde is a working-class, American expatriate who moves easily among the diverse inhabitants of Marseille's Quayside; his first action in the novel is in defense of St. Dominique. Big Blonde has "no interest in the workers' unions" (*RM*, 94), but, as Holcomb and Maxwell observe, he represents a kind of chain-breaking "socialist colossus": an embodiment of the drawing at the Communist Seamen's Club that hangs below images of Marx and Lenin and depicts "two terrible giants, one white, the other black, both bracing themselves to break the chains that bound them" (*RM*, 76).[37] If Lafala's return to Africa presents a dead end, then hope is to be located in characters like St. Dominique and Big Blonde: in queer-affirming, interracial, international, organized Marxism.

Writings composed after *Romance in Marseille* suggest that McKay's altered notion of primitivism was, at least to a certain extent, enduring and not unique to his most recently published novel. In *Amiable with Big Teeth* (completed 1941), a satire documenting the efforts of Harlem intellectuals to organize in support of Ethiopia under fascist Italian control, McKay critiques both the stereotyping of Ethiopians by African Americans and the performative primitivism of characters like Professor Koazhy, who appears at the novel's opening in "barbaric fantastic costume" and feels a "primitive joy in extravagantly exhibiting himself."[38] In the character of Lij Alamaya, as in Lafala, McKay again depicts an African in many ways more "modern" and "civilized" than those he encounters in Harlem.

Romance in Marseille is one of several works by writers associated with the Harlem Renaissance to be published for the first time or republished after a long hiatus in recent years. *Amiable with Big Teeth* and Zora Neale Hurston's *Barracoon: The Story of the Last Slave* saw their first publication in 2017 and 2018, respectively, while a new collection of Hurston's short stories, *Hitting a Straight Lick with a Crooked Stick*, and a new edition of Jessie Redmon Fauset's *There is Confusion* (first published 1924) have both been published in 2020. These "new" Harlem Renaissance works embody the simultaneity of the nonsimultaneous; they appear to us at once as old works with a particular history, as time capsules unearthed and poised to reveal some past mystery, yet they also emerge as strikingly fresh, novel works: the New Negro made new once again eight or nine decades on.

Of all these works, *Romance in Marseille*, with its unprecedented and prescient treatment of queer characters, disability, radical politics, and, as this article has demonstrated, the relation between "the primitive" and "civilization," seems poised to exercise perhaps the greatest impact on prevailing views and interpretations of the Harlem Renaissance. Exactly what this impact will entail remains to be seen. It will likely necessitate a discussion of whether or not the work and/or its author should even be considered and categorized primarily as belonging to the Harlem Renaissance. Whatever the future critical fortunes of McKay and *Romance in Marseille*, it is clear that this long-absent novel both raises a number of new debates and necessitates the reexamination of old ones.

LAURA RYAN recently completed her PhD on D. H. Lawrence and the Harlem Renaissance at the University of Manchester.

Notes

1   McKay, *Romance in Marseille* (hereafter cited as *RM*), 53.

2   McKay, *Home to Harlem* (hereafter cited as *HH*), 272.

3   Huggins, *Harlem Renaissance*, 172–73.

4   Etherington, *Literary Primitivism*, 135.

5   Holcomb, *Claude McKay, Code Name Sasha*, 17. Holcomb describes these three novels as "three little black bombs to be hurled into the discourses of state nationalism, racism, capitalism, and imperialism" (19).

6   Etherington, *Literary Primitivism*, 38.

7   Etherington, *Literary Primitivism*, xiii, 35.

8   Etherington, *Literary Primitivism*, xiii, 35.

9   McKay, "A Negro Writer to His Critics," 392.

10 Etherington, *Literary Primitivism*, xv.

11 Cooper, *Claude McKay*, 239.

12 See Marx, "Forgotten Jungle Songs."

13 Marx, "Forgotten Jungle Songs," 79.

14 Marx, "Forgotten Jungle Songs," 81.

15 McKay, *Banjo*, 207 (hereafter cited as *B*).

16 McCabe, "The Multifaceted Politics of Primitivism in Harlem Renaissance Writing," 485.

17 Holcomb, *Claude McKay, Code Name Sasha*, 138.

18 McKay, "A Negro Writer to His Critics," 392.

19 McKay, "A Negro Writer to His Critics," 393.

20 Holcomb and Maxwell, introduction, xxxi.

21 McKay, quoted in Edwards, *The Practice of Diaspora*, 210.

22 Etherington, *Literary Primitivism*, 148.

23 Etherington, *Literary Primitivism*, 152.

24 Etherington, *Literary Primitivism*, 8.

25 Bloch's principal use of this concept is in a 1932 essay on the rise of National Socialism in Germany, which he calls "the classical land of non-simultaneity" ("Nonsynchronism and the Obligation to Its Dialectics," 29).

26 This description of Marrakech is echoed in McKay's 1937 autobiography, in which he likens the city to "an immense cradle of experiment in the marriage of civilized life and primitive life" (*A Long Way from Home*, 234).

27 Quoted in Holcomb and Maxwell, introduction, xxiii–xxiv.

28 See Holcomb and Maxwell, introduction, xxiv.

29 Rosenberg, *Nationalism and the Formation of Caribbean Literature*, 91.

30 Holcomb and Maxwell, introduction, xxi.

31 Dawahare, *Nationalism, Marxism, and African American Literature*, 95–96.

32 Hughes, "One More 'S' in the USA," in *Collected Poems*, 176.

33 Hughes, *The Big Sea*, 178.

34 Hughes, *The Ways of White Folks*.

35 Wall, *Women of the Harlem Renaissance*, 9.

36 Holcomb, *Claude McKay, Code Name Sasha*, 12.

37 Holcomb and Maxwell, introduction, xxxiv.

38 McKay, *Amiable with Big Teeth*, 6, 14.

Works Cited

Bloch, Ernst. "Nonsynchronism and the Obligation to Its Dialectics," translated by Mark Ritter. *New German Critique*, no. 11 (1977): 22–38.

Cooper, Wayne F. *Claude McKay: Rebel Sojourner in the Harlem Renaissance*. Baton Rouge: Louisiana State University Press, 1996.

Dawahare, Anthony. *Nationalism, Marxism, and African American Literature between the Wars: A New Pandora's Box*. Jackson: University Press of Mississippi, 2003.

Edwards, Brent Hayes. *The Practice of Diaspora: Literature, Translation, and the Rise of Black Internationalism*. Cambridge, MA: Harvard University Press, 2003.

Etherington, Ben. *Literary Primitivism*. Stanford, CA: Stanford University Press, 2017.

Holcomb, Gary Edward. *Claude McKay, Code Name Sasha*. Gainesville: University Press of Florida, 2009.

Holcomb, Gary Edward, and William J. Maxwell. Introduction to McKay, *Romance in Marseille*, vii–xxxix.

Huggins, Nathan Irvin. *Harlem Renaissance*. New York: Oxford University Press, 1973.

Hughes, Langston. *The Big Sea*, edited by Joseph McLaren. Columbia: University of Missouri Press, 2002.

Hughes, Langston. *The Collected Poems of Langston Hughes*, edited by Arnold Rampersad. New York: Vintage, 1995.

Hughes, Langston. *The Ways of White Folks*. New York: Vintage, 1990.

Marx, Edward. "Forgotten Jungle Songs: Primitivist Strategies of the Harlem Renaissance." *Langston Hughes Review* 14, nos. 1–2 (1996): 79–93.

McCabe, Tracy. "The Multifaceted Politics of Primitivism in Harlem Renaissance Writing." *Soundings: An Interdisciplinary Journal* 80, no. 4 (1997): 475–97.

McKay, Claude. *Amiable with Big Teeth*. New York: Penguin, 2017.

McKay, Claude. *Banana Bottom*. Chatham, NJ: Chatham Bookseller, 1970.

McKay, Claude. *Banjo: A Story without a Plot*. London: Serpent's Tail, 2008.

McKay, Claude. *Home to Harlem*. Boston: Northeastern University Press, 1987.

McKay, Claude. *A Long Way from Home*. New Brunswick, NJ: Rutgers University Press, 2007.

McKay, Claude. "A Negro Writer to His Critics." In *The New Negro: Readings on Race, Representation, and African American Culture, 1892–1938*, edited by Henry Louis Gates Jr. and Gene Andrew Jarrett, 390–93. Princeton, NJ: Princeton University Press, 2007.

McKay, Claude. *Romance in Marseille*, edited by Gary Edward Holcomb and William J. Maxwell. New York: Penguin, 2020.

Reade Rosenberg, Leah. *Nationalism and the Formation of Caribbean Literature*. Basingstoke: Palgrave Macmillan, 2007.

Wall, Cheryl A. *Women of the Harlem Renaissance*. Bloomington: Indiana University Press, 1995.

Marseille Exposed

Under Surveillance in Claude McKay's
Banjo and *Romance in Marseille*

STEPHANIE J. BROWN

Abstract   This article examines the representation of surveillance in Claude McKay's *Romance in Marseille* and the influence of surveillance on the novel's aesthetics. It uses McKay's 1929 novel *Banjo* as a prior representation of Marseille that establishes the historical constraints under which characters in *Romance* navigate the social world of Quayside, the city's international working-class quarter. The article argues that McKay depicts an important moment in which state and corporate actors create networks of transnational surveillance that aim at securing an advantageous global distribution of labor for capital. McKay's novel examines the mechanisms through which surveillance controls the mobility of racialized and gendered bodies, and depicts the strategies of resistance that such characters deploy more and less successfully against these often-violent mechanisms.

Keywords   surveillance, modernism, Claude McKay, *Romance in Marseille*, gender

Acts of surveillance pervade Claude McKay's newly issued novel *Romance in Marseille*.[1] This may be unsurprising in light of McKay's decades-long experience as a subject of state surveillance,[2] especially given that *Romance* traces the fallout of a historical incident of surveillance: in mid-1920s Marseille, McKay encountered Nelson Simon Dede, a Nigerian sailor who stowed away on a ship sailing from Marseille and was then caught by ship's security officers and imprisoned in a ship's lavatory so cold that he lost his feet to exposure.[3] Dede's story influenced two of McKay's novels: it informs the minor character Taloufa in *Banjo* (1929), who in turn becomes the prototype for *Romance*'s protagonist, Lafala.[4] *Romance* begins in New York with Lafala, like the historical Dede, winning a lawsuit against the company on whose ship he stowed away. The company surveils Lafala in their attempt to thwart his lawsuit, but after the verdict this surveillance devolves into a shadowy pursuit of corporate vengeance that tracks Lafala back across the Atlantic to Marseille. Lafala spends much of the novel evading the company's surveillance agents and kidnapping attempts. Eventually, he suffers imprisonment by the Marseille

ENGLISH LANGUAGE NOTES

59:1, April 2021 DOI 10.1215/00138282-8815005
© 2021 Regents of the University of Colorado

police at the company's behest before returning to Africa to escape an increasingly global system of surveillance operated in the name of capital.

This article considers *Romance in Marseille* alongside McKay's earlier Marseille novel *Banjo* to argue that McKay depicts surveillance as a set of overlapping practices by various agents—the state, the transnational corporation, and a range of other private interests—that constrain the flourishing of Black migrant lives in the transatlantic world. In particular, it is the corporation's increasingly global reach into already existing systems of surveillance—from migration checks at national borders to social surveillance among more local interests in Marseille and New York—that constrain *Romance*'s characters. I argue that attending closely to the strategies Lafala and his lover Aslima develop for resisting surveillance clarifies the predicament in which Black migrants find themselves under surveillance capitalism.

Defining Surveillance in *Banjo* and *Romance in Marseille*

If surveillance can be broadly defined as the practice of watching so as to collect data about observed subjects, often, though not necessarily, with the intent of acting on information thus obtained, then *Banjo* and *Romance* portray an abundance of surveillance agents, operating sometimes independently of one another and sometimes in concert, at various scales—from the nation or the transnational space in which agents deployed by capitalism circulate, to the city, down to the sexual liaison or even the interiority of an individual. *Romance* narrates surveillance experiences as *multiple and ongoing*—iterative but also arising from a variety of sources. Importantly for McKay's characters, this surveillance is focalized through what the surveillance scholar Simone Browne refers to as "racializing surveillance": "those moments when enactments of surveillance reify boundaries, borders, and bodies along racial lines, and where the outcome is often discriminatory treatment."[5] Browne's work emphasizes that surveillance has historically been aimed at controlling the mobility of racialized people in the service of capitalism;[6] McKay's novel vividly documents how racializing surveillance entangles characters in overlapping surveillance networks, with the result of intensifying surveillance's effects. Each surveillant act attempts to render its object legible to observers, but, as *Romance* reveals, the incoherence of these networks' competing demands and the radically different scales of the domains across which those demands operate also create deadly consequences for the surveilled subject.

In such conditions, it may be tempting to look to narratives of interiority that recuperate a plenitude or fullness for the surveilled subject in order to reveal how such subjects exceed surveillance's instrumental rendering. For example, Ruha Benjamin proposes that closely attending to the experiences of the surveilled can correct such dehumanizing effects: "If surveillance treats people like a 'surface,' then countering this form of violent exposure can entail listening deeply to the everyday encounters of those who are forcibly watched."[7] Benjamin points readers to a path McKay emphatically does not take. *Romance* refuses to tell such a redemptive story or give its characters' tools that would allow them to counter the violence

Benjamin describes; nor does McKay's narrative, as distinct from his characters, perform such a "deep listening." Instead, his novel dramatizes the specific ways in which surveillant environments require that the experience of self be reduced to a reckoning with *surface*, forcing characters to prioritize forms of self-conceptualization, modes of perception, and precautionary ways of navigating the world that allegedly secure their safety by surrendering to the imperatives of surveillance. *Romance's* stylistic emphases—on opacity, on representations of bodies and speech rather than interiority, and on surveillant acts of sorting, categorization, confinement—establish racialized surveillance as an inescapable form of authority that makes characters vulnerable to manipulation, violence, and death.

McKay had long been aware of how racializing surveillance functions. His work as a constable in Jamaica in 1911 allowed him to observe firsthand how policing used systematic surveillance backed by the force of law to dictate the movement of labor for the benefit of capitalist overseers (in this case, the Jamaican plantocracy).[8] Significantly, McKay described his unfitness for this work in terms of its uncongenial forms of seeing: in his words, he turned "a blind eye to what it was my manifest duty to see."[9] Policing workers' papers trained McKay to see how the dictates of capital determined the treatment of laborers, and how racialization affected their mobility—concerns that became increasingly pressing in his novels.

Banjo and *Romance* share a Marseillais setting, and both involve their characters in conflict with the police and with state surveillance systems in the forms of national borders, papers of identification, and customs officers. There is, however, a transformation in how surveillance and its agents are represented between the two novels. A distinction arises between policing in *Banjo* and the pervasiveness of surveillance in *Romance* based on the multiplicity of surveillance projects to which the latter novel's characters are subject. The situation of restricted mobility in which *Banjo's* characters find themselves by the end of that novel leads to this distinction.

Banjo and the End of Vagabondage

Banjo initially makes much of the liberating possibilities of being a vagabond, opening with a status quo under which characters have outmaneuvered the prescriptive demands of the state.[10] Nissa Ren Cannon argues that *Banjo* "emphasiz-[es] the potency of amended papers over originals" to enable cross-border movement and claims that the passport's openness to amendment "allows Banjo to resist the nation's defining vision of identity."[11] Banjo's characters cultivate a shared repertoire of strategies to amend their documents, and using these strategies directly correlates to outcomes: ultimately, "all of the characters who are allowed to end the novel happily do so through a refusal to conform to the dictates of their documents."[12]

Nevertheless, *Banjo's* internationalism, enabled as it is by these strategies of amendment, identifies possibilities for community that slip away by the end of the novel's second part, with the third and final part forcefully staging the negation of cosmopolitanism's radical potential. In foregrounding moments of successful negotiation of the state's surveillance apparatuses, the novel's depiction of the community of beach boys invests their vagabondage with various forms of utopian potential, whether queer, economic, political, artistic, or some combination of these. However, as the novel progresses, state authorities undermine this utopian potential, making their own uses of the amendable nature of state documents.

In the third part, we see this capacity turned against several characters, including Taloufa, who becomes Lafala in *Romance*. As the mobility that enables *Banjo's* approximation of a café-centered public sphere dissipates, its concrete realization of a vagabond utopia crumbles. The beach boys scatter accordingly, a plot point that reflects the historical decrease in the number and mobility of Black mariners in the late 1920s.[13] *Banjo* emphasizes that the British Empire's administrators *intend* to immobilize colonial subjects elsewhere: Taloufa, for example, returns to Marseille near the novel's end, having failed to disembark in London. "He was permitted to land only to see about his affairs and under supervision. Colored subjects were not wanted in Britain."[14]

Why has the position of the beach boys become so acute? The situation of migrant workers became increasingly untenable as the postwar labor shortages in European countries eased, the global economic depression took hold, and visa regimes intended to restrict the movement of Black workers reasserted themselves once their labor was no longer needed. While the reimposition of national borders disperses the Quayside community by branding its members with "nationality doubtful" status (*B*, 311), racialized police violence asserts new internal borders across Marseille as well. McKay's intellectual stand-in character Ray interprets his arrest and beating by the Marseille police as a sign of renewed virulence in the measures meant to keep Black migrants in place. He surmises that "it was moving out of the Ditch that caused the policeman to take me for a criminal nosing round the quarter of respectability. . . . Better had I stayed down here with Banjo and the boys where the white bastards thought I ought to be" (*B*, 278–79). Ray's exclusion is permanent. While *Banjo* allows the reader to watch him interpreting and evaluating the novel's conversations about race, vagabondage, "civilization," and community, there is no such perspective in *Romance*, which, by contrast, lacks the intellectual probing that Ray pursues. Instead, intellectual debates diminish into ineffectual bickering between the communist organizer Étienne St. Dominique and the "minor [colonial] cleric" Falope Sbaye (*RM*, 75).

In an additional turn of the screw in *Banjo's* late chapters, Ray's acquaintance, known only as the chauffeur, reveals that we have not been privy to key details of the Marseillais economy. The chauffeur has been running a band of boys in the city who "steal, murder, love in all ways, lie, and spy" (*B*, 299), all of which funds his purchase of property and respectability. The visibility of the police has been a decoy, allowing Banjo, Ray, and the reader to understand surveillance as tied to state interests and to see the corruption of the police as an unintended source of social instability. In fact, however, one secret of Marseille's economic structure is the presence of "unofficial" actors, such as the chauffeur who gains wealth from surveillance turned blackmail and channels it to the suburbs. When Banjo notes that he could have become equally respectable by purchasing land in these suburbs when he arrived, Ray contradicts him, pointing out that he lacks the chauffeur's "instinct for civilization," including the middle-class aspirations that undergird his support for "firm colonial policy" (B, 289). The chauffeur's "civilized" chauvinism against racialized French colonial subjects, combined with his surveillant knowledge of Marseille's social networks, provides opportunities for assimilation not open to Black characters.

Exposure in *Romance*'s Marseille

Surveillance's role in *Banjo*'s Marseille can be productively compared to that in *Romance* with help from Hille Koskela's theory that "surveillance actually *makes* space a container."[15] According to Koskela:

> The alienated who look from behind the camera see the space under
> surveillance through the monitor . . . and they look at people as if they were
> objects. . . . The technical equipment that separates the two sides of
> surveillance makes it difficult for the space to be recognized as a lived,
> experienced space. This particular technologization of space is affecting the
> nature of space: space is regarded as if it were merely a passive container where
> the watched objects exist. It is insensitive to . . . feelings or intentions. . . .
> Furthermore, the space under surveillance is always confined . . . and, while
> one is in it, one is seen as an inactive object of surveillance. . . . In this space
> people are reduced to socially inactive producers of bodily movements and
> analysed as if looked at from above.[16]

For Koskela, surveillance is a form of mediation that "affects the nature of space" by relaying only some types of data from the container to the observer, thus turning the field of view into a "contained" space that refuses "lived experience, feelings or intentions." This framing directs the *observer's* experience of the "objects" inside by providing limited information, configured to avoid the possibility that the watched objects are potential subjects.

Koskela's theory provides a fairly precise description of how *Romance* frames the moment of Lafala's return to Marseille. Unlike the voice of *Banjo*, *Romance*'s narrative voice consistently replicates this mediating and alienating function of surveillance equipment, presenting the reader with a surveillant experience of the port of Marseille. In New York, McKay writes, Lafala "had been hankering all along for the caves and dens of Marseille with a desire to show himself there again as a personage" (*RM*, 28). This passage prepares us to read Marseille as a visual display in which pleasure comes from "showing oneself" to advantage as a legible "personage." The opening of chapter 7 affirms this perspective:

> Wide open in the shape of an enormous fan splashed with violent colors,
> Marseille laid bare to the glory of the meridian sun, like a fever consuming the
> senses, alluring and repelling, full of the unending pageantry of ships and
> of men.
>
> Magnificent Mediterranean harbor. Port of seamen's dreams and their
> nightmares. Port of the bum's delight, the enchanted Breakwater. Port of
> innumerable ships, blowing out, booming in, riding the docks, blessing the

town with sweaty activity and giving sustenance to worker and boss, peddler and prostitute, pimp and panhandler. Part of the fascinating, forbidding and tumultuous Quayside against which the thick scum of life forms and bubbles and breaks in a syrup of passion and desire. (*RM*, 29)

It is worth comparing this passage to *Banjo*'s view of Marseille for a sense of the radically different aesthetics through which Marseille is constructed as a backdrop:

> There was a barbarous international romance in the ways of Marseille that was vividly significant of the great modern movement of life. Small, with a population apparently too great for it, Europe's best back door, discharging and receiving its traffic to the Orient and Africa, favorite port of seamen on French leave, infested with ratty beings of the Mediterranean countries, overrun with guides, cocottes, procurers, repelling and attracting in its white-fanged vileness under its picturesqueness, the town seemed to proclaim to the world that the grandest thing about modern life was that it was bawdy. (*B*, 69)

The port of Marseille in *Banjo* is rife with ambiguities, and McKay's narrator indicates its depths without declaring that they can be plumbed. Simultaneously "barbarous" and "modern"; a visual trick that boasts a population its physical dimensions cannot support; a diaphanous picturesqueness overlaying a hinted-at vileness: the closest you can get to certainty is to say that Marseille "seems to be proclaiming" the grand bawdiness of this "best back door" (double entendre, it seems safe to say, intended). The undecidability of *Banjo*'s Marseille emerges in part from the uncertain status of those who arrive through an unsurveilled back door where, as the term *French leave* suggests, no one looks too closely at anyone's demobilization papers. Although this impression is revealed to be inaccurate by the painstaking documentation of characters' visas, *Banjo*'s Marseille is the distinctly less legible sibling to *Romance*'s port of "pageantry." *Romance*'s emphasis on surfaces mimics a surveillant mode of seeing, one in which the submarine must rise to the surface, "bubbl[ing] and break[ing] in a syrup of passion and desire" instantiated in physical form, in order to become clinically legible through inscription into one of the available social categories: "seamen . . . bum . . . worker and boss, peddler and prostitute, pimp and panhandler." This emphasis on surfaces goes hand in hand with a thematic epidermalization of Black identity.[17] In *Romance*, *Banjo*'s long conversations about the *meaning* of race are displaced by moments of visual revelation: Lafala's heavenly dream of a fantastic "transfiguration" that would simultaneously deracialize and restore him, for instance, or Aslima's vision of the "loving feast" as she "gaze[s] out over the big bay" at Quayside (*RM*, 6, 61, 60).

In the transition between novels, the perceived nature of Marseille changes. Previously a penetrable locale with internal depths that functions as a back door to the rest of the world—a point of ingress, but also an escape route—*Romance*'s darker vision sees Marseille as a container in which Black characters face various forms of immobilization in mutually reinforcing scopic regimes. The breadth of *Banjo*'s curiosity about the diverse experiences consolidated under the signifier "blackness"—how it feels, whether it might ground a political identity or even ontology—is flattened in *Romance* by concerns about how it *circulates* and is monetized, most obviously in Lafala's preoccupation with the fungibility of his lost legs and with the money he receives as compensation for that loss. To circulate, to be monetized, to be fungible—all depend on epidermalizing Blackness as a stable, corporeal, and reliably legible characteristic from which to launch a series of transactions.

From its opening pages, *Romance* presents exposure to an overlapping set of surveillance practices as the primary cause of the vulnerabilities that plague its characters. The novel grapples with the lost freedom of movement of Afro-diasporic characters who seek community outside the terms of capitalist modernity. It builds a surface-oriented aesthetic that maps these characters as sites captured by intersecting surveillance interests that take them as objects. *Romance*'s corporate actors deploy surveillance to immobilize Black labor in the place where it is most valuable and vulnerable to the demands of the labor market. Corporate surveillance, for its part, aims at sovereignty over the movement of Black bodies and punishes transgressions against the maximization of profit/value whenever possible. McKay depicts corporate surveillance tactics that simultaneously exploit state resources, such as migration legislation and police violence, and when necessary evade state surveillance to achieve company goals.

In consequence, Lafala enters transatlantic circuits of surveillance that encompass New York, Marseille, and, eventually, West and North Africa. After the amputation of his legs, he comes to experience New York as a space in which he has little control over surveillance that targets him, in part because his situation requires him to expose himself to a number of powerful parties in order to attain redress for his injuries.

The surveillance scholar Kirstie Ball has theorized "exposure" as a concept that "may be used to frame the subjective experience of surveillance." She identifies exposure as a structural effect of "contemporary institutional configurations" working themselves out "at the level of the individual" subject.[18] Considering exposure in *Romance* reveals that surveillance does not merely create vulnerability; it also generates an affective experience of the self that is exposed to these "institutional configurations" and that guides how characters perceive the choices available to them. The sense of exposure shapes the responses of subjects to surveillance, including, importantly, their perceptions of their bodily experiences while under observation.

In a situation in which multiple surveillance actors operate, the sense of exposure can quickly change valence depending on which of those actors is dominant. During his trial, for example, exposure from the Black press helps Lafala's chances by publicizing his "pathetic story" (*RM*, 12). But when he wins his financial settlement, press coverage accidentally makes him a target for fiscal exploitation by readers. Ultimately, the shipping company and the court officials in charge of overseeing his settlement determine his safety and destination. The shipping company kidnaps and attempts to deport him in an effort to prevent his case from being settled—an attempt thwarted by his lawyer's anticipatory countersurveillance. In settling his case, the court determines that Lafala must be returned to Marseille, his port of origin as a stowaway, according to "the international usage" in such cases (*RM,* 15). It also writes the settlement in terms that encourage him to return home to West Africa. Exposure here entails the forced subordination of Lafala's agency to his stowaway status. Arriving in Marseille, Lafala finds "the freedom of the Quayside . . . practically granted to" him (*RM,* 31), but by this point the reader has a clear enough picture of the overlapping circles of surveillance surrounding him to hear in that *practically* more of an "almost" than an "in practice." In Marseille these circles include networks comprising surveillance agents (gangs and their networks of informants, state agents, police, corporations, communists, pimps, other busybodies). Surveillance that aims to monetize the intelligence it collects pervades Marseille and maneuvers the novel's characters into situations where they are the most vulnerable to its effects.

If, as Ball suggests, exposure makes the individual a surface on which "institutional configurations" articulate their demands, then public space structured by the dictates of surveillance entails fewer opportunities for building community and communal forms that might effectively resist such imperatives. This difficulty, in turn, shapes characters' experiences of those communities. When considering Étienne's plan to attract Quayside inhabitants to the Seamen's club for "recreation and reading and lectures," Lafala explicitly depoliticizes the inhabitants of Quayside, noting that he never thought "of such toilers achieving anything different or changing the way of life that seemed as eternal as the rhythm of the ways along Quayside which they so much resembled" (*RM,* 74, 77). The absence of viable philosophical or political modes of shared meaning-making restricts *Romance*'s characters to forms of inquiry that can be answered by reading "resemblances." These practical exigencies limit the narrator's scope to legible networks of characters and the circulation of intelligence—knowledge about individuals and their actions that may be exploitable for fiscal or other forms of gain—rather than the elaboration of ideas. Even apparently intellectual debates such as Étienne and Falope's provide potentially compromising data about the characters—data that are valuable because of their potential for future exploitation rather than because they create opportunities for the novel to take up ideas in any sustained way.

In *Romance* reading for patterns and "resemblances" coincides with the emergence of the *transnational* corporation as a direct and powerful surveillance agent, one able to mobilize Marseille's corrupt, racist police force to surveil and incarcerate characters on its behalf. In New York, Lafala's lawyer warns him that his safety depends on keeping his movements secret, insisting that he should not "go back to the port you stowed away from, for you can never tell what they might do to you there" (*RM,* 16). Although Lafala is forcibly returned, this warning guides his conduct while navigating Marseille. The somatic experience of surveillance and the spaces in which it occurs differ on the basis of whether or not a person expects to face consequences for their surveilled activities;[19] Lafala thus remains wary of both police and company spies, suspicious men who make him, attuned as he has become to the dangers of exposure, "uncomfortably aware of being the object of observation and comment" (*RM,* 75). Unfortunately for him, national boundaries prove no hindrance to the shipping company. Returning to a Marseille that functions as a closed container and feels increasingly like a trap, Lafala tries and fails to convey his sense of exposure to surveillance to Étienne and Falope, who incorrectly assure him that it is an affair of the "political police" alone (*RM*, 78). Although Lafala takes evasive countersurveillance measures, "hastily hustl[ing] out" of a taxi into the "crowded square in the center of Marseille," the company's men succeed in making him "vanish like a spark in the air" in the closing lines of the second part (*RM*, 79).

Romance places this second, successful kidnapping attempt in close proximity to an episode of colonial surveillance. This proximity suggests that specifically paternalist colonial ideologies, outdated and insufficiently capitalist in their modes of apprehension, are no match for the resources of the modern, globalized corporation. Immediately before his kidnapping, Lafala visits his agent, the "important white person . . . entitled to represent [him] formally" in legal matters in Marseille, whose "sentiment toward Negroes was based upon *Uncle Tom's Cabin* and David Livingstone. And he took a sort of patriarchal interest in the black boys drifting into Marseille . . . so long as they were good children" (*RM*, 20, 71–72). Unfortunately for Lafala, this agent's "patriarchal interest" extends only to policing the color line and establishing that the woman Lafala proposes to take back to Africa with him is not white: "It would never do for a black man to take a white woman back to an African colony, especially a woman of Quayside who would certainly be a disgrace to the European colony and make it look morally small in the eyes of the natives" (*RM*, 72). Myopically obsessed with the sexual politics of empire, and focusing his infantilizing surveillance efforts accordingly, the agent fails to grasp the economic interests involved or their danger to Lafala, for whom he is responsible.

Étienne eventually secures Lafala's release from prison, but Lafala's sense of vulnerability leaves him mistrustful of everyone and determined to return to Africa. He frames this decision as a move back to "the bush," a space he imagines as outside "civilization" (*RM*, 114) where he could escape a globalizing economy that uses surveillance to optimize the smooth distribution of labor. After his departure, Rock and Diup, two "fixtures of the Quayside," report to the other characters that they spotted him on a ship and said their good-byes, after which he "done sailed away" to Africa (*RM*, 35, 127). With this secondhand farewell scene, the narrator gives no indication of how Lafala's return to the bush will play out.

Importantly, this was not the novel's original ending: McKay's 1929 draft and a letter to his editor recount a conclusion in which Lafala "eluded the 'political police' and vanished back into the obscure back streets" of Quayside.[20] The revised ending suggests that escaping surveillance in Quayside's warrens may have no longer struck McKay as a plausible or aesthetically coherent narrative resolution by the early 1930s. But if Marseille finally offers no way out of the novel's closed system of surveillance, a conversation early in the novel suggests that Africa may not be the refuge Lafala seeks, either. On hearing of Lafala's plan to return, Diup figures modern Africa not as a dark continent but as one captured by a global capitalist surveillance. He advises Lafala that white scrutiny reaches into the otherwise lawless bush, and that he should "stay here where Civilization can protect you and leave jungle Africa to white men. . . . White man don't like black man with brains nor money near him in jungleland" (*RM*, 36). These terms echo McKay's autobiographical account of his experiences with British and French colonial surveillance in Tunisia while writing *Romance*: "Even in Africa I was confronted by the specter, the white terror always pursuing the black. There was no escape anywhere from the white hound of Civilization."[21] From early on McKay's reader has been informed of the ubiquity of surveillance that racializes landownership as white and Black bodies as labor. In West Africa, Lafala, no longer a bushman but an African with capital, will likely be read as a threat to white corporate control of the continent's natural resources. As he passes beyond its horizon, the novel anticipates surveillance greeting him anew in "jungleland."

Compulsory Exposure and the Strategic Undecidability of Women

Lafala's departure is not, however, where the novel ends. Instead, its conclusion turns to Aslima's reaction to her abrupt abandonment by Lafala and her almost certain death at the hands of Titin. This ending emphasizes an important question about surveillance that the novel resolves through her plotline: If navigating surveilled spaces entails various forms of exposure, can strategic opacity mitigate the vulnerabilities such exposure creates?

In response to the colonizing West's imperative to transparency, the postcolonial theorist Édouard Glissant has "clamor[ed] for the right to opacity for everyone." Opacity, for Glissant, is "the most perennial guarantee of participation and confluence"; it maintains the possibility of relation by saving us from being immobilized in "unequivocal courses and irreversible choices."[22] Glissant does not specifically theorize surveillance per se, but his concern with resisting colonial forms of "reductive transparency"[23] and his framing of opacity as a right that allows forms of depth, futurity, and shared possibility for colonized subjects neatly illuminate what Aslima is up to as she, like Glissant, cultivates strategies of survival under surveillant capitalist modernity.

Before the novel begins, Lafala stows away as a result of Aslima robbing him, and her presence in Marseille likewise prompts his return. He confronts her, and the pair are reconciled, although not without suspicion of each other's motives, the threats of greed and revenge still operative in their interactions. They decide to return to Africa together and to allay Titin's suspicion by behaving as if Aslima were conning the guileless Lafala. She maintains this charade when he disappears into police custody, even as she attempts to make certain that Titin hasn't kidnapped and tortured Lafala to get at his money. When Lafala reappears, Titin promises to marry Aslima if she swindles him, while she and Lafala plan to leave for Africa together. When a colonial agent thwarts this plan, Lafala proposes an alternative: he will send Aslima "back home" to her family (*RM*, 123). After she explains that this is impossible because she has no family or home to return to, they renew their decision to travel together, and the last direct representation of Lafala in the novel shows him determined to "stick to her and be a contented pig in a pen, wallowing with joy in the mud" (*RM*, 125). When Titin finds that Lafala has sailed off without Aslima, leaving behind money for her to "return home" instead, he confronts her.

Titin arrives to find her "listless . . . silent and mocking" at being abandoned (*RM*, 129). He issues what she mistakes for a threat against Lafala, and she attacks him, provoking him, in the novel's dramatic closing image, to shoot her while "cursing and calling upon hell to swallow her soul" (*RM*, 130).

In McKay's novels women are particularly vulnerable to violence, and in Marseille they "bear the brunt of anxiety and violence that the 'vagabond international' might have generated."[24] Just as *Banjo* dismisses its vagabond community, the possibility of friendly comradeship between the sexes, represented in the character of Latnah, dissipates in an ending that notoriously reduces women to "a conjunction," with Banjo sagely noting that "theah's things we can git away with all the time and she just kain't" (*B*, 326).[25] In both *Banjo* and *Romance*, the consequences for women who try to "git away with things" are disproportionate and extreme. If, as McKay claimed, he hadn't "gone over the old *Banjo* ground [in *Romance*]" and in fact "especially tried to avoid that," then the structural repetition of closure through the abandonment of women is pointedly significant.[26] Ending both novels with abandoned women gives their elimination the ring of the inevitable.

In *Romance*, *Banjo*'s acknowledgment of the constricted mobility of women, and their vulnerability to arbitrary violence, is taken for granted. Instead of demonstrating this vulnerability, *Romance* examines how surveillance contributes to gendered violence by making its main female characters sex workers, cogs in an industry that generates capital by using surveillance to tightly circumscribe women's geographic mobility and economic opportunity. While women are a "conjunction" in *Banjo*, that conjunction threatens to take the form of a black box in *Romance*: the prostitute becomes the site at which inscrutable forms of exchange take place. Sex work links the already unpredictable effects of intimacy to debt and to often-equivocal forms of attachment, creating points of illegibility on the city's surveilled surface and introducing uncertainties into attempts to map characters' relationships. Prostitutes, in their plurality of connections and their monetizing of intimacy, require concentrated monitoring under a maxim of surveillance practice: the greater the indeterminacies around a relationship, and the more conjunctions at which the parties involved are located, the more closely they must be watched. This is why Titin participates in a secret "fellowship in Quayside . . . [,] an international association, a kind of loose federation of men of common mind and ideals who kept in touch with one another by secret correspondence, keeping tabs on their protégées" (*RM*, 64).

The novel makes it clear that Titin has ensnared Aslima in a dynamic common to those who provide benefits to dependents that they then surveil. John Gilliom terms this dynamic "a power struggle over the compulsory visibility" of the disempowered beneficiary.[27] While Titin has practical reasons for surveilling Aslima, the novel often depicts characters—Babel, Lafala's agent; the prostitute La Fleur Noire; even casual observers—speculating about the nature of her attachment to Lafala. The opacity of Aslima's motives generates a fascination among these characters, who then narrate her actions to one another, insistently attempting to fix her with familiar tropes. Aslima chooses a unique strategic response to this form of exposure: accepting that she will be subject to public attention, she cultivates an opacity about her motives that ensures that even though her *choices* inevitably become public knowledge, their *meaning* remains inscrutable.

Significantly, this strategy is predicated on Aslima's awareness that vagabond-age is not an option. As "a child of North Africa out of Marrakesh . . . [,] Aslima was born a slave" to an enslaved Sudanese mother (*RM*, 44).[28] She is, by virtue of this status and her gender, equally unable to access the kinds of state protections that *Banjo*'s vagabonds manipulate.[29] If McKay's other Arab-African female characters "embodied the hybrid internationalism of the black transnational journey without ever being able to participate in it themselves," then this predicament is particularly ironic, and cruel in Aslima's case.[30] Aslima follows a vagabond path from Marra-kesh, where she is kidnapped, to Fez, Casablanca, Algeria, and finally Marseille. Unlike McKay's other vagabonds, however, she moves while in captivity to the men who purport to own her, from her kidnappers, to the "colored sub-officer from the French West Indies" who buys her out of a brothel (*RM*, 45), to Titin. In a parallel to Lafala's interactions with the shipping company, powerful men control her mobility while apparently having no trouble moving (her) across borders. Borders do not dis-rupt her enslaved status: nothing changes when she is taken from enslavement in North Africa to a place where Titin's claims on her are legally tenuous. Her lack of agency belies the seemingly vagabond nature of her route, and despite telling Titin that the Arab men of Quayside will protect her out of ethnic sentiment, Aslima knows that she "has no secret relations with the Arabs" that would substantiate such a claim (*RM*, 89).

State surveillance in Marseille likewise makes her status as prostitute, if not as a slave, permanent, defining her via public, legal categorization as a "woman whose identity was the yellow card of prostitution" (*RM*, 90). In a novel whose characters are constantly required to show their papers, this highly visible sign brands her in the eyes of the French as "a woman without family, without home, without name" beyond the horizon of any imagined future: "Aslima could never escape from her record as prostitute. If she had a son it would be a whoreson. Wherever she went and whatever she did . . . the police record . . . would trace her down to the third and fourth generation" (*RM*, 90). She is fully aware of how this branding functions, recriminating with Titin that prostitutes are "not human beings in your eyes. You're all crazy about marrying a pure girl, *une jeune fille de famille*" (*RM*, 90). Her emphasis on family ties (*de famille*) reminds readers that reestablishing her kinship ties is impossible. Her family's identity is a mystery, and even if locating relatives were possible, reincorporating her into protective family structures is not. Her illeg-ibility in familial terms, in tandem with her legibility as a prostitute, leaves her exposed to the brand of the yellow card.[31] She tells Lafala as much when he suggests repatriating her to Marrakesh: "I have no home to go back to. No parents, no rela-tives. I would be a stranger going back alone" (*RM*, 123). Aslima's decision to fight surveillance with opacity is accordingly made under duress.

It is also, in one sense, a successful decision: the surveillant narrator's voice that reads characters via surfaces and public acts is notably cagey when assessing Aslima, as is evident in judgments like this one: "It *appeared as if* Aslima's liaison with Lafala was incapacitating her as the hardiest hustler of Quayside" (*RM*, 58;

my emphasis). Refusing to weigh in definitively on the truth status of such observations, the narrator is generally reduced to reading Aslima's surface and marking the opaqueness of her intentions. Aslima carefully maintains multiple accounts of her actions for different audiences in Marseille, and McKay leaves the reader with few interpretive resources beyond the information that can be gleaned through surveilling her actions.

The few glimpses of Aslima's interiority granted the reader are, crucially, not moments of decision. Readers have access to her emotional reactions to Titin's demand that she swear to her honesty, for example: "How detestable he was, asking her to swear before the church, Aslima thought. She swore with her mouth, but her heart went out to her own God. . . . She uttered a silent prayer that the lost dominions of her [Muslim] people might be restored" (*RM*, 68–69). Here we learn that Aslima retains an attachment to Islam, information interesting enough to distract us from noticing that we have learned nothing about her immediate intentions. Likewise, in the aftermath of Lafala's proposal that she accompany him to Africa, she has a "revelation of a different scene" that superimposes on the sight of Marseille's sunset a "loving feast" in an "antique white-washed city," a visual phantasmagoria of Orientalist tropes whose abundance overwhelms her interpretive abilities as well as the narrator's: "What a vision! Awful and sweet! Oh, I wonder if it meant good or bad?" (*RM*, 60, 61, 60, 62). When she seeks out Lafala immediately after her vision, it is not to answer his proposal but to describe her dream, again deferring an irrevocable declaration of intentions.

Aslima is the only character whose intentions remain ambiguous for the duration of the novel, and this scene suggests that ambiguity, cultivated as a survival tactic, makes definitive choices impossible. Like Scheherazade in *The Arabian Nights*, Aslima's opacity is sustained through a series of deferrals that must continue indefinitely in order to remain effective. In contrast, *Romance*'s male characters view Aslima's opacity as a mystery needing resolution for a variety of reasons, many of which have to do with calculating what kind and degree of risk she poses to their various plans or how valuable she and her labor might be. They consistently try to force her into choices that would reveal enough to render her intelligible. Titin, for example, complains that after reuniting with Lafala she no longer "hustles on the side" (*RM*, 59)—an attempt to force her back into a more easily surveillable form of prostitution. Lafala tracks the status of their relationship through the apparent openness of her behavior. Pleased when "Aslima revealed herself to him as she had never done before nor to anybody in Marseille," Lafala's pleasure is tempered by his recognition of risk: "He became afraid of this happiness. . . . But this time he wasn't going to fall that way like an overripe fruit. No, not for Aslima" (*RM*, 34). His determination to repatriate her to Morocco despite her protests is an attempt to impose a resolution to their relationship that ignores her desires and reality. He imagines returning her to a familial space in which paternal surveillance will both redeem her and replace the life of "making pig-honey together" that she proposes in their last moments together (*RM*, 124). Even as he is "sent home" by the surveillant corporate powers directing his own movements, he hopes to compensate for this loss of agency by doing the same to Aslima.[32]

Just as Latnah is abandoned once she can no longer function effectively as a conjunction in *Banjo*, *Romance*'s ending reveals that, for women, losing one's carefully cultivated indeterminacy means death. Aslima is ultimately forced into a grave choice, and her decision to leave for Africa with Lafala reveals both her desire to be safely exposed and a belief that she might find such safety in romantic intimacy. To her dismay and destruction, she is abandoned and dehumanized as a "mad-woman" and killed as "a precious wild beast" (*RM*, 129). While *Romance* is riddled with "displays of nonchalant misogyny," it renders salient the special predicament of women and the consequent constraints on their agency under scopic regimes of surveillance.[33] It may not always do so with sympathy, but it certainly does so with clarity.

Conclusion

The collision of surveillance interests in *Romance in Marseille* is, in one sense, fruitless. The shipping company never retrieves its money from Lafala, Titin's "fellowship" fails to help him monetize Aslima's labor, and the judiciary in New York and police violence in Marseille act in ways largely uncorrelated to the state interests they purportedly serve. Nonetheless, this collision produces effects: changes in the nature and experience of public space in Marseille, Lafala's exilic "return" to West Africa, and Aslima's death. In the end, *Romance in Marseille* proves most invested in displaying the deadly collateral effects of a surveillance system that attempts to derive value from the efficient management of bodies. The gratuitousness of these collateral effects, and their failure to create value for the capitalist powers they purportedly serve, must be considered alongside the novel's work to display the binds surveillance creates for its disenfranchised characters. What emerges is a capitalist modernity that can create no value from the incidents in Marseille, unfazed by its failure at this local scale because certain of success globally. Destroying the affective communal bonds of *Banjo*, dismembering both the physical body of the Black worker and tenuous forms of diasporic Black intimacy that the liaison between Aslima and Lafala suggests, the corporate organization of public space in the interest of surveillance and control yields nothing but casual cruelty.

STEPHANIE J. BROWN is assistant professor of English and affiliated faculty member of the Gender and Women's Studies and Social, Cultural, and Critical Theory programs at the University of Arizona. Her current book project, tentatively titled *Watching Women: State Surveillance and Feminist Activism in Early Twentieth Century Britain*, uses archival research to document British activists' responses to forms of state surveillance that emerged to target female activists in Britain during those decades.

Notes

1   McKay, *Romance in Marseille* (hereafter cited as *RM*).

2   The most sustained of these accounts of various states' interest in McKay are Maxwell, *F.B. Eyes*, and Holcomb, *Claude McKay, Code Name Sasha*.

3   Cooper, *Claude McKay*, 237–79.

4   The novel's early drafts refer to Lafala as Taloufa.

5   Browne, *Dark Matters*, 16.

6   Although he doesn't explicitly use surveillance as a framework, Cedric Robinson in *Black Marxism* offers a foundational reading of how

the careful monitoring of mobility is necessary to the logics of racial capitalism.

7   Benjamin, *Race after Technology*, 128.
8   Cooper, *Claude McKay*, 34. When slavery ended in Jamaica, policing was one mechanism that kept Black Jamaican laborers on the plantations and at the bottom of the island's social, political, and economic power structures (Johnson, "Patterns of Policing," 71, 75).
9   McKay, *Complete Poems*, 295. The quote is from McKay's preface to *Constab Ballads*.
10 On vagabondage, see Vadde, *Chimeras of Form*, 112–33.
11 Cannon, "'Unique Plan,'" 144.
12 Cannon, "'Unique Plan,'" 149.
13 Stephens, *Black Empire*, 192.
14 McKay, *Banjo*, 311 (hereafter cited as *B*).
15 Koskela, "'The Gaze without Eyes,'" 250.
16 Koskela, "'The Gaze without Eyes,'" 250–51.
17 Browne's reading of Fanon's *Black Skin, White Masks* defines "epidermalization" as "the imposition of race on the body" that "fixes and frames blackness as an object of surveillance" (*Dark Matters*, 7).
18 Ball, "Exposure," 640.
19 Gilliom, "Struggling with Surveillance," 125–26.
20 Holcomb and Maxwell, introduction, xlv.
21 McKay, *A Long Way from Home*, 304.
22 Glissant, *Poetics of Relation*, 190, 191, 194.
23 Glissant, *Poetics of Relation*, 161.
24 Reed, "'A Woman Is a Conjunction,'" 762.
25 For an extended reading of this image, see Reed, "'A Woman Is a Conjunction.'"
26 Letter quoted in Fabre, "Beyond Banjo," 45.
27 Gilliom, *Overseers of the Poor*, 105.
28 McKay had observed and was "not at all upset by the lingering forms of [female] slavery still practiced in Morocco" (Cooper, *Claude McKay*, 251).
29 By the 1920s the British Foreign Office and other European nations were increasingly using passport offices to identify cases of "white slavery" (Salter, *Rights of Passage*, 31). Unfortunately, similar concern was not expressed for African trafficking victims.
30 Stephens, *Black Empire*, 171.
31 For an extended discussion of how racializing surveillance wields the brand against Black subjects, see Browne's chapter "B®anding Blackness" (*Dark Matters*, 89–130).
32 A historical possibility that I cannot quite resolve in my thinking about Aslima is that, had she returned with Lafala to Nigeria, she might have been present for the Aba Women's Revolt of 1929–30 and the founding of the Egba Women's Alliance in the 1930s. Each of these events asserted women's political agency in the conduct of the colonial Nigerian state (Agbese, "Maintaining Power," 23–25) and offered radically different configurations of women's aspirations than those on offer in McKay's representations of Africa.
33 Holcomb and Maxwell, introduction, xxvii.

Works Cited

Agbese, Aje-Ori. "Maintaining Power in the Face of Political, Economics, and Social Discrimination: The Tale of Nigerian Women." *Women and Language* 26, no. 1 (2003): 18–25.

Ball, Kirstie. "Exposure." *Information, Communication and Society* 12, no. 5 (2009): 639–57.

Benjamin, Ruha. *Race after Technology: Abolitionist Tools for the New Jim Code*. New York: Polity, 2019.

Browne, Simone. *Dark Matters: On the Surveillance of Blackness*. Durham, NC: Duke University Press, 2015.

Cannon, Nissa Ren. "'A Unique Plan of Getting Deported': Claude McKay's *Banjo* and the Marked Passport." *Symploke* 25, nos. 1–2 (2017): 141–53.

Cooper, Wayne F. *Claude McKay: Rebel Sojourner in the Harlem Renaissance*. Detroit: Wayne State University Press, 1987.

Fabre, Michael. "Beyond *Banjo*: Claude McKay's African Experience." *Commonwealth* 5 (1981): 37–52.

Gilliom, John. *Overseers of the Poor: Surveillance, Resistance, and the Limits of Privacy*. Chicago: University of Chicago Press, 2001.

Gilliom, John. "Struggling with Surveillance: Resistance, Consciousness, and Identity." In *The New Politics of Surveillance and Visibility*, edited by Kevin D. Haggerty and Richard V. Ericson, 111–39. Toronto: University of Toronto Press, 2006.

Glissant, Édouard. *Poetics of Relation*, translated by Betsy Wing. Ann Arbor: University of Michigan Press, 1997.

Holcomb, Gary Edward. *Claude McKay, Code Name Sasha: Queer Black Marxism and the Harlem Renaissance*. Gainesville: University Press of Florida, 2007.

Holcomb, Gary Edward, and William J. Maxwell. Introduction to *Romance in Marseille*, vii–xxxix. New York: Penguin, 2020.

Johnson, Howard. "Patterns of Policing in the Post-emancipation British Caribbean, 1835–1895." In *Policing the Empire: Government, Authority, and Control, 1830–1940*, edited by David M. Anderson and David Killingray, 71–89. Manchester: Manchester University Press, 1991.

Koskela, Hille. "'The Gaze without Eyes': Video-Surveillance and the Changing Nature of Urban Space." *Progress in Human Geography* 24, no. 2 (2000): 243–65.

Maxwell, William J. *F.B. Eyes: How J. Edgar Hoover's Ghostreaders Framed African American Literature.* Princeton, NJ: Princeton University Press, 2015.

McKay, Claude. *Banjo: A Story without a Plot.* New York: Harcourt Brace, 1929.

McKay, Claude. *Complete Poems,* edited by William J. Maxwell. Urbana: University of Illinois Press, 2000.

McKay, Claude. *A Long Way from Home.* New York: Arno, 1969.

McKay, Claude. *Romance in Marseille,* edited by Gary Edward Holcomb and William J. Maxwell. New York: Penguin, 2020.

Reed, Anthony. "'A Woman Is a Conjunction': The Ends of Improvisation in Claude McKay's *Banjo: A Story without a Plot.*" *Callaloo* 36, no. 3 (2013): 758–72.

Robinson, Cedric J. *Black Marxism: The Making of the Black Radical Tradition.* Chapel Hill: University of North Carolina Press, 2000.

Salter, Mark B. *Rights of Passage: The Passport in International Relations.* Boulder, CO: Rienner, 2003.

Stephens, Michelle Ann. *Black Empire: The Masculine Global Imaginary of Caribbean Intellectuals in the United States, 1914–1962.* Durham, NC: Duke University Press, 2005.

Vadde, Aarthi. *Chimeras of Form: Modernist Internationalism beyond Europe, 1914–2016.* New York: Columbia University Press, 2017.

Claude McKay's Bad Nationalists

Colonial Passport Controls and Shipping Damages in *Romance in Marseille*

RICH COLE

Abstract   This article examines Claude McKay's 1928 journey to Africa under colonial occupation and uncovers how these true events partly inspired his late work of expatriate fiction, *Romance in Marseille*. By bringing together migration studies with literary history, the article challenges and expands existing research that suggests that McKay's writings register the impulse for a nomadic wandering away from oppressive forms of identity control set up in the wake of World War I. The article contends that Claude McKay's renegade cast of "bad nationalist" characters registers a generative tension between the imperial national forms the author encountered in North Africa and the Black nationalist vision of Marcus Garvey's Back-to-Africa campaign. Reading the dialectics of bad nationalisms and Black internationalisms, the article explores how the utopian promise for Black liberation by returning back to Africa, central to the New Negro project of Black advancement, frequently becomes entangled in McKay's transnational stowaway fiction with conflicting calls for reparations, liabilities, and shipping damages.
Keywords   Black Internationalism, Claude McKay, Harlem Renaissance, Pan-Africanism, migration studies

Oh Marcus Garvey! They who hated you
Like hell have now embalmed you in a book,
Your words that made them squirm from yellow to blue,
They have now placed you into a special nook
Of culture
—Claude McKay, *The Cycle*

Whenever authors of the Negro race write good literature
for publication the white publishers refuse to publish it, but
wherever the Negro is sufficiently known to attract attention
he is advised to write in the way that the white man wants.
That is just what happened to Claude McKay.
—Marcus Garvey, *Negro World*

ENGLISH LANGUAGE NOTES
59:1, April 2021 DOI 10.1215/00138282-8815016
© 2021 Regents of the University of Colorado

I n late September 1928 the Harlem Renaissance writer Claude McKay boarded a ship on the southern coast of Spain. This sea voyage marked the decisive leg of his travel plans to visit Africa for the first time. Anticipation to connect with his ancestral homeland had grown steadily, though he did exercise enough self-discipline over the preceding summer months to draft his second novel, *Banjo* (1929), before plunging into the new adventure. When he finally commenced the sea journey, crossed into the territorial waters of North Africa, and disembarked through a Moroccan port of entry, McKay's initial feelings of relief that he had at last broken free of the rule-bound strictures of bureaucratized life in Europe were almost immediately tested. Soon after his arrival in Africa, McKay became involved in a minor altercation on the streets of Fez. A confrontation with a messenger from the British government caused McKay to self-identify as "a bad nationalist."[1]

McKay was confronted by a North African man hired by the British government to keep tabs on persons traveling in the region. McKay's memoir *A Long Way from Home* (1937) recounts how this man had identified him in a crowded market-place and eventually pulled him aside:

> A *chaoush* (native doorman and messenger) from the British Consulate had accosted me in a *souk* one day and asked whether I was American. I said I was born in the West Indies and lived in the United States and that I was an American, even though I was a British subject, but I preferred to think of myself as an internationalist. The *chaoush* said he didn't understand what was an internationalist. I laughed and said that an internationalist is a bad nationalist. (*LW*, 300)

McKay boasted in jest that he was a bad nationalist without immediately recognizing the transgressive nature of his own declaration. "I had said I was . . . a bad nationalist," McKay qualifies, "just by way of a joke without thinking of its radical implications" (*LW*, 300). His commitment to look for international networks of political affiliation beyond the strictures of conventional borderlines is phrased in such a way that it effaces the primacy of organizational power held by the modern nation-state to exercise control over its own citizens both at home and abroad. Yet McKay's wordplay did not illicit the desired effect to lighten the mood of his confrontation on the street. Annoyed, the messenger working for the British Consulate spoke back to McKay assertively. He "replied gravely: 'All the Moors call you an American, and if you are British, you should come and register at the Consulate'" (*LW*, 300).

McKay's verbal slip to a stranger in the busy Moroccan marketplace about being "an internationalist . . . a bad nationalist," albeit a joke, revealed a repressed undercurrent of political deviance informing his radical writings and vagabond geographic movements, all of which had cogently manifested itself in just two raw words as a hidden truth—*bad nationalist*. As the negation indicates, McKay did not readily ascribe to the proliferation of bureaucratic regulations in the interwar period concerning national forms of identity documentation. Deprioritizing his own natural-born citizenship as the principal marker of his identification in the modern world demonstrates a reluctance to equate a fixed conception of nation-hood or legal personhood with the continuity of the human subject.

No wonder the North African messenger expressed frustrations that McKay's national loyalties were hard to pin down. Their conflict in the street over following proper entry protocols when traveling abroad was further underscored by McKay's deliberate decision not to follow the messenger's stern instructions. Although McKay was certainly aware of the communist overtones of branding himself an internation-alist, he recalled, "I did not go to register at the Consulate" in Fez; "I thought that it was enough that my passport was in working order" (*LW*, 301). His reluctance to follow mandatory guidelines to register and self-identify as a British subject when traveling abroad challenged the ascendancy of modern border control measures coextensive with the national form of state power. One of the problems McKay observed with the upsurge in excessive national partisanship during the interwar period was that the formation of these kinds of exclusive and exclusionary distinc-tions between inhabitants as belonging to a specific place threatened to destroy global lines of solidarity between workers—many of whom also identified as colo-nial subjects of empire. Nandita Sharma elaborates on the pattern of immigration controls designed to separate "nationals from migrants," observing that imple-menting tactics of national belonging "became a crucial aspect of the governmen-tality of nation-states. Migrants were the foil against which nations could be mobilized and on whose shoulders the source of very real miseries—and immiseration—of worker-citizens could be placed."[2] Displacement of blame onto the backs of racial-ized outsiders, foreigners, immigrants, refugees, vagabonds, outcasts, expatriates, and diasporic subjects functioned to reconfigure the loyalties of naturalized citi-zens and, in turn, weakened the advancements of both global labor and international race alliances. In addition, McKay's surprise that the passport regime was now actively policed by local Moroccans living under the repressive situation of colonial rule only further confirmed his suspicions about the evacuation of freedom from within the modern global order of ruling imperial powers. "This commitment to territorial integrity," states Adom Getachew, "was largely aimed at warding off violent successions," but in North Africa it also had the effect of excluding claims to self-determination by local members of indigenous groups because many of these territories, like Morocco, were governed by external colonial rule rather than by their own political units.[3] The French protectorate in Morocco, to which I will return, was largely emboldened by its own administrative measures of interven-tion that experimented with various strategies for cooperation and development in North Africa. French colonial administrators enacted and put into practice the lofty humanist objective of population improvement through the implementation of a widespread social restructuring better suited for economic development and political modernization. These were the nodal points of a new governmental ratio-nality, which, quite effectively, reconceptualized the French imperial nation-state as a modern global power with the capabilities of setting up its own managerial branches in developing overseas territories, imposing administrative changes along-side governmental surveillance bound up in a network of movement controls, mandates, and dependencies that operated as an integrated form of structural dispossession in the colonies. Non-European territories like Morocco were excluded from the full rights of membership in the international system, but, simultaneously, they remained subject to the obligations of modern governance, which included the responsibilities to enact clearly defined borders and to install modern immigration controls.

This last point brings us to a crucial distinction intrinsic to McKay's unease with the proliferation of identity documentation and border security measures. For a Jamaican-born individual to declare himself a British national—a subject of the British Empire even when traveling on the African continent—was to reiterate the uneven terms of the interwar international society. Partial recognition of this kind was granted to Jamaicans, but it was a recognition that functioned to dispossess this group of non-European peoples of the possibility for self-determination. The larger issue at stake here is the extent to which partial membership for non-European territories was circumscribed in such a way that it reinforced racial divides. Colonized peoples of color were denied full rights of membership, and the colonies they belonged to were further encumbered with onerous obligations to become developed before gaining a seat at the bargaining table of the great world powers. Border controls, ID cards, and identity checks were expected to be implemented across the developing colonies. These measures kept tabs on the movements of foreign outsiders, immigrants, and dissidents. The new network of controls also functioned to track local insurgent forces fighting for national self-determination. Above all, for McKay, the emergence of the modern national system prevented the possibility for a more international conception of collective solidarity and freedom to emerge across border lines for workers and colonized peoples. In *Claude McKay, Code Name Sasha: Queer Black Marxism and the Harlem Renaissance* (2007), Gary Edward Holcomb reads the image of the "bad nationalist" in Althusserian terms: "Once again the reader encounters a McKay character who is a 'bad nationalist,' . . . an Althusserian bad subject, the human subject who is incapable of being interpellated by the linguistics of the nation."[4] In view of his ostensible break with the linguistic protocols of imperial nationalism by the time he visited Africa, McKay's later writings pose problems. His subsequent character development of the figure of the bad nationalist in his ensuing literary works demonstrates an attempt to foreground, challenge, and expose a structural and recurring crisis that emerged in efforts by states to nationalize their sovereignty in the interwar era with highly restrictive and regulative citizenship control measures. I am particularly interested in how the well-developed Althusserian scene of interpellation that McKay experienced when hailed on the Moroccan street exposed the following contradiction at the core of modern national belonging: the idea of the progressive realization of freedom in an emerging world of nation-states required that all members of the population, regardless of standing, must paradoxically adhere to the gradual perfection of restrictive movement controls implemented by the repressive state apparatus. Exposing this national contradiction, marked by a persistent governmental irrationality between supposedly guaranteeing some rights and liberties while restricting sovereign borders and the freedom of movement both within and between territories, disrupts given historical chronologies coextensive with nation-building and complicates abstract promises of freedom supposedly guaranteed by the modern nation-state system. McKay further reveals that after he shirked his administrative responsibility to report to the consul and be counted, the force of coercion soon reappeared in front of him again, this time in a more authoritative form.

Following his strange encounter on the street, McKay was quickly summoned by police, transported to the consul, and interrogated by a ranking French official in the territory, who alleged that McKay was a Bolshevik spy and Black radical propagandist. McKay's biographer, Wayne Cooper, observes that the colonial powers "viewed his racial and political militancy as a definite threat. He was accordingly . . . advised to stop associating with the natives."[5] Officials raised concerns about McKay's influencing presence among Africans on the continent and threatened him with deportation from the North African territory. At some point during these tense interrogations, McKay talked his way out of expulsion from Africa by convincing the imperial bureaucrats in charge that he was simply on holiday, not acting as a Bolshevik secret agent or propagandist New Negro agitator, and, likely much more persuasive in a legal frame of reference, he carried a British passport with certain privileges of immunity (*LW*, 302).

McKay evaded expulsion, but clearly his motivations for falling back on his primary national identification were not guided by patriotism or allegiance to the imperial Union Jack—or to any other national flag, for that matter. The reason was chiefly pragmatic. He faced extradition from the territory. McKay communicates the restrictive parameters of his own bad-nationalist outlook when he admits that the modern concept of national culture had so strongly intensified across the globe in the wake of geopolitical realignments after World War I that he was regularly left with few choices but "scrupulously complying with official regulations regarding passports, identity cards and visas, etc." He immediately adds the caveat, however, that "in all my traveling in strange places, I have always relied on my own personality as the best passport" (*LW*, 301). It may seem counterintuitive, or even hypocritical, for a self-professed bad nationalist to still carry a citizenship document and then to immediately follow such an admission with a statement of disavowal indicating that he didn't fully prioritize the formalities of official documentation, either. But such contradictions do offer perspective on both the governmental logic of the passport system and the real-life, anxious, everyday interactions with national forms that caused McKay to stage instances of resistance to subvert and confuse the tracking systems of federal authorities. His nomadic wanderings, if only offering up a partial release, demonstrate an inclination to be freed up just enough to prioritize his own imperfect "bad" instincts for globality as the best passport to challenge some of the more predictable and clunky logics of national forms. "Bad nationalism" thus emerges in McKay's lexicon as a response to the pressures to conform to the dominant discourse of national governance in the 1920s that simultaneously produced and challenged his own right to belong in the modern world.

My overall purpose in this essay is to examine the ways in which Claude McKay's bad nationalism registers a generative tension between his encounters

with imperial national forms in North Africa as well as to question the political efficacy of Black nationalist campaigns for a return back to Africa. These two opposing nationalist visions collide in McKay's fiction. The following discussion consequently has two main parts. It begins with a short overview of McKay's encounters
with the passport systems set up by the imperial regimes in Morocco and then analyzes how McKay's fiction activates the residual Garveyite energies marked by an
enthusiasm for a return to African origins. Critics repeatedly overlook the significance of McKay's experiences specific to the modernizing late-colonial context of
Morocco. Discussions have instead focused overwhelmingly on McKay's "magic pilgrimage" to Soviet Russia in the early twenties.[6] But what about colonial Africa?
How do his novels written in the late twenties correspond to his travels to Africa in
1928? How are we to situate Claude McKay's complicated relationship with the New
Negro movement for Black advancement without examining his encounters that
the administrative systems of colonial rule set up in Africa by imperial governments to extend their control by rendering both individual citizens and subjects of
empire "available for governance" to a higher degree than ever before?[7] Offering a
corrective, I argue that McKay's fictional cast of Black expats in his novels—bad
nationalists who move between seaports and skirt passport controls—repeatedly
bump up against competing expectations to align with modern movement controls
as well as the social pressures to share enthusiasm about a return back to African
origins. Particular attention is given to McKay's *Romance in Marseille* (ca. 1929–33;
2020), a stowaway novel deeply preoccupied with the intricacies of diasporic movement and the institutions of movement control—from the opening scene describing Lafala in the "immigrant hospital" on Ellis Island, where he learns from
fellow political refugees about Garveyite plans for New Negro uplift, to the concluding sequence of the West African sailor's heartbreaking solo journey back to
the continent from which he was snatched by European missionaries as a young
child.[8] This dialectical interplay between competing national forms—imperial
nationalism and Black nationalism—allowed McKay to test the limits associated
with constructions of inhabitants belonging to a specific place while exploring
the spaces between geographic points to sketch the radical possibility to move
between and beyond nationalist concerns as necessary to open a more common,
worldly place where the historical capacity for freedom is more effectively realized.

Contemporary critics have tended to read these currents of "vagabond internationalism" in McKay's life and works by paying attention to how migration served
as both a real and a figurative practice by which the Black writer sought to push back
against external forms of identity recognition.[9] By crossing borders, exposing the
gaps between nation-states, and pursuing international alliances for Black workers,
McKay demonstrated a desire to slide outside the forms of population control mon-
itored by imperial bureaucratic practices and ultimately to break up the monetary
pact of worldwide colonialism. Bridget Chalk notes that by voluntarily "claiming
he is American despite his official British status, McKay brazenly asserts that national
identity as a category cannot account for him because his transience exempts him
from loyalty to any one nation."[10] Examining McKay's preference to voluntarily
identify as an American constitutes a valuable insight precisely because this "play-

fully transgressive demarcation" subverts the tracking power of European bureaucratic authority in Africa, challenging "state imperatives of identity and mobility" and carving out alternative forms of belonging insofar as the gesture of his elective, opt-in or opt-out, flexible citizenship "refuses the sort of cohesive self-presentation required for colonial mobility in a setting marked by the incessant policing of identity."[11] In making these important observations about McKay's suspicions toward the procedures and protocols of colonial governmentality, however, Chalk elides a significant historical detail.

The colonial subject in question was not born in England or America. McKay was born in Jamaica as a subject of British colonial rule. This geographic qualification matters for understanding McKay's self-presentation as a bad nationalist for the simple reason that from the day he was born on the island of Jamaica, officially recorded on his birth papers as September 15, 1889,[12] he was bestowed with a kind of provisional national belonging contingent on the external governmental authority of the British Empire for documentation and authorization.

The closing pages of *Banjo* echo this modern demand for recognition. Taloufa lands at a port of entry only to discover that the British government has installed new entry criteria along with refined official documentation protocols used to categorize and screen Black migrants. The new British system of entry discriminates against nonwhites using an exclusionary logic of racial classifications. "This was the chief topic of serious talk among colored seamen in all the ports," McKay states. "Black and brown men being sent back" to their homelands after being denied entry.[13] *Banjo* is likely referring to the 1925 Coloured Alien Seamen Order. The law was thought to be promulgated by the National Union of Seamen, run by white bosses, and quickly passed by members of the British Parliament in 1925 to block foreign seamen from employment. The maritime legislation contained a special order for British coastal officers and consular officials to ensure that all undocumented Black seamen were registered as aliens. Thus it implicitly targeted Black sailors born in the colonial outposts of the British Empire. "Race discrimination originated and was encouraged at the highest levels of government," Laura Tabili explains, "in response to converging pressures from historical actors within and outside the state." As a result of the Coloured Alien Seamen Order, she adds, "the meaning of what it was to be 'coloured' or Black was reformulated in the process of state policy making," and "many Black British subjects [born abroad] were registered as aliens, impairing their ability to get work, and many were threatened with deportation."[14] In *Banjo* these Black sailors under threat of deportation "showed one another their papers," and comparing their identity documents led to an unsettling discovery: "The majority of their papers were distinguished by the official phrase: Nationally Doubtful" (*B*, 312). In this fictionalized treatment of modern immigration protocols, McKay even envisions a multitiered passport system. "Colored" seamen who "had lost their papers in low-down places to touts, hold-up men, and passport fabricators, and were unable or too ignorant to show exact proof of their birthplace, were furnished with new 'Nationally Doubtful' papers" (*B*, 312). Documents were stamped in government ink. But the designation itself is effectively a noncategory, a dubious marker reserved for stateless persons, indicative of the

rightless condition that Hannah Arendt famously theorized as the exilic predicament of "no-man's-land" for placeless persons without full membership and cast
adrift outside the regular national order.[15]

Banjo, of course, opens with a discussion of the consequences of improper
documentation. The character Ginger "had lost his seaman's papers. He had been
in prison for vagabondage and served with a writ of expulsion. But he had destroyed
the writ and swiped the papers of another seaman" (*B*, 5). The cultural sceneography
of "colored" sailors jostling with and betraying one another as they crossed constricted ports of entry falls into a literary pattern that Harris Feinsod classifies as
the interwar "genre of proletarian maritime novels written around the global portal
system." "Leftist publishers and worker book clubs" regularly featured these novels
about the "transoceanic social experiences" of economic migrants who bounced
between short-term jobs as longshoremen and sailors. The stories "detailed the rising tide of interferences endured by the homeless seafarers entangled in global cultural commerce, labor, and immigration."[16] Surveying the novels set in the interwar global port system, Feinsod draws specific attention to a devastatingly honest
remark by the American sailor Gerard Gales: "If you don't belong to a country in
these times, you had better jump in the sea."[17] The rootless predicament of statelessness emerges in lockstep with the precarious condition of rightlessness. Both are
defined by Arendt in *The Origins of Totalitarianism* (1951) as resulting from a lack
of political membership. Arendt tracks the emerging condition caused by the displacement of people in Europe, reserving the term *stateless* for two distinct but
interrelated groups of modern persons: to describe those refugees who formally
lost their nationality and also those unable to hold the paperwork necessary to benefit from citizenship rights. Ayten Gundogdu clarifies: "What brought together
these people, who otherwise held different kinds of juridical status," as "refugees,
asylum seekers, economic immigrants, even naturalized citizens who faced the
threat of denaturalization in times of emergency," was that they became deprived
of their legal personhood, along with their place in the world, "when they all were
ejected from 'the old trinity of state-people-territory,' and Arendt argued that this
exclusion left them in a condition of rightlessness."[18] Of course, for many modern
refugees, and especially for persons of color, the loss of official paperwork simply
codified in explicit terms what was already implicitly true about bureaucratic constructions of identity. A questionable standing and right to fully belong in the modern nation-state system meant that such persons must repeatedly prove their identity and trace back their national origins with a verifiable paper trail, and this
national purity test prioritized pure-blooded natural citizens, with lasting consequences for those of lesser race who fell through the cracks.

McKay's novel communicates the underlying, implicit understanding rendered by bureaucrats in invisible ink: "Colored subjects were not wanted in Britain"
(*B*, 311). Even "colored" subjects with proper documentation, like Jamaican-born
expatriates, were simply unwanted. The force behind McKay's bad nationalism is
therefore not merely, or not only, that his vagabond transnational migrations constituted a playful subversive gesture to evade, renounce, or challenge the ways
in which the bureaucratic structures of modern statehood tracked and policed

national identities. The corollary issue is that as a marginalized Black Jamaican subject of empire, he had always been categorized in public life as a bad nationalist—a *citizen not quite*—geographically marginalized, born outside England's territorial borders as a person of color from the West Indies, not yet a full-blooded British citizen, and never quite good enough to qualify for full citizenship.[19] McKay's Freudian slip thus exposed a contradictory civil status of belonging.

The antagonism of territorial natives against their migrant others cuts a number of ways, but attending to the specific, modernizing late-colonial context of Morocco requires a historical examination rooted in concerns about how the fortification of borders and movement controls helped ensure that new trade routes of capitalist exchange would not financially disadvantage ruling empires. McKay's article "North African Triangle," published in the *Nation*, looks at France's colonial extension into Africa. He observes that this territorial expansion triggered a fundamental conflict between two competing modes of material production. French "big business" began to increase its profit margins by buying and selling cheap goods produced in North Africa. But the danger was that these commodities produced abroad "using cheap native labor" threatened to outpace France's local production and destabilize its domestic labor force. Anxiety about the looming crisis of goods "undersold on the French market" was shared by all parties in the French parliament. "Governments rose and fell in Paris," McKay notes, "but all agreed that Frenchmen must be protected from the threat of cheap African importations." To safeguard the "French market" and the "French peasantry," he adds, "a cartel plan was set up for the French colonies, and North Africa was required to supply commodities to France on this quota system."[20] Trade quotas offered an effective way for the French protectorate to monitor and limit the export of Moroccan commodities like wheat.[21] A second, related measure was also implemented. To further harden national borders, economic regulations on the movement of goods were coupled with significant rules and restrictions on the movement of peoples between territories.

McKay questioned the pervasive structures of imperial governance responsible for the tightening up of political space. He was not alone in expressing his discomfort with the nationalization of state sovereignty and the restriction of mobility between territories. Jesper Gulddal's recent investigation into the history of the modern passport has uncovered the following pattern as it played out in the interwar period:

> The outbreak of the First World War triggered a wholesale reintroduction of
> passport requirements as a means of protecting the integrity of national
> borders. These efforts to control mobility were originally touted as temporary
> measures to remain in place only for the duration of the war. In reality,
> movement control had come to stay. This was partly due to issues directly
> associated with the end of the war, such as the perceived need to protect
> domestic labor markets.[22]

McKay advances this line of historical investigation beyond the special situation of the Great War, noting that after the Armistice a new paper war of passports and entry visas was conducted for the purposes of invading, occupying, and dividing all remaining territories in the late-colonial scramble for Africa. He pays particular attention to the rise of modern border control as a highly capable instrument used by imperial administrators to suppress anticolonial freedom struggles. "The French Republic," McKay observes, "decided that it could not permit the existence of an independent native state contiguous to its Moroccan protectorate." Once movement restrictions were set up, McKay writes, "conditions became worse for the natives. Instead of more freedom of movement" to self-organize and develop radical networks of affiliation, "passport regulations became more stringent. Things tightened up . . . it was no longer the clearing house for nationalist thought."[23] Asymmetrical power relations implemented by the French protectorate hampered the possibility for North Africa to act as a dwelling place where certain forms of state-mandated identity, such as native and foreigner, or race and nation, might give way to what Nandita Sharma has termed "a livelihood *without exclusion*."[24]

No less significant for historically reconstructing decisive events in the life of a writer affiliated with the New Negro cultural movement is the evidence confirming that Claude McKay had traveled to Africa in hopes of finding his own transformational experience. Before his unpleasant detainment by colonial representatives, Africa seems to have offered him sanctuary, if only for a fleeting moment. When McKay first set foot on African soil, his arrival felt nothing short of a homecoming. In his memoir chapter "When a Negro Goes Native," McKay remarked that his visit to Africa finally placed him "among kindred spirits" (*LW*, 300). "For the first time in my life," he exclaimed, "I felt myself singularly free of color-consciousness" (*LW*, 300). His racial burden as a colonized subject of empire had apparently lifted—if only temporarily. McKay's memoir dramatizes the cosmopolitan scene in North Africa as a diverse cultural patchwork. He was intoxicated by the spice markets, ancient craftworks, sunbaked city walls, and bright mosaics. Morocco was a fusion of Arabs, Blacks, and many shades between. But how do we square McKay's brief but emphatic firsthand account of his newfound African sanctuary with his prior denouncements of Black nationalists who called for a return to Africa? There are some clues to be found in his plans for the journey.

Textual evidence confirms that McKay's plans to visit the continent were deeply informed by his interactions with the roving African sailors and dockworkers he met in the south of France. McKay was a regular at a Senegalese bar located on the bustling quayside of Marseille. The bar owner, whose "social outlook" was "African Nationalist," routinely introduced McKay to his fellow "countrymen" (*LW*, 278). McKay drew on this social network to figure out "the ways and means of a holiday somewhere in Africa" to see the continent firsthand (*LW*, 295). He openly discussed his travel intentions with fellow regulars. When a Senegalese bar patron suggested instead taking a holiday in Paris, "where one can amuse oneself," gamble, drink, fornicate, and carouse until money runs out, McKay rejected the hollowness of this travel suggestion. "I didn't feel attracted to Paris," he recalled, "but to Africa." Another bar patron piped up to deliver more instructive advice: "A Martinique sailor, whose boat had just arrived from Casablanca, said that Africa was alright and that Morocco was the best place. He said he had visited every big port in

Africa, and he preferred Morocco. He lived there. He said, 'If you're going to Africa, come to Morocco'" (*LW*, 295). Following a long stopover in Barcelona, McKay eventually made it to Morocco. His old "Martiniquan Moroccan" acquaintance soon introduced him to the members of the Gueanoua, "the only group of pure Negroes in Morocco. Men and women marry black, and it is the only religious order that has women members. If one is not a pure black he cannot belong to the Gueanoua. They say that the strict keeping of this rule makes the Gueanoua magic powerful. The fetish rites are West African and are transmitted from generation to generation" (*LW*, 297). McKay learned that the Gueanoua people "have a special place in the social life of Morocco" (*LW*, 297). But his curiosities to visit other sights and to experience new rhythms quickly outweighed any convictions he may have carried for an immediate return to "pure black" origins. He also expressed some confusion that the rituals practiced by the Black population in Casablanca bore an uncanny resemblance to the folk religion of myalism, a belief system associated with African ancestry and practiced in his Caribbean place of birth. "The first shock I registered," he wrote, "was the realization that they looked exactly like certain peasants of Jamaica. . . . The only difference was in their clothing" (*LW*, 296–97). The question of home, of course, was a complex subject for McKay, and he soon drifted onward.[25] His decision to leave happened after he learned more about the hospitality extended by his "Martiniquan Moroccan" host. The Black sailor did in fact speak fluent "Arab and Senegalese," which impressed McKay, as did the extravagant lifestyle, but he was soon disappointed to discover that the Black sailor was asserting his national identity as a French citizen in the colonial territory in order to earn "between forty and fifty francs a day—about six times what the native doing the same work got. Thus the black sailor was really living 'white' in Africa" (*LW*, 298).

Dissatisfied and restless, McKay soon left Casablanca to travel farther and deeper into North Africa. A group of local students told him to visit Fez, where "you will find the heart of Morocco."[26] As soon as he arrived, McKay recalled, "I went completely native" (*LW*, 299). His days were "occupied sampling the treasures of the city and its environment." But his growing connections also felt like he was falling under the spell of an irresistible intoxication.[27] "The mosaics of Morocco went to my head like a red wine," McKay confessed (*LW*, 299). Authentic or not, his explorations were cut short by the altercation with the government officials. In a letter McKay admitted, "I did not want to leave if it were not that the French are masters there. . . . I dislike them because they are the most nationalistic people in the world, and they are never tired of saying that they are the nation destined to keep the torch of civilization burning."[28]

The fact that this scene of national interpellation arose on the streets of continental Africa further troubles our critical ability to read it. Hadn't McKay traveled to Africa to escape these kinds of fixed essential categories set up and policed by the rival imperial powers in the great worldwide competition to stake out territories, set up borders, and to tightly control national boundaries between population groups? To be sure, some present-day researchers might direct us toward the substantial mass of evidence verifying that by the time McKay arrived in North Africa in 1928 the oppressive exercise of civil conquest was well under way.[29] No wonder McKay voices his saddened disappointment and displeasure that in Africa "I suddenly found myself right up against European intervention and prescription" (*LW*, 299). It seemed the dream was dead long before his arrival.

McKay evaded immediate deportation, but his ensuing novel, *Romance in Marseille*, was deeply informed by the accusation that he was a working spy. Signaling a formal departure from *Banjo: A Story without a Plot*, his subsequent novel spins together the narrative threads of multiple plots of deception for his dedicated readers to untangle. What holds all these plot machinations and conspiracies together is their narrative proximity to the main character, Lafala, a West African sailor who circulated nomadically between geographic locales on both sides of the Atlantic. The stock emblem of the spy as a *bad nationalist*, engaged in surreptitious acts of treason against the modern state, is transposed into the figure of the stowaway in the conspiratorial world of McKay's late work of expatriate fiction.

The stowaway—a transatlantic mole who embarks on an illegal crossing without payment and hopes to remain undetected—mobilizes, energizes, and exposes the link between criminality and immigration. Typically, the thrill of the stowaway saga is a function of their anonymity. The stowaway must skillfully avoid detection before the ship shoves off. Once under sail, the adventure novel turns to the subject of the nautical expedition. But the racialized undertones in McKay's novel demonstrate the risks involved for Black stowaways who cannot easily "pass" for affluent white passengers on the steam liner. Hence the pressures to avoid detection for the Black stowaway extend between the points of departure and arrival. Black criminality is here linked with access to free mobility. Of course, there are also general commonalities more universal to the stowaway genre. Outwitting and outmaneuvering the modern fixation with identity documentation, and operating on the high seas beyond the state powers of detection, the stowaway embarks on secret journeys, prioritizing personal rites of passage over the rights of modern citizens to cross territorial borders through legal ports of entry. Equally important, the stowaway, who refuses to pay for a ticket and rides for free, circumvents the global pact between modern commerce and modern nation-states in the capitalist world-system. The stowaway narrative draws attention to the fact that borders are not simply, or not only, upheld by the political power of nation-states alone. Transatlantic shipping corporations must turn a profit. These large-scale commercial ventures require immense amounts of financial capital to build and maintain transportation infrastructure across clearly defined and carefully controlled seaways. In a bid to stake out, protect, and expand their economic power over the world's seaways, companies running a commercial fleet of ocean liners hire security guards, erect fences, and enact a myriad of other regulative measures for the transport of persons across shipping corridors in exchange for ticket payment. These are the kinds of narrative stakes that play out when the stowaway illegally boards a ship for free.

The originality of McKay's novel is attributable to how its narrative sequence radically reinvents the stowaway genre. Rather than presenting a straightforward linear sequence typical of the stowaway craze in the 1920s, McKay's novel does not follow the typical narrative arc from illegal boarding to eventual arrival at the port of destination, documenting in between the evasive maneuvers made during the crossing. What the novel presents readers with instead is a delayed narrative chronology that tracks the long aftermath of an illegal sea voyage that went sour. McKay's novel opens with the protagonist Lafala marooned in a hospital ward on dry land recounting his botched stowaway attempt. It charts the long historical arc of repercussions after this stowaway was caught and paid the price for his free passage with the loss of his main tool of locomotion—his legs—typically used by the clandestine traveler to secretly board the ships and to move about the vessel's compartments undetected. A cast of characters engage in actions and conspiracies as necessary to assert their power over the original historical event of Lafala's illegal stowaway journey. Holcomb further points out:

> *Romance in Marseille* not only consists of several parallel running plot lines but is, as well, copious with plotting in the locutions of collateral through related meaning: scheming, calumny, betrayal, rumor peddling, threats against security, intelligence gathering, attempts at blackmail, character assassination—in summary, the stock inventory of espionage conduct. Characters undertake cabals, intrigues, and machinations against one another in order to procure some mastery over their corner of the sexual commerce of the Marseilles waterfront slum. Every structure of the narrative reinforces this notion. The composition of the story drifts to and fro, like the greasy quayside breakers, between characters plotting conspiracies and voices interacting in dialectical materialist dialogues. In other words, *Romance in Marseille*'s modulation iteratively shifts between the politically hazardous environment of conspiracy and intelligence collection and the conceptual, conditional, rationally disposed world.[30]

McKay's transatlantic novel sets memorable supporting actors on conspiratorial collision courses with one another. In one particularly high-stakes narrative conflict, a greedy American personal-injury lawyer conspires against his own amputee client in a scheme to pocket the majority of a lump-sum financial settlement won through negotiations with the bosses of the negligent shipping company on the hook for liable damages. On the other side of the pond, French police officials engage in a suspenseful cat-and-mouse game as they search the Quayside docks for elusive and cunning undocumented immigrants referred to in French parlance as *sans-papiers*. These regimented patrols formed a crucial part of the French national government's intensifying efforts in the 1920s to fortify its own borders against foreigners, spies, expats, exiles, and refugees—in sum, bad nationalists seeking illegal refuge. Equally important, too, this intensified, xenophobic crackdown on and detainment of undocumented Black migrant workers was understood by many natural-born French citizens to be warranted retribution for illegal border crossers. The rejection of immigrants presented a magical solution to job shortage crisis after the war. The "us versus them" message reached frenzied levels. An unintended consequence of the rise of xenophobic discourse, however, was its blurring of the line of demarcation between citizen and state. Messages were disseminated by French workers and bureaucratic administrators alike as they entered into a closed feed-back loop designed to shut out foreigners and, consequently, to authorize the press-ing need for the government to extend the reach of its own national authority into the untidy corners of everyday life to impose order. The gradual deployment of these techniques also had a notable impact on the relationships between foreign dock-workers, often dividing them. Work became scarce, and money was in short supply. McKay's disabled male protagonist comes to recognize and express sorrowful regret over the increasingly instrumentalized quality of his interactions with his old com-rades on the docks. In part, the origins of such observations stem back to the finan-cial reward he was allotted effectively in exchange for the amputation of his legs. As McKay phrases it, "There was fortune in Lafala's misfortune" (*RM*, 17). Rival Black newspapers announced his winnings in more spectacular terms:

> The *Bellows of the Belt* shouted:
> AFRICAN DAMAGED FIFTY THOUSAND DOLLARS
> But it was outdone by the *United Negro* which ran:
> AFRICAN LEGS BRING ONE HUNDRED THOUSAND DOLLARS
> The African had conquered Aframerica with a whoop. (*RM*, 19)

The second news headline, a parody of Marcus Garvey's *Negro World* weekly news-paper, estimated the value of the settlement to be double the amount first reported by the Black-owned Harlem gossip leaflet. Printing inflated numbers was, of course, a common practice used in the propaganda campaign mounted by the Universal Negro Improvement Association (UNIA) to unite some "400,000,000 Negroes of the world."[31] This population statistic was hardly verifiable, but sensational presen-tations like these drew widespread attention and followers to Garvey's Back-to-Africa campaign. Both news reports were accurate to suggest that Lafala won a legal settlement. Funds had been awarded from the transatlantic shipping com-pany for the injuries sustained after an officer of the ship found Lafala stowed away on board and promptly locked the illegal passenger in a cold latrine for the duration of the transatlantic sea journey.

Lafala would never dance again, but, ironically, he also made a fortune from the unfortunate circumstances that cost him his legs. Early on in the text he excit-edly observes: "It was the first sign of hope for the future that he had seen. He had never before thought of gaining something from such a loss, never dreamed there was the slightest chance" (*RM*, 9). His rags-to-riches story, as a genre marked by personal upward mobility in the capitalist economic system, is replete with obliga-tory scenes in which Lafala's newfound financial wealth has been accompanied with a rise in social capital among the Quaysiders. But this upswing in his social stand-ing also triggers the unexpected feeling of not fully belonging among the common ranks of the undocumented Black migrant workers—bad nationalists—on the docks. The story makes clear that others aren't so lucky. His close friend, Babel, is forced to concede that "Lafala should have a new standard of life according to his means. The vagabond life was all right for a man without property or position, but responsibility and vagabondage could not go together" (*RM*, 109). Chronicling how class differences become quickly naturalized, or at least accepted as inescapable social facts, even among the Black seafarers on the docks, the novel demonstrates that any wealth gained from the personal liability suit sets Lafala's responsibilities apart from the other disenfranchised members of the population still down on their luck. Babel even argues that his friend's personal duties and social responsibilities now lie beyond the dockyards: "Lafala had offered him some money but he had refused it, saying that however much Lafala had, he would not accept any, because Lafala's legs were amputated and all his funds were necessary to him" (*RM*, 109–10). Such lines demonstrate Babel's unwavering loyalty to his old friend as much as they announce the diminished possibilities for the recently disabled Black mariner to attain viable employment as a double amputee in the modern industrial economy. Widespread discrimination based on disability has suppressed and concealed the social duty for modern employers to make accommodations in the workplace. Additionally, not every individual in the story remains as loyal a friend as Babel.

Lafala is troubled by the suspicion that a few of his old comrades are scheming for a piece of the pie. He is talked about more often, even in his absence, and his reputation now precedes him. After he wins a settlement case in America, the novel details the swirling rumors, many of them false, that greet Lafala on his arrival back to the French dockside:

> The freedom of Quayside was practically granted to Lafala on his return. As a onetime habitué it was a big event for him to come back to the old haunt with the status of a personage. There was all sorts of wild talk about him. Some said he was officially protected and had been granted a large tract of land somewhere in the deep bush of Africa. Others said he was going to acquire real estate in Marseille. (*RM*, 31)

Wild speculations about Lafala's financial reward precipitated a dramatic change in his social position among his old comrades. He left the docks down on his luck and returns to Marseille surprised to find that the Quaysiders have taken a keen interest in the litigative jackpot he won after his stowaway attempt went south.

Even his former lover, Aslima, the Moroccan courtesan whom Lafala admits once betrayed him when she "robbed him and escaped him" (*RM*, 42), shows a renewed romantic interest in the now disabled and wealthy sailor on his return to France. Lafala cannot discern whether Aslima's love for him is true and sincere or whether her actions are secretly motivated by a cunning scheme to gain access to his wealth and double-cross him a second time. Contrasting scenes in the novel come to reveal that Aslima's loyalties remain starkly divided between her tender affections for Lafala and that of her controlling pimp, Titin, a menacing brute who in private conversations influences, controls, and berates the Moroccan woman born into sexual servitude. This unusual love triangle is further complicated by Titin's unmistakable attempts to use Aslima's powers of attraction as romantic leverage to swindle the Black amputee, whom he shamelessly mocks with derogatory nicknames. Titin tells Aslima to rekindle her relationship "with Pied-Coupé. Give me that money" (*RM*, 47). But succeeding in the act of theft also involves playing the long game.

"Lafala had very little money in his possession," Aslima reports to Titin midway through the novel. "He received money only from the official agent who was looking after his affairs. And she was waiting too and working herself into his confidence" (*RM*, 47). Although she tells Titin that "she has to be very clever and sincere-like because of the first trick she had turned on Lafala," these sinister confessions are juxtaposed with scenes where Aslima remains clearly conflicted about which side she wants to permanently join. For his part, Lafala actively launches a multifaceted campaign of influence—part passion, part reason—to try to win both Aslima's heart and her mind with confidence. He asks her to end the love-hate standoff once and for all: "Why don't you quit Titin and come with me?" She responds, "Where? Quit Titin to go where?" Lafala immediately suggests, "Back to Africa with me for a change. Wouldn't you like to go back?" (*RM*, 42). At first, the two laugh off the idea of accompanying each other back to their African homeland. But the mention of Africa does provide an important clue to how the novel will end. References to the continent foreshadow the concluding sequence when the disabled West African sailor makes his own escape back to his homeland. This revelation is announced in the closing pages: "Lafala had secretly sailed away from Aslima and Quayside." His quiet departure ensures that he is "gone with all the money and the great deep sea between them" (*RM*, 127–29).

A key piece of the puzzle that McKay leaves for readers to fit into place is that Lafala sided with a white official responsible for dispensing his money, and by doing so he knowingly betrayed a fellow African on the docks. Some observers might argue, of course, that the heartbroken West African sailor was simply repaying the unkind gesture made by Aslima when she crossed him ages ago and left him for broke. No doubt the score was now settled. Her bloody death at the hands of the greedy pimp Titin happens in the wake of Lafala's unexpected departure. But reading the novel as a straightforward revenge plot cannot account for the compromised state of affairs in which Lafala finds himself before leaving Marseille. In fact, Lafala had seriously contemplated bringing Aslima with him in tow. His friends Babel and St. Dominique swiftly took turns trying "to talk Lafala out of the crazy idea" of her accompanying him back to Africa (*RM*, 127). "Impossible!" Falope interrupted. "How could you think of taking a girl like Aslima back to Africa now?" (*RM*, 113). But the novel also testifies to the more pragmatic consideration that the official would grant Lafala's safe passage back to his home port in West Africa only if he left his intimate affairs behind. For as quiet as it is kept, this final migration is hardly determined by chance. When pressed on the question as to why Lafala did not simply bypass Marseille altogether and go straight back to Africa, Lafala confesses: "I had no choice. I was sent back here" (*RM*, 105). His pay dirt came with unexpected strings attached. More to the point, he reluctantly consented to the bitter betrayal of a member of his own race for a free passage home, however much this choice also ironically signaled his own compromised agency.

There appears to be historical parallels here with McKay's own feelings of betrayal at the hands of the Moroccan messenger who reported him to the consulate—a fellow African whom McKay had mistakenly assumed would put color before national duty. The expatriate novelist fills out this episode in his memoir by noting that he had mistakenly assumed that the native African man living under the threat of boundless Euro-imperial expansion would share his suspicions about the pressures of conforming to national protocols used to extend the outward reach of empire into new territories. In Africa, McKay writes with surprise, "I suddenly found myself right up against European intervention and prescription" (*LW*, 300). The social-political dynamic at stake here is that Africa could not persist as a mental sanctuary or abstract refuge free from the wreckage of imperial damages. Bureaucratic control had taken over the continent. Moreover, McKay's character Lafala was a *bad African nationalist* for taking his solo Garveyite journey back to Africa, because this was an individual financial consideration, not a collective endeavor for the advancement of the Black community. It is an elegant paradox that McKay has crafted. Lafala's yearnings for international race affiliation and solidarity between members of the Black diaspora were left abandoned with the workers on the Quayside docks when he boarded the ship home to Africa. The novel comes full circle at the end with the permanently wounded Lafala now inflicting an injury on others. Recall that the opening scene in the "immigrant hospital" features a nostalgic requiem for Lafala's "dancing legs" now amputated. Of course, other kinds of detachment are dramatized at the hospital. We learn: "As a kid boy, the missionaries brought him from the bush to town where they livened and taught. His legs were put in pants and soon, soon he learned among other things the delight of legs. . . . Dancing on toes, dancing on the heels, dancing flat-footed. Lafala's dancing legs had carried him from Africa to Europe, from Europe to America" (*RM*, 3–4). He was first severed from his homeland by missionaries and taken to Europe. After that he kept on walking. His diasporic wanderings on ships between ports soon felt as natural as walking on solid ground. The motif of the immigrant hospital further resonates because it functions as a reminder of the place where "Lafala first heard the other Negroes discussing the Back-to-Africa news and wondering what would become of it." Indeed, Lafala listened to the "universal excitement" of Black advancement "and was stirred too. Return. . . . Return. . . . Turn away from strange scenes and false gods to find salvation in native things" (*RM*, 4–5). The reference to native things bears a striking resemblance to McKay's memoir chapter "When a Negro Goes Native" discussed above.

No less significant for historically reconstructing the decisive events in the life of a writer affiliated with the New Negro cultural movement is that in September 1928, the same month that McKay boarded the ship to Morocco, Marcus Garvey, president-general of the UNIA and bombastic voice behind the Back-to-Africa movement, wrote a scathing editorial review of McKay's first novel *Home to Harlem*. Although the novel had found early commercial success, Garvey scolded his fellow Jamaican expatriate in the *Negro World* newspaper. "The book of Claude McKay's is a damnable libel against the Negro," Garvey announced.[32] Several features of the novel prompted this reading. Hard-fought efforts by members of the New Negro movement to engage in Pan-African liberation projects were transformed in the novel into liberatory acts as trivial as walking into a loud and bouncy Harlem nightclub. Garvey also voiced his displeasure that the common story of a poor Black migrant worker had been turned into a salable commodity for white booksellers. Garvey evidently saw unmistakable biographical parallels between *Home to Harlem* and "Claude McKay, the Jamaican Negro" whose own life experiences working dangerous longshoreman jobs overseas for low pay now lined the pages of his first novel. "White publishers use these Negroes," the Black leader observed, "to write the kind of stuff that they desire to feed the public with so that the Negro can still be regarded as a monkey, some imbecilic creature." No less candid was Garvey's general overview of the current state of New Negro writing in 1928:

> Fellowmen of the Negro Race, Greeting:
>
> It is my duty to bring to your attention this week a grave evil that afflicts us as a people at this time. Our race, within recent years, has developed a new group of writers who have been prostituting their intelligence, under the direction of the white man, to bring out and show up those worse traits of our people. Several of these writers are American and West Indian Negroes. They have been writing books, novels and poems, under the advice of white publishers, to portray to the world the looseness, laxity and immorality that are peculiar to our group, for the purpose of these publishers circulating the libel against us among the white peoples of the world, to further hold us up to ridicule and contempt and universal prejudice.[33]

It remains an odd oversight in McKay scholarship that an extensive book review personally written by the leader of the Back-to-Africa movement is so routinely overlooked by critics.

Of course, Garvey was hardly alone in admonishing Black writers for publishing what he deemed poorly conceived literary works. Critical discussions have instead focused on Garvey's rival political opponent, the NAACP leader W. E. B. Du Bois, who famously made the incendiary remark that McKay's best-selling novel "nauseates me, and after the dirtiest parts of its filth I feel distinctly like taking a bath."[34] Garvey probably read Du Bois's review before writing his own critical appraisal a few months later. In typical Garvey fashion, he did not miss the opportunity to take a combative jab at his rival "W. E. B. Du Bois, of America," leader of the elitist Black intelligentsia in the country, before noting that "Walter White, [James] Weldon Johnson, Eric Walron[d] of British Guiana, and others, have written similar books, while we have had recently a large number of sappy poems from the rising poets."[35] Rather than further addressing the pitfalls and failures of the wider New Negro cultural renaissance, however, Garvey aims the main critical force of his review at his fellow Jamaican Claude McKay.

A notable difference between these two reviews by rival Black leaders is that Du Bois was particularly concerned with *Home to Harlem*'s inability to stray away from popular caricatures of working-class Black life. McKay's novel, Du Bois charges, had "projected its own fantasies of 'utter licentiousness' onto 'black Harlem.'"[36] McKay's gritty portrayal of lower-class Harlem, capital of the Black world, featured a cast of transient railway cooks, dishwashers, porters, and servers who frequent nightspots and cabarets. In presenting these gritty, unhygienic depictions of Black life, McKay had strayed from upholding the moral standard of the Black writer as a ranking member of the *talented tenth*, tasked with an important cultural role to provide guideposts through aspirational portrayals of the folk spirit, required to lift up the Black population and ultimately to rise above social disenfranchisement.

But where Du Bois criticized the novel's "utter licentiousness," Garvey focused on what he deemed its libelous contents. Garvey was hardly unfamiliar with the term *libel* and its inferences in the legal rhetoric of damages and financial compensation for defamation. Only a few years earlier, the UNIA leader himself was sued for libel, convicted by a US federal judge in the Southern District of New York, and sentenced to prison after the Black Star Line Steamship Corporation became financially insolvent. Garvey was embittered when his plan to realize his Back-to-Africa scheme had been targeted by the Federal Bureau of Investigation. The book review, written from his jail cell, lashed back at "libellers against the black race," particularly those who got in the way of his Pan-African vision to unite and emancipate Blacks scattered across the world.

For McKay, this review penned by a fellow Jamaican expat marked a serious betrayal of trust. He had, in fact, previously written and published his own *Negro World* articles, and he had mailed several letters to Garvey between 1919 and 1920.[37] These letters exhibit McKay's clear attempts to influence and steer Garvey's populist Black movement toward the communist cause of a worker revolution. McKay obviously understood that Garveyism was antithetical to communism, despite its anticolonial aspect, but the immense popularity of the New Negro movement quickly became too large to sidestep. Garvey in April 1919 announced his plans to launch the capitalist Black Star Line venture, which gained steam even as McKay pleaded with his fellow Jamaican to change course and direct the Black-owned companies toward communism. When these attempts failed, McKay took great pleasure in publishing an article in the *Liberator* extolling Garvey's arrest by federal authorities, calling it a "fitting climax" for the "universal advertising manager" after "five years of stupendous vaudeville."[38] McKay added that the "most puzzling thing about the 'Back to Africa' propaganda is the leader's repudiation of all the fundamentals of the black worker's economic struggle."[39] It is not without a certain amount of irony, then, that McKay's own protagonist in *Romance in Marseille* would travel back to Africa with a fat bank account and leave his fellow Black workers behind on the docks. Revenge or not, McKay exposed a hollowed-out Garveyite vision of Black redemption and questioned its moral pitfalls. More immediately clear is that McKay was livid after reading the reviews of his first novel. His rebuttal reads as follows: "If my brethren had taken the trouble to look a little into my obscure life they would have discovered that years before I had recaptured the spirit of Jamaican peasants in verse, rendering their primitive joys, their loves and hates, their work and play, their dialect. And what I did in prose for Harlem was very similar to what I have done for Jamaica in verse."[40] McKay resented the supposedly thoughtful "colored elite," which had not taken his long career seriously enough. These complaints about McKay's unjust critical reception as a novelist were mostly directed at the Black bourgeois intelligentsia, probably Du Bois in particular. He reserved a different treatment for the populist leader Garvey.

Indeed, McKay held a dialectical view of Black mass movement led by his fellow Jamaican. In the *Liberator* McKay observed that "coming to New York in 1917, Garvey struck the black belt like a cyclone, and there lay the foundation of the Universal Negro Improvement Association and the Black Star Line."[41] But the immense power of the populist vision was limited by the poorly conceived dialectical terms of its construction. McKay added, "It is rather strange that Garvey's political ideas should be so curiously bourgeois-obsolete and fantastically utopian," considering that "Garvey's background is very industrial."[42] Garvey first represented Black workers as a union leader in Jamaica during an industrial printer's strike. McKay wondered why a Black leader calling for revolutionary change would champion the very capitalist vision that was responsible for the exploitation and disenfranchisement of Black workers.

It was not by chance that McKay's stowaway protagonist owned shares in Garvey's Black Star Line business venture. In *Banjo* the Quaysiders learn that the West African sailor "bought a hundred dollars of Black Star Line shares" (*B*, 91). He held twenty shares of stock in the Negro shipping line, sold at five dollars each. But his dream of becoming part owner of a Negro ship made Lafala a frequent target of ridicule. Banjo, in particular, cannot help but cynically call out "the Marcus Garvey Back-to-Africa movement," even ridiculing the West African sailor for purchasing those shares: "And what does he think now that they got the fat block a that black swindler in the jail-house?" (*B*, 76, 91). But not everyone in the bar idly listened to Banjo make libelous claims about the Black leader. "'Garvey was good for all Negroes,' the barkeep turned upon Banjo—'Negroes in America and in Europe and in Africa'" (*B*, 77). The Garveyite vision later resurfaces in *Romance in Marseille*. Here the Black stowaway Lafala is further educated on the unrealizable potential of Black-owned ships to connect members of the African diaspora with their own commercial shipping routes and to set up a new society in Africa. The Black communist St. Dominique, who effectively functions in the novel as McKay's alter ego, draws a definitive conclusion on the catastrophic fate of the Garveyite vision to unite the Black population. In doing so, he communicates a distinction between the Black emigration movement and the need for all the workers of the world to unite, workers of every color, who must stay where they are to fight for global change by securing local victories:

> The Back-to-Africa movement is different. It began like a religious revival and
> is dying out the same way. Because it wasn't founded on the facts and the needs
> of our time. It was a race movement. But we can't go back to Africa. *You* can as
> an individual. But we can't as a people. Our movement is a bigger thing. Each
> group of workers must stay where it is but all fight the battle of class struggle
> for the new society. (*RM*, 77)

The dream to create a new society by returning to Africa was founded on an anachronistic vision to the extent that Garvey envisioned the continent as a tabula rasa untainted by the twin modern forces of colonial expansion and capitalist modernity.

Garvey was correct, however, that publishers were wary of Black authors who took seriously the role of literature as a social document capable of exposing the ugly and unsettling contradictions causing the disenfranchisement of large swaths of the population. We know this because McKay found no publisher for *Romance in Marseille* during his lifetime. Garvey adds, "Mr. Claude McKay has had a career highly colored with the romance that belongs to all wanderers."[43] But the romance of the Black wanderer—the vagabond internationalism—that McKay provides in his expatriate novel eventually ends with the tragic, forced return of the West African deportee back to his African homeland. Symbolically, it might be argued that Lafala effectively won back payments for having been displaced by colonial missionaries as a young boy and transported off the continent against his will. This primal scene in the personal history of his own colonization unleashed a chain of unfortunate events in Lafala's life leading up to his failed stowaway adventure. Reparations for the transatlantic shipping damages were undoubtably awarded to a rightful person. The act of litigative justice itself counts as a success consistent with the tenets of liberal individualism, for it reopened the promise of a future horizon. But such promises could just as easily force the realization that there was no longer a recognizable home or community back in Africa for Lafala to return to. The circumstances also draw into question why the same luxury of a return journey was not granted to Aslima, murdered in Marseille. Not only that, but Lafala's payout from the shipping company did not fully grant him the privilege of global mobility free of a fear of impunity; rather, his forced repatriation back to Africa came with strings attached. He muses, "I am one independent cuss," only to follow in an evasive tone, "The money is alright" (*RM*, 52–53). These disclosures draw attention to the constant worry of securing his personal fortune from loss, but they also reflect the duty or burden to protect other bad nationalists in Africa from the money's divisive, magical, intoxicating power.

⋯⋯⋯

RICH COLE teaches literature and writing at Alberta University of the Arts.

Notes

1   McKay, *A Long Way from Home*, 300 (hereafter cited as *LW*).
2   Sharma, *Home Rule*, 88.
3   Getachew, *Worldmaking after Empire*, 86.
4   Holcomb, *Claude McKay, Code Name Sasha*, 150.
5   Cooper, *Claude McKay*, 252.
6   For the origins of McKay's phrase, see Lang, "Claude McKay."
7   See Gulddal, "*Das Totenschiff*," 296.
8   McKay, *Romance in Marseille*, 5 (hereafter cited as *RM*).
9   Brent Hayes Edwards has developed a sophisticated reading of McKay's "vagabond internationalism": a critical framework used to examine the author's recurrent use of the word *vagabond* as it "must be understood not as what Ray," McKay's alter ego in *Banjo*, "dismisses as 'mere unexcited drifting, a purposeless live for the moment, negative' mode of existence . . . but instead the vibrant resistance of the black boys to the forces that would contain them." This remains a useful distinction, because the prioritization of necessary transits, diasporic movements, and crossings over wistful wanderlust calls attention to the pressures of identity control that, left otherwise unresisted, will hold in place the new restrictions on mobility accompanying the drawing of new national lines in Europe in the wake of World War I. The term *bad nationalist*, however, never

appears in Edwards's theorization of Black internationalism, nor is McKay's back-to-Africa journey discussed. See Edwards, *The Practice of Diaspora*, 206. For supplemental appraisals, see Vadde, "Stories without Plots"; and Nickels, "Claude McKay and Dissident Internationalism."

10   Chalk, "Sensible of Being *Étrangers*," 361.

11   Chalk, "Sensible of Being *Étrangers*," 361, 367, 361.

12   This is the date recorded on the original birth certificate held by the Island Record Office. Locating this record has resolved a controversy among McKay scholars, who for years struggled to determine McKay's "true" birthday. For a good summary of this controversy and a facsimile of McKay's birth record, see "Appendix" in James, *A Fierce Hatred of Injustice*, 152–61.

13   McKay, *Banjo*, 311 (hereafter cited as *B*).

14   Tabili adds that many historians "tend to overestimate the union's role in policy formation," and her article instead argues that the abuse associated with race discrimination was "neither a spontaneous outbreak of popular racism nor merely localized abuse of power by provincial police and officials" ("The Construction of Race Difference," 57).

15   Arendt, "Guests from No-Man's-Land," 211.

16   See Feinsod, "Death Ships," n.p.

17   Quoted in Feinsod, "Death Ships," n.p.

18   Gundogdu, *Rightlessness in an Age of Rights*, 2.

19   For a good examination of the Black experience of being treated as a foreigner in one's home country and covertly excluded as a *citizen-not-quite*, see Waligora-Davis, *Sanctuary*.

20   McKay, "North African Triangle," in *The Passion*, 291.

21   Many historians will substantiate McKay's claim here. See, e.g., Swearingen, "In Pursuit of the Granary of Rome."

22   Gulddal, "*Das Totenschiff*," 296.

23   McKay, "North African Triangle," 286.

24   Sharma's critique of the myth of nationalism concludes with the demand that all peoples cast aside the differences between natives and migrants to create a common ground by "seeking neither territory nor sovereignty but *land* and the ability to enjoy a livelihood on it *without exclusion*" (*Home Rule*, 286).

25   After his vacation McKay eventually returned to Morocco and made his home in Tangier from 1930 to 1934. He announced the move in a letter to Max Eastman: "I quit France in December for Morocco." North Africa was not perfect, but McKay confided that it offered the most satisfactory place to write: "I need to settle down and no place has satisfied me since I left home as much as Morocco." By 1933, however, his publishing royalties had dried up, and he felt trapped. He expressed his desire to leave North Africa for good (quoted in Bishop, "Claude McKay's Songs of Morocco").

26   "It is our capital city," they added. "You haven't seen Morocco until you see Fez" (*LW*, 298).

27   McKay wrote several poems named for Moroccan cities, among them "Fez." His memoir also includes a poem published as "A Farewell to Morocco," with the lines: "How strangely I was brought beneath your spell! / But willingly / A captive I / Remained to be." Maxwell observes that "McKay introduces the poem with a dose of appreciative Orientalism" (endnote in McKay, *Collected Poems*, 362–64). McKay admits that the "maze of *souks* and bazaars with unfamiliar patterns of wares was like an oriental fantasy" (*LW*, 298).

28   McKay, *The Passion*, 148.

29   Moroccan territory was being shepherded through the requisite prenatal phases of economic development, but only to the extent that its entrance into the modern capitalist world-system would remain structurally dependent on the intervention and prescription of a superior national power like France. The irreversible effects date back at least as far as the 1912 official signing of the French protectorate treaty. For reasons of historical accuracy, it must be further noted that not all the archival evidence recorded during the period of colonial expansion in North Africa was expressly negative. A scholarly article published in the July 1919 issue of the *Geographical Review* praises in wholly uncritical terms the civilizing mission undertaken by French imperial officers to broker "co-operation" among smaller populations of North African "natives" meant to strike up a "mutual advantage" in accordance with the tenets of liberal progressivism as this bold intervention "implies respect for native tradition" but also "does not exclude the introduction of changes necessary to put this people in the way of modern life." Such efforts were accomplished using laws of expropriation, coldly implemented by French bureaucrats, to intervene in property disputes between members of local groups. This ensured that the land changed hands as necessary to advance the territory from a patchwork of distinct regional communities with interwoven monetary histories into an integrated modern industrial economic system with roads, railways, sanitation systems, large-scale agricultural practices, and so on. See de Tarde, "The Work of France in Morocco," 30.

30   Holcomb, *Claude McKay, Code Name Sasha*, 177.

31   This population statistic features, for instance, in a speech delivered by Marcus Garvey in New York on November 25, 1922 ("The Principles of the Universal Negro Improvement Association," 148).

32   Garvey, "Editorial," 238.

33   Garvey, "Editorial," 238.

34   Du Bois quoted in Maxwell, "Banjo Meets the Dark Princess," 170.

35   Garvey, "Editorial," 238.

36   Du Bois quoted in Maxwell, "Banjo Meets the Dark Princess," 170.

37   James recently unearthed two such letters. For transcripts, see "Letters from London in Black and Red."

38   McKay, *The Passion*, 69.

39   McKay, *The Passion*, 68.

40   McKay, *The Passion*, 135.

41   McKay, "Garvey as a Negro Moses," 8.

42   McKay, "Garvey as a Negro Moses," 8.

43   Garvey, "Editorial," 239.

Works Cited

Arendt, Hannah. "Guests from No-Man's-Land." In *The Jewish Writings*, edited by Jerome Kohn and Ron H. Feldman, 211–13. New York: Schocken, 2007.

Bishop, Jacqueline. "Claude McKay's Songs of Morocco." *Black Renaissance/Renaissance Noire* 14, no. 1 (2014): 68–75.

Chalk, Bridget. "Sensible of Being *Étrangers*: Plots and Identity Papers in *Banjo*." *Twentieth-Century Literature* 55, no. 3 (2009): 357–77.

Cooper, Wayne. *Claude McKay: Rebel Sojourner in the Harlem Renaissance*. New York: Schocken, 1987.

de Tarde, Alfred. "The Work of France in Morocco." *Geographical Review* 8, no. 1 (1919): 1–30.

Edwards, Brent Hayes. *The Practice of Diaspora: Literature, Translation, and the Rise of Black Internationalism*. Cambridge, MA: Harvard University Press, 2003.

Feinsod, Harris. "Death Ships: The Cruel Translations of the Interwar Maritime Novel." *Modernism/Modernity Print Plus*, vol. 3, cycle 3, August 20, 2018. modernismmodernity.org /forums/posts/death-ships#_ednref23.

Garvey, Marcus. "Editorial by Marcus Garvey in the *Negro World*." In vol. 7 of *The Marcus Garvey and Universal Improvement Association Papers*, edited by Robert Hill, 238–42. Berkeley: University of California Press, 1990.

Garvey, Marcus. "The Principles of the Universal Negro Improvement Association." In vol. 5 of *The Marcus Garvey and Universal Negro Improvement Association Papers*, edited by Robert Hill, 143–49. Berkeley: University of California Press, 1986.

Getachew, Adom. *Worldmaking after Empire: The Rise and Fall of Self-Determination*. Princeton, NJ: Princeton University Press, 2019.

Gulddal, Jesper. "*Das Totenschiff* and the Chronotope of Movement Control." *German Life and Letters* 66, no. 3 (2013): 292–307.

Gundogdu, Ayten. *Rightlessness in an Age of Rights: Hannah Arendt and the Contemporary Struggles of Migrants*. New York: Oxford University Press, 2015.

Holcomb, Gary Edward. *Claude McKay, Code Name Sasha: Queer Black Marxism and the Harlem Renaissance*. Gainesville: University Press of Florida, 2007.

James, Winston. *A Fierce Hatred of Injustice: Claude McKay's Jamaica and His Poetry of Rebellion*. London: Verso, 2000.

James, Winston. "Letters from London in Black and Red: Claude McKay, Marcus Garvey, and the *Negro World*." *History Workshop Journal*, no. 85 (2018): 281–93.

Lang, Phyllis Martin. "Claude McKay: Evidence of a Magic Pilgrimage." *CLA Journal* 16, no. 4 (1973): 475–84.

Maxwell, William J. "Banjo Meets the Dark Princess: Claude McKay, W. E. B. Du Bois, and the Transnational Novel of the Harlem Renaissance." In *The Cambridge Companion to the Harlem Renaissance*, edited by George Hutchinson, 170–83. Cambridge: Cambridge University Press, 2007.

McKay, Claude. *Banjo: A Story without a Plot*. Orlando, FL: Harcourt Brace, 1957.

McKay, Claude. *Complete Poems*, edited by William J. Maxwell. Urbana: University of Illinois Press, 2004.

McKay, Claude. "Garvey as a Negro Moses." *Liberator*, April 1922, 8.

McKay, Claude. *A Long Way from Home*. London: Pluto, 1970.

McKay, Claude. *The Passion of Claude McKay: Selected Poetry and Prose*, edited by Wayne Cooper. New York: Schocken, 1973.

McKay, Claude. *Romance in Marseille*, edited by Gary Edward Holcomb and William J. Maxwell. New York: Penguin, 2020.

Nickels, Joel. "Claude McKay and Dissident Internationalism." *Cultural Critique*, no. 87 (2014): 1–37.

Sharma, Nandita. *Home Rule: National Sovereignty and the Separation of Natives and Migrants*. Durham, NC: Duke University Press, 2020.

Swearingen, Will D. "In Pursuit of the Granary of Rome: France's Wheat Policy in Morocco, 1915–1931." *International Journal of Middle East Studies* 17, no. 3 (1985): 347–63.

Tabili, Laura. "The Construction of Race Difference in Twentieth-Century Britain: The Special Restriction (Coloured Alien Seamen) Order, 1925." *Journal of British Studies* 33, no. 1 (1994): 54–98.

Vadde, Aarthi. "Stories without Plots: The Nomadic Collectivism of Claude McKay and George Lamming." In *Chimeras of Form: Modernist Internationalism beyond Europe, 1914–2016*, 108–48. New York: Columbia University Press, 2017.

Waligora-Davis, Nicole. *Sanctuary: African Americans and Empire*. New York: Oxford University Press, 2011.

"No Man's Ocean Ever Did Get the Best of Me"

The Oceanic Journeys and Maritime Modernism of *Romance in Marseille*

NISSA REN CANNON

Abstract   By the late 1920s steam travel was faster, more comfortable, and more afford-able than ever before, and there were more shipping lines, operating more ships, than in the past. The major lines could not compete with one another in terms of cost or speed, so they wooed customers by focusing on passenger comfort, attempting to one-up each other's luxury. It is in this context that Claude McKay wrote a novel about an African seaman who makes two miserable passages across the Atlantic—the first as a stow-away, the second in first class. This article reads McKay's novel as a revision of the narra-tive of liberating and luxurious ocean travel promoted by the shipping lines and argues that *Romance in Marseille* offers novel possibilities and implications for maritime and oceanic studies because it asks readers to recognize overlaps between different forms of mobility and, in characteristic McKay fashion, to resist reductive interpretation.
Keywords   steamship, maritime modernism, Claude McKay, travel

In 1930 the Fabre Line, one of over seventy shipping companies competing to transport people and goods across the Atlantic, promised potential passengers cabins that were "roomy, airy, and all outside," while promoting their ships' "refined environment, cleanliness in all departments on board, fine French cuisine and pleasing service of the officers and crew."[1] A year before, Claude McKay, inspired in part by an incident aboard a Fabre Line ship in the 1920s, had begun writing a novel featuring a transatlantic crossing as different as imaginable from these sales pitches. McKay's work, first published nearly ninety years after it was written, cen-ters on an African emigrant named Lafala, who stows away from Marseille to New York, hoping that his black skin will disguise him in the "gloominess of the bun-ker."[2] When discovered by the ship's crew, Lafala is imprisoned in a space even less like the "airy" rooms the shipping lines' promotional materials promised: a "miserable" and "very cold" W.C., where his legs are catastrophically frostbitten, leaving doctors to "save his life only by cutting [them] off" (*RM*, 5). In what follows,

ENGLISH LANGUAGE NOTES

59:1, April 2021   DOI 10.1215/00138282-8815027
© 2021 Regents of the University of Colorado

I will situate McKay's novel in the context of interwar ocean travel, reading it as a revision of the narrative of liberating and luxurious mobility promoted by shipping lines in the period. I will also position the book in relation to an expanding body of literary scholarship on the oceanic and the maritime to argue that *Romance in Marseille* introduces a perspective thus far absent from these fields. The novel refuses the narratives of lavish comfort the shipping lines promoted yet demonstrates the misguidedness of any attempt to see all narratives of Black bodies crossing the Atlantic as directly reflective of the Middle Passage. By asking readers to recognize overlaps between different experiences of mobility, McKay's novel suggests that we should avoid reducing the transatlantic crossing to a space of either simple leisure or labor, offering a perspective on identity and power that refuses reductive binaries.

Romance in Marseille is a short book—published at just 130 pages—divided into three sections. Sea journeys bookend the novel as well as open each of its parts. In their introduction to the 2020 Penguin Classics edition, Gary Edward Holcomb and William J. Maxwell highlight McKay's work in "diagramming [the novel's] arcs and plot points," underscoring the value of dwelling on the significant role of ocean journeys in both the book's plot and form.[3] The novel's first crossing is the one Lafala remembers from his New York hospital bed in a flashback beginning on the first chapter's second page. Readers learn that Lafala "stowed away from Marseille" on a ship bound for New York, after being betrayed by Aslima, the "burning brown mixed of Arab and Negro and other wanton bloods" with whom he was in love (*RM*, 4). During this journey the crew "found him" hiding in the ship's bunker, and "he was locked up in a miserable place" where he was unable to communicate with his captors that his "legs were frozen stiff" (*RM*, 5). When Lafala arrived in New York, his legs had to be amputated below the knees. The events of this first crossing set up the rest of *Romance in Marseille*'s central plotline, in which Lafala, with the help of a lawyer, sues the shipping company for his injuries; is awarded financial compensation (concluding the book's first part); returns to Marseille to await his payment (the book's second and third parts); and finally takes his fortune back to Africa, returning to "the jungle . . . with a little civilization in [his] pocket" (the novel's finale; *RM*, 36).

The book's second transatlantic crossing opens its second part. This time, unlike his furtive first crossing, Lafala sails "at the company's expense, first class" after winning his suit, "mak[ing] good use of all that the company was paying for" (*RM*, 27). Yet Lafala has lost his figurative sea legs along with his literal ones: he is miserably seasick, and his desire to take advantage of the company's generosity backfires: "His long-disciplined body . . . reacted against the sudden abuse, and his bowels roared resentment against too much first-class food." What should be a voyage of comfort instead leaves Lafala looking back fondly at the "many voyages he had made" as a sailor "without ever getting sick" (*RM*, 27).

Romance in Marseille's third and final crossing transpires largely off the page but is no less important to the story. At the book's end Lafala achieves his goal of sailing "back to make good" in Africa with his new fortune (*RM*, 36). As Marseille Quaysiders Diup and Rock watch his ship leave, Lafala departs alone. Despite having seemingly reconciled with the once-treacherous Aslima—the two spend much of the novel's second and third parts publicly and privately proclaiming their passion for each other—Lafala suddenly changes course and, without warning Aslima, decides not to bring her back to Africa with him. While Lafala sails "without any tears shed" (*RM*, 127), his decision has tragic results for Aslima. When her pimp, Titin, learns that she has betrayed him with her commitments to Lafala, he shoots her, "cursing and calling upon hell to swallow her soul" (*RM*, 130).

The centrality of these oceanic crossings to the book's plot and form makes *Romance in Marseille* something of an outlier in interwar literature, which has a tendency not to dwell on shipboard space and time.[4] While transatlantic crossings are mainstays of the period's nonfiction and letters—and so instrumental to the era that Maxwell has described conventional modernist studies as positioning the "Cunard Line . . . as the chronotope of transatlantic modernity"[5]—this experience is notably absent from much of the fiction commonly classified as Anglophone modernism. For example, such canonical novels as E. M. Forster's *A Passage to India* (1924), Ernest Hemingway's *The Sun Also Rises* (1926), F. Scott Fitzgerald's *Tender Is the Night* (1934), and Djuna Barnes's *Nightwood* (1936) all are populated by characters who have recently sailed across an ocean, but barely mention these crossings.

The paucity of oceanic travel in fiction stands in stark contrast to the historical facts, with Harris Feinsod describing ship voyages as "a more pedestrian reality for writers of the modernist period than . . . for any period before or after."[6] By the late 1920s, when *Romance in Marseille* is set, steam travel was faster, more comfortable, and more affordable for middle- and upper-class passengers than it had ever been, and there were more shipping lines, operating more ships, than ever before.[7] Technological and historical developments contributed to dramatic changes in the experience and opportunities for passenger travel in the early twentieth century. One reason for this was the increase in ships' sizes: in 1900 the largest ocean liner was fifteen thousand tons, while by 1914 it had more than tripled, to fifty thousand.[8] This meant space for more goods and also for many more people aboard each ship. Yet as liners reached these enormous sizes, immigrants' demand for passage, which shipping lines had relied on for income, dropped precipitously. The United States' enactment of the Dillingham immigration restrictions in 1921 and the Johnson-Reed Act in 1924 dramatically limited the number of passengers allowed to immigrate to the United States, leaving lines unable to fill the vast spaces they had allotted to steerage.

The lines responded by reconstituting much of this space as a new travel class, which they named "tourist third."[9] This new class offered many of the comforts previously enjoyed only by first-class ticket holders—including private berths and fancy dining options—at lower costs. Once an experience limited primarily to immigrants and the wealthy, transatlantic travel became accessibly middle class. The introduction of this new travel class coincided with a series of historical shifts that dramatically increased the number of Americans traveling overseas. In 1921 Europe reopened to tourists after wartime limitations, and the US dollar's strength inspired Americans who had never been abroad to board ships. Around the same time, "Junior Year Abroad" programs launched, sending thousands of university students to Europe each year, and these primarily female students were part of a trend of women increasingly gaining the autonomy to travel without male escorts, a fact the shipping lines acknowledged through appeals aimed directly at female travelers.[10]

The major shipping lines could not compete with one another in terms of cost or speed; they operated with slim profit margins on most tickets and ran ships with comparable engine power. But they recognized that they could win customers by focusing on passenger comfort and attempted to one-up each other in luxury and glamor.[11] Within enormous luxury liners there was ample room for an array of spaces and services, and lines hired renowned architects and designers to create lavish interiors and exteriors.[12] In *Of Time and the River* Thomas Wolfe regards a docked ship in detail and catalogs its many features, including "storeyed decks and promenades as wide as city streets, the fabulous variety and opulence of her public rooms, her vast lounges and salons, her restaurants, grills, and cafes, her libraries, writing-rooms, ballrooms, swimming-pools, her imperial suites with broad beds, private decks, sitting-rooms, gleaming baths."[13]

Shipping companies advertised heavily to recruit passengers and distinguish their services from one another. One particularly large ship—the United States Line's aptly named SS *Leviathan*—touted its Ritz Carlton restaurant, a "'phone in every room . . . , American plumbing, lighting and heating," as well as a "Roman swimming pool" and the ship's own band.[14] When the French Line relaunched its SS *France* as a luxury liner in 1924, its pictorial advertising featured photos of its sundeck, grand stairway, "Salon Louis XIV," and "Boudoir of a De Luxe suite." The line promised Americans booking passage back to the United States from Paris, "the voyage home will be a continuation of your trip to Europe. You will absorb the refined atmosphere of the *France* in its delightful customs, manners, music, cuisine and surroundings—a fitting climax to your trip abroad."[15] Comfort was an amenity emphasized both on and off the ships: a 1923 pitch from the French Line, for example, focused on the ease of embarkation, promising "no long annoying wait in the cold on a bobbing tender. The embarkation facilities of the French Line are the finest in France."[16]

Among the many lines operating in the 1920s was the Compagnie Française de Navigation à Vapeur Cyprien Fabre, better known by the abbreviated "Fabre Line." It was an incident aboard a Fabre Line ship that provided some of the real-life inspiration for McKay's novel. Beginning a sequence that will sound familiar to *Romance in Marseille*'s readers, the Nigerian sailor Nelson Simeon Dede stowed away on a ship bound for New York in 1926. He was discovered on board by the crew and locked up in the ship's water closet, lost his feet to frostbite, was awarded a settlement by the Fabre Line, and was later jailed for his earlier transgression of stowing away.[17] McKay initially met Dede in Marseille in 1926, before these events, and became reacquainted with him in 1928, intervening with authorities on Dede's behalf to help him be released from jail.[18] The plot of *Romance in Marseille* parallels these events, down to the intervention of an educated and literary Caribbean man—the fictional Étienne St. Dominique—who aids in securing Lafala's freedom.

While McKay does not specifically name the Fabre Line in *Romance in Marseille*, the parallels between Dede's story and Lafala's invite special scrutiny of this company. The Fabre Line was the oldest passenger line connecting the Mediterranean with North America, and introduced their Marseille–to–New York service in 1881.[19] In addition to transatlantic passenger travel, the line offered cruises around the Mediterranean, facilitating both regional and global movement of goods and people. In 1930 Fabre Line ships sailing from New York and Boston made stops in many Mediterranean ports before landing in Marseille. These included Ponta Delgada, Madeira, and Lisbon; British Gibraltar and Palestine; French-colonized Algiers and Beirut, as well as Monaco and Ajaccio; Palermo, Messina, Siracusa, and Naples; Athens and Rhodes; Constantinople; and Alexandria. [20] In *Romance in Marseille* Aslima's mixed background is representative of the intra-Mediterranean maritime connectivity and commerce made possible—as well as exploitable—by the Fabre Line. She was raised in Marrakech, taken to Casablanca and Algeria by a soldier who "paid a few hundred francs to take her away" (*RM*, 45), became involved with a Corsican pimp, and was sold to a brothel in Marseille. The furnishings of Aslima's apartment reflect this deceptively easy transnationalism: her bedroom is dominated by a "water pitcher . . . made in Spain and the bowl in France," which create an atmosphere "effectively African" (*RM*, 46).

The Fabre Line's promotional materials yield a particularly ghoulish reading with Dede and Lafala's voyages in mind. The line had long made passenger safety one of its selling points. In 1914, for instance, the souvenir postcards they distributed featured the phrase "Over Thirty-Two Years Existence Without a Single Accident or Loss of Life to Any Passenger."[21] This theme was still present in a 1930 brochure that promised that the line's ships were "stable and ride the sea remarkably well, which is an absolute guarantee of well-being for the passenger."[22] This brochure, in fact, does more than simply guarantee passengers' continued health by proffering "such a complete diversion from one's daily habits that the curative effect on those subject to it is always miraculous."[23] Lafala's experiences on board—the loss of his feet and later the unpleasant seasickness—seem to explicitly refute these assurances of passenger safety and comfort.

McKay also appears to criticize the Fabre Line's insistence on the open-air capaciousness of its ships. Promotional pamphlets from 1930 highlight passengers' access to large, open spaces, including "numerous private and general bathrooms, commodious writing and reading saloons, an elegant smoking room, two café balconies, and ample deck space."[24] They display images of sunshine streaming through windows on a lounge deck, and a dining room with all the curtains pulled open to showcase the panorama of the sea. When the Fabre Line tells potential passengers that its ship's "cabins are roomy, airy, and all outside," Dede and Lafala's dark confinements are placed in stark relief,[25] and it is hard not to think of Lafala's total isolation in the hold when the brochure assures potential customers that "solitude is no longer sought by our contemporaries either on trips or elsewhere. . . . The friendships gained while travelling are often one of the greatest pleasures of the trip."[26]

Romance in Marseille's engagement with oceanic voyages is not limited to stowaways and paying passengers, since maritime laborers are the book's most numerous seafarers. Indeed, several of McKay's novels feature sailors and dockworkers: *Home to Harlem* opens with protagonist Jake Brown working aboard a freighter; *Banjo* is set among the dockworkers of Marseille; and, prior to stowing away, *Romance in Marseille*'s Lafala is a sailor, traveling "from port to port, crossing and recrossing the Atlantic" (*RM*, 27). Marseille is presented in *Romance* in terms of these maritime workers, described as the "port of seamen's dreams and their nightmares. Port of the bums' delight, the enchanted breakwater. Port of innumerable ships, blowing out, booming in, riding the docks, blessing the town with sweaty activity" (*RM*, 29).

While the dockworkers in McKay's novels are an international, multiethnic group, it is important to acknowledge the glaring adjectival qualification to Lafala's position as passenger: namely, his Blackness. This position makes him invisible in both shipping lines' promotional materials and many of the literary texts I have mentioned, but accounts of the racism experienced by Black passengers were a feature of African American newspapers when *Romance* was penned. For example, in 1930 the *Chicago Defender* reported that the French Line was forced to disavow the actions of one of the company's agents, who had claimed that Black people "were not accepted as passengers in tourist third class on the French line steamships."[27] When the NAACP reached out to the French Line for comment, the line's assistant general passenger manager insisted that their company "does not discriminate in color," offering as evidence the fact that several touring companies of Black performers had recently sailed with them.

In 1932 the *Chicago Defender* ran a story about discrimination against a "successful young physician and his charming wife" who were suing the Cunard Line for denying them their already-paid places aboard the RMS *Mauretania*. The physician had booked tickets by phone, and the paper reported that "the company, unaware that he was Colored, issued him a certificate guaranteeing passage and accommodations on the boat" before refusing to allow the pair to board. The newspaper pointed out the irony that the Cunard Line's heiress, "the tempestuous Hon. Nancy Cunard," was a "great and demonstrative friend of [Black] people."[28] Nancy Cunard was well aware of this history of discrimination: according to Langston Hughes, when he told her that he "had come to France on a Cunard Line vessel, thinking it would please her," he discovered that "she had never set foot on a Cunard liner and never intended to do so," since "the line segregated Negroes. Instead, she travelled on the French boats."[29]

The Cunard Line's racism predated Nancy Cunard. In his second autobiography, *My Bondage and My Freedom* (1855), Frederick Douglass recounted that when a friend tried to book passage to England on a Cunard Line ship on his behalf, he was told that Douglass "could not be received on board as a cabin passenger" and must instead travel in steerage.[30] Alasdair Pettinger writes that "the decks of a transatlantic steamer were negotiated spaces, in which custom and routine made it relatively easy to impose racial segregation." But while segregation on ships certainly took place, it was, in Pettinger's words, "by no means inevitable," in the nineteenth century or the twentieth.[31]

Although discriminated against by the shipping line, Douglass records a warm welcome from his fellow passengers during the same crossing, and James

Weldon Johnson's 1912 *Autobiography of an Ex-Colored Man* depicts a transatlantic journey in which prejudice encountered on a ship is aberrant enough to be commented on. In line with these experiences, an African American high school teacher named Willis N. Huggins detailed his trip on the French Line's SS *Paris* in a 1924 article in the *Chicago Defender*. He celebrated his fellow passengers who "threw color prejudice overboard" and praised a shipboard talk by a New York University professor who proclaimed that "men and women of all races are gathered on board this vessel and living in peace and harmony. If they can so live for seven days they can so live for seven weeks, seven years, aye, they can so live forever."[32]

Where McKay troubles the shipping companies' narrative of passenger travel as easy and comfortable by writing about the difficulty and discomfort they inflict on Black bodies, Marcus Garvey's Black Star Line attempted to circumvent white shipping lines entirely. Promising "a line of steamships to run between America, Africa, the West Indies, Canada, South and Central America, Carrying Freight and Passengers,"[33] the Black Star Line was, in W. E. B. Du Bois's estimation, "a brilliant suggestion and Garvey's only original contribution to the race problem."[34] Although Garvey's plans for the line focused primarily on its role in commerce—framing it to investors as a way to raise capital for Black people and better their situation—it was always intended to be a passenger line as well, and one that sought to resolve the segregation present on other ships. The following back-and-forth appears in a transcript from the US government's inquiries into Garvey's activities: "Does [the Black Star Line] discriminate between whites and blacks?" the questioner asks, to which the reply is, "We have taken white passengers." When again asked "Have you any rule against taking white passengers?," the respondent answers, "No; the present captain is a white man."[35]

From 1919 through 1922 Garvey's ships, staffed mainly by Black captains and Black crews, fulfilled his goal of carrying passengers and goods to ports in the West Indies. His proclamation that "stocks [are] sold only to Negroes," and that the Black Star Line would "open up untold possibilities for the race," suggests a vision of a world free from the dominance of the white-owned shipping companies.[36] Although the line's finances were poorly managed, forcing it to shutter before many of Garvey's promises were fulfilled, it remained a symbol for race-based repatriation for decades. Alongside McKay's novelistic critique of the shipping lines' authority stands Garvey's material challenge to their absolute power to control bodies and narratives.

Having briefly situated *Romance in Marseille* in relation to interwar steam travel, I will next consider it in relation to two critical fields with which I believe it can be productively engaged: maritime studies and oceanic studies. While naming these as scholarly areas of discourse is a relatively recent practice, I argue that McKay's novel anticipates some of the tenets of the research now done under their auspices. For one thing, by upending the optimistic narrative the shipping lines promoted, McKay uses his maritime setting to invert a familiar vision of the world, much as oceanic studies takes as one of its dominant epistemological interventions a similar reorientation. By this, I am referring to the rethinking of the nation the ocean makes possible—a move that has allowed Atlantic studies, Mediterranean

studies, and, more recently, Pacific studies to become familiar frameworks for discussing geographic connections beyond national paradigms. As Michelle Burnham
explains in the case of American studies, an "aquatic approach . . . is . . . something like the geographic equivalent to a photographic negative, producing a shift
in perspective that revises the terms and alters the features of what had been a clear
and familiar image of the globe and of America's place in it."[37]

In this revised global vision, the ocean becomes a means of uniting countries
and continents rather than of separating them, like the interconnected nature of
the Mediterranean that makes McKay's Marseille possible. This geographic paradigm may have become de rigueur in literary criticism only in recent decades, but
some of its conceits were already familiar to the twentieth-century shipping lines
that enabled global movement. For instance, an aquatic reimagining of the world
is visible in the image featured on the Fabre Line's 1930 promotional materials,
which displays a map dominated by an open ocean surrounded by just the tips
of continents, sliced through with the bold line of the Fabre Line's transatlantic
route—an image violating the conventional perspective of a map centered on the
continents familiar to its intended viewers.[38]

Much of the literary criticism invested in the maritime—including seminal
book-length works *The Novel and the Sea* (2010), by Margaret Cohen, and *The View
from the Mast-Head: Maritime Imagination and Antebellum American Sea Narratives*
(2008), by Hester Blum—has focused on writing from the nineteenth century and
earlier. More recently, the centrality of the ocean to the twenty-first century's global
refugee crisis has yielded scholarship on contemporary fiction's treatment of oceanic travel. Yet the space between these historical bookends led Nicole Rizzuto to
assert in 2019 that "the interwar period appears to be a dead zone in the history of
seafaring literature."[39] Rizzuto, alongside others, has been working to correct this
oversight, part of a small but growing body of work on maritime literature of the
modernist period.[40]

Yet this scholarship on maritime modernism, too, leaves something of a gap
where *Romance in Marseille* dwells. Rizzuto, Feinsod, and Maxwell Uphaus have
each concentrated on the figure of the laborer at sea, with Feinsod identifying
"a historically specific global corpus of interwar fictions, all written between 1922
and 1934, that sought to write stateless dockworkers, coalers, ordinary seamen,
wharf rats, and migrant laborers into the discourse of globalization."[41] Separately,
a similarly small pool of literary critics—including Mark Rennella and Whitney
Walton, Shawna Ross, Anna Snaith, Tamara Wagner, and Faye Hammill—have
investigated luxury-liner travel in the period.[42] McKay's novel, with its interest in
both the figure of the maritime laborer and the first-class passenger—not to mention the stowaway—seems to exceed the concerns of each of these groups. In writing about these different forms of mobility side by side, the book offers the opportunity to think about them as overlapping, rather than wholly distinct, phenomena.

The ideas emerging from maritime and oceanic studies provide other useful
interpretive possibilities for McKay's text. They can help readers contextualize the
power struggle within the novel between the shipping company and the individual

and can situate Lafala's moral ambiguity—a point of discomfort—in relation to the text's larger themes and those that run through McKay's oeuvre. One idea consistently at the heart of oceanic and maritime studies is that the ocean is a site that refuses reductive interpretation. In the introduction to the scholarly collection *Sea Changes: Historicizing the Ocean* (2003), Bernhard Klein and Gesa Mackenthun describe the ocean:

> As enormous as its roles have been contradictory: the sea has served as an
> agent of colonial oppression but also of indigenous resistance and native
> empowerment, it has been a site of loss, dispersal, and enforced migration but
> also of new forms of solidarity and affective kinship, a paradigm of modern
> capitalism but also of its creative reinterpretation, a figure of death but also
> of life.[43]

Terri Gordon-Zolov and Amy Sodaro's assertion that "the sea embodies dystopian despair, violence, and degradation, but also hope, coexistence, and possibility" similarly sums up the seeming contradictions embodied through the ocean.[44] The tendency already discussed within the field to refuse national paradigms in favor of international ones—which Blum describes as "the relative irrelevance of state affiliations in the maritime world"[45]—presents a similar demand to reconcile the purportedly antithetical.

Reading *Romance in Marseille* in relation to these maritime contradictions allows some seemingly opposing positions in the novel to appear less baffling and more integral to the text. One of the novel's structuring tensions surrounds power: when the shipping company's actions rob Lafala of his legs yet grant him the money to fulfill his dream of buying land in Africa, can the company claim totalizing control over the individual, or is this subverted by the individual ultimately getting what they want? At first glance, it is the shipping line that remains in control on board and on land. The company enforces both mobility and immobility, transporting Lafala across the ocean while also completely halting his movement, first through his confinement in the hospital and then in the limbo of awaiting his settlement money in Marseille. Yet despite this control over Lafala's movements, the shipping company's power is never entire. Lafala's misadventure takes place alongside that of his "partner in stowing away," a "huge West Indian from a British island" named Babel, whose story opens the book's third part. Babel is "routed out of his hiding place a day after Lafala had been discovered" and, without the necessity of being left at the hospital in New York, taken directly back to his port of embarkation. But "when [Babel's] boat appeared in full view of Marseille and the officers were busy preparing for the visit of port officials, he leaped overboard and dived to safety"—wresting control of his own mobility rather than complying with the company's will (*RM*, 83). This ability to take advantage of the resources those in power think they control continues in a ploy McKay repeats from his earlier novel, *Banjo*: Babel secures free room and board from "an agent in Genoa who put up stranded seamen" under the pretense that he is seeking work (*RM*, 84). When Holcomb and

Maxwell describe the novel as "a work of stowaway fiction . . . [,] a reflection on the art of improvised movement around a black world rediscovering its far-flung corners and relations," it is just this kind of subversion of ostensibly powerful forces they are describing.[46]

It is important to note, of course, that these rebellions take Babel only so far. Eventually, the shipping line jails both him and Lafala for their initial attempt to gain free passage to New York. But these possibilities for McKay's characters to benefit from the systems intended to control them continue to suggest that institutional power is not totalizing. It is ultimately the work of an individual that frees Lafala and Babel from jail, when St. Dominique—McKay's biographical stand-in—takes up their cause and convinces the company to let them go. Throughout Lafala's and Babel's lives the individual and the company vie for power, with neither the clear victor—a situation analogous to the often-contradictory power relations, and resistance to easy binaries, scholarship has recognized in maritime relations.

The recognition that the state of the world is inherently contradictory can also be brought to bear on what is perhaps the novel's most pressing interpretive question: how are readers expected to respond to Lafala's moral ambiguity? As a character, Lafala ricochets between provoking compassion and repelling it. He is first introduced at his most sympathetic, bedridden "like a sawed-off stump and ponder[ing] the loss of his legs," at the moment when this loss has both literally and figuratively cut him off from his past (RM, 3). Yet within the balance of the novel's first part, Lafala betrays the people helping him, making it hard to stay on his side. After Lafala wins his suit against the shipping company, he backs out of the contract with his lawyer, denying him the money he has promised. Lafala's actions affect not just his white Jewish lawyer but the professed "race man" (RM, 23)—named Black Angel, no less—who initially led Lafala to the lawyer. When Black Angel comes pleading to Lafala, reminding him that "I done earned what was promised to me," Lafala betrays his ally, insisting that "I can't start paying out money like that" (RM, 24). Later in the novel McKay repeats this pattern of building and betraying sympathy. Lafala is clearly wronged by the shipping line through the double jeopardy of being imprisoned for a crime for which he has already paid dearly with his legs. Yet soon after he is released from jail, he breaks his promise to Aslima, which leads to her death at Titin's hands. Just as the tension between the individual and the institution in the novel remains unresolved, readers must accept the persistence of contradictions in Lafala's character—a position those invested in the ideas of maritime and oceanic studies find themselves familiar with.

I want to suggest that both of these interpretive inconsistencies are part of a larger project that McKay's life and work both undertake: systematically refusing binary and reductive meanings. An anecdote in his 1937 autobiography, *A Long Way from Home*, displays the author's refusal to be confined to any single facet of his identity. McKay tells an immigration official that "I was born in the West Indies and lived in the United States and . . . was an American, even though I was a British subject, but I preferred to think of myself as an internationalist."[47] McKay's reluctance to conform to an easily identifiable sexuality, too—as explored extensively in Holcomb's *Code Name Sasha* (2007)—appears to be part of this same refusal of the reductive.

Beyond the biographical, much of McKay's writing similarly frustrates attempts at consistent interpretation. There is the violent divide in reactions to *Home to Harlem* immediately after its publication—from Langston Hughes's resounding praise to Du Bois's conclusion that "after the dirtier parts of its filth I feel distinctly like taking a bath"[48]—and *Banjo*'s rejection of any extant form of Black internationalism, as it demands new models of racial solidarity. Even McKay's attempts to reconcile the traditional form of the sonnet with modern themes and materials in his poetry might be seen as part of this refusal.

"No man's ocean ever did get the best of me in my sound feet, footloose days," declares McKay's Lafala, looking back wistfully at his days of labor from the purported comfort of the first-class deck (*RM*, 27). The Euro-American shipping lines' visions of interwar travel—in which overseas journeys are easy, quick, and comfortable—are contradicted by Lafala's experience, in which ocean transport is uncomfortable, marked not by speed but by the lengthy periods of immobility it makes necessary. This rejection of the lines' narrative of straightforward mobility is just one of the ways in which *Romance in Marseille* anticipates twenty-first-century conversations in oceanic and maritime studies. Like McKay's novel, these conversations foreground interpretive contradictions and geographic reimaginings. *Romance* offers new possibilities for those studying interwar maritime culture as well. It represents things and relationships that have thus far remained just outside the scope of much of the work in this area: hybrid figures of both labor and leisure, and the rare Black man traveling first class. Considering *Romance in Marseille* in the historical and critical context of ocean travel offers a compelling opportunity to recognize the complexity and irreducibility of figures and spaces of interwar oceanic mobility—an opportunity ripe with promise for future scholars.

NISSA REN CANNON teaches in the Program in Writing and Rhetoric at Stanford University. Her research focuses on transatlantic modernism, citizenship, and print culture. Her work has appeared in *symplokē*, the *Journal of Modern Periodical Studies*, and *Modernism/ Modernity*'s print plus platform and is forthcoming in *Cultural History*.

Notes

1   "Fabre Line S.S. *Alesia* Cabin Class Passenger List—19 June 1930," Gjenvick Gjonvik Archives, www.gjenvick.com/Passengers /FabreLine/Alesia-PassengerList-1930-06-19 .html; "Fabre Line Mediterranean Cruises 1930," Jas. W. Elwell and Co., Inc. General Agents.

2   McKay, *Romance in Marseille*, 5 (hereafter cited as *RM*).

3   Holcomb and Maxwell, introduction, xxv.

4   I mean not to imply that this experience is entirely absent from the era's fiction but simply to say that it is underrepresented in relation to its logistical importance. The most common place to find a fictionalized representation of shipboard space in the interwar period is in the era's detective fiction, although there are also notable interwar examples from such authors as Virginia Woolf, John Dos Passos, Sinclair Lewis, F. Scott Fitzgerald, Evelyn Waugh, and Katherine Mansfield.

5   Maxwell, "Global Poetics and State-Sponsored Transnationalism," 360.

6   Feinsod, "Vehicular Networks and the Modernist Seaways," 687.

7   For historical overviews of passenger travel in the interwar period, see Coons and Varias, *Tourist Third Cabin*; and Brinnin, *The Sway of the Grand Saloon*.

8   Roka, "Building the *Titanic*," 61.

9   Coons and Varias, *Tourist Third Cabin*, 25.

10   For more on study-abroad programs and female travelers in the 1920s, see Walton, "Internationalism and the Junior Year Abroad."

11   Feys, *The Battle for the Migrants*, 155.

12   For more on liner design, see Wealleans, *Designing Liners*.

13   Wolfe, *Of Time and the River*, 886.

14   *Chicago Tribune European Edition*, "The Luxury Ship."

15   *Chicago Tribune European Edition Sunday Magazine*, "S.S. Paris," 12.

16   *Ex Libris*, "French Line," 21.

17   Holcomb and Maxwell, introduction, xi.

18   Holcomb and Maxwell, introduction, xix.

19   Jennings and Conley, *Aboard the Fabre Line to Providence*.

20   "Fabre Line Mediterranean Cruises 1930."

21   "Fabre Line T.S.S. *Canada* Passenger List 16 April 1914," Gjenvick Gjonvik Archives, www .gjenvick.com/Passengers/FabreLine/Canada -PassengerList-1914-04-16.html.

22   "Fabre Line Mediterranean Cruises 1930."

23   "Fabre Line Mediterranean Cruises 1930."

24   "Fabre Line S.S. *Alesia* Cabin Class Passenger List."

25   "Fabre Line S.S. *Alesia* Cabin Class Passenger List."

26   "Fabre Line Mediterranean Cruises 1930."

27   *Chicago Defender*, "No Segregation on French Liners."

28   *Chicago Defender*, "Tourists Barred from Abroad by Cunard Line."

29   Hughes, *I Wonder as I Wander*, 318.

30   Douglass, *My Bondage*, 366.

31   Pettinger, "At Sea—Coloured Passenger," 160.

32   Huggins, "Ten Weeks in Europe."

33   Hill, "The Negro in the Realm of Commerce," 136.

34   Du Bois, "The Black Star Line."

35   Hill, "Report on *Black Star Line v. The Chicago Defender*," 356–57.

36   Hill, "The Negro in the Realm of Commerce," 136.

37   Burnham, *Transoceanic America*, 3.

38   "Fabre Line Mediterranean Cruises 1930."

39   Rizzuto, "Maritime Optics," 129.

40   I do not mean to treat "maritime studies" and "oceanic studies" as synonymous. Instead, for the purposes of this article, I hope to highlight the places where they overlap.

41   Feinsod, "Death Ships." See also Rizzuto, "Maritime Modernism"; and Uphaus, "Hurry Up and Wait."

42   Rennella and Walton, "Planned Serendipity"; Ross, "'History, Mystery, Leisure, Pleasure'"; Snaith, *Modernist Voyages*; Wagner, "Children on Board"; Hammill, "Ocean Liners in Literature and Onstage."

43   Klein and Mackenthun, *Sea Changes*, 2.

44   Gordon-Zolov and Sodaro, introduction, 12.

45   Blum, "The Prospect of Oceanic Studies," 671. Laura Winkiel sees a similar destabilization in Virginia Woolf's *The Waves*, where the sea "problematizes the fundamental grounds upon which material existence is actualized" ("A Queer Ecology of the Sea," 146).

46   Holcomb and Maxwell, introduction, xiv.

47   McKay, *A Long Way from Home*, 300.

48   Du Bois, "Two Novels."

Works Cited

Blum, Hester. "The Prospect of Oceanic Studies." *PMLA* 125, no. 3 (2010): 670–77.

Brinnin, John Malcolm. *The Sway of the Grand Saloon: A Social History of the North Atlantic*. New York: Barnes and Noble Books, 2000.

Burnham, Michelle. *Transoceanic America: Risk, Writing, and Revolution in the Global Pacific*. New York: Oxford University Press, 2019.

Chicago Defender. "No Segregation on French Liners." May 24, 1930.

Chicago Defender. "Tourists Barred from Abroad by Cunard Line." August 6, 1932.

Chicago Tribune European Edition. "The Luxury Ship." May 10, 1925.

Chicago Tribune European Edition Sunday Magazine. "S.S. Paris." April 6, 1924, 12.

Coons, Lorraine, and Alexander Varias. *Tourist Third Cabin: Steamship Travel in the Interwar Years*. New York: Palgrave Macmillan, 2003.

Douglass, Frederick. *My Bondage and My Freedom*. New York, 1857.

Du Bois, W. E. B. "The Black Star Line." *Crisis*, September 1922.

Du Bois, W. E. B. "Two Novels: Nella Larsen, Quicksand & Claude McKay, Home to Harlem." *Crisis*, June 1928.

Ex Libris. "French Line." July 1923, 21.

Feinsod, Harris. "Death Ships: The Cruel Translations of the Interwar Maritime Novel." *Modernism/Modernity Print Plus* 3, no. 3 (2018). doi.org/10.26597/mod.0063.

Feinsod, Harris. "Vehicular Networks and the Modernist Seaways: Crane, Lorca, Novo, Hughes." *American Literary History* 27, no. 4 (2015): 683–716.

Feys, Torsten. *The Battle for the Migrants: The Introduction of Steamshipping on the North Atlantic and Its Impact on the European Exodus*. St. John's, NL: International Maritime Economic History Association, 2013.

Gordon-Zolov, Terri, and Amy Sodaro. Introduction to "At Sea," edited by Terri Gordon-Zolov and Amy Sodaro. Special issue, *Women's Studies Quarterly* 45, nos. 1–2 (2017): 12–26.

Hammill, Faye. "Ocean Liners in Literature and Onstage." Lecture, Victoria and Albert Museum, London, April 27, 2018.

Hill, Robert A., ed. "Report on *Black Star Line v. The Chicago Defender*." In vol. 2 of *The Marcus Garvey and Universal Negro Improvement Association Papers*, edited by Robert A. Hill, 349–71. Berkeley: University of California Press, 1983.

Holcomb, Gary Edward, and William J. Maxwell. Introduction to McKay, *Romance in Marseille*, vii–xxxix.

Huggins, Willis N. "Ten Weeks in Europe." *Chicago Defender*, December 13, 1924.

Hughes, Langston. *I Wonder as I Wander*. New York: Hill and Wang, 1993.

Jennings, William, and Patrick T. Conley. *Aboard the Fabre Line to Providence: Immigration to Rhode Island*. Charleston, SC: History Press, 2013.

Klein, Bernhard, and Gesa Mackenthun, eds. *Sea Changes: Historicizing the Ocean*. London: Routledge, 2003.

Maxwell, William J. "Global Poetics and State-Sponsored Transnationalism: A Reply to Jahan Ramazani." *American Literary History* 18, no. 2 (2006): 360–64.

McKay, Claude. *A Long Way from Home*. New York: Arno, 1969.

McKay, Claude. *Romance in Marseille*, edited by Gary Edward Holcomb and William J. Maxwell. New York: Penguin, 2020.

Pettinger, Alasdair. "At Sea—Coloured Passenger." In Klein and McKenthum, *Sea Changes*, 149–66.

Rennella, Mark, and Whitney Walton. "Planned Serendipity: American Travelers and the Transatlantic Voyage in the Nineteenth and Twentieth Centuries." *Journal of Social History* 38, no. 2 (2004): 365–83.

Rizzuto, Nicole. "Maritime Modernism: The Aqueous Form of Virginia Woolf's *The Waves*." *Modernist Cultures* 11, no. 2 (2016): 268–92.

Rizzuto, Nicole. "Maritime Optics in Sea-War Fiction between the Wars." *English Language Notes* 57, no. 1 (2019): 129–39.

Roka, William B. "Building the *Titanic* for Mr. Morgan: How the Rise of the American Economy in the Early Twentieth Century Created a Travelling High Society That Spurred the Development of the North Atlantic Superliner." *Traversea* 3 (2013): 61–76. traversea.journal.library.uta.edu/index.php /traversea/article/view/20.

Ross, Shawna. "'History, Mystery, Leisure, Pleasure': Evelyn Waugh, Bruno Latour, and the Ocean Liner." In *Literary Cartographies*, edited by Robert T. Tally, 111–25. New York: Palgrave Macmillan, 2014.

Snaith, Anna. *Modernist Voyages: Colonial Women Writers in London, 1890–1945*. Cambridge: Cambridge University Press, 2014.

Uphaus, Maxwell. "Hurry Up and Wait: *The Nigger of the 'Narcissus'* and the Maritime in Modernism." *Modernist Cultures* 12, no. 2 (2017): 173–97.

Wagner, Tamara S. "Children on Board: Transoceanic Crossings in Victorian Literature." In *Transport in British Fiction*, edited by Adrienne E. Gavin and Andrew F. Humphries, 69–83. New York: Palgrave Macmillan, 2015.

Walton, Whitney. "Internationalism and the Junior Year Abroad: American Students in France in the 1920s and 1930s." *Diplomatic History* 29, no. 2 (2005): 255–78.

Wealleans, Anne. *Designing Liners: A History of Interior Design Afloat*. New York: Routledge, 2006.

Winkiel, Laura. "A Queer Ecology of the Sea: Reading Virginia Woolf's *The Waves*." *Feminist Modernist Studies* 2, no. 2 (2019): 141–63.

Wolfe, Thomas. *Of Time and the River: A Legend of Man's Hunger in His Youth*. New York: Scribner's Sons, 1935.

Shoreline Thinking

Alluvial Entanglements in *Romance in Marseille*

LAURA WINKIEL

Abstract This article explores the relation between the dockside denizens of Claude McKay's Marseille and the violent history of slavery and racism. It takes a *longue durée* approach to modernism by arguing that the previous five hundred years of colonization and conquest of Black and Indigenous life continue to constrain the possibilities of freedom imagined in the art and literature of the early twentieth century. Using Édouard Glissant's poetics of relation, it considers how the shoreline in *Romance in Marseille* provides a fecund location for sifting through the residues of slavery to salvage possibilities for living otherwise than the racist state demands. In so doing, *Romance in Marseille* goes further than McKay's other novels in asserting that Black femininity must be central to a Black reinvention of the human.

Keywords Claude McKay, Édouard Glissant, Middle Passage, fungibility, slavery

All this was like an unknown tongue to Lafala, but interesting to hear. His civilized contacts had been limited to the flotsam and jetsam of port life, people who went with the drift like the scum and froth of the tides breaking on the shore, their thinking confined to the immediate needs of a day's work down the docks or a trip on the boat or any other means of procuring money for flopping, feeding, loving.[1]

In the above quote from Claude McKay's circa 1929–33 novel, *Romance in Marseille*, Lafala refers to Black and Red internationalism as "an unknown tongue." It widens his conceptual horizon, but only to an extent. Rather than dwell on the abstractions of the Marxist theory of world revolution that render his presence at the Seaman's Club symbolic, he reflects on the "flotsam and jetsam of port life" who had heretofore comprised his "civilized contacts."[2] The metaphor flotsam and jetsam associates these people with debris from ships, whether deliberately discarded (jetsam) or accidently lost (flotsam). This article argues that the figure of the "flotsam and jetsam of port life" conjures a Middle Passage history of abyssal loss and human commodification.[3] What other people have been deliberately discarded

ENGLISH LANGUAGE NOTES

59:1, April 2021 DOI 10.1215/00138282-8815038
© 2021 Regents of the University of Colorado

into the sea? Who else have lost themselves through suicide among the waves?[4] Granted, one might take flotsam and jetsam to be just a metaphor; however, this essay will demonstrate that McKay's novel interrogates the social logic and history of racialized disposability alluded to by these terms. Paradoxically, the novel also suggests that this long history of expendability contains the seeds of a transformation of Black life via lateral and reciprocal relations with humans and nonhumans alike.[5] In the quotation above, the flotsam and jetsam "went with the drift like scum and froth of the tides breaking on the shore." McKay figures the Quayside population as intimately affected by externalities. These forces move them, and they, in turn, affect their environment and others. In using terms of unwanted microscopic plant life and overlooked spume (a froth caused by dissolved organic matter churned up by the sea), McKay casts these drifting "civilized contacts" as nonhuman thingness.[6] As such, the figures turn abjection and disposability into dynamic self-creation by embodying a living, mixing, mobile force: "flopping, feeding, loving." By presenting the mutable, shifting collective of transients and day laborers in transitive, unanchored terms, the novel experiments with envisioning subjectivity in terms other than those of the liberal subject.

Unlike autonomous, liberal subjects who are held to act unilaterally on the world they find outside themselves, "flotsam and jetsam" evokes the legacy of slavery, whereby captive peoples are stripped of agency and autonomy. Slavery effected a "transubstantiation of things" by turning bodies into fungible (exchangeable), thingified objects.[7] Captive bodies were turned into commodities that served as "abstract and empty vessel[s] vulnerable to the projection of others' feelings, ideas, desires, and values."[8] They were emptied of subjectivity and became instead screens for any impulse or image that white supremacy cast on them. Because slaves were never autonomous, they and their descendants, as McKay shows, reinvent subjectivity as malleable and permeable to others and to their surroundings. They revalue and recast the very fungibility to which they were subjected. Such reinvention enacts a nonnormative, resistant relation to racial supremacy. In the McKay quotation above, the same fungibility that turns humans into refuse also describes a motley crew who embrace their designation as disposable and unwanted to transform that exclusion into a riotous experiment of living otherwise.[9] They act in concert with their surroundings, "feeding, flopping, loving," to produce what Saidiya Hartman calls "a complete program of disorder . . . tumult, upheaval, open rebellion."[10] These transversal relations (i.e., open-ended and under the radar) produce a radical Black collectivity: queer, interracial, international, embodied, sensual, and resistant.[11] Finally, by situating Lafala's "civilized contacts" on the shore, the novel insists on a mobile geography: shifting, unstable, porous, and sedimented with layers of historical accumulation. McKay shows how the shoreline is both a zone of pleasure and sexual freedom and a tightly patrolled border where the state regulates the influx of danger: from disease, immorality, sedition, unwanted peoples, contraband cargoes, and more.[12] Using the Caribbean theorist Édouard Glissant's poetics of relation, this article explores how the shoreline in *Romance in Marseille* provides a fecund location for sifting through the residues of slavery to salvage possibilities for living otherwise than the racist state demands.

This interpretation of *Romance in Marseille* centers on the long history of slavery, a critical move that goes against the grain of most readings of McKay's novel, with its defiantly modern, urban dockworkers, prostitutes, and drifters who enact the new and the now. Instead, this essay takes a *longue durée* approach to modernism in which the previous five hundred years of colonization and conquest of Black and Indigenous life continue to constrain the possibilities of freedom imagined in the art and literature of the early twentieth century. This article also joins recent critical work on maritime modernisms in its efforts to bring to the fore the repressed geographies and histories of the oceans and their role in advancing empire, colonization, and slavery (see also Cannon's essay in this special issue).[13] It refrains from charting the movements of ships or the lives of sailors and instead argues that the sea itself provides a way of rethinking the human. It builds on Hester Blum's suggestion that the oceans provide "a methodological model for nonlinear or nonplanar thought."[14] In this endeavor, Blum draws on the groundbreaking work of the geographer Philip E. Steinberg, who argues that we need to develop models of knowledge in which the oceans are "continually being reconstituted by a variety of elements: the non-human and the human, the biological and the geophysical, the historic and the contemporary."[15] Thinking the oceanic requires what Glissant calls "the other of Thought," a nontranscendent encounter with an unfathomable totality that alters the subject by opening it to an "aesthetics of turbulence,"[16] this undoing of self dissolves certainties of knowing and being. As such, the sea—and its shoreline—provides a space for other modes of relating to humans and nonhumans alike. From this alternate realm, *Romance in Marseille* reconfigures its drifters as being liminal to national, racial, gender, and sexual normative categories that attach to territorializing societies. So, despite its emphasis on Blackness formed through the legacy of slavery, Lafala's "civilized contacts" are multiracial and multinational. The character Étienne St. Dominique says, "We're all divided, all have a dual personality, black, brown, yellow, white" (*RM*, 102). Given the port setting of these comments, we can think of this conflicted state of being through an oceanic frame. On the one hand, the violence of racial capitalism aims to imprison humans within clearly defined and enforced categories of racial supremacy and gender normativity. On the other hand, the chaos of the sea, with its endless drawing toward and apart from the shore, emphasizes what Blum calls the "unfixed, ungraspable contours" of the sensuous, plurivocal, nonlinear aquatic realm.[17] The sea, in this lens, is agential. Water is "an active participant in mediating intimacies and creating pleasure."[18] These twin forces, the centripetal order of state-sanctioned violence and the unmaking of those categories through shoreline mixing and oceanic erotics, produce in the characters who populate *Romance in Marseille*'s dual personalities who are either at war with the normative state apparatus or succumb to its power.

Tracing the heretofore unremarked presence in modernism of this long history reveals the complex temporality of what Hartman calls "the afterlife of slavery," the lived sense that "all of it is now," as Toni Morrison memorably writes.[19] Decades before Morrison, McKay already recognizes this complexity in the quotation above as he encodes slave history within the resolute contingency of the day laborers. Lafala represents the drifters' temporal horizon as being strictly limited to "the immediate needs of a day's work," achieved via improvised, flexible labor and exchange. Soon after, he admits that he had never considered "such toilers achieving anything different or changing the way of life that seemed as eternal as the rhythm of the waves alongside Quayside which they so much resembled" (*RM*, 77). Putting these two temporalities together, it becomes clear that the grinding everyday poverty and insecurity of the dockside inhabitants seems insurmountable *because* these people seem as "eternal as the rhythm of the waves." They *seem* to be outside history because they are associated *with* the waves through the slave abyss.

Abyss

We turn next to a consideration of Glissant's meditation on how the historical trauma of slavery, that is, the "refuse" status of Black life, can be the site of resistance to racial supremacy's need to fix, surveil, and confine Blackness as fundamentally abject. As discussed above, Lafala notes that the Quayside inhabitants "went with the drift" like the "scum and froth of the tides." He associates the port's prostitutes, beggars, pimps, sailors, and day laborers with unwanted plant life and agitated seawater. This description suggests a floating account of what Glissant calls "a whole alluvium," sediments of the Middle Passage that wash up on shore. Such alluvium, "indistinct and unexplored," is usually discounted as waste (*PR*, 111). It appears formless; its opacity rebuffs possession or exchange. Therein, as Glissant argues, lies its promise.

In a crucial rewriting of Caribbean poetics and history, Glissant posits the Middle Passage as the "abyssal" beginnings of Caribbean thought:

> Experience of the abyss lies inside and outside the abyss. The torment of those
> who never escaped it: straight from the belly of the slave ship into the violent
> belly of the ocean depths they went. But their ordeal did not die; it quickened
> into this continuous/discontinuous thing: the panic of the new land, the
> haunting of the former land, finally the alliance with the imposed land,
> suffered and redeemed. The unconscious memory of the abyss served as the
> alluvium for these metamorphoses. (*PR*, 7)

The abyss is both literal and sedimented into the history, memory, and location of the Caribbean archipelago. It is the watery grave of the estimated 1.8 million men, women, and children thrown or suicided overboard the slave ships *and* the residual trace of the abyss that is metamorphosed into, as Sylvia Wynter puts it, "new natives in a new world."[20] The newness is paradoxically born in terror and loss and afterward comes to sediment traces from Africa on the imposed land. The abyss does not break from a past; rather, it emerges after any known point of reference—a natal alienation from land, ancestors, and cosmologies—has been obliterated from memory. John E. Drabinski glosses this arrival as follows: "This new time and birth is the end of the sea at the sand, an end of the terror and the beginning of the terrifying, the life of trauma for the living. . . . The dead mark the living and their sense of what it means to go on, but as a peculiar and utterly devastating absence."[21] The enslaved survivors and their descendants were both dehumanized by the plantation economies in which they found themselves and rehumanized by "rerooting" in the Caribbean archipelago. This rerooting is open, discontinuous, and shot through with the trace of the abyss. The trace can be felt throughout the afflicted land of the Caribbean as panic, haunting, suffering, and cultural transformation (creolization) arrived at through what Glissant calls *relation*.

Glissant defines relation as "the creativity of marginalized peoples who today confront the ideal of transparent universality, imposed by the West [a project, not a place], with secretive and multiple manifestations of Diversity."[22] By *secretive*, Glissant makes indirect reference to his concept of "opacity." Opacity refers to the resistance and alterity of the knowledge and being of subaltern collectivities as opposed to the demand for transparent universality by the West.[23] By *alterity*, I do not intend to evoke poststructuralism's static figure of the absolute other who is permanently foreclosed from language and hence exoticized. Rather, the alterity of colonized peoples refers to a poetic or imaginative force, an errancy, that refuses stasis. Relation is dynamic, unpredictable, multiple, lateral, and unbounded. The importance of this mobile and opaque complexity is that it evades colonizing categories of knowledge. The colonizers, Glissant argues, depend on territorial, nation-based knowledge. The "root" of their worldview is dualistic: citizens versus barbarians, master versus slave, West versus the rest. Such a geography of reason, grounded in European civilization and religion, orders the world according to its narcissistic view, foreclosing difference that fails to support the myth of its superior status.

In contrast to its foreclosure in European thought, abyssal history animates the narrative of *Romance in Marseille*. The flotsam and jetsam enact a riotous upheaval against the omnipresence of state-sponsored violence, confinement, deportation, and harassment. McKay's novel upends the geography of reason to disclose a poetics of relation—lateral, reciprocal, and creative—between the human and nonhuman. In so doing, it attempts to disturb the smooth unfolding of narrative and the conventional assumptions of literary form in favor of the nonlinear, entangled, and disposable.[24] Too often, critics assume that Black modernist texts break from the past in a manner consistent with European modernity and its rupture with tradition. The signature term of the Harlem Renaissance, the *New Negro*, suggests as much. The *New Negro* rejects the debacle of the post-Reconstruction era and instead proclaims a new militancy in the African American freedom struggle, as exemplified by McKay's famous sonnet "If We Must Die." New Negro writers, the critical consensus maintains, celebrate the freedoms possible in modern, urban Black life and turn away from the slave past. In her groundbreaking study of the global afterlives of slave narratives in contemporary Anglophone novels, Yogita Goyal repeats this assumption, claiming that it wasn't until the 1960s that writers began to revisit the slave past "after a gap of almost a century, barring exceptions like Arna Bontemp's 1936 *Black Thunder*."[25] Certainly, this claim can be upheld in terms of an explicit, realist retelling of slave history. But by foregrounding the abyssal history of the slave past, the absent presence of the Middle Passage, McKay's novel explores the ongoing afterlife of slavery and locates a poetics of relation from within its inherited structures, especially the commodification and mutilation of disposable persons. This article asks, How does McKay transform the biologically inferior status of human "refuse" that is Black life within racialized capitalism from waste to the alluvial entanglements of Black life lived otherwise?

More than any of McKay's other works, *Romance in Marseille* directly interrogates the afterlife of slavery in early twentieth-century Afro-diasporic cultures. Lafala's stowaway passage from Marseille to New York City results in his captivity and the loss of his legs caused by the crew. The settlement he receives from the shipping company for his double amputation exchanges his body parts for money. The announcements in the Black press resonate uncomfortably with slave auction catalogues and plantation account books, for instance: "AFRICAN LEGS BRING ONE HUNDRED THOUSAND DOLLARS" (*RM*, 19). Moreover, Lafala appears to accept his passive, objectified role within the system that has not only mutilated him but also subjected him to manipulation by his multiple handlers: Black Angel, who finds the appropriate lawyer for the case; the Jewish lawyer who defends him and wants half of the settlement money; the company; and the official who represents Lafala's colonial or protected status (it's never clear which he falls under). And this manipulation continues in Marseille by the shipping company and Lafala's agent, friends, and enemies. Finally, Lafala's background, while not the complete natal alienation of slavery, implies a fundamental rootlessness due to colonial cultural reprogramming. Colonial missionaries removed Lafala from his village at a young age so that he could be educated in a mission school in a larger town, thereby destroying Lafala's authentic belonging to his Indigenous tribal community. The statelessness and familial homelessness, as well as his physical mutilation, are remarked on through his lawyer's third-person account of how Lafala's abject status will appear before a New York judge: "Poor African boy without any relatives taken away from his people when he was so young he did not even remember them, without family, without country even, without legs" (*RM*, 11–12). The resultant effect is that Lafala declares, "You are a good lawyer; this gentleman is a big official. I am nothing" (*RM*, 22). Swallowed up by a white world, Lafala drifts along, buffeted by the whims of others.

Lafala's love interest, Aslima, also exhibits a constrained sense of agency that can be attributed to her status as a sex slave in Morocco and as a prostitute in Marseille. Aslima was born a slave in North Africa. Her mother was "a robust Sudanese who was sold a slave to the Moors," of whom Aslima has only "a shadowy remembrance" (*RM*, 44). Aslima's childhood is short; at an early age, she is kidnapped to serve "as a decorative thing in the house of a wise old courtesan" until she can fetch a large price as a virgin sex slave (*RM*, 44). Next, a French West Indian soldier buys her to be his concubine in Casablanca and later moves her to Algeria. Finally, a Corsican "tout," acting as her protector, takes her to Marseille and sells her to a "loving house" (*RM*, 45). Aslima drifts from house to house until she strikes out on her own, with the protection of her pimp, Titin. Lafala, enthralled once again with Aslima on his return visit to Marseille, invites her to go "Back to Africa" with him (*RM*, 42). Such an invitation echoes Marcus Garvey's rallying cry of a popular Black internationalism and identifies both Lafala and Aslima as products of slavery and members of an extended Black diaspora. Even more, Aslima combines Pan-Africanism with Orientalism, given her association with the Islamic and animist cultures of North Africa, where she grew up. Such racial blending works to displace a Black/white binary into a multiracial and multinational continuum of diasporic identities.[26] The Asiatic dimension of Aslima's character provides a sensuous and exotic eroticism that at times allows her to escape her commodified sexuality.

The question of whether to live otherwise than the white world demands, to exert however constrained an agency, drives the plot: Will Lafala take Aslima with him back to Africa? Who will double-cross whom, or will true love win? The motivation of each character is opaque. Each is faced with the choice between money and sensuous, redemptive love. The uncertainty of the outcome drives the plot and confronts the reader with the unknowability of human actions. The difficulty is particularly clear in Lafala's case. After he is released from the Marseille prison where he was held by the shipping company for the crime of stowing away, his agent advises him to "leave Marseille at once to avoid further complications." The agent speaks out of shock after learning that Aslima "was just a colored creature of the dives of Quayside" (*RM*, 122). The agent's racist misogyny accords with Lafala's practical impulse to protect his money and outweighs "the sensual" aspect of his character in the "clear and sobering daylight" on the morning that Lafala is to leave Marseille (*RM*, 127). Although Lafala is "overwhelmed in love" with Aslima, he takes action to preserve his newfound wealth and status by abandoning Aslima and leaving her money to salve his guilty conscience (*RM*, 125). His choice speaks to the "dual personality" of living in a white world: namely, the conflict between the prizes offered under racialized capitalism, on the one hand, and the precarious possibility of living otherwise, on the other. Meanwhile, Aslima's motivations also remain murky, at least to Titin, until the denouement. While this opacity mimics the hard-boiled detective novel, when we account for the Middle Passage history and disposable status of the Quayside population that subtends this plot, the possibilities of living otherwise—fleeting, ephemeral, excessive—are far more subversive than a potboiler whodunit can convey. These "experiments in freedom" that are staged in the novel, riotous conduct, queer sexuality, gaming the system, form a "beautiful [counter]plot against the plantation" (*WL*, 17, 34). The counterplot depends on embracing contingent, lateral relations with human "refuse"—the queer, the stranger, and the whore—to succeed.

Alluvium

The possibility of a collective transformation from racialized refuse to living otherwise together in *Romance in Marseille* depends on what Glissant terms "alluvium." According to Glissant, "the unconscious memory" of the Middle Passage provides "a whole alluvium" or the poetic relations and affectual practices of Black life (*PR*, 7, 111). Glissant refers to "the unconscious memory" as "the asceticism of crossing this way the land-sea that, unknown to you, is the planet Earth, feeling a language vanish, the word of the gods vanish, and the sealed image of even the most everyday object, of even the most familiar animal, vanish. The evanescent taste of what you ate. The hounded scent of ochre earth and savannas" (*PR*, 7). Glissant's "unconscious memory" is a forgotten "chasm" that is "furrowed with fugitive memories" (*PR*, 7). There is neither origin nor ground here but only loss and uncertain remembrance. The chasm paradoxically figures an absence that "in the end became knowledge" (*PR*, 8). Glissant figures memory as akin to the sea: indeterminate, groundless, yet material and present. The absence of origins, rather than producing nothingness or nonbeing, instead proliferates possibilities: Africa becomes "the birthplace of multiplicity" and the Caribbean becomes a "cradle of multiple diasporas."[27] Freed from fixed meanings, origins, genealogies, and territories, alluvium conjoins multiple sources, overlapping memories and practices, and fosters a poetics of relation built on unknowing. Glissant states that the peoples who found themselves so displaced, who forgot the chasm, "nevertheless wove this sail (a veil)" (*PR*, 7). They weave together stories and rituals whose figuration as a veil highlights an opacity of knowing. This opacity nonetheless provides for a new sort of chronotope: a way to sail a craft (a narrative) where "at the bow there is still something we now share: this murmur, cloud or rain or peaceful smoke" (*PR*, 9). Evanescent, boundless, and filled with unformed sound and a dispersed yet meaningful atmosphere, a postslavery poetics of relation is affective and fleeting and carries with it both the devastating absence of forgotten traumas *and* the possibilities of living otherwise together. The chasm that is the legacy of the Middle Passage produces the crosscultural nature of Glissant's poetics of relation that is predicated on knowledge that is open-ended, shared, and contingent: "Beyond its chasm we gamble on the unknown" (*PR*, 8). Such absence, shot through with fugitive memories (that can range from tragicomic references such as "African legs bring one hundred thousand dollars" to the simple refusal to plan for the future), becomes a mode by which Black and multiracial life unfolds, as we find in *Romance in Marseille*.

The absent presence of slavery in *Romance in Marseille* manifests through the racial state: frequent, unanticipated arrests; the condemnation of the drifting unemployed for attempting to live outside the racist structures of labor; the criminalization of prostitutes, communist organizers, and queer subjects; and the policing of national boundaries that entails the deportation of those without the necessary papers. These efforts halt movement, inject uncertainty, and devalue the community's experiments in living. In addition, the fugitive memory of the Middle Passage haunts Lafala's double amputation. The palimpsest of suffering, both past and present, has the effect of collapsing time frames and disrupting chronological history. It draws on an alluvium that sediments Black suffering and collective rejuvenation. The point is underscored when Lafala attends the reception at the Toutva-Bien to celebrate his release from jail: "Everybody was close together in a thick juice melted by wine and music." The beguine was playing, "always living [*sic*] this heady Martinique dance, blood cousin to the other West Indian folk dances, the Aframerican shuffle and the African swaying" (*RM*, 107). Time and space are collapsed into one heady celebration where music and dancing evoke both African and Afro-diasporic practices. The crowd merges into a potent being-in-common, people dissolving into one another, while the music evokes a Black Atlantic mobility that articulates a "blood" kinship or racial memory with other Pan-African music.[28]

Lafala is literally carried off by the current of erotic, sensual energy: "The beguine rhythm caught him by the middle, drop by drop. The music swelled up and down with a sweep and rushed him off his feet" (*RM*, 108). Ironically, it is the pull of the music that propels Lafala *to* his feet as he attempts to dance for the first time since his amputations. But he can do so only by relying on the force of the music and crowd and on his dependence on Aslima: "He found it was not so difficult after all with Aslima carrying him along" (*RM*, 108). The pun on *beguine*, as both a dance and slang for sexual attraction, transforms Aslima into a bulwark for Lafala as she "stiffened her breast to bear him up" (*RM*, 108). She becomes a feminine ship floating on a sea of restorative Black life. The scene underscores Lafala's physical dependence on the Quayside community, and Aslima in particular, to rejuvenate him. After all, he seems to walk without assistance elsewhere in the novel. The dance displays the necessity of Aslima's Black femininity to transvalue Lafala's vulnerable and dependent masculinity. So, too, the festivity renders him a full participant in the multiracial collective. The celebration at Tout-va-Bien is experienced as an entanglement of bodies, energies, and elemental rhythms, music without, wine within, that allow subjects to become porous and slippery against one another in a living, mixing, mobile force. The alluvial scene occurs despite and within the ever-present racist structures that seek to eliminate such wayward activity and compel obedience to the servitude of menial labor and sexual commodification.

Later in *Poetics of Relation* alluvium becomes something more than an absence. It refers to a shoreline sedimentation of the overlooked practices of Black life. As mentioned above, relation refuses transparency and visibility. Its opacity is not, Glissant states, the tain of the mirror "[by] which Western humanity reflected the world in its own image." Instead, "there is opacity now at the bottom of the mirror, a whole alluvium deposited by populations, silt that is fertile but, in actual fact, indistinct and unexplored even today" (*PR*, 111). The inert tain of the mirror is disavowed by the colonizer in his insistence on the transparency of the native, whereas, for Glissant, alluvium is living, creative, and diverse. While Blackness is created by means of the abyss that violently severed captives from their geographic and cultural ties to the ancestral land, Glissant underscores a rehumanizing reattachment to New World ecologies. The horrific deformation of personhood in racialized slavery—social death, as Orlando Patterson terms it—at the same time "presses an inhuman categorization and the inhuman earth into intimacy."[29] *A whole alluvium* alludes to the fertile richness of land, water, and bodies joined together for survival and creation. It is sedimented in an ongoing process that is contingent and unpredictable. Importantly, alluvium is both inscrutable and resistant to coloniality; it decenters European knowledge by means of a creative, dynamic synthesis. The assemblage is unpredictable in its becoming because its form is open, embodied, and intra-active; that is, it is shaped as much by nonhuman matter as by human intention, and that intra-action is ongoing.[30]

That Afro-diasporic subjects resist colonial and neocolonial power is indicated by Glissant's insistence on the "*right* to opacity." Drabinski argues that this phrase indicates its "anticolonial force, and therefore its resistance to certain senses of knowing and understanding that would seek to absorb, reactivate, and possess; it is resistance to the dialectic of legibility and illegibility."[31] What resists visuality is the composted amalgamation of cultural mixing and loss, a merging of land and water, sand and salt, absent past and given present. The mixture becomes a productive fecundity that carries the imaginative and material power to transfigure the very concept of the world. It is "the constant reinvention of not just meaning but the meaning of meaning in the New World."[32] In effect, the very grounds for comparison, reason, and value dissolve, necessitating a radical rethinking of meaning: what one attempts to convey by language. Opacity continually alters the aims and intention of signification. Such a Caribbean creolizing force reconfigures the geography of reason and revalues relations between humans and the nonhuman. McKay further displaces the geography of reason by acknowledging the diasporic aftereffects of slavery in Africa and Europe. Caribbean creolization extends its project into the "old" world.

A crucial alluvial entanglement in *Romance in Marseille* occurs through the resignification and revaluation of the term *pig*. During their first sexual encounter on Lafala's return to Marseille, Aslima remarks, "'I've been a pig all my life. . . . But with you I don't feel that it's just a mud bath. I feel like we're clean pigs'" (*RM*, 41). Their racial association with animality and filth interrogates the human as it is defined by Europe. Aslima scrubs Black sexuality clean from its association with dirt, immorality, and licentiousness. Together, Lafala and Aslima "reconstruct intimate life" from the racialized confines begun on the slave ship and the plantation. Hartman says of these sexually revolutionary practices: "The bedroom was a domain of thought in deed and a site of enacting, exceeding, undoing, and remaking relations of power" (*WL*, 61). Aslima in particular reinvents herself as a creative, loving human entangled joyfully with another in a manner that negates her social position as a disposable, vilified prostitute of color. Yet she does not mimic a (white) autonomous subject who claims to have full agency over their surrounds. Aslima configures herself and Lafala in lateral, mutual terms. Neither condemns the other for their Blackness, disability, or profession. Their partial agency, arising out of their confinement within raced and gendered systems of power, finds freedom only by embracing and exploring the very derogatory terms with which they are associated. Such metaphorical and historical proximity to dirt and animality emphasizes the fungibility of their Black bodies in their formlessness, permeability, and unmoored location. By affirming this designation rather than condemning it, the novel proposes a sexualized, scandalous, rebellious liaison that wallows in its sensual, pleasurable, and liberating force. This reconsideration of sexuality is especially important for Aslima.

In more general terms, McKay's novels occasion a broad rethinking of the human through the very process of dehumanization. Jennifer F. Wang argues that McKay's association in *Home to Harlem* of working-class Black subjects with animals is a "racial-form-of-life [in which] . . . revitalization emerges out of the revisioning of biological and organic life ('living itself')."[33] The suggestion that Black reinvention of the human proceeds by revisioning its relation to biological and organic life makes Aslima's declaration to Lafala, "I want to convince you that I am human at bottom," resonate with the long history of Black (and female) dehumanization (*RM*, 41). Her assertion revalues and reimagines the alluvial location to which Black life has been consigned. *At bottom, as refuse, as flesh, I am human.* To grasp the revolutionary potential of this alluvial reinvention of the human, it's important to keep in mind the racial chasm, as Hartman stresses:

> *The Negress* occupied a different rung of existence than the mistress and the
> lady of the house, the very term signaled a break or caesura in species life, a
> variant in the human, an antagonism or dimorphism more fundamental than
> man and woman. Yet, was there an opportunity . . . in the refusal to emulate

and mimic the standards of who and what you were directed and commanded
to be (but never would be)? It was difficult to put this visceral and abiding
sense of existing otherwise, at odds with the given, into words. (*WL*, 274–75)

It is McKay's genius that he *did* put the revolutionary potential of alluvial
entanglements—sexual, fungible, human and nonhuman, shifting and open—
into words in his novels. *Romance in Marseille* goes further than his other novels
in taking seriously how Black femininity, as it exists otherwise, must be central to
the Black reinvention of the human. The final section of this essay discusses in
more depth how Aslima is the fulcrum around which the novel's "experiments in
freedom that unfolded within slavery's shadow" take place (*WL*, 17).

Fungibility

Glissant's "womb abyss" deploys a familiar feminine gendering of the ship at sea to
highlight a maternal rather than paternal presence in the formation of Black Atlantic histories.[34] But it neglects the ship's ungendering of captive bodies that renders
them commodified property and erases the sexual violence that occurs on board
ship. A critique of Glissant's gender blindness is crucial because *Romance in Marseille* is concerned with how Black women hold the keys to unmaking the white
world. We next return to the question of fungibility so that we can better understand Aslima's importance in reenvisioning Black life in McKay's novel.

Atlantic slavery initiated the structural transformation of people into commodities. Foundational to chattel slavery in the New World was the abstract exchangeability of humans on the market. The term used by Portuguese slave traders that
allowed for the exchangeability of human persons was *pieza*. The Portuguese traders defined a *pieza* as a twenty-five-year-old male African in good health.[35] All other
captives were made relative to this unit of measure. For instance, three small children together could equal a *pieza*. Older Africans and those with disabilities could
be counted as "refuse" and thrown into the bargain for free or be rejected entirely.
Stephanie Smallwood describes this transformation of living human beings into
objects of exchange as beginning at the African littoral, just outside the slave forts
and prior to boarding the slave ship. As the slave ship captains selected Africans to
be transported to the Americas, they "reduced people to the sum of their biological
parts, thereby scaling life down to an arithmetical equation and finding the lowest
common denominator."[36] The reduction of people to biology sets the stage for racist
evolutionary science in the nineteenth century. To return to the conversation in
Romance in Marseille that began this article, when St. Dominique informs Lafala
that "[his] race represented the very lowest level of humanity, biologically and spiritually speaking," we can certainly read his words as chiming with evolutionary history and racist science (*RM*, 76).[37] St. Dominique's statement associates Blackness
with biology and immanence, a failure of the Black race to transcend their so-called
barbaric conditions. Reading against the grain, as I believe the novel's irony in this
scene suggests, I am arguing that it is precisely the association of Blackness with
biology and immanence that provides the basis for McKay's Black liberatory aesthetics. Lafala, after all, rejects the Seaman's Club and the hierarchical structure of
its world-historical narrative that is represented by St. Dominique.

The racial hierarchy depends on the physical and social violence of abstract equivalence that reduced the captives, in the eyes of the captors, to things, or as Orlando Patterson says, to "liminal beings" condemned to "social death."[38] To their captors, the captives' value lay in the potential extraction of labor power in the Americas and, in the case of female slaves, in their potential to reproduce property.[39] Their exchangeability on the market "outweighed any social value they might have."[40] External exchange value places value outside the now empty, valueless nonperson of the captive. Like the commodity form that Marx analyzes, the slave commodity has value only in relation to other equivalent units of value, that is, in relation to other slaves on the market. In sum, the African captives' lives became reduced under the slave system they entered on the shores of the West African coast to their equivalent value as a *pieza* of labor power: a piece, a quantitative unit; a what, not a who. That the Atlantic slave trade forced the ontological transformation of captive Africans into Blackness, from human to thing, is crucial for understanding the sea change of the modern world: specifically, how Blackness, produced in the afterlife of slavery, continues to confine and constrain the denizens of the French seaport in McKay's *Romance in Marseille*.

As a "thing" expelled from the category of human, the slave is not static and fixed as is an object within the Cartesian system of knowledge. Rather, it is fungible, meaning that because slaves were valued strictly through their exchangeability, their actual bodies and persons possessed an extraordinary "metaphorical aptitude" that Hartman glosses as the slaves' ability to be endlessly replaced (because they are all equivalent) and also because, as a commodity, they were considered always sexually available.[41] Such vulnerability and powerlessness arise because "power and projection produce certain bodies as other, thereby granting them a mysterious quality of desirability, which is always already undergirded by violence and the assumption of possession."[42] Though the slave system and its afterlife project this availability onto Black female (and other) bodies, their domination was and is never total. Tiffany Lethabo King argues that "fungibility is, in fact, a product of White anxiety and representation, an attempt to 'get in front of' or anticipate Black fugitive movement" (*BS*, 25). The system of turning people into property depended on deploying physical and social violence that was ongoing, inventive, excessive, and repeated. In response to white violence, "Black struggle's resistance to and maneuvering within fungibility is as unpredictable and uncontainable" (*BS*, 24). King continues: "Black fungibility can denote and connote pure flux, process, and potential. To be rendered Black and fungible under conquest is to be rendered porous, undulating, fluttering, sensuous, and in a space and state at-the-edge and outside of normative configurations of sex, gender, sexuality, space, and time to stabilize and fix the human category" (*BS*, 23). Fungibility, then, has two modes: the first as a tool for white domination as it commodifies others; the second as Black resistance against those same forces by means of embracing nonnormativity and nonlinearity (the past and future in the present).

Fungibility as a tool for white domination has a long history. Sexual violence against Black bodies was neither a crime on the slave ship nor within the plantation regime. That Glissant does not explicitly engage with sexual violence reflects the afterlife of slavery, namely, that sexual violence against Black women (and certainly

also Black men) remains profoundly widespread and unspoken, that is, accepted
with impunity throughout most of the twentieth century. Hartman writes, "The
repression and negation of this act of violence are central not only to the pained constitution of blackness but also to the figuration and the deployment of sexuality in
the context of captivity."[43] While no longer a de facto slave, Aslima's seamless transition from slavery to sexual slavery allows McKay to comment on the violence and
domination that Aslima continues to face in her work as a prostitute in Marseille. Her
status as "a stranger" and her profession of lending her body for impersonal sexual
congress reflects the extreme marginality of her social position (RM, 91, 123).[44]
Such precarity shows itself when Aslima suggests to her pimp, Titin, that they
marry. Titin reflects to himself, "It was an unthinkable thing—the idea of marrying
a whore, a woman whose card of identity was the yellow one of prostitution, a
woman without family, without home, without name" (RM, 90). Denied kinship,
permanently labeled adversely by the state, and existing in a state of natal alienation,
Aslima cannot escape her status as a commodity. She exists solely to be the vessel
for the projection of others' desires for possession and domination until she is
rejected for even this role. Thinking about Aslima's suggestion of marriage, Titin
reflects (via free indirect narration): "There were certain Quaysiders who were mar-
ried to professional prostitutes but they were creatures of brothels and allied places
of the same status as the inmates. Titin referred to such men as degenerates and
perverts. He felt sick in the guts from the suggestion at his becoming a member
of that class of men" (RM, 91). Titin's categorization of those who love prostitutes
queers Lafala and relegates both him and Aslima to the lowest ranks of society.
Lafala becomes viscerally abhorrent and morally outrageous in the view of those
who uphold the social order, including those, like Titin, who are parasites on the
very women whom they condemn.

The effect of this abuse is to render Aslima barely legible. The fungibility to
which she is reduced produces a countercharge that is erotic and transformative
but unspoken. As King says above, fungibility that comprises Black resistance is
"porous, undulating, fluttering, sensuous, and in a space and state at-the-edge and
outside of normal configurations of sex, gender, sexuality, space, and time to stabilize and fix the human category." Aslima offers resistance by means of her body and
its connection to nonhuman life. She elicits a sensuous and ecstatic, erotic state in
Lafala, who remarks, "Under her coarse and hard exterior there was always that rare
green and fruity quality which had so intoxicated him when they first met" (RM,
113). Together, Aslima and Lafala reinvent the human as coterminous with the nonhuman world, "rare green and fruity." They enact a nonnormative sexuality that
transports them elsewhere, through the deprivations of a Middle Passage absence,
and through the alluvium of their disposable and degraded status, to a reconfigura-
tion of Black life. Audre Lorde speaks of the erotic as an overlooked resource that
has been "vilified, abused, and devalued within western society."[45] The word, she
states, "comes from the Greek word eros, the personification of love in all its
aspects—born of Chaos, and personifying creative power and harmony" (SO, 55).
Lorde calls eros a "lifeforce" and associates it with women, though it can easily be
broadened to account for many forms of embodied resistance to Cartesian dual-

ism (*SO*, 55). Eros evokes a wider reality than Enlightenment thought allows. Its formlessness—what Lorde calls "a chaos of our strongest feelings"—joins together with sensual, spiritual, physical, emotional, and creative energies across individuals and beyond the limit of the spoken (*SO*, 54). Aslima enacts an erotic fungibility of flux and potentiality even as she suspects that she'll be sacrificed to the dominant order that confines her.

In presenting the setting for Aslima's vision of her sacrifice, McKay transposes Caribbean creolization onto North African Islamic and animist cultures so as to render time and space nonlinear and nonplanar. The geographic lamination of Africa, the Caribbean, and the East render disparate places and times simultaneous and overdetermined. The multiplied setting is exemplified by McKay's having drafted much of *Romance in Marseille* while living in Morocco. It renders a sense of diasporic mobility that is nearly as shifting and mutable as the sea itself. East and West, past and present, mingle sharply in Aslima's hallucinatory nocturnal vision on the Marseille wharf. As she sits near the shoreline, overlooking the bay, enveloped in darkness and obscurity,

> A red light appeared in the horizon revealing to her a different scene. She was in the heart of an antique white-washed city. And there was loud mounting music of voices as if a thousand golden-throated muezzins were calling in one mighty chorus. . . . There followed a loving feast. . . .
>
> When the feasting was finished the belly-moving beat of the drum roused the people again after an interval of rest to dancing and chanting over and over again repeating and reiterating from pattern to pattern unraveling the threads of life from the most intricate to the simplest to the naked bottom as if in evocation of the first gods who emerged out of the ancient unfathomed womb of Africa to procreate and spread over the vast surface of the land. (*RM*, 60–61)

Though the simile in the first sentence, "as if a thousand golden-throated muezzins were calling," suggests an Islamic religious celebration and the feast of Iftar during the holy month of Ramadan, we learn instead that the crowds, some enslaved and some free, gather together to worship "the Sword of Life." Africa and Islam meet, conjoin, and creolize through the mixing of slaves and freepersons from within and beyond the Islamic world. The vision is overwrought, as the crowd worships "a flaming sword suspended from the center of the dome," but it serves two functions. The first is to assert an African life force, a shared "racial memory" of the "threads of life."[46] These threads are unraveled to the "naked bottom," the facts of reproduction and death. The second is to foreshadow the novel's ending.

The passage insists on both its sensuous and erotic features in the present moment and a sedimentation of deep time and the now. "*As if* in evocation of the first gods" both invokes a prehistorical time and cancels it in favor of a lurid description in the present. As the participants dance and chant, their civilized facade is stripped away to reveal their elemental selves: naked, spontaneous, and uninhibited. Similarly, "the naked bottom" is compared to the gods emerging from "the ancient unfathomable womb of Africa." The comparison is structurally similar to

Glissant's alluvium that sediments "the unconscious memory" of the Middle Passage, especially when Glissant figures the slave ship as a "womb abyss" in birthing African captives as slaves (*PR*, 6). Significantly, both McKay and Glissant convert nonhuman sites into gendered ones to link materiality—the landscape of Africa; the infrastructure of the slave ship—with feminized Blackness. This assemblage then allows for the reclamation of the flesh in the vision above and when Aslima repeatedly insists, as discussed above, that she and Lafala are pigs wallowing in the mud. The alluvial, figured as mud, silt, the womb, and seaborne detritus, in North Africa as well as the Caribbean and Marseille, refers to life stripped to its most basic elements and celebrated as such: a collective, creative, embodied energy that strengthens the pan Afro-Orientalist liaison in resistance to Western colonization. The second function of this vision is to preordain the plot twists to come. Aslima's vision is her fate. In the hallucination, she is among the group who would be offered up "body and soul as a sacrifice" (*RM*, 62). The vision foreshadows the plot denouement when Aslima, after learning that Lafala left for Africa without her, attacks her pimp with a knife because he threatens to kill Lafala. Titin riddles her body with bullets, thereby making Aslima into a sacrificial offering to Lafala's altar of monied prestige. Aslima shows the limits of Black femininity in the face of racialized capitalism. She remains in the chaos of oceanic eros and reveals the "unfixed, ungraspable contours" of fluid sensuality and self-abnegating love.[47] Hartman underscores the potentiality of Aslima's life experience that cannot yet be realized:

> The most significant absence of all in the dramaturgy of struggle, in the
> cosmic shattered history of black life, in the unfolding plot of the wretched,
> was that of [the black] woman. . . . If the text of the human was written over
> and against [the black man], she fell out of the order of representation all
> together. Neither subject nor object, but a mute silenced thing, like an
> impossible metaphor or a beached whale or as a form yet to be named.
> (*WL*, 259)

McKay cannot fully represent Aslima. She remains opaque, her physical presence—erotic, sensual, alluvial—hinting at the form "yet to be named" of Black humanity. Her last moments, as she is riddled by bullets from Titin's gun, exemplify the "unanchored, malleable, and open signs" of Black fungibility: "She threw up her hands like a bird of prey about to swoop down upon a victim and pitched headlong to the door" (*BS*, 22; *RM*, 130). Aslima is reduced to flesh—torn and bleeding—and she simultaneously refers to another way of being. She appears as an avenging animal, fluttering, porous, and beyond the racist categories to which she is assigned. She signifies both racist confinement and the possibility of transforming that confinement into an alluvial entanglement with human and nonhuman alike.

Revaluing Black femininity whose flesh has been written over by colonial masters, Lafala links Aslima's body to the fecund earth in an alluvial form that gives shape to Black as well as pan-Afro-Oriental freedom and futurity. On their final night together, Lafala marvels: "It was as if Aslima had all the time reserved a secret cell in her being and had unlocked it now for him alone to enter. And how like a rare tropical garden it was where every fruit was delicious to taste" (*RM*, 125). Her body and soul are figuratively linked to "a rare tropical garden," not, I think, to simply link Black femininity with nature, but to assemble the human and nonhuman in a coterminous and transformative relation. McKay inverts colonial fantasies of the female captive body, associated with the domination of the land, into the mutual enjoyment of self and land in an affirming, creative, intimate sharing. Aslima, after all, must make herself vulnerable—unlock her being—for this experience to occur. However, this mutuality is not to last. As Aslima's body is torn apart by bullets, it returns to mere flesh and its association with waste. McKay's novel implies that Black alluvial life is precarious under conditions of racial capitalism. But, as Aslima shows, it must be attempted against all odds.

LAURA WINKIEL is associate professor of English at the University of Colorado Boulder. She is author of *Modernism, Race, and Manifestos* (2008) and *Modernism: The Basics* (2017) and coeditor of *Geomodernisms: Race, Modernism, Modernity* (2005). She served as senior editor of *English Language Notes* for seven years, during which she edited three special issues, including "Hydro-criticism," published in April 2019. She held the position of president of the Modernist Studies Association in 2017–18. She is presently at work on a book called *Modernism and the Middle Passage*.

Notes

1 McKay, *Romance in Marseille*, 76 (hereafter cited as *RM*).

2 When Lafala visits the Seaman's and Worker's Club, his guide and Marxist revolutionary pedagogue St. Dominique, an educated mixed-race ("mulatto") worker from Martinique, narrates the significance of Lafala's presence: "Lafala's being there with his yellow and white comrades was a symbol of the all-embracing purpose of the new social ideal. Lafala's race represented the very lowest level of humanity, biologically and spiritually speaking. But there was no hindrance to its full participation in the coming [universal] social order" (*RM*, 76).

3 "The slave ship was a strange and potent combination of war machine, mobile prison, and factory. . . . Sailors . . . 'produced' slaves within the ship as factory, doubling their economic value as they moved them from a market on the eastern Atlantic to one on the west and helping to create the labor power that animated a growing world economy in the eighteenth century and after. In producing workers for the plantation, the ship-factory also produced 'race'" (Rediker, *Slave Ship*, 9–10). To be sure, this process began even before embarkation, on the shores of West Africa,

where captives were first purchased and made fungible. See Smallwood, *Saltwater Slavery*, chap. 2.

4 These questions allude to the infamous *Zong* case as well as to the large number of suicides during the Middle Passage; see, e.g., Baucom, *Specters of the Atlantic*; Philip, *Zong!*; and Snyder, *The Power to Die*. One must add, following Sharpe's *In the Wake*, that contemporary refugees frequently meet similar fates on overcrowded, unsafe, and unwanted vessels. See also Emma Christopher, Cassandra Pybus, and Marcus Rediker, *Many Middle Passages*, for a global history of forced migrations that question the exceptional status of the Atlantic trade.

5 On finding power through trauma, Scott asks, "What is the potential for useful political, personal, psychological resource in racialization-through-abjection as historical legacy, as ancestral experience?" (*Extravagant Abjection*, 6). Specifically, his book explores Black sexuality "as a vehicle for, and the realization of, black freedom and power" (7). On lateral relations with the nonhuman, Chen and Luciano explore how the photographer Laura Aguilar questions what constitutes the human by positing an erotic, queer relation to the

nonhuman land. Queer theory, Chen and Luciano state, tends to interrogate the nature of the "human" in its relation to the queer, both in their attention to "how sexual norms . . . constitute and regulate hierarchies of humanness, and as they work to unsettle those norms and the default forms of humanness they uphold" ("Introduction," 186). This unsettling of norms, they argue, extends to relations with nonhuman surrounds.

6   A useful definition of things as opposed to objects comes from Brown: "The passage into materialism . . . requires acknowledging 'things' outside the subject/object trajectory, which means thinking sensation in its distinction from cognition. . . . To the degree that the 'thing' registers the undignified mutability of objects, and thus the excess of the object (a capacity to be other than it is), the 'thing' names a mutual mediation (and a slide between objective and subjective predication) that appears as the object's difference from itself" ("The Secret Life of Things," 1–2).

7   Snorton, *Black on Both Sides*, 6.

8   Hartman, *Scenes of Subjection*, 21.

9   We can also understand fungibility-as-resistance as having always accompanied the slave ship masters' attempts to render African captives into pure, exchangeable quantities of human labor. The slave ship used the depersonalizing nowhere of the waters, the violent threat of drowning and sharks, and the horrendous confinement in the holds to commodify humans into racialized refuse. But something else occurred on those ships: namely, what Tinsley refers to as "the brown-skinned, fluid-bodied experiences now called *blackness* and *queerness* [that] surfaced in intercontinental, maritime contact hundreds of years ago: in the seventeenth century, in the Atlantic Ocean. . . . The black Atlantic has always been the queer Atlantic" ("Black Atlantic," 191). That queerness arose from the need to survive captivity and to resist commodification, Tinsley says, "by *feeling* and *feeling for* their co-occupants [in the sex-segregated holds] on these ships" (192). This eroticism took place against the backdrop of violent dehumanization on board ship and against the threat of death by drowning.

10   Hartman, *Wayward Lives*, 61–62 (hereafter cited as *WL*).

11   Glissant defines "transversality" as submerged forms of relationality that need not be visible to have effects (*Caribbean Discourse*, 66–67). Transversality also encompasses the quality of open-ended activity and affectivity: passing, cruising, flopping, feeding, loving. The "trans"

here, as Snorton poses it, is a transitive grammar, "the expression of an action that requires a direct object to complete its sense of meaning" (*Black on Both Sides*, 6). See Snorton's discussion of transversality (9–11).

12   Samuelson, "Coastal Form," 17; Hofmeyr, "Provisional Notes."

13   See especially Winkiel, "Hydro-criticism," and the cluster in it called "Hydro-critical Practices: Modernism and the Sea."

14   Blum, "Introduction," 151.

15   Blum, "Introduction," 151. See also Steinberg, "Of Other Seas," 157.

16   Glissant, *Poetics of Relation*, 54–55 (hereafter cited as *PR*).

17   Blum, "Introduction," 151.

18   Chow and Bushman, "Hydro-eroticism," 98.

19   "If slavery persists as an issue in the political life of black America, it is not because of an antiquarian obsession with bygone days or the burden of a too-long memory, but because black lives are still imperiled and devalued by a racial calculus and a political arithmetic that were entrenched centuries ago. This is the afterlife of slavery—skewed life chances, limited access to health and education, premature death, incarceration and impoverishment," states Hartman, *Lose Your Mother*, 6. "All of it is now   it is always now   there will never be a time when I am not crouching and watching others who are crouching too," to quote Morrison, *Beloved*, 210.

20   Wynter's formulation problematically erases the Indigenous presence already existing in the "New" World (*Black Metamorphosis*). Several important recent studies have engaged with the overlapping but discrete predicaments of First Peoples and Blacks in North America and the Caribbean: see Rivkin, *Fictions of Land and Flesh*; Wilderson, *Red, White, and Black*; and King, *The Black Shoals* (hereafter cited as *BS*).

21   Drabinski, *Glissant and the Middle Passage*, 52.

22   Glissant, *Caribbean Discourse*, 2.

23   See also Musser's discussion of Glissant, whom she quotes: "'Thought of self and thought of other here become obsolete in their duality.' Glissant's argument [in *Poetics of Relation*] that lingering in opacity offers a way around the cleavage between self and Other because it refuses a prioritization of either and forces a reckoning with unknowability is central to the stakes that underlie brown jouissance" (*Sensual Excess*, 14). I am focusing on the anticolonialism in McKay's novel, while Musser examines contemporary Black visual and performance artists.

24   I use the term *entanglement* following Barad: "Matter and meaning are not separate

elements. They are inextricably fused together, and no event, no matter how energetic, can tear them asunder. . . . Mattering is simultaneously a matter of substance and significance, most evidently perhaps when it is the nature of matter that is in question, when the smallest parts of matter are found to be capable of exploding deeply entrenched ideas and large cities. Perhaps this is why contemporary physics makes the inescapable entanglement of matters of being, knowing, and doing, of ontology, epistemology, and ethics, of fact and value, so tangible, so poignant" (*Meeting the Universe Halfway*, 3). While Barad's archive consists of subatomic particles and wave theory, feminist new materialism has taken up her work on the undecidability of matter and meaning and the question of subjective perspective vis-à-vis the object being studied to foreground the liveliness of matter. This liveliness transforms received notions of causality and agency and highlights the ways in which subjectivity is situated within a complex, interlocking multitude of systems that are both internal and external to the subject.

25 Goyal, *Afterlives*, 22.

26 On Afro-Orientalism in McKay's work, see Borst, "Signifyin(g) Afro-Orientalism"; and, more broadly, Mullen, *Afro-Orientalism*.

27 Bradley and Marassa, "Awakening to the World," 113.

28 On "racial memory," see n. 46 below.

29 Yusoff, *A Billion Black Anthropocenes or None*, xii.

30 On intra-action, see Barad, *Meeting the Universe Halfway*.

31 Drabinski, *Glissant and the Middle Passage*, 13.

32 Drabinski, *Glissant and the Middle Passage*, 13.

33 Wang, "Anachronistic Life," 791.

34 For histories of the Black Atlantic that foreground Black masculinity, see Gilroy, *The Black Atlantic*; and Stephens, *Black Empire*.

35 Wynter, "Beyond the Categories," 63. See also Hantel, "Plasticity and Fungibility," 97.

36 Smallwood, *Saltwater Slavery*, 43.

37 See the longer quotation in n. 2.

38 Patterson, *Slavery and Social Death*, 51. It's important to note, for the purposes of my larger argument, that Patterson recasts the slave's socially dead status (socially dead relative to the dominant white society) as what allows the slave to "[live] on the margin between community and chaos, life and death, the sacred and the secular" (51). Elsewhere Patterson characterizes the slave as "neither human nor inhuman, neither man nor beast, neither dead nor alive, the enemy within who was neither member nor true alien" (46).

Hence the slave is both fungible and alluvially entangled.

39 See Morgan, *Laboring Women*.

40 Smallwood, *Saltwater Slavery*, 52.

41 Hartman, *Scenes of Subjection*, 7.

42 Musser, *Sensual Excess*, 6.

43 Hartman, *Scenes of Subjection*, 80.

44 It's notable that Lafala is also labeled a stranger—the term Hartman uses to define a slave (*Lose Your Mother*, 5); see also Patterson, *Slavery and Social Death*, 39—by Aslima when she recounts his first arrival in Marseille and why she thought it was appropriate to steal his money (*RM*, 33).

45 Lorde, *Sister Outsider*, 53 (hereafter cited as *SO*).

46 While the phrase *racial memory* suggests a problematic racial essentialism, it's important to historicize the term. It partakes of a project of racial vitalism most closely associated with the Négritude writers Aimé Césaire, Léopold Sédar Senghor, and Léon Gontran Damas, who held McKay's novel *Banjo* (1929) in high esteem. Racial vitalism attempts to know and describe the category of life as something beyond the mechanical, the rational, and the dualist subject-object split. In so doing, it seeks to define the human in terms other than those developed in post-Enlightenment Europe. Its modern sources include Romantic organicism and, slightly later, evolutionary biology. The latter had special relevance for McKay's reclamation of Black life. Jones writes, "Biology opened up the possibility of defining life in terms of memory, and the discovery of a deep ethnological past in the context of social Darwinian anthropology made it possible to speculate on the memories of racial groups" (*Racial Discourses*, 6). In short, vitalism, as it was formulated in the early twentieth century and used by writers including McKay, involved an intuition of racial memory. Access to this memory could be known only "through aesthetic experience or deeper and immediate self-knowledge," a recovery of authentic existence through an active wresting of truth out of memory (114).

47 Blum, "Introduction," 151.

Works Cited

Barad, Karen. *Meeting the Universe Halfway: Quantum Physics and the Entanglement of Matter and Meaning*. Durham, NC: Duke University Press, 2007.

Baucom, Ian. *Specters of the Atlantic: Finance Capital, Slavery, and the Philosophy of History*. Durham, NC: Duke University Press, 2005.

Blum, Hester. "Introduction: Oceanic Studies." *Atlantic Studies* 10, no. 2 (2013): 151–55.

Borst, Allan G. "Signifyin(g) Afro-Orientalism: The Jazz Addict Subculture of *Nigger Heaven* and *Home to Harlem.*" *Modernism/Modernity* 16, no. 4 (2009): 685–707.

Bradley, Rizvana, and Damien-Adia Marassa. "Awakening to the World: Relation, Totality, and Writing from Below." *Discourse* 36, no. 1 (2014): 112–31.

Brown, Bill. "The Secret Life of Things (Virginia Woolf and the Matter of Modernism)." *Modernism/Modernity* 6, no. 2 (1999): 1–28.

Chow, Jeremy, and Brandi Bushman. "Hydro-eroticism." In Winkiel, "Hydro-criticism," 96–115.

Christopher, Emma, Cassandra Pybus, and Marcus Rediker, eds. *Many Middle Passages: Forced Migration and the Making of the Modern World.* Berkeley: University of California Press, 2007.

Drabinski, John E. *Glissant and the Middle Passage: Philosophy, Beginning, Abyss.* Minneapolis: University of Minnesota Press, 2019.

Gilroy, Paul. *The Black Atlantic: Modernity and Double Consciousness.* Cambridge, MA: Harvard University Press, 1993.

Glissant, Édouard. *Caribbean Discourse: Selected Essays,* translated by J. Michael Dash. Charlottesville: University of Virginia Press, 1989.

Glissant, Édouard. *Poetics of Relation,* translated by Betsy Wing. Ann Arbor: University of Michigan Press, 1997.

Goyal, Yogita. *Runaway Genres: The Global Afterlives of Slavery.* New York: New York University Press, 2019.

Hantel, Max. "Plasticity and Fungibility: On Sylvia Wynter's Pieza Framework." *Social Text,* no. 143 (2020): 97–119.

Hartman, Saidiya V. *Lose Your Mother: A Journey along the Atlantic Slave Route.* New York: Farrar, Straus and Giroux, 2008.

Hartman, Saidiya V. *Scenes of Subjection: Terror, Slavery, and Self-Making in Nineteenth-Century America.* New York: Oxford University Press, 1997.

Hartman, Saidiya V. *Wayward Lives, Beautiful Experiments.* New York: Norton, 2019.

Hofmeyr, Isabel. "Provisional Notes on Hydrocolonialism." In Winkiel, "Hydro-criticism," 11–20.

Jones, Donna V. *The Racial Discourses of Life Philosophy: Négritude, Vitalism, and Modernity.* New York: Columbia University Press, 2010.

King, Tiffany Lethabo. *The Black Shoals: Offshore Formations of Black and Native Studies.* Durham, NC: Duke University Press, 2019.

Lorde, Audre. *Sister Outsider: Essays and Speeches.* Berkeley, CA: Crossing, 1984.

Luciano, Dana, and Mel Y. Chen. "Has the Queer Ever Been Human?" In "Queer Inhumanisms," edited by Mel Y. Chen and Dana Luciano. Special issue, *GLQ* 21, nos. 2–3 (2015): 183–207.

McKay, Claude. *Romance in Marseille,* edited by Gary Edward Holcomb and William J. Maxwell. New York: Penguin, 2020.

Morgan, Jennifer L. *Laboring Women: Reproduction and Gender in New World Slavery.* Philadelphia: University of Pennsylvania Press, 2004.

Morrison, Toni. *Beloved.* New York: Penguin, 1987.

Mullen, Bill V. *Afro-Orientalism.* Minneapolis: University of Minnesota Press, 2004.

Musser, Amber Jamilla. *Sensual Excess: Queer Femininity and Brown Jouissance.* New York: New York University Press, 2018.

Patterson, Orlando. *Slavery and Social Death: A Comparative Study.* Cambridge, MA: Harvard University Press, 1982.

Philip, M. NourbeSe. *Zong!* Middleton, CT: Wesleyan University Press, 2011.

Rediker, Marcus. *The Slave Ship: A Human History.* New York: Penguin, 2008.

Rivkin, Mark. *Fictions of Land and Flesh: Blackness, Indigeneity, Speculation.* Durham, NC: Duke University Press, 2019.

Samuelson, Meg. "Coastal Form: Amphibian Positions, Wider Worlds, and Planetary Horizons on the African Indian Ocean Littoral." *Comparative Literature* 69, no. 1 (2017): 16–24.

Scott, Darieck. *Extravagant Abjection: Blackness, Power, and Sexuality in the African American Literary Imagination.* New York: New York University Press, 2010.

Sharpe, Christina. *In the Wake: On Blackness and Being.* Durham, NC: Duke University Press, 2016.

Smallwood, Stephanie. *Saltwater Slavery: A Middle Passage from Africa to American Diaspora.* Cambridge, MA: Harvard University Press, 2007.

Snorton, Riley C. *Black on Both Sides: A Racial History of Trans Identity.* Minneapolis: University of Minnesota Press, 2017.

Snyder, Terri L. *The Power to Die: Slavery and Suicide in British North America.* Chicago: University of Chicago Press, 2015.

Steinberg, Philip E. "Of Other Seas: Metaphors and Materialities in Maritime Regions." *Atlantic Studies* 10, no. 2 (2013): 156–69.

Stephens, Michelle Ann. *Black Empire: The Masculine Global Imaginary of Caribbean Intellectuals in the United States, 1914–1962.* Durham, NC: Duke University Press, 2005.

Tinsley, Omise'eke Natasha. "Black Atlantic, Queer
    Atlantic: Queer Imaginings of the Middle
    Passage." *GLQ* 14, nos. 2–4 (2008): 191–215.
Wang, Jennifer F. "Anachronistic Life: Racial
    Vitalism and 'Unhistorical' Temporality in
    Claude McKay's *Home to Harlem.*" *Modernism/
    Modernity* 26, no. 4 (2019): 785–803.
Wilderson, Frank B., III. *Red, White, and Black:
    Cinema and the Structure of U.S. Antagonisms.*
    Durham, NC: Duke University Press, 2010.
Winkiel, Laura, ed. "Hydro-criticism." Special issue,
    ELN 57, no. 1 (2019).
Wynter, Sylvia. "Beyond the Categories of the
    Master Conception: The Counterdoctrine of
    the Jamesian Poiesis." In *C. L. R. James's
    Caribbean*, edited by Paget Henry and Paul
    Buhle, 63–91. Durham, NC: Duke University
    Press, 1992.
Wynter, Sylvia. *Black Metamorphosis: New Natives in
    a New World.* Schomburg Center for Research
    in Black Culture, New York, n.d. [1970s].
Yusoff, Kathryn. *A Billion Black Anthropocenes or
    None.* Minneapolis: University of Minnesota
    Press, 2018.

Mooring Aslima

Afro-Orientalist Diaspora in Claude McKay's Pan-Atlantic Mediterranean Modernism

ZAINAB CHEEMA

Abstract   In Claude McKay's *Romance in Marseille*, the entanglement of Spain and Morocco emerges through the diasporic figure of Aslima, the Moroccan sex worker. This essay examines McKay's Maurophilia, which he circuitously refers to as "Afro-Orientalism" in his various writings. Maurophilia not only foregrounds Aslima's associations with Spain and Morocco but also highlights McKay's engagement with transhistorical Mediterranean diasporas, including the intra-African slave trade and Iberian Moriscos and conversos settling in North Africa following the Reconquista. This essay argues that while Aslima's associations with Moorish-Iberian performance styles influence McKay's modernist poetics and radical aspirations for a global pandiasporic Black alliance, *Romance in Marseille* ultimately forecloses the prospect of a pan-Mediterranean, Black Atlantic globalism because of contradictions of gender and religion.

Keywords   Maurophilia, transdiaspora, Orientalism, Spain, Morocco

C laude McKay began writing *Romance in Marseille* in late 1929 in Barcelona and revised the novel for publication during his tenure in Morocco. While McKay, the author of the Marseille-set *Banjo* (1929), once again turned to the south of France to stage the internationalism represented by his queer, Black, vagabond and laboring-class characters, the imprint of Spain and Morocco's discursive space layered on the French Mediterranean in the later novel should not be underestimated. A number of scholars have discussed the influence of Spain and Morocco on McKay's transnational literary production.[1] However, as Michael K. Walonen has observed, there remains a gap in critical literature discussing the Mediterranean as a framework shaping McKay's work.[2] Scholarly criticism has not yet sufficiently excavated the way in which cultural formations of Moorishness relate McKay's representations of Iberian and North African discursive spaces, his interwoven portrait of what Fernand Braudel called "the great bi-continent" of Spain and North Africa.[3] The significance of this issue is especially charged since McKay gestures toward the imprint of Iberian and North African cultural flows on his self-fashioning, and toward the influence of their entangled histories on his

ENGLISH LANGUAGE NOTES

59:1, April 2021   DOI 10.1215/00138282-8815049
© 2021 Regents of the University of Colorado

conjoining of Atlantic diasporic with Mediterranean elements in his Black modernist poetics. In *Romance in Marseille* the entanglement of Spain and Morocco emerges through the diasporic figure of Aslima, the Moroccan sex worker whom Lafala loves and leaves over the course of the novel.[4] In this essay I read Aslima's in-between positionality in Marseille through the framework of trans-Mediterranean diaspora linking Iberia and North Africa from the eighth-century Islamicate conquest of Iberia and Provence to the waves of expulsion of Iberian Moors, Jews, conversos, and Moriscos resulting from the Reconquista and Inquisitions.

Additionally, I examine how Lafala's relationship with Aslima mediates McKay's negotiations between Atlantic and Mediterranean spaces of diaspora and cultural production. Michelle Stephens calls attention to the Orientalized woman in McKay's work as a conjunction who enables the allegorical imagination of queer Black transnationalism at the expense of women's embodied inclusion in Black radical futurities.[5] Smita Das notes that the position of Orientalized Black women in McKay's novels is partly determined by the racialized and gendered striations in French colonial policy.[6] While these observations apply to Aslima, this essay primarily examines the heroine of *Romance in Marseille* through the lens of McKay's Maurophilia, which he circuitously references as "Afro-Orientalism" in his various writings. Maurophilia foregrounds not only the racial and cultural privileging of Spain and Morocco in McKay's work but also highlights McKay's engagement with an alternate diasporic space underlying the topography of *Romance in Marseille*. Barbara Fuchs has described Maurophilia as "the urgent negotiation of a Moorishness that is not only a historiographical relic but a vivid presence in quotidian Spanish culture."[7] In *Romance in Marseille* McKay's Maurophilia toward Spain and Morocco deconstructs racialized systems of exclusion in the Atlantic through the hybridizing fantasy that Al-Andalus or Moorish Spain[8] materializes the cultural and racial *mestizaje* of Europe with Africa.

In the first part of this essay I read Aslima's white Arab father and Black Sudanese mother as embodying McKay's engagement with transhistorical Mediterranean diasporas between Spain, North Africa, and sub-Saharan Africa. The second half of the essay reads Aslima and Lafala's relationship as a symbol of the regenerative utopia of a global Black Atlantic-Mediterranean alliance—an alliance with which McKay engages with but ultimately forecloses in his writings. This section discusses how diasporic Afro-Oriental soundscapes shape the modernist poetics of both Aslima's messianic dream vision and McKay's related poem "A Farewell to Morocco." I show how these texts foreground an aesthetic fusion of Afraamerican and Afro-Oriental poetics representing Atlantic-Mediterranean diasporas, only to emphasize their political separation.

Aslima and the Conjunction of Mediterranean Diasporas

In "Creolization in the Americas" Édouard Glissant positions the Mediterranean as a foil for the Atlantic in his discussion of Caribbean creolization. In Glissant's concept of creolization, the pluralistic bricolage of the languages and cultures of diasporic Caribbean peoples is defined against Mediterranean tendencies toward a singular hegemony shaped by the homogenizing movements of empire.[9] In *Romance in Marseille*, however, McKay offers a counterimage to this portrait of the Mediterranean through Aslima's embodiment of trans-Mediterranean diasporas. More recent scholarship also highlights the Mediterranean basin as a place of transcultural convergence that challenges unitary and homogenizing frameworks for localized, performative aspects of Mediterranean identity,[10] a conception closer to McKay's sense of the space. I argue that McKay sees Aslima's Afro-Oriental identity as shaped by the transcultural intersections of three major diasporic flows to Morocco: the sub-Saharan African slave trade; the exile of Spanish Moors migrating during the Iberian frontier wars; and the expulsion of Spanish Moriscos and conversos by the Spanish monarchy in the early seventeenth century.

Aslima embodies transhistorical Mediterranean diasporas through her miscegenated genealogy: her white Arab father hails from the northern regions of Morocco, while her Sudanese mother, the novel tells us, "had been sold a slave to the Moors in Marrakesh."[11] Aslima's parents, respectively from the Hispanophone north and Africanist south of Morocco, are not only biographical context for the character but also allegories for the diasporic flows shaping the racial and cultural *mestizaje* of Morocco. Aslima's mother embodies McKay's engagement with the ancient sub-Saharan slave trade in Morocco, particularly in cities such as Marrakesh, a central depot for the intra-African slave trade. In a 1929 letter to his agent, William Aspenwall Bradley, written from Nice, McKay observes that "in Marrakesh you'll get a slight idea of what tropical Africa must be, because it is still semi-savage with the Arabs always coming into the city from the Souss country and slaves from the Sudan and the Senegal bush."[12]

Saidiya Hartmann notes that the epistemic condition of slavery is the historical erasure that emerges from the diasporic loss and forgetting of one's mother.[13] Accordingly, Aslima's "shadowy" memories of her mother (*RM*, 44) before she too is captured as a child by slave traders and brought to Fez and Casablanca allude to the violence and dislocation of the intra-African slave trade shaping Morocco's racial heterogeneity and cultural bricolage. The diaspora of Black West Africans in Morocco, the majority of whom were forcefully transported across the Sahara and sold in Morocco, shares some important traits with the African transatlantic diaspora.[14] As with Atlantic diasporas, the intra-African slave trade shaped Marrakesh as culturally and racially miscegenated. This racial miscegenation is corporally incarnated in Aslima's "chocolate-brown complexion" and "burning brown . . . [mixture] of Arab and Negro and other wanton bloods perhaps that had created her a barbaric creature" (*RM*, 40, 4).[15] Aslima's maternal genealogy embodies the cultural flows of the intra-African slave trade as well as its structures of dislocation and violence. Her initial separation from the shadowy figure of her enslaved mother ricochets into the character's exploitative migrations upward through Morocco into Marseille and across a series of exploitative sexual contracts.[16]

For McKay, Afro-Orientalism is also constituted through a long history of violent, diasporic dislocations across Iberia–North Africa. If Aslima's mother embodies the migrations between Morocco and sub-Saharan Africa, Aslima's father represents the *longue durée* of diasporic movements between North Africa and Europe. McKay calls Aslima's father a Moor, meaning a North African man tracing a European lineage to Al-Andalus, or Moorish Spain. McKay often referred to white North Africans in his writings, stressing the similarity of their appearance to Europeans. In *Romance in Marseille* the absent white Moor father is somatically marked in the color coding of Aslima's miscegenated "chocolate-brown" and "burning brown" beauty. Her unnamed father marks an equally violent history of dislocation: the waves of Moors and, later, Moriscos escaping from the Iberian Peninsula to North Africa during the Reconquista and Spanish Inquisition. Beyond the novel McKay's lyric odes to Moroccan cities betray an attraction for urban centers settled by Moorish and Sephardic immigrants. His poems "Xauen," "Tetuan," "Tanger," and "Fez"[17] celebrate urban centers whose cultural identity was prominently shaped by the Jewish and Andalusian quarters settled by Iberian migrants, and that developed into creolized enclaves of diasporic cultural memories and practices. In his sonnet "Fez" McKay would enigmatically recall an Arab paramour "of beauty African in shape and form, / With glowing fire of Andalusian eyes"—a lover whose color coding echoes Aslima's own "burning brown" mixture of African and Arab blood.

In *Romance in Marseille* McKay drapes Moorish Spain's cultural landscape over the topos of Marseille like a palimpsest, foregrounding how transhistorical Afro-Oriental diasporic flows shaped the landscape of twentieth-century Europe's late colonial empire. As Jonathan Shannon has noted, Al-Andalus or Moorish Spain is "a fluid and shifting geographical, historical, political, and cultural cartography" shaped by multiple and overlapping historical memories associated with medieval Spain.[18] This fluctuating space appears in a crucial scene in the novel, when Titin attempts to force Aslima to swear near the Cathedral of Notre Dame that she will ally with him in double-crossing Lafala. Aslima equivocates by invoking Morocco's diasporic memories of Moorish Spain, outwardly complying with Titin's request but inwardly calling on the multiple sediments of conquest and cultural memory underlying the cathedral and the topos of Marseille itself. "She had heard the story of the warriors of the golden age of her people conquering all that romantic stretch of earth between the Pillars of Hercules and Marseille. And there was a legend that the cathedral was built on the site of a mosque, over the bones, maybe, of a marabout. And she uttered a silent prayer that the lost dominions of her people might be restored" (*RM*, 69). Aslima's prayer opens up the queer temporality of *Romance in Marseille*, McKay's folding of multiple temporalities and historical currents within early twentieth-century landscapes of colonialism and capitalism. The ghostly bones of the marabout reveal the Cathedral of Notre Dame as an architectural metonymy of Marseille, transforming the city into a transhistorical palimpsest for the Moorish cultural flows underlying Provence, Iberia, and North Africa. Aslima's invocation of the ghostly remnants of the Moorish fortress-mausoleum evokes Sevilla's La Giralda, the ornamental Moorish minaret repurposed into a church bell tower, which McKay referred to a number of times in his correspondence with Bradley.[19] McKay's letters attest to his fascination with La Giralda; the architectural shard of the Moorish minaret attached to the Cathedral of Seville seems to him a metaphor of the black cultural and racial foundations to European civilizations."[20] In a 1929 letter to Bradley sent from Marseille, McKay notes that "the Alhambra, the Cathedral at Cordova and all the other Moorish works in Spain seemed more interesting to me *after* I had been in Morocco and seen the Arabs chez eux." The letter then describes "the fine Arabesques and paneling" of the Alhambra plastered over by "the fanatic Philip II (?)," and how twentieth-century renovation efforts at the palace gave him "a shock to see on one side delicate and decorative work with the other side covered up by grey forbidding renaissance plaster."[21] In McKay's attempt to remove more of the plaster, his invocation of the diasporic relics in the fortress-mosque rebuilt as a cathedral underscores the identity of Africa as Europe's queer origin point. Here *Romance in Marseille* deconstructs hegemonic formations of late European colonialism by recasting Europe as the subject as much as the agent of the Mediterranean's entangled histories of conquest, displacement and migration.

Through her racially mixed beauty and diasporic genealogies, Aslima incarnates McKay's Maurophilia: his attraction to Moorish Spain as the embodiment of the *mestizaje* of African and European civilizations, an affection shared by other Harlem Renaissance writers such as W. E. B. Du Bois and Langston Hughes. As Barbara Fuchs defines it, Maurophilia refers to sixteenth-century Europe's exoticization of Spain through other aspects of Moorishness incorporated in Spain's quotidian cultural landscape.[22] Historically, Maurophilia has been intertwined with the Black Legend of Spanish cruelty, propaganda that traced Spain's exceptional cruelty against Amerindians to the racial contamination of Spanish blood with Moorish and Jewish blood during the eight centuries of Moorish rule in Iberia. While the Black Legend was originally spread by English and Dutch empires attempting to wrest Spain's control of the Atlantic, the United States appropriated it in the nineteenth century while competing with Spain for control of its Caribbean and South American colonies. For McKay, Hughes, and other Black modernist writers, Maurophilia centered on exoticizing Spanish otherness in Europe, both the Black Legend of Spain's Moorish-Jewish-African miscegenation and the exoticization of Spain and North Africa's racial entanglements. McKay alluded to this exoticizing of the Black Legend of racial kinship between Spain and Morocco when privately describing his Mediterranean cruising. "It's that Spanish dignity that puts the 'maricones' in the bordelo," he suggested to Bradley in a 1929 letter from Antwerp. In his next sentence McKay explains that "you find them in the bordelo in Morocco too, extremely beautiful boys . . . ultra raffiné in that harchaise atmosphere having nothing at all in common with the petites tantes of Paris."[23] McKay indexes the erotic appeal of Spanish and Moroccan masculinity under a single category defined against the French racial type.

McKay's Orientalism privileges Moorish Spain as the signifier of a "perfect miscegenation" (*LW*, 237) of Afro-European hybridities in bodily and architectural form, an ideal mix that unmoors Europe's colonial constructions of African savagery and barbarity. While *Romance in Marseille* does not name or describe Aslima's Moorish father, McKay perhaps offers a telling portrait in *A Long Way from Home*. Moroccans of the northern regions, this memoir observes, are "blue-eyed and blonde-haired types resembling Nordics, except that they are rather bronzed. But they are all remarkably free of any color obsessions or ideas of discrimination. They are *Africans*" (*LW*, 255; italics mine).[24] Late imperial Catholic Spain's racialized codes of *limpieza de sangre* or blood purity would affiliate Aslima's father with the Blackness and racial impurity variously imputed to Jews, Moors, Blacks, and heretics, regardless of his phenotypical whiteness. In contrast, McKay views the descendants of Iberian immigrants to Morocco as incarnations of miscegenated African and European lineages stretching from the medieval period to the twentieth century.

As Jacob Rama Berman and others have noted, McKay selectively appropriates Anglo-American Orientalism toward both Spain and Morocco in his correspondence and writings. Morocco and Aslima are frequently associated with the barbarism, exotic "native" color, and sensuality characteristic in French and Anglo-American Orientalist representations of the Maghreb. Nevertheless, McKay's Maurophilia is also grounded in an awareness of the violence of the Afro-Oriental diasporic histories that constituted the bodies, sounds, and cultural forms he admired. The dislocations and diasporic flows inflecting Aslima's personal displacements as a Moroccan sex worker in the south of France in the 1920s are inscribed in the character's original name: Zhima. Writing to Bradley about the unlikability of Lafala (who at this point in the drafting process was called Taloufa), McKay admits the centrality of his Moroccan paramour: "It's the girl Zhima who runs away with the story and after her Marty."[25] Notably, "Zhima" is McKay's transcription of *ahl al-dhimma* or *dhimmi*: non-Muslim People of the Book who lived as subjects to Islamicate kingdoms.[26] The irony of Aslima's original name, of course, is that it allegorizes her marginal status as a Moor in early twentieth-century Europe. She is a minority and border subject in Marseille, vulnerable to the uncertainty and violence of European colonial peripheries. While McKay's aestheticization of Aslima reflects his Maurophilia toward African-European miscegenation, his crafting of Aslima's maternal and paternal genealogies shows that this aesthetic bricolage is located in material histories of the dislocation of sub-Saharan slaves, Moors, Jews, Moriscos, and conversos along the Iberian-Moroccan corridor. As a *dhimmi* in Marseille, Aslima embodies how historical Afro-Oriental diasporas are intertwined with the early twentieth-century vagabond republic of laborers, beach boys, sex workers, pimps, and musicians in Mediterranean port cities.

Modernist Fusions: The Diasporic Soundscapes of Aslima's Dream Vision and "A Farewell to Morocco"

In much of his work McKay employs the categories of "Afro-Orientalism" and "Afraamericanism" to indicate two alternate historical currents of Black diaspora. In the latter, the pan-Atlantic slave trade shapes creole Black Americas; in the former, the Iberian-Moroccan bicontinent stages Africa's and Europe's entangled histories. Aslima and Lafala's relationship thus opens up a transhistorical hinge of possibility, the fusion of Afro-Oriental and Afraamerican diasporas as an aesthetic, ideological, and political bulwark against European capitalist modernity. The use of romance plots to materialize a recuperative alliance between African Africans and the global South against European racism and colonialism has been explored in other Harlem Renaissance writing, most notably W. E. B. Du Bois's *Dark Princess*. While McKay teases this possibility in *Romance in Marseille* through Lafala and

Aslima's plans to marry and escape to Africa, he ultimately refuses it. Nevertheless, the junction between Afro-Orientalism and Afraamericanism imprints itself on the experimentalism of his modernist aesthetics, particularly in his lyric fusion of jazz poetics with Moroccan diasporic soundscapes. This section of the essay accordingly reads Aslima's dream vision against McKay's poem "A Farewell to Morocco," delving into the political failure and lyric generativity that McKay inscribes at this transdiasporic junction.

Modernist aesthetics were frequently grounded in rupture, dislocation, and experimental variegation over closure. Sympathetically, McKay's description of Aslima's dream vision foretelling her separation from Lafala reflects the modernist fusion of Moroccan soundscapes with the syncopation, polyrhythmicality, and open-endedness of his Harlem jazz poetry. In both Aslima's vision and the farewell poem, McKay appropriates Afro-Oriental sounds and images of loss and dislocation from the diverse Moroccan soundscapes to which he had been exposed. Leaving an increasingly aggressive Titin—Aslima's pimp—to go find Lafala, Aslima has a prophetic vision while seated on a bench near the shore. In a trancelike state, she envisions a Moroccan festival in a "white-washed city," where a nighttime procession of loose-robed men and women and children march as to a midnight ritual, "stamping and dancing to barbaric music." The apparition ends in a traditional Andalusian palace courtyard, featuring "a vast marble and malachite court of beautiful balconies filled with kindred people and all the people marched around a gushing fountain dipping their hands in limpid water. And perfume was shed down upon them from on high. There followed a loving feast . . . under lights like variegated flowers and shrouded in clouds of rarest incense" (*RM*, 61). The imagery of monumental architecture evokes the diasporic Andalusian palace-garden complexes that fascinated McKay along the Iberian-Moroccan corridor in cities including Fez, Marrakesh, Cordoba, Seville, and Granada. The nightly feasting and dancing rituals suggest Ramadan, where dusk ends the fast and opens nightlong feasting. The scene aggressively blends registers of the sacred and secular: alongside popular feasting, dusk in Ramadan initiates musical soirees organized by Sufi orders, which feature chanting and dancing set to sacred music.

In this dream vision, McKay also samples Moroccan soundscapes that are closely affiliated with the Afro-Oriental diasporic currents embodied by Aslima's lost mother and father. In particular, McKay combines imagery and rhythms of Gnawa and Andalusian music, two Moroccan musical traditions that respectively embody the sub-Saharan and Iberian diasporas. Images of ornamental gardens, water, and perfume are all tropes in Andalusian Arabic poetics of loss, which Iberian exiles memorialized in a repertoire of strophic songs that traveled to North Africa. Developing from the mixed orality of peninsular Spain's soundscapes, particularly the multilingual code-switching of poetic muwashshah and zajal, the traumatic migration of this sonic repertoire to North Africa froze into what has popularly become known as the Andalusian musical tradition (*al-mūsīqā al-andalusiyya*).[27] In Morocco this song canon is closely associated with the cultural identity of Iberian Moorish emigres. As Aslima's dream progresses, McKay syncopates these stock images encoding lyric longing and loss for Spain with the sounds and rhythms of Morocco's sub-Saharan slave music: the Gnawa. At one point, Aslima sees that

> when the feasting was finished the belly-moving beat of the drum roused the people again after an interval of rest to dancing and chanting over and over again repeating and reiterating from pattern to pattern unraveling the threads of life from the most intricate to the simplest to the naked bottom as if in evocation of the first gods who emerged out of the ancient unfathomed womb of Africa to procreate and spread over the vast surface of the land. (*RM*, 61)

This depiction mirrors McKay's description elsewhere of witnessing a Gnawa performance in Morocco. *Gnawa* refers both to the descendants of West African slaves funneled to Morocco in the trans-Saharan slave trade and to their Sufi spiritual order and West Africa influenced musical style.[28] In his autobiography McKay describes watching "some Guinea sorcerers (or Gueanoua, as they are called in Morocco)" perform an exorcism. The music was made by a single lute and a big bass drum and sounded like muffled thunder in the belly of the earth," while the dancing resembled "a kind of primitive rhumba" (*LW*, 228). In short, Aslima's dream vision brings together McKay's sampling and syncopation of different Moroccan musical soundscapes affiliated with the Afro-Oriental diasporas of the trans-Saharan slave trade and Iberian-Maghrebi migrations. This syncopation becomes a crucial part of McKay's modernist experimentation and his creating through prose a hybrid synesthesia that rhythmically integrates musical and ethnographic traditions. In Aslima's dream McKay's aesthetics make a political point: his excavation of primordial Africanist rhythms underlying the Morocco's Iberian-Moorish musical repertoires insists on a miscegenated soundscape, mashing up acoustics and ethnographic flows that are performed as distinct and separate in Morocco.

The first half of Aslima's dream vision in *Romance in Marseille* parallels the themes and imagery of the poem "A Farewell to Morocco,"[29] in which McKay detailed his nostalgic longing for Moroccan festive life following his return to America:

> Oh friends, my friends! When Ramadan returns
> And daily fast and feasting through the night,
> With chants and music honey-dripping sweets,
> And fatmahs shaking their flamenco feet,
> >   My thoughts will wing
> >   The waves of air
> >   To be with you.
> Oh when the cannon sounds to break the fast,
> And children chorus madly their relief,
> And you together group to feast at last,
> You'll feel my hungry spirit in your midst,

> Released from me
> A prisoner,
> To fly to you.
> And when you go beneath the orange trees,
> To mark and serenade the crescent growth,
> With droning lute and shivering mandolin
> And drop the scented blossoms in your cups!
> Oh make one tune,
> One melody
> Of love for me. (*LW*, 259)

This modified modernist sonnet, which adapts the Andalusi poetic style, finds McKay appropriating images from strophic love songs of loss for Iberian palace gardens to fashion his own lyrics of diasporic haunting. As with Aslima's dream vision, however, the time space of this ode is a heterotopic one, an ecstatic synesthesia of McKay's travels in Morocco distilled with a deconstructed sonnet form. As in Aslima's dream, McKay crafts a tone of Oriental romanticism through Maurophilic imagery of ritual feasting in Andalusian style garden courtyards with orange trees, mandolins, lutes, and scented flowers. He fuses the polyrhythmic hauntings of the jazz sonnet with the Andalusian poetics of elegy, the latter employed by Iberian Muslim and Jewish poets such as al-Saraqusṭī and Moses ibn Ezra, who fled their cities to escape the armies of Christian princes. In this elegiac form, symbolic imagery of the lost Andalusian palace garden encodes a traumatic site of memory.[30] In the version of "A Farewell to Morocco" printed in *A Long Way from Home*, McKay declares "Habeeb, Habeeba, I may never return," referring to both the male and the female rendering of the Arabic word for "beloved" while returning to the memory-scape of "vistas opening to an infinite way / Of perfect love" of his Ramadan nights (*LW*, 260). In his borrowing of these Andalusian tropes, McKay closely interweaves his own passage across Afro-Oriental and Afraamerican spaces with diasporic cultural flows between Spain and Morocco.

The formal innovations in McKay's hybrid mashup of the modernized English sonnet and the Arabophone lyric elegy uniquely personalize the queer temporality of diasporic dislocation. Among other things, "A Farewell to Morocco" is a shape poem whose form simulates the cannons discharged in Morocco at daybreak during Ramadan, announcing the end of fasting, a phenomenon he refers to in the second stanza quoted above. In particular, each blank verse quartet simulates the cannon with its muzzle, and each attached tercet, truncated through enjambment, evokes the mount. The cannon imprints into the very shape of the poem the time space of the palace garden feast. With its intercultural borrowings of western European and Iberian-Moroccan lyric forms and imagery, the poem intimately positions McKay within the mixed acoustics and polytemporal interstices between Afro-Oriental and Afraamerican diasporas. "A Farewell to Morocco" personifies McKay's Maurophilic longings for Morocco on the shores of New York through the alter ego of the prisoner, who he imagines is released from the self-divided poet. The escaped prisoner was a common feature of nineteenth-century Barbary captivity narratives as well as maroon narratives of Caribbean slavery. With the help of this and other borrowings, McKay's polyrhythm, syncopation, and improvisational hybridization intermixes the traumatic histories of the Mediterranean and Atlantic diasporas.

Yet in both Aslima's dream vision and "A Farewell to Morocco," McKay explores but ultimately retreats from the transdiasporic union of Afro-Orientalism and Afro-Americanism. The second half of Aslima's dream vision becomes apocalyptic, as she envisions her separation from Lafala and her violent death. The scene of feasting transforms into a vast congregation under an "immense dome studded with all the jewels of earth and reflecting all the colors of life" (*RM*, 61). The description is suggestive of the material appearance of the monumental Iberian-Moroccan architecture that had enchanted McKay. It also echoes McKay's descriptions of Aslima and Lafala's lovemaking, which are shaded as "a riotous sensation of crimson and green, yellow and honey and all the kindred colors of love and passion" (*RM*, 124). If Lafala and Aslima's romantic relationship represents a transdiasporic alliance, Aslima's vision foretells its failure, which is then realized in Lafala's sailing away from Marseille without her and her tragic death at Titin's hands. As the political significance of this romantic relationship is not realized, it's hard to conceive exactly what form it would have taken. Perhaps as in Du Bois's *Dark Princess*, their child would symbolize a messianic incorporation who channels energies across these diasporas in a movement against European colonialism. While the political implication of Lafala and Aslima's romance is finally withdrawn, their affair lyrically opens up a space of modernist suspension and dislocation for McKay, himself a voyager across Atlantic and Mediterranean spaces.

In Aslima's dream, the image of the flaming Sword of Life suspended from the center of the dome is syncretic, fusing biblical and Islamic cosmological references. It conjoins the flaming swords of biblical angels, the Sword of Damocles and the Tree of Life with—quite possibly—the Arabic name for the star cluster of Orion's Sword, identified in Arabic and Latin astrological books as *sayf al-jabbār*,[31] or the "sword of the giant."[32] The flaming sword of life becomes a figure of time and loss, to which subjects sacrifice the "budding flower of childhood, fruit of adolescence, honey of maturity, wine of experience, vinegar of disillusion, bitter broth of cynicism, lamentation of blasted hopes," or in Aslima's case, her full "body and soul" (*RM*, 62). As Holcomb and Maxwell observe in their edition of novel, the vision predicts Aslima's martyrdom on Lafala's behalf (*RM*, 154n2). The congregation of people worshipping the flaming Sword of Life channels Judeo-Christian-Islamic eschatology inflecting apocalyptic images of the end of time and the Day of Judgment: "All the people of the earth were assembled under that dome and worshipping that sword. Some were slaves and some were free; some were wanton and some were happy. Some were strange and some were sad; some were lighthearted and some were heavy-burdened" (*RM*, 61). While this imagery is eschatological, McKay repurposes it to construct the transhistorical time space of the pan-Atlantic Mediterranean Black diaspora. Here I return to the intertext of the Orion star cluster, which helped mariners navigate between east and west: the astral image of Orion's Sword suspended in the cosmic dome of Aslima's dream vision possibly maps the space in which this congregated humanity is assembled on the waterways of dislocation (and at times escape and redemption) for the slaves, captives, exiles, refugees, laborers, and sex workers shuttling between Africa, Europe, and the

Americas. Moreover, the eschatological image of the Sword of Life is in itself a *diasporic* figuration: in Arabic, the graphemes for the word *sayf*, or "sword," are the same as the word *sīf*, or "shore of the sea or of a great river,"[33] thus overlapping the lexical significations of cutting and separation with that of the littoral and maritime space. The transdiasporic rupture opened by the messianic nature of Aslima's dream is layered on her separation from Lafala—and McKay's from Morocco—all joining the sword as a conjoined image of both shore and separation that signifies the haunted in-betweenness of Mediterranean and Atlantic history.

McKay underlines his own lyric haunting through the thematic interlacing between "A Farewell to Morocco" and Aslima's dream vision in *Romance in Marseille*. As I have argued, McKay's modernist innovations of form, acoustics, and imagery in these two texts demonstrate the influence of Morocco's soundscapes on his imagination. The correspondences between "A Farewell to Morocco" and the dream vision in *Romance in Marseille* display the innovation and generativity of McKay's translation of trans-Mediterranean cultural productions into modernist form. McKay ends "A Farewell to Morocco" with a familiar *Mektoub*, or "It is written":

> Keeping your happy vigil through the night,
> With tales and music whiling by the hours,
> You may recall my joy to be with you,
> Until the watchers passed from house to house
> > And bugle call
> > And muffled drum
> > Proclaimed the day![34] . . .
> > > —Mektoub. (*LW*, 259–60)

In *Romance in Marseille* Aslima utters the same phrase when she learns that Lafala has sailed from Marseille: "Aslima said nothing. She had turned away from the woman at the bar and now she left the café repeating to herself 'Mektoub! Mektoub!' (Destiny! Destiny!)" (*RM*, 128). On the one hand, McKay's doubled use of *Mektoub* points to his romanticization of "Oriental fatalism," a widely circulating trope in nineteenth- and early twentieth-century narratives of Barbary captivity, Near Eastern travel, and Orientalist romance.[35] On the other, the theme of destiny and loss is also a trope of Andalusian diasporic lyric poetry, in which the symbolic imageries of mourning for the traces of the absent beloved channels traumatic memories of lost cities and homelands in Iberia. McKay's quasi-Orientalist "Mektoub" also indicates his exposure to these poetic tropes through Ibero-Moroccan music and his appropriation of them to fashion the modernist Afro-Oriental lyricism of these two texts. The closure of his poem summons Iberian-Andalusian lyricism and Gnawan "muffled drum" acoustics to mark the Black modernist poet's own final separation from North African shores, threading his own subjectivity into these transhistorical flows.

As discussed above, McKay's portrait of Aslima in the French port city of Marseille operates as an allegory of what he called Afro-Orientalism—namely, Moorish

Africa's shaping by multiple diasporas moving between Europe and Africa at large around the Mediterranean Sea. Similarly, Lafala appears to embody the historical experiences and markings of Afraamericanism and other circum-Atlantic diasporas between Africa and the Americas. As with Du Bois's Afro-Indian alliance in *Dark Princess*, Aslima and Lafala's union might represent the Black globalism to which McKay hints in the sonic metaphor of the syncopated love song of "A Farewell to Morocco": "Oh make one tune, / One melody / Of love for me." The question remains, however, why McKay retreats from the possibility of a pan-Atlantic-Mediterranean alliance both in his own history and in the fictional one of *Romance in Marseille*. This is a complicated question, and its answer can be only tentative here. One clue can be found in the grammatical form of Aslima's name: in Arabic, *aslima* is the dual command for the verb *aslama*, namely, to accept or submit to Islam. In the allegorical meaning of his tragic heroine's name, McKay may communicate the sense that fully committing to Afro-Oriental syncopations would not be possible without his own Muslim conversion. Despite his Maurophilic attraction toward Afro-Oriental racial and cultural miscegenations, McKay may ultimately foreclose the political possibilities of a pan-Atlantic-Mediterranean diasporic alliance because he did not see Islam as compatible with his own identity as a vagabond Harlem poet. This possibility is influenced by the complex politics of McKay's Orientalism, through which he strategically appropriates but surrenders to the European colonial objectification of North Africa.[36] McKay's surveillance by French and Anglo-American colonial authorities also influenced this representation of Lafala and Aslima's tragic relationship. Aslima's highly symbolic death at the hands of the French Corsican Titin overlaps with McKay's own persecution at the hands of colonial authorities in Morocco.

Lafala's final departure from Aslima and from Morocco itself opens up lyric spaces of fusion and experimentation, allowing McKay to weave together the rhythm and form of the sonnet, blues, and jazz with such diasporic Afro-Oriental soundscapes as Andalusian lyric elegy and Gnawa. While McKay departs from the political junction of Afraamerican and Afro-Oriental diasporas, he opens up a generative space of modernist rupture that continues to hold his imagination. While Lafala leaves Aslima behind in voyaging to Africa, it is not quite a clean break: correspondingly, in the sonnet verse in "A Farewell to Morocco," the cannon announcing the end of the fast also triggers a ghostly return of McKay's alter ego to Afro-Oriental shores, "Released from me / A prisoner, / To fly to you." Despite his choice of the Atlantic, McKay's longings for Afro-Oriental spaces and times fracture the topos of a singular "home" directing his traveling, generating the plethora of ghostly selves suspended in his Ramadan love song like so many fragmented reflections in a baroque hall of mirrors. McKay fashions his lyric alter ego as a flying prisoner, a figure that combines Atlantic slave tales of enslaved Africans flying back home with lyric images of return taken from the soundscapes of Morocco's Iberian and sub-Saharan diasporas. This alter ego, released by McKay to journey between Black Atlantic and Mediterranean space times, illustrates the generative miscegenation of Afro-Oriental and Afraamerican diasporas in his art even as he prefers, at last, to keep the political and historical trajectories of these littorals sundered.

ZAINAB CHEEMA is adjunct professorial lecturer at American University. Her research interests include early modern critical race studies, seventeenth-century Anglo-Iberian print culture and history of the book, entangled alliances and transimperial relations, antiracist pedagogies, and Black modernist literature.

Notes

1 Bishop, "Claude McKay's Songs of Morocco"; Holcomb, "Diaspora Cruises," 725–30; Berman, *American Arabesque*, 138–39.

2 Walonen, "Land of Racial Confluence and Spatial Accessibility," 75.

3 Braudel, *The Mediterranean and the Mediterranean World*, 1:117.

4 The influence of Aslima over *Romance in Marseille* cannot be overemphasized. In his correspondence with literary agent William Bradley about the novel, McKay himself admits that "the Arab girl is growing bigger than I ever dreamed and running away with the book and me." See McKay to Bradley, March 18, 1930, William A. Bradley Literary Agency Records 1909–1982, Harry Ransom Center, University of Texas at Austin. All cited letters from McKay to Bradley are housed here.

5 Stephens, *Black Empire*, 167–68.

6 Das, "Subjecting Pleasure," 713.

7 Fuchs, *Exotic Nation*, 5.

8 In this essay I generally prefer to use the historically and culturally imprecise term of *Moorish Spain* over the equally imprecise term of *Al-Andalus* for a number of reasons, including the fact that Moorish Spain is a closer transcription of how McKay and other Harlem Renaissance writers refer to the period.

9 Glissant, "Creolization in the Americas," 81.

10 Boetsch and Ferrié, "Ancient Survivals, Comparatism, and Diffusion," 9–11. I owe the quote to Walonen, "Land of Racial Confluence and Spatial Accessibility," 80.

11 McKay, *Romance in Marseille*, 44 (hereafter cited as *RM*).

12 McKay to Bradley, March 25, 1929.

13 Hartman, *Lose Your Mother*, 116.

14 El Hamel, *Black Morocco*, 270.

15 McKay highlighted other correspondences between Afro-Oriental and Black Atlantic slavery when engaging with the Gnawa musicians of intra-African slave trade, who hybridized diasporic forms of sub-Saharan music with Sufi mystical soundscapes; in his autobiography he described the homologies between the Caribbean vodun of his Jamaica and the "Guinea sorcerers" of the Gnawan Sufi orders. See McKay, *A Long Way from Home*, 228 (hereafter cited as *LW*).

16 McKay would return to the theme of the intra-African slave trade in Morocco after his own return to America from Morocco, filling out a rejected application for a Guggenheim Fellowship in 1937 in which he proposed to study the Senegalese roots of Morocco. See Cooper, *Claude McKay*, 296.

17 McKay, *Complete Poems*, 225–28.

18 Shannon, "Performing al-Andalus," 25. Shannon notes that Al-Andalus sometimes refers to the whole of Spain, sometimes to southern Iberia and Morocco, and sometimes to the Spanish autonomous region of Andalucía, including the modern Spanish cities that bear the names of the medieval city-states (or *ta'ifa* kingdoms) of Córdoba, Granada, Málaga, Sevilla, Valencia, and so on.

19 McKay to Bradley, March 14, 1929.

20 In one letter to Bradley, McKay invokes La Giralda as the architectural signifier of the pan-Iberia-Moroccan Black power embodied by the Marinid sultan, Abu al-Hassan Ali ibn Othman: "I went to Sevilla, of course, to see the Giralda that legend attributes to the Black Sultan as also the Hassan Tower and the Koutoubia at Marrakesh. I don't know if I told you that I wanted to make the legend the chief interest of my Moroccan book." McKay to Bradley, March 14, 1929.

21 McKay to Bradley, December 21, 1929.

22 Fuchs, *Exotic Nation*, 5.

23 McKay to Bradley, July 5, 1929.

24 Jacob Rama Berman notes that McKay significantly conflates the heterogeneous ethnoracial landscape of Morocco, glossing over the racial tensions between Arabs and Berbers (*American Arabesque*, 173).

25 McKay to Bradley, March 14, 1929.

26 *Oxford Islamic Studies Online*, s.v. "dhimmi."

27 For more information on Morocco's Andalusian music tradition and its diasporic context, see Davila, *The Andalusi Turn*, 149–69; and Davila, *The Andalusian Music in Fez*.

28 El Hamel, *Black Morocco*, 270. For more information about Gnawa, see also Aidi, "Claude McKay and Gnawa Music"; and Kapchan, *Traveling Spirit Masters*.

29 The earlier version of the poem collected in the *Complete Poems* anthology is titled "Morocco." In

his autobiography McKay reproduces an edited and expanded version of the poem, renaming it "A Farewell to Morocco." See *LW*, 258–60.

30 Elinson, *Looking Back at al-Andalus*, 20–21.

31 Lane, *An Arabic-English Lexicon*, 4:1485. There is no recognizable Arabic poetic, mystical, or historical reference for *sayf al-Ḥayāt* or "Sword of Life." There are regnal titles such as "Sayf al-Mulūk" (Sword of the Nations) and historical names such as "Sayf al-Dīn" (Sword of the Religion), but these seem inapplicable here. Given that the sword in Aslima's vision is suspended in a cosmic dome, there could be a connection to Arabic astronomy and the star cluster of "sayf al-jabbār" or Orion's Sword. *Sayf al-jabbār* is found in a number of classical Arabic astronomy treatises and is also referenced in Henry Wadsworth Longfellow's poem "The Occultation of Orion": "Begirt with many a blazing star / Stood the great giant Algebar / Orion, hunter of the beast! / His sword hung gleaming by his side" (*Poems and Other Writings*, 43). Dorothee Metlitzki writes that "Saif al-jabbār, the Sword of the Powerful One, is the name of the three central stars in Orion which were considered as forming a sword hanging at the giant's waist. All stars in the constellation are listed as sons or children of *al-jabbār*, which is also called *al-jauzā*, in the Arabic *Almagest*" (*The Matter of Araby in Medieval England*, 79).

32 *Al-Jabbār* in the astronomical context refers to the astral figure of Orion as Hunter-giant. In addition, it is one of the ninety-nine names of God in Islamic mysticism.

33 Lane, *An Arabic-English Lexicon*, 4:1485. While letters for *sayf* and *sīf* are the same, they have different diacritics and thus are vowelized differently. The more common word for "shore" is *sāḥil*. In Arabic, words containing the same lexical roots share semantic resonances and interconnections across their differences in meaning.

34 This is the final stanza of the original version of the poem, which was published in 1937 under the title "Morocco." In McKay's expanded version of the poem titled "A Farewell to Morocco," he adds a number of stanzas whose presence I am indicating by the ellipsis. "A Farewell to Morocco" ends with "—Mektoub." but "Morocco" does not.

35 Berman, *American Arabesque*, 1.

36 Berman, *American Arabesque*, 139.

Works Cited

Ahmad, Dohra. "'More than Romance': Genre and Geography in 'Dark Princess.'" *ELH* 69, no. 3 (2002): 775–803.

Aidi, Hisham. "Claude McKay and Gnawa Music." *New Yorker*, September 2, 2014. www .newyorker.com/culture/culture-desk/claude -mckay-gnawa-music.

Berman, Jacob Rama. *American Arabesque: Arabs, Islam and the Nineteenth-Century Imaginary*. New York: New York University Press, 2012.

Bishop, Jacqueline. "Claude McKay's Songs of Morocco." *Black Renaissance/Renaissance Noire* 14, no. 1 (2014): 68–75.

Boetsch, Gilles, and Jean-Noel Ferrié. "Ancient Survivals, Comparatism, and Diffusion: Remarks on the Formation of the Mediterranean Cultural Area." In *The Mediterranean Reconsidered: Representations, Emergences, Recompositions*, edited by Mauro Pernissi and Ratiba Hadj Moussa, 9–11. Gatineau: Canadian Museum of Civilization, 2005.

Braudel, Fernand. *The Mediterranean and the Mediterranean World in the Age of Philip II*, translated by Siân Reynolds. 2 vols. Berkeley: University of California Press, 1995.

Colmeiro, José F. "Exorcising Exoticism: 'Carmen' and the Construction of Oriental Spain." *Comparative Literature* 54, no. 2 (2002): 127–44.

Cooper, Wayne F. *Claude McKay: Rebel Sojourner in the Harlem Renaissance*. Baton Rouge: Louisiana State University Press, 1987.

Das, Smita. "Subjecting Pleasure: Claude McKay's Narratives of Transracial Desire." *Journal of Black Studies* 44, no. 7 (2013): 706–24.

Davila, Carl. "The Andalusi Turn: The Nūba in Mediterranean History." *Mediterranean Studies* 23, no. 2 (2015): 149–69.

Davila, Carl. "The Andalusian Music in Fez: The Preservation of a Mixed Oral Tradition." PhD diss., Yale University, 2006.

Edwards, Brent Hayes. *The Practice of Diaspora: Literature, Translation, and the Rise of Black Internationalism*. Cambridge, MA: Harvard University Press, 2003.

El Hamel, Chouki. *Black Morocco: A History of Slavery, Race, and Islam*. Cambridge: Cambridge University Press, 2013.

Elinson, Alexander E. *Looking Back at Al-Andalus: The Poetics of Loss and Nostalgia in Medieval Arabic and Hebrew Literature*. Leiden: Brill, 2009.

Fuchs, Barbara. *Exotic Nation: Maurophilia and the Construction of Early Modern Spain*. Philadelphia: University of Pennsylvania Press, 2009.

García-Arenal, Mercedes, and Gerard Wiegers, eds. *The Expulsion of the Moriscos from Spain: A Mediterranean Diaspora*, translated by Consuelo López-Morillas and Martin Beagles. Leiden: Brill, 2014.

Gikandi, Simon. *Writing in Limbo: Modernism and Caribbean Literature*. Ithaca, NY: Cornell University Press, 1992.

Glissant, Édouard. "Creolization in the Making of the Americas." *Caribbean Quarterly* 54, nos. 1–2 (2008): 81–89.

Hartman, Saidiya V. *Lose Your Mother: A Journey along the Atlantic Slave Route*. New York: Farrar, Straus and Giroux, 2008.

Holcomb, Gary Edward. *Claude McKay, Code Name Sasha: Queer Black Marxism and the Harlem Renaissance*. Gainesville: University Press of Florida, 2007.

Holcomb, Gary Edward. "Diaspora Cruises: Queer Black Proletarianism in Claude McKay's *A Long Way from Home*." *Modern Fiction Studies* 49, no. 4 (2003): 714–45.

Kapchan, Deborah. *Traveling Spirit Masters: Moroccan Gnawa Trance and Music in the Global Marketplace*. Middletown, CT: Wesleyan University Press, 2007.

Lane, Edward William. *An Arabic-English Lexicon*. 8 vols. London, 1863–93.

Longfellow, Henry Wadsworth. *Poems and Other Writings*, edited by J. D. McClatchy. New York: Literary Classics of the United States, 2000.

McKay, Claude. *Complete Poems*, edited by William J. Maxwell. Urbana: University of Illinois Press, 2004.

McKay, Claude. *A Long Way from Home*, edited by Gene Andrew Jarrett. New Brunswick, NJ: Rutgers University Press, 2007.

McKay, Claude. *Romance in Marseille*, edited by Gary Edward Holcomb and William J. Maxwell. New York: Penguin, 2020.

Metlitzki, Dorothee. *The Matter of Araby in Medieval England*. New Haven, CT: Yale University Press, 1977.

Shannon, Jonathan H. "Performing al-Andalus, Remembering al-Andalus: Mediterranean Soundings from Mashriq to Maghrib." *Journal of American Folklore*, no. 477 (2007): 308–34.

Stephens, Michelle Ann. *Black Empire: The Masculine Global Imaginary of Caribbean Intellectuals in the United States, 1914–1962*. Durham, NC: Duke University Press, 2005.

Walonen, Michael K. "Land of Racial Confluence and Spatial Accessibility: Claude McKay's Sense of Mediterranean Place." In *Geocritical Explorations: Space, Place, and Mapping in Literary and Cultural Studies*, edited by Robert T. Tally Jr., 75–86. New York: Palgrave Macmillan, 2011.

Lyric Commodification
in McKay's Morocco

DAVID B. HOBBS

Abstract Reassessing Claude McKay's writing about North Africa, this article contends that McKay saw sites in this region as uniquely felicitous to staging conversations
between global socialism and the Black diasporic avant-garde. His attention to site-specific
interracial urban cultures serves as a counterpoint to the Depression-fueled Pan-Africanism
that increasingly defined W. E. B. Du Bois's editorials for the *Crisis*. At the same time,
McKay's persistent interest in the activities of the *Liberator* suggests a surprising
resonance between their aesthetics to his locodescriptive verse. Bringing these strands
together, the article finds that McKay did not seek a synesthetic resolution to the question of organizing an urban community or an integrationist racial future but, rather, sought
to highlight the importance of dissensus despite global uncertainty. The article considers
McKay's formal poetics and fiction together, comparing his visual tactics with the French
and British Colonial Expositions' "panoramas."
Keywords   lyric, urban, sonnet, Morocco, modernism

> What is Africa to me:
> Copper sun or scarlet sea,
> Jungle star or jungle track,
> Strong bronze men, or regal black
> Women from whose loins I sprang
> When the birds of Eden sang?
> —Countee Cullen, "Heritage"

It's easy to understand why Countee Cullen's "Heritage" (1925) became a touchstone for Black Anglophone poets in the early twentieth century.[1] At once
fantastic and frustrated, biblical and erotic, mindful of the continent's complex
multihued cultures even as it claims curiosity more than understanding, Cullen's
investigation eludes resolution because it desires a specific answer to an expansive
and shifting question. Caryl Phillips is quite right to see the "Eden" at this excerpt's
terminus as an indication of a broader "dreaming of repairing the rupture in their

personal and social history that had been caused by the institution of slavery," and it makes sense that Alain Locke included the poem in *The New Negro*, not in the selection of Cullen's poetry but in the section titled "The Negro Digs Up His Past."[2] But the belief that such a question could have a specific answer lies, at least in part, in the presumptions that undergird the "selfhood" that shapes so much of lyric poetry. A coherent speaker demands a coherent history, yet Cullen's discomforted questioner finds these histories multiple, fugitive, and, somewhat surprisingly, urban:

> So I lie, who find no peace
> Night or day, no slight release
> From the unremittent beat
> Made by cruel padded feet
> Walking through my body's street.[3]

Where the poem began with the jungle and the pair bond, the impetus to continue comes from the multitude endlessly pacing an "inner" city—a conjunction of embodiment, fragmentation, and urban space that may not surprise scholars of modernism but nevertheless tends not to be the way that Africa is imagined, even by the speaker. The drama of the question lies with "their" restlessness as much as his or hers or theirs.

A few years later Cullen would inflect "Heritage" with firsthand experience. Traveling Europe with Harold Jackman, to whom Cullen had dedicated the poem, they had the chance to visit Algeria and took it—breaking an appointment with Claude McKay, who arrived in Paris shortly after they had left. [4] Cullen describes the trip in breezy fragments in his column for *Opportunity*:

> We are back in our hotel . . . it is early morning . . . our room is high with
> a great circular balcony from which we can see in every direction. Algiers
> spreading out like a large white fan, its white roofs shining and flashing in the
> early morning sun, the entire panorama one of bewildering beauty, if one
> could only forget the dirt and disease which stalks the Arab population. . . .
> Suddenly there is a knock at the door. We open to one of our boat companions,
> a young German aviator. In halting English he explains that he would like to
> indulge in a sun bath on our balcony in the hope that he might tan himself
> to what he considers our marvelous complexion. . . . Will we allow him?
> My companion and I exchange smiles. No similar premium has ever been
> placed on our color where we came from. . . . Bitters and sweets, aloe and
> honeysuckle.[5]

Cullen's saucy ellipses are characteristic of these letters from abroad, but they chime with the slackening of the color line. We never do discover whether or not he allowed the German aviator to join them. The qualified "panorama . . . of bewildering beauty," however, echoes Cullen's description of the celebrated Bal Nègre nightclub in Paris in the same article—a "gliding, twisting panorama" in which he and Jackman notice that "these Negroes have become Europeanized in dress and manner."[6]

Brent Hayes Edwards contrasts Cullen's "somewhat patronizing" description of the nightclub with Paulette Nardal's keen attention to the rhetoric of dance but, in doing so, misses the possibility of a colonial critique that spans the article.[7] In both cases, Cullen appeals to a technology of compressed and theatrical exoticism that was, at the time, inextricable from the way that American and European audiences came to understand Black life in the United States and in Africa.[8] He even refers to the nightclub as "Bal Colonial."[9]

But I want to focus on the "premium" placed on Cullen's skin tone, which qualifies McKay's own experience in the Maghreb. Recalling his first trip to Morocco in 1928—his return voyage to Paris practically passing Cullen's ship to Algiers—McKay leaps from the superficial sights and sounds of the marketplace in Fez to a revelation about how he experienced his identity differently in this new territory: "The mosaics of Morocco went to my head like rare wine. . . . I was never tired of listening to the native musicians playing African variations of the oriental melodies in the Moroccan cafés. For the first time in my life I felt myself singularly free of color-consciousness."[10] McKay's testimonial is striking for several reasons, but the realities of French colonial occupation demand primary attention. General Hubert Lyautey, the colonial administrator of Morocco, had shifted the local capital from Fez to Rabat and sought to extend and deepen preexisting segregation practices, enlisting the Parisian architect Henry Prost to develop "one of the most elaborate experiments of racial segregation in the history of city splitting" shortly after assuming control in 1912.[11] Lyautey was also keen to downplay his responsibility, at least to a gentile reading public. Traveling with Lyautey in 1920, Edith Wharton suggests that the very vibrancy that McKay finds in Fez's markets was the residual effect of a Muslim pogrom instead of a colonial tactic: "Happily for the inhabitants, [the massacre] has disappeared into rebuilding. North African Jews are still compelled to live in ghettos, into which they are locked at night, as in France and Germany in the Middle Ages."[12] Compromised as it is, Wharton's record nevertheless deepens the mystery of McKay's first response, as much as Cullen's responses suggests a similar, albeit more jaundiced, renegotiation of color and place.

As the newly available novel *Romance in Marseille* indicates, McKay was very much aware of the racial segregation of the Maghreb (and its manipulations). While his description of the early history of his Moroccan femme fatale, Aslima, leans on many of the same Orientalist tropes that appear in his memoir—and there will be more to say about these marketplace scenes in a moment—a later passage is far more pertinent. Aslima begins to avoid sex work and spend more time with the novel's hero, Lafala, and consequently her money starts to grow thin and she angers her pimp, Titin. With nowhere to turn, she tries to find her way to Lafala's hotel but cannot and is left alone on the Quayside with night rolling in. Suddenly, she finds herself selected for a human sacrifice in a whitewashed city that recalls Tétouan more than Marseille, and as she tries to call for help, "a high wall ar[ises] shutting her off and all was darkness," and only when she awakens does she realize that this has been a dream.[13] The recovery of *Romance in Marseille* provides an opportunity to read a fuller impression of McKay's years in Africa and offers a chance to draw on his fiction to help understand his much-neglected late poetry, which superficially lacks the socialist heft as well as the sarcasm and play that have attracted so many recent readers. But his contemporaneous sonnets, describing Tétouan and Fez as well as Marrakech, Chefchaouen, and Tangier, brilliantly draw on a similar sense of restriction, using it to craft a cautious but indelible sense of Black liberation within the urban grid and to comment on the commodification of lyric poetry. Indeed, all five of these poems were intended for a suite titled "Cities," which McKay tried to publish after returning to the United States in 1933.[14]

This article has two goals. The first is to demonstrate that the poems that McKay wrote in the early 1930s represent a conscious effort to adapt the lyric to his political convictions and global experience. Sonnets were and are inevitably grouped as *lyric*—Peter Howarth describes the form as "epitomizing compact lyric perfection" for late nineteenth- and early twentieth-century readers, while Heather Dubrow says that the sonnet is "not merely an instance but also a textbook example, even a prototype of the lyric mode."[15] But how *these* sonnets are lyric, and what the "lyricization" of their content means for McKay's depiction of North African cities, remains unexplored. In undertaking such an exploration, I mean to unsettle the prevailing scholarly narrative of McKay's career, in which he transitions from primarily a poet in the 1910s and early 1920s to a best-selling novelist in the late 1920s and the 1930s. Even though *Romance in Marseille* provides the occasion for this issue, McKay limns his enduring belief in his poetry's efficacy as well as the constraints that produced his career shift in a rather modest letter to his friend and editor Max Eastman in August 1933: "I guess I could do poetry still if I were not bound by prose to make a living."[16] I am beginning with the assumption—based on the shared subject matter of these poems as well as the restricted patterns to which they conform—that this group represents an *attempt* at something heretofore unrecognized and that a closer analysis of that group of poems will make that attempt clearer.

But the fact that this shared subject matter *is* urban life leads to my second goal. I argue that the panorama, with its abstracted, depersonalized, and colonial connotations, acted as a symbol or blueprint for alternative Black sociality in the modernist era. Part of what registers as *strange*, in these sonnets, is their lack of attention to the specific, individual experiences that populate his novels. While my first section concentrates on McKay's separation of the sonnet from the progressive structure of "thought" with which it is normally associated, my second explores these "unthought" sonnets as targeted interventions into a broader conversation about Black life within city space. McKay's North African sonnets do not avoid race—far from it—but seem mindful of the ways that racial disparity has been constructed differently in different settings. The *urban* content of these sonnets is essential to understanding this sensibility, and McKay's locodescriptive concentration on the marketplace activates contemporaneous sociological investigations into the origins of "the city" as well as the then-popular use of panorama form as a method of rendering an impression of city life as its own kind of commodity. This is especially true of the colonial expositions that brought simulacra of Fez and Tangier and Marrakech into European cities like Marseille and London, which the Black American press covered avidly.[17]

That McKay is a writer of the city is beyond question. But scholarly attention remains focused on his relationship with Harlem, even though much of his corpus was written outside it and about other places, and he worried about kinds of limits that New York and Harlem could impose. In fact, McKay dreaded returning to the place that we still most frequently read him through, writing to Eastman earlier in 1933: "Fact is I am afraid of the idea of returning for good. For now I can't live like in the days before *The Liberator*. I'll have to find myself among the 'Niggerati' as I hear they call themselves in Harlem. And I think it will be more losing than finding."[18] By looking more closely at McKay's sonnets about North African cities, we can better know what he worried about losing when he returned to Harlem, as well as what produced his persistent love for cities and "their changing moods."[19]

But I started with Cullen and "Heritage" to give a sense of a wider story. Because of the *Crisis*'s importance in shaping Black Americans' impressions of Africa, and because *Romance in Marseille* and McKay's Moroccan sonnets were written after W. E. B. Du Bois's much-discussed pan of *Home to Harlem*, it would be difficult to discuss McKay's global Black sociality without Du Bois's own evolving views. Cullen offers a (biased) middle point between these two figures—an unlikely son-in-law to one and a sometimes friend and stalwart fan to the other, neither as skeptical about the Maghreb as Du Bois nor as profoundly affected as McKay.

Enclosing the Sestet

> I love all cities, I love their foreign ways.
> Their tyranny over the life of man.
> —Claude McKay, *Complete Poems*

During the twelve years McKay spent in Europe and North Africa, his friends maintained his reputation by foregrounding the fineness of his poetic craft. Shortly after Cullen became his assistant in 1926, *Opportunity* editor Charles S. Johnson wrote to McKay that he was "more than commonly interested in having American readers reestablish that keen and delightful direct contact with you through your verse, which your absence has broken."[20] Between 1931 and 1933 Langston Hughes tried to publish two articles about McKay. In the first he recovers McKay from the "devastating criticisms" of *Home to Harlem* by redirecting attention to his first American poetry collection, *Harlem Shadows* (1922), which Hughes says "contain[s] the finest sonnets any member of our race has ever written."[21] His next is even more effusive, opining that McKay's "sonnets are among the finest in contemporary English" in a draft succinctly titled "Claude McKay: The Best."[22] And even though Eastman had told McKay that the manuscript for *Home to Harlem* "felt like 1000 dollars in [my] pocket," he more frequently queried McKay's verse.[23] "Do you ever write any more poetry?" Eastman asked, in a note accompanying some of his own poems, sent to McKay in Tangier in 1930.[24]

McKay did, of course, and with a major shift in form. He was introduced to American readers as a poet of "Sonnets and Songs" in the *Liberator* in July 1919, and from the very beginning his sonnets tend to conclude with a strong, memorable couplet.[25] "The Little Peoples," for instance, shifts from an octet about the "little nations that are weak and white" to a sestet about the damage that this insecurity wreaks on the darker-skinned world, adopting what Christopher Spaide calls the "generational 'we'":

> We to the ancient gods of greed and lust
> Must still be offered up as sacrifice:
> Oh, we who design to live but will not dare,
> The white world's burden must forever bear![26]

In "A Capitalist at Dinner," also included in that *Liberator* suite, McKay begins by describing a specific "ugly . . . heavy, overfed" capitalist and wonders whether "creatures *like* this money-fool" will "forever rule." If so, McKay decides, "then let proud mothers cease from giving birth; / Let human beings perish from the earth."[27] Both poems are laid out as octet-sestet, yet both rhyme *abab cdcd efef gg*, and while both seem to change their focus between octet and sestet, both also evince a strong rhetorical shift in the concluding couplet. These poems are difficult to sort into the conventional Shakespearean-Petrarchan sonnet binary, but primarily because they evince elements of both forms, a sort of hybrid suited to McKay's vocative first-person plurals.

In his "Cities" sonnets, however, McKay begins to write sestets that are not only self-sufficient but self-contained. Throughout the entire collection, these poems conclude by rhyming *efgfge* or *fghghf*, with the rhyme on the first and final lines serving as a phonetic boundary. Where we typically expect the sonnet to move from a proposition to its complication, McKay frustrates this sense of momentum and separates each poem's uneven halves, even as he tends to use a colon to signal a sort of equation between them. This operation has less of an impact on the opening stanza, in which we expect an idea to progress into *something* but do not necessarily seek to predict the direction and tone of that progression. But it gives the sestet a strange, constricted feeling. To highlight the unlikeliness of this rhyme pattern, Lewis Sterner's contemporaneous *The Sonnet in American Literature* (1930)—an exhaustive doctoral dissertation that studied prosodic trends up to the year of its submission, isolating dozens of "hybrid" forms—offers no indication of a similar scheme. This form, it appears, is entirely McKay's own.[28]

For a sense of how this constriction impacts the poem as a whole, here is "Tetuan." McKay visited the city, now known as Tétouan, in 1931 and "witnessed a wonderful demonstration of amity and fraternity between the native Moorish and civilian Spanish populations."[29] For clarity's sake, I have indicated the rhyme scheme in the margin:

The conquering Moor an homage paid to Spain	a
And the Alhambra lifted up its towers!	b
Africa's fingers tipped with miracles,	c
And quivering with Arabian designs,	d
Traced words and figures like exotic flowers,	b

Sultanas' chambers of rare tapestries,	e
Filigree marvels from Koranic lines	d
Mosaics chanting notes like tropic rain.	a
And Spain repaid the tribute ages after:	f
To Tetuan, that fort of struggle and strife,	g
Where chagrined Andalusian Moors retired,	h
She brought a fountain bubbling with new life,	g
Whose crystal charm won even the Muslim pride,	h
And filled it sparkling with flamenco laughter.	f[30]

This potted history of Moorish expansion into the Iberian peninsula and the subsequent Spanish colonization of eastern Morocco provides a stark tonal shift from McKay's early sonnets as well as a new form. Simply put, it's hard to know what McKay is doing here, and even though Tétouan would have been relatively inaccessible to his readers, there is hardly enough here to get a clear impression of the town, especially because the octet is about a palace in Spain. Timo Müller, in *The African American Sonnet: A Literary History*, argues that McKay's North African sonnets are propelled by the "uneasy relationship between McKay's anticolonialism and his individualist transnationalism," but I don't see how the relationship between anticolonialism and individualist transnationalism is "uneasy"—here, or elsewhere—to say nothing of the maladroit Orientalism in phrases like *Filigree marvels from Koranic lines*.[31] But more to the point, this sonnet feels temporally and syntactically *sluggish*, with most lines containing complete clauses and lacking a clear sense of parataxis between them.[32] We should probably grant McKay a silent contrast between Tétouan's "flamenco laughter" and the agonized colonial administration of nearby Tangier, but this poem is still without the political urgency of his *Harlem Shadows*.[33] The bloodlessness of the critique is underscored by binding the sestet with opening and closing rhymes on *after* and *laughter*, which suggest that the "struggle and strife" are healed over time, even though Spain's occupation of Tétouan was a relatively recent development and McKay elsewhere alludes to colonial violence directly.

But "Tetuan" is *not* apolitical, and more closely considering the sonnet form is key to understanding the politics of this shift. The sonnet offers a close relationship with several long literary histories, and we also understand it to carry an expectation of harmony between scheme and cognition. As Paul Muldoon put it recently: "The sonnet, like most of us, can just about deal with one to two thoughts at a time. We have thought 1. In addition to thought 1 we have thought 2, or by contrast, we have thought 2. It's precisely because of what might be construed as its dullness that the sonnet has managed to be so durable."[34] McKay often brings this sense of cognition together with literary history, as in "The White City" (1921), which opens with a brooding octet containing allusions to *The Taming of the Shrew* and *Paradise Lost* and then shifts into a visionary description: "I see the mighty city through a mist— / The strident trains that speed the goaded mass."[35] The *volta* not only marks a shift between thoughts 1 and 2 but tells us how to read the shift between them—in "The White City," the opening first-person singular reflection on a "life-long hate" that will not "bend an inch" (via Shakespeare) tells us that the subsequent perceptions are informed by this hatred. When the speaker is "contemplat[ing]" the "spires and towers vapor-kissed," we understand that his love of this almost Gothic city stems from a kind of attunement. In McKay's *Liberator* suite, these shifts tend toward contrast, with "The Little People," "A Capitalist at Dinner," and "If We Must Die" progressing from the behaviors of the white ruling class to the conditions of the oppressed.

McKay's late scheme thwarts the conceit that the first idea should *develop* through addition or contrast. Between the octet and sestet, "Tetuan" jumps forward in history with combined resignation ("And Spain repaid the tribute ages after") and hope ("bubbling with new life"). The progress in these sonnets is not just frustrated but frustrat*ing*, not dull because they conform to convention but uncooperative because they appear to be missing their fundamental "turn." Instead of mimicking the way that we "can just about deal with one to two thoughts at a time," McKay offers sonnets that are not progressive or contrastive but episodic or accretive. In effect, his new sonnet form relocates Tétouan into what Saidiya Hartman refers to as the "position of the unthought," whose radicalness she glosses by emphasizing the way that "so much of our political vocabulary/imaginary/desires have been implicitly integrationist even when we imagine our claims are radical."[36] McKay's "Tetuan" won't be integrated but rather creates a sort of dissonance with the expectations created by its form. The impression is less that Tétouan is an unfit subject for a sonnet than that the sonnet as it previously existed was too committed to cognitive resolution to adequately reflect McKay's North African subject.

This enclosure offers a global extension from Sonya Posmentier's argument about the importance of the "provision ground"—a plot of land assigned to enslaved persons for subsistence farming—to McKay's *Harlem Shadows*–era sonnets. Posmentier characterizes the sonnet form as "shar[ing] the burdens and possibilities of . . . agricultural spaces, taking shape in relationship to a colonial tradition while defining a black expressive form that resists its own utility within the post-plantation aesthetic economy."[37] This description seems to allow for growth and change within the given "plot" of conventions that McKay (or any poet) develops, instead of seeing the fact of identified parameters as primarily restrictive. Following Posmentier, McKay's new form is better understood as a cultivated change instead of a radical remaking. But where Posmentier sees the sonnet form *itself* as an "enclosure"—albeit one that allows McKay to "break from that history" of slavery— McKay's African sonnet form is interested in subdivisions.[38] This social relationship between the enclosed, uneven halves of the sonnet seems more like the way that McKay describes the divided city of Tétouan itself: "The ancient walls merge into the new without pain. The Spanish Morocco buildings give more lightness to the native Moroccan, and the architectural effect of the whole is a miracle of perfect miscegenation."[39] Fusing diachronic divisions with a sense of racial amity, these walls separate but also seem to foster a "lightness" that would be difficult in a united space. There is reason to be skeptical of McKay's "miracle," but it seems significant that McKay locates this "miracle" beyond the colonial purview of the British

Empire. Indeed, following that description of Tétouan, McKay tells us that he felt no discrimination, because he purposefully "avoided British territory" in North Africa.[40] McKay's North African sonnets are still "taking shape in relationship to a colonial tradition" (per Posmentier), but they seem more deeply aware of the ways that those traditions differ in different former colonies, particularly with respect to the experience of race.

In McKay's "Cities" form, the sonnet becomes less about development, either from proposition to complication or from thesis to antithesis, and more about the fact of difference. In doing so, McKay suggests a relationship between octet and sestet more *social* than cognitive—that is, the two uneven halves of the poem interact in a manner that has less to do with one becoming the other, or with holding both in mind at once, and more to do with figuring out how they have come to coexist and can continue to do so. This is, perhaps, the best way of understanding the near-absent speakers in these poems, with pronouns appearing to mark observations but rarely investing the scenes with evaluations or philosophical extensions.

Experimental "Lyrical Taste" and City Sonnets as Commodities

> The quality of being inevitably and honestly square may become a dreadful thing, however. And it makes this form inappropriate for persons who have not at least a certain degree of lyrical taste. In the hands of such persons a sonnet is not a poem, but an enterprise.
> —Max Eastman, "Preface about Sonnets"

There is a tendency to treat Black formal poetics ethnographically, which calls attention to how rarely *other* formal poetics are treated in this manner. Timo Müller makes this tendency stark in an article for *American Literature* that preceded his monograph: "Since they did not have a unified tradition to continue or reject, poets like Gwendolyn Brooks, Robert Hayden, and Melvin Tolson drew on a variety of sources, most importantly high modernist formal experimentation and Black vernacular speech, which they combined in a self-consciously artificial manner."[41] Without supporting evidence, the belief that the working-class Brooks, who did not attend a four-year university, would share the same literary tradition as Hayden, who studied with W. H. Auden at the University of Michigan during his master's degree and taught in universities for his entire career, cannot be taken seriously and would hardly be admitted for poets of any other background.[42] And McKay's own training was sui generis—Winston James provides a detailed analysis of his strange tutelage, first under the direction of his older brother, a "committed freethinker and socialist," and then by a Cambridge-educated chaplain with whom he "read and discussed Berkeley, Hume, and Spencer, among others," before McKay came to the Tuskegee Institute in 1912 to study agriculture.[43] It would be difficult to imagine even a fellow Jamaican émigré sharing McKay's sense of "tradition," let alone diverse Black sonneteers like Langston Hughes and Jean Toomer.

Instead, I want to borrow a reframing approach from queer theory. In his pathbreaking work on identity and genre in *The Queen's Throat*, Wayne Koestenbaum takes opera's popularity with gay men as an occasion to investigate the formal goals and affordance of the *opera* instead of as an aperture for understanding cosmopolitan male queerness. Along similar lines, investigating formal poetry by Black poets might more productively yield answers about *the sonnet* and its status in the 1920s and 1930s than conclusions about Blackness. However, this belief that Black poets *should* share a single orientation has seemingly existed for as long as poetry by Black poets, and McKay was acutely aware of its prevalence.

McKay's belief that the "ultra modernists in poetry and prose . . . lack that high mental equipment that makes for clarity of expression of a high order" has too often been taken as a far-reaching condemnation of literary experimentation.[44] But McKay made waves as an editor at the *Liberator* for accepting poetry—sonnets—that was too experimental:

> One day I had sorted and read until my brain was fagged and I hadn't found a single startling line. Then I picked up a thin sheaf and discovered some verses which stimulated me like an elixir. They were mostly sonnets, a little modernistic, without capitals, a little voluptuous, yet restrained and strangely precise, with a flavor of Latin eroticism and decadence. They were signed, E.E. Cummings.
>
> . . . I was particularly excited by one called *"Maison."* It created something like an exquisite miniature palace of Chinese porcelain. The palace was so real that it rose up out of the page, but the author had also placed in it a little egg so rotten that you could smell it.
>
> . . . I wanted to make a spread of the verses in *The Liberator*, but Robert Minor was substituting as editor-in-chief that month and he had a violent reaction against the verses. I remember Minor's saying to me that if I liked such poems I was more of a decadent than a social revolutionist.[45]

Cummings's poem appeared in the July 1921 issue of the *Liberator* and bears little resemblance to McKay's own writing. Eschewing stable grammar and adopting a much more restricted vocabulary, "Maison" is superficially a fantastical love poem:

> my love is building a magic, a discreet
> tower of magic and (as I guess)
> when Farmer Death (whom fairies hate) shall
> crumble the mouth-flower fleet[46]

The explicit weirdness of Cummings's notation and syntax tend to take top billing, and certainly much could be said about that strange last line. But Cummings is also burlesquing the sonnet's expected progress of thought-then-addition-or-contrast by interjecting parenthetical swerves throughout. Here, though, the sense of self-doubt *intensifies* the sonnet's focus on cognition, so while Cummings is distressing the same convention as McKay does in his new sonnet form, Cummings is doing so in a different way. This is not only a point of surprising resonance between McKay and Cummings but indicative of a wider group of socialist sonnet experiments. Louis Zukofsky's corona "A-7" was written around the same time, while Eastman's own collections always included a section of sonnets, and most issues of the *Liberator* and the *New Masses* include variations on the form by a host of writers.

McKay certainly belongs in this group of left-leaning experiments with the form, but the very unlikeliness of this potential subgenre highlights broader shortcomings in the way we understand modernist poetic production and distribution, which might clarify the relationship between McKay's African sonnet form and the wider conversation about poetic commodification. Per this section's epigraph, McKay's friend Eastman believed that the sonnet "is not a poem, but an enterprise" when written by poets without "lyrical taste." The question of who was allowed to have this "lyrical taste," or how that taste might differ according to experience and identity, is left unasked by Eastman, but McKay's pre-African experience illuminates the stakes of writing in this form and the kinds of assumptions about a Black lyrical "taste" being made by McKay's other socialist interlocutors. Not only did McKay's championing of Cummings's sonnet lead to Robert Minor doubting his revolutionary convictions, but Minor questioned McKay's identity as well. The disagreement develops into Minor suggesting that McKay's appreciation indicates a failure to appear authentically Black, albeit in highly racist terms. "Robert Minor said he could not visualize me as a real Negro. He thought of a Negro as of a rugged tree in the forest."[47] Hurtful and hateful, Minor's criticism indicates the kind of racist-aesthetic logic that operated within McKay's socialist milieu, a belief that decorousness, subtlety, and even strangeness itself should be unappealing to "a real Negro."[48]

McKay's "Cities" should be read through this expectation—even considered as written against it. Both his vocabulary and his attention in these poems incline toward a sensuousness that seems "decadent." But in focusing on Africa, especially on market scenes in the cities of the Maghreb, McKay makes the case that these topoi *can* be revolutionary with sufficient attention to the coincidence of commerce and global disparity. Put another way, McKay's North African sonnets are interested in the geopolitics of conspicuous consumption—which Thorstein Veblen characterized as representing "a larger element" of city life, as opposed to country life, and as "more imperative" to city life as well—and use the same elements of Minor's critique to investigate this phenomenon.[49] Here, for instance, is "Marrakesh," which opens with a description of the very walls that McKay's rhyme scheme recalls:

High ramparts, tombs and mosques and mansions vaunting
Above the myriad huts of straw and clay,
Against the palms and olive branches singing,
Beneath the circling Atlas grand and hoary
Barbaric strength of swarthy sultans' sway—
While walls re-echo with the bell-like ringing
Of Muezzins' voices chanting Allah's glory,
And ghosts of warriors ancient flags are flaunting:

> The Berber youngsters pitch their little tents
> And skip gazelle-like for the approving throng
> Of nomads purchasing the city's joys—
> African drum beat, oriental song,
> Salome-sensual dance of jeweled boys,
> Amidst the ruins of austere monuments.[50]

Certainly "decadent," this is in a different key from the self-consciously Wildean works about Harlem by Richard Bruce Nugent or Wallace Thurman, who tend to write with ennui and sarcasm about social and sexual encounters between class equivalents. McKay's lines are sexual, even queer, in a way that his *Harlem Shadows*–era poetry typically is not, but they advertise an imbalanced, Islamophilic sexual economy in which "the city's joys" include "jeweled boys" as well as exoticizing "African drum beat[s]" and "oriental song." In "Fez" McKay makes the intercontinental foundation of this sexual economy clear by referring to a "dream erotic / Of beauty African in shape and form."[51] And we can make a reasonable guess as to the origin of the "nomads" purchasing these "joys": we would ordinarily expect the Berbers to be described as nomads, but here it seems more plausible that McKay is talking about the "throngs" of European and American tourists who began visiting the Maghreb after the establishment of the Spanish protectorate in 1912.[52] But while a previous iteration of the sonnet might beckon a facile irony between the visual-descriptive octet and the enclosed, commercial sestet, as if these battlements and warriors were helpless to protect Marrakech from an economic "invasion," McKay's social form suggests an uneasy stalemate. It is less a question of opposition than one of complicity—these walls, too, attract the tourists, even if they can't be bought in quite the same way.

McKay entangles this investigation with the coincident discussion of the sonnet *itself* as a commodified poetic identity—a seemingly antimodern form that had an outsized importance in the Depression's global literary economy. Ezra Pound's famous description of the sonnet as "the *devil*" emerges from a specific context, in which the early Depression heightened an awareness of poets' complicity in the commodification of poetry.[53] Christopher Nealon has described Pound's *ABC of Reading* as an attempted call to action:

> The explicatory text from this period that has proven more lasting, of course,
> is 1934's *ABC of Reading*, which sets out not only a syllabus for its readers but
> a technique for reading texts. This technique is famously "economic," not
> least because it is driven by numbers at every level, from the single poem,
> to anthologies of poems, even to the general category of "poetry." . . . The
> pleasure in reading this advice, even today, is in Pound's readiness to
> disaggregate the "units" of literature into components one level down: breaking
> anthologies into poems, poems into lines, and lines (in other exercises) into
> words.[54]

Pound may have provided the most economically minded warning against poetic commodification (however dubious and idiosyncratic his understanding of economics might otherwise be), but he was in good company. Other poets and critics seemed especially suspicious of formal poetry's easy commodification through republishing efforts like anthologies. But critics have tended to ignore the possibility of the poet's own awareness of the relationship between form, circulation, and reception, taking the use of recognizable verse forms as an indication of poetic commodification yet rarely considering commodification as an important tactic. But I'm not sure how to read McKay's sonnets of Maghreb market scenes without receiving some indication that he is critiquing the unthinking consumption of exotic commodities. That McKay isn't only experimenting with the form that contained his most celebrated, declamatory lines but that he is interrogating the ways that these kinds of poems circulate.

It is on these *tactical* grounds that McKay's African sonnets provide an opportunity to revisit and refine Houston Baker's characterization of McKay's formal poems as examples of "mastered masks."[55] Indeed, Baker coins this description as a way of understanding McKay's and Cullen's contributions to *The New Negro*:

> The trick of McKay and Cullen was what one of my colleagues calls the
> denigration of form—a necessary ("forced," as it were) adoption of the standard
> that results in an effective *blackening*. Locke was never of the opinion that
> Western *standards* in art were anything other than adequate goals for high
> Afro-American cultural achievement. And the revaluation of the Afro-
> American based on artistic accomplishment for which he calls mandated,
> in his view, a willingness on the part of black spokespersons to aspire toward
> such standards. Hence, one would have to present *recognizably* standard forms,
> and get what black mileage one could out of subtle, or, by contrast, straining
> (like McKay's rebellious cries) variations and deepening of these forms.[56]

McKay's *New Negro* sonnets all conform to his *Harlem Shadows*–era scheme, and Baker's second parenthetical reminds us that the rousing and rallying couplets that mark those poems might be viewed less as heroic culminations than as the "black mileage" proffered by the standard. In this case, the North African sonnets show us a McKay who no longer feels the responsibility to meet "standards," instead writing beyond a circumscribed racial-national paradigm and offering a poetic form that, while *recognizable*, is nevertheless wholly his own. McKay's swerve away from those "rebellious cries" may indicate a refusal to continue to commodify that rhetorical register, to write sonnets of increasingly capacious critique without the outrage that the standard previously afforded. This form is a new mask, one that unambiguously presents the disqualifying decadence that put McKay at odds with his comrades, and one that also eschews the "achievement" that Locke envisioned so that the poems might better interrogate commodification itself.

McKay's North African Panoramas and Afterward

> Tangier is suffering from the uncertainty of its status.
> —*New York Tribune*, "Tangier Suffers and Decays"

The Depression seems to have deepened the association of scope and poverty that Cullen activates in his rooftop description of Algiers's "panorama." The architectural theorist M. Christine Boyer has argued that the panorama's capacity for rendering large plazas as interior spaces—an inversion of "outside in" (instead of inside out) that captures the city's impact on sustained relationships and on group formation as well as oblique encounters in crowded plazas—initially allowed a subtext of "optimism [to] reign."[57] But by *One Way Street* (1928), Walter Benjamin turns to the panorama for "a tour through the German inflation," finding in the form's wide view an analogue for the many ways that the economic crisis was discussed in Weimar Berlin, using it to unearth the cruel optimism lurking beneath statements like "Things can't go on like this."[58] Even as Benjamin reaches for the panorama as a powerful metaphor, there seems to be an unavoidable risk in its capaciousness.

At the same time, panoramas continued to serve a powerful colonial agenda. They formed the main attractions in the colonial exhibitions that continued through the 1920s and 1930s, and despite the obviousness of this agenda, these exhibitions attracted Black American curiosity. Indeed, one of the few articles to pay attention to specific African sites in Du Bois's *Crisis* based its descriptions not on a trip to the continent but on the simulacra that appeared in the Marseille colonial exhibition in 1922. Du Bois sent William S. Nelson, who was studying at the Seminaire Protestant in Paris, to cover the exhibition, and in rhapsodic terms Nelson describes the "panorama" constructions that allowed the exhibition's designers to render sublimity within the exhibition hall:[59]

> North Africa. The palaces of Morocco, Algeria, and Tunis present a panorama, indeed interesting and instructive. The walls of the palace of Morocco inclose [*sic*] the reproduction of a quarter in a Moroccan town where the Moroccans and Arabs fashion before the eyes of the curious innumerable objects of art. In the entrance hall of this palace hangs a portrait of the Sultan, who, according to an inscription on the wall "has been permitted to retain his rights and prerogatives as sovereign and his religious prestige as chief of the Mohammedan community," and, who, but recently avowed for France on the part of Morocco, Morocco's "indefectible attachment." Near the portrait of the Sultan hangs that of Marshall Lyautey. . . . Behind the walls of the palace of Tunis is reproduced a native street, tramped by brilliantly uniformed Tunisian soldiers and flanked by the booths of native merchants displaying a tempting variety of hand-worked articles. The palace is replete with an exposition of the principal products of Tunis, its carpets, sponges, tobaccos, narghiles or Turkish pipes, its potteries and objects in copper and precious metals, its wines, dates

and fish. Exportations from Tunis are shown to have increased by 400% from 1912 to 1921. A reproduction of a corner in the city of Tunis by means of a panorama, with its Arab market and numerous small merchants picturesquely sheltered, offers an interesting glance at life characteristically Tunisian.[60]

In this lengthy but brisk excerpt, Nelson gives us a sense of the ways that the colonial mission was justified through the exciting variety of exotic commodities that it offered as well as through raw economic reportage. There is no sense of the average person's accommodations or life beyond the bazaar—instead, the spectator moves perpetually from palace to marketplace to palace, with the human scale of these spaces continually revised. Think of how strange it must have been to encounter "brilliantly uniformed Tunisian soldiers" marching inside of a fish-eyed recreation of a North African town. Yet somehow the panorama renders North African space as apprehensible, as livable, but also as controllable by colonial authority.

That Du Bois should run such an underqualified article comes as something of a shock. Just a few years earlier, in an editorial expressing concern about the expansion of colonization following the First World War, Du Bois suggests that Morocco was the first territory to fall to European predation. "Europe had begun to look with covetous eyes toward Africa as early as 1415, when the Portuguese at the Battle of Ceuta gained a foothold in Morocco."[61] This sentiment deepens over time, but only in part. Du Bois had been skeptical of Marcus Garvey's Back-to-Africa movement in the 1910s and 1920s, but the Depression pushes Du Bois to believe that conditions in the United States are untenable. By 1933's "Pan-Africa and the New Radical Philosophy," Du Bois is arguing that "when it becomes an economic problem, a stark matter of bread and butter, then if this young, black American is going to survive and live a life, he must calmly face the fact that however much he is an American there are interests which draw him nearer to the dark people outside of America than to his white fellow citizens."[62] But Du Bois did not seem to consider the Maghreb part of Africa, as far as Black Americans were concerned. He never traveled to North Africa, and his later writings about the region are inflected with a belief in a clash of civilizations that is starkly unnuanced. In *Black Folk, Then and Now* (1939), his research yields a significantly less tolerant picture than McKay's or Cullen's travels, emphasizing the "impossibility of self-defense [from Islam] on the part of the various centers of culture."[63] However, at least part of McKay's feeling "singularly free of color-consciousness" comes from the local celebration of Black poetry, written in classical Arabic: "When I was introduced as a poet there was not a suspicion of surprise among the natives. Instead I was surprised by their flattering remarks: 'A poet! *Mezziane! Mezziane!* Our greatest poet, Antar, was a Negro.'"[64] If the Maghreb was inhospitable to a broader Black return in the early Depression, it seems to have easily felt like a poetic home.

In "Tanger," the longest and most overtly political of McKay's North African poems, he intensifies this "panoramic" approach by stacking his sonnets. In three numbered sections, which recall the three European powers sharing colonial control of the city, McKay characterizes this "gateway" city thus:

> Morocco's severed head is Europe's ball
> Kicked from goal to goal and all around—
> In the African game of the European.[65]

Each section begins with a different "prospect" of the city, first from the European continent, then from the Mediterranean sea, and finally from the hills behind the city. And in this final section, we get the reflecting speaker that the other sonnets avoid:

> Tanger! A Rock of Ages painted white.
> And oh, I found within your native niche
> A beauty pregnant of life's pristine womb,
> Whose fingers, dripping with experience,
> Caressed my spirit and held it growing rich,
> While, on your bosom asleep, I heard the drum
> Of Africa upswelling from the dense
> Dim deeps to stir you far upon the height.
>
> Oh, I have felt the breaking wave on wave
> Of ages washing up against your base,
> From warm Sahara, heart of dark Soudan,
> The clash and clamor of time, the human race
> Within the cradle Mediterranean,
> Round yon high symbol of the Berber brave![66]

Part of McKay's sustained focus can be credited to Tangier's familiarity to his readers. Whereas most would not have ventured far beyond it, Wharton dismissively described the city as the "cosmopolitan, frowsy, familiar Tangier, that every tourist has visited."[67] But McKay is developing an association between the acute effects of the Depression and the longer histories of colonialization exploitation. Earlier in the poem McKay takes on North African tourism directly:

> The tourists stop to gaze at you in chains
> And purchase from the souks a souvenir,
> Thinking your soul breathes in a servile guide.[68]

Where McKay's other African sonnets sketched tensions between specific urban sites and broader geopolitical forces, this poem moves with awkward centripetal motion around an organizing center, more interested in what is (or isn't) visible within this sustained panorama. In the opening line we cannot help but expect the second line of the hymn—"Rock of Ages, cleft for me, / Let me hide myself in Thee"—but find a "niche" instead of a cleavage, a kind of social belonging, instead of an opportunity to be concealed. Likewise, there is some uncertainty in the personification being described in the octet's first lines. Do the "fingers" belong to Tangier, or to a specific "beauty"? But the unnerving impression made by the "fingers, dripping with experience" does not depend on a specific owner. Instead, we get the sense that resistance has a real, sanguinary cost.

When McKay returns to New York, his urban panoramas begin to speak back. Abandoning his new sonnet form, McKay's Depression-era poetry about New York records the intrusive force of advertising, exploring a similar relationship between urban space and commodity culture but with an added focus on the cruelty of being told to consume when one does not have the means to do so. In the rolling quatrains of "New York," McKay turns from the sweeping vistas that marked his Maghreb sonnets to the billboards dotting the sides of the buildings:

> Oh wonder steel and stone that make New York
> A grandeur such as Egypt knew of old!
> The free white mind soared daringly to work,
> And obelisks prick the sky with spires of gold!
>
> But oh the city shouts! A thousand signs,
> Buildings and lots and shattered businesses,
> And stuff too intimate for printed lines,
> Clutched in the grip of dragon-clawed distress.[69]

While "New York" shifts dramatically, from an ode to urban ingenuity in the first stanza to the desperation of the city's poor in the second, the "free white mind" prepares us for this shift. "Free" here means free from need more than free to imagine—which is also to say, free from a sense of awareness of the shared social conditions of the people around him. McKay, in returning to Harlem, saw both the intensity of the Depression but also the intensity of that denial, and turns away from the sonnet form that he crafted while abroad.

· ·

DAVID B. HOBBS is assistant professor of English at the University of Lethbridge (Canada). He writes about poetry, urban studies, and social movements, with articles in (or forthcoming in) the *Journal of Modern Literature*, *Modernism/Modernity*, the *Boston Review*, the *New York Review of Books*, the *Nation*, and elsewhere.

Acknowledgments

My boundless thanks to Gary Edward Holcomb and William J. Maxwell for convening this issue, to Jini Kim Watson for pushing me to sharpen my argument while broadening my scope, and to Chris Mazzara for his heroic editing skills.

Notes

1   Cullen, "Heritage," in *Collected Poems*, 28. See Charles Molesworth's discussion of the poem's reception (*Bid Him Sing*, 73–78). Maya Angelou goes further, suggesting that "Heritage," Claude McKay's "White Houses," and Sterling Brown's "Strong Men" were "guiding lights to the colonized African poets" as well as Caribbean writers (*Letter to My Daughter*, 156).

2   Phillips, "Africa," 10; Cullen, "Heritage," in *The New Negro*.

3   Cullen, "Heritage," in *Collected Poems*, 30.

4   Molesworth, *Bid Him Sing*, 164–65.

5   Cullen, "The Dark Tower," 273; original ellipses.

6   Cullen, "The Dark Tower," 272.

7   Edwards, *The Practice of Diaspora*, 175.

8   While this article will concentrate on the use of panorama re-creations in colonial exhibitions,

Nancy Bentley finds that "elaborate re-creations of plantation life, including massive 'panoramas' of Old South scenes, toured widely in the North and West [during the last decades of the nineteenth century] and were featured at world fairs" (*Frantic Panoramas*, 196).

9   Cullen, "The Dark Tower," 273.

10   McKay, *A Long Way from Home*, 299–300.

11   Picker, *Racial Cities*, 24.

12   Wharton, *In Morocco*, 53.

13   McKay, *Romance in Marseille*, 62. White modernists like the Bowleses tended to focus on gender divisions within North African Muslim households, and Wharton uses the term *segregation* only in this sense.

14   This suite was, at least for a time, intended to form the opening of an expanded edition of *Harlem Shadows*, but McKay would not release another poetry collection until his posthumous *Selected Poems* (1953). For details about "Cities," see Maxwell, "Notes."

15   Howarth, "The Modern Sonnet," 225; Dubrow, "Sonnet and Lyric Mode," 25.

16   Here McKay seems to refer to opinion essays more than novels, as he was also unable to find a publisher for *Romance in Marseille* ("Letter to Max Eastman, 19 August 1933," Max Eastman Papers, McKay Manuscripts, Lilly Library, Indiana University).

17   By "origins of 'the city,'" I am thinking specifically of Max Weber's writing about "the Nature of the City" (first published in the second volume of the posthumous collection *Wirtschaft und Gesellschaft* [1921], translated into English as the stand-alone volume *The City* [1958]).

18   McKay's use of the term *Niggerati* succinctly indicates his continued interest in Harlem's literary community as well as his divergence from that community's sensibility. Coined in 1926 by Zora Neale Hurston and Wallace Thurman as a way of distinguishing their generation of Harlem writers—often used to refer to "Niggeratti Manor," Thurman's building on 136th Street—the term is, clearly, a portmanteau of *nigger* and *literati*. But as a way of highlighting the bohemian impecuniousness of these younger writers, Thurman transcribes it with an extra *t*, which he limns in his 1932 novel *Infants of the Spring*: "'Niggeratti Manor,' Stephen repeated. 'I don't quite get it.' 'You wouldn't, Steve.' 'All of us can't be as clever as you, Paul.' 'I bet Ray gets it . . . Don't you?' 'Niggeratti Manor . . . hmmm . . . quite appropriate, I would say. God knows we're ratty enough'" (*Infants of the Spring*, 40). McKay's "exile" began in late 1922, so his very use of the term is a bit surprising, if entirely explicable through his correspondence

and the magazines sent to him. But he seems to miss some of the playful irony that the term's coiners intended, suggesting something homogenizing ("losing") rather than rebellious and incandescent ("Letter to Max Eastman, 28 June 1933," Max Eastman Papers). See also Rabaka, *The Negritude Movement*, 85–86n33.

19   McKay, *Complete Poems*, 223.

20   Charles S. Johnson, "Letter to Claude McKay, 12 November 1926," Claude McKay Papers, JWJ MSS 27, Box 5, Folder 164, Beinecke Library, Yale University.

21   Hughes, "Negro Art," 46.

22   Hughes, "Claude McKay," 53.

23   McKay quotes "felt like 1000 . . ." back to Eastman in a letter dated 1 December 1930, Max Eastman Papers.

24   Max Eastman, "Letter to Claude McKay, 19 October 1930," Claude McKay Papers, JWJ MSS 27, Box 3, Folder 67.

25   Earlier publications—such as "The Harlem Dancer," in the October 1917 (and final) issue of Waldo Frank's *Seven Arts*—were pseudonymous (in this case, credited to "Eli Edwards").

26   Spaide, "Wallace Stevens."

27   McKay, "Sonnets and Songs," 20–21.

28   There is one possible, although unlikely, precedent: a very early sonnet by Alfred Lord Tennyson, "O, were I loved as I desire to be!," contains an *efgfge* sestet, according to F. E. L. Priestly (*Tennyson's Poetry*, 32), but its octet rhymes *abba cdcd*, and McKay never cites Tennyson as an influence, although an endnote by Wayne F. Cooper suggests that McKay occasionally "unconsciously imitated" Tennyson along with Burns, Shelley, and others in his early dialect poetry ("Notes," 332). See also Sterner, "The Sonnet."

29   McKay, *A Long Way from Home*, 325.

30   McKay, *Complete Poems*, 227.

31   Müller, *African American Sonnet*, 67.

32   McKay even maintains the rhymeless "miracles" and "tapestries" across several drafts. See "Cities," typescript and typescript carbon, corrected, Claude McKay Papers, JWJ MSS 27, Box 12, Folders 381–82.

33   Spain, France, and Britain "shared" Tangier through the "Tangier Statutes": a 1923 *New York Times* article, "The Problem of Tangier," outlines the three colonial empires' competing claims on Tangier without ever discussing the Moroccans' own interest.

34   Muldoon, "Contemporary Poets," 9.

35   McKay, *Complete Poems*, 162. Cary Nelson identifies these allusions as well as one to Wordsworth's "Composed upon Westminster Bridge, Sept. 3 1802," in the notes to "The White City" in *Anthology of Modern American*

36 Hartman, "Position of the Unthought," 184–85.

37 Posmentier, "Provision Ground in New York," 276.

38 Posmentier, "Provision Ground in New York," 277.

39 McKay, *A Long Way from Home*, 308.

40 McKay, *A Long Way from Home*, 308.

41 Müller, "Vernacular Sonnet," 253.

42 George E. Kent offers details on Brooks's two years at Wilson Junior College (*A Life of Gwendolyn Brooks*, chap. 2), while Derek Smith pays special attention to the ways that Hayden's poems "Frederick Douglass," "The Ballad of Nat Turner," and "Rungate, Rungate" developed during "his study under W. H. Auden and his conversion to the Bahá'í Faith in 1941–43" (*Robert Hayden in Verse*, 121).

43 James, *A Fierce Hatred of Injustice*, 27, 36.

44 McKay, "Letter to Max Eastman (25 April 1932)," 151. There are many reasons to be skeptical of this statement—McKay was agreeing with Eastman, his primary means of financial support, who was in the process of sponsoring McKay for a Guggenheim grant—but McKay also goes on to criticize T. S. Eliot, while venerating James Joyce. This letter's outsize impact on McKay scholarship is at least partly due to access, as it is anthologized in *The Passion of Claude McKay* (1973).

45 McKay, *A Long Way from Home*, 102–3.

46 Cummings, "Maison." When Cummings published "Maison" in his collection *Tulips & Chimneys* (1922), he eliminated the spaces on either end of the parentheses, inserted stanza breaks after "guess)" and "shall," and removed the title; it appears as "XII" in the sequence "SONNETS—ACTUALITIES."

47 McKay, *A Long Way from Home*, 103.

48 McKay writes about this expectation quite directly in *Negroes in America*, 67–69, the prose volume he published in the Soviet Union in 1923.

49 Veblen, *Leisure Class*, 87–88.

50 McKay, *Complete Poems*, 227.

51 McKay, *Complete Poems*, 226.

52 See Scherle, "Morocco."

53 Pound, *ABC of Reading*, 157.

54 Nealon, *The Matter of Capital*, 47–48.

55 Baker, *Modernism*, 85.

56 Baker, *Modernism*, 85–86.

57 Boyer, *The City of Collective Memory*, 43.

58 Benjamin, *One Way Street*, 33.

59 William S. Nelson, "Letter to W.E.B. DuBois (28 April 1922)," W. E. B. Du Bois Papers

Digital Collection (MS 312), Special Collections and University Archives, University of Massachusetts Amherst Libraries.

60 Nelson, "French Colonial Exposition," 118.

61 Du Bois, "Editorial," 164.

62 Du Bois, "Pan-Africa," 247. It's probably worth mentioning that Du Bois's first trip to Africa begins with landing at Monrovia, Liberia, on December 22, 1923—in his diary he recorded the precise minute (3:22 p.m.) that he first saw Africa (Lewis, *W.E.B. Du Bois*, 118)—although he continued to condemn Garveyist stances on an African return for years afterward.

63 Du Bois, *Black Folk*, 38–39.

64 McKay, *A Long Way from Home*, 89.

65 McKay, *Complete Poems*, 225.

66 McKay, *Complete Poems*, 225–26.

67 Wharton, *In Morocco*, 1.

68 McKay, *Complete Poems*, 225.

69 McKay, *Complete Poems*, 239–40.

Works Cited

Angelou, Maya. *Letter to My Daughter*. New York: Random House, 2008.

Baker, Houston A., Jr. *Modernism and the Harlem Renaissance*. Chicago: University of Chicago Press, 1987.

Benjamin, Walter. *One Way Street*, edited by Michael W. Jennings, translated by Edmund Jephcott. Cambridge, MA: Belknap Press of Harvard University Press, 2016.

Bentley, Nancy. *Frantic Panoramas*. Philadelphia: University of Pennsylvania Press, 2009.

Boyer, M. Christine. *The City of Collective Memory*. Cambridge, MA: MIT Press, 1996.

Cooper, Wayne F. "Notes to Ch. 3: Poetry, 1912–1925." In *The Passion of Claude McKay*, 332. New York: Schocken, 1973.

Cullen, Countee. "The Dark Tower." *Opportunity* 6, no. 9 (1928): 272–73.

Cullen, Countee. "Heritage." In *Collected Poems*, edited by Major Jackson, 28–32. New York: Library of America, 2013.

Cullen, Countee. "Heritage." In *The New Negro*, edited by Alain Locke, 250–54. New York: Boni, 1925.

Cummings, E. E. "Maison." *Liberator* 4, no. 7 (1921): 24.

Du Bois, W. E. B. *Black Folk, Then and Now*, edited by Henry Louis Gates Jr. Oxford: Oxford University Press, 2007.

Du Bois, W. E. B. "Editorial." *Crisis* 17, no. 4 (1919): 163–66.

Du Bois, W. E. B. "Pan-Africa and New Radical Philosophy." *Crisis* 40, no. 11 (1933): 247, 262.

Dubrow, Heather. "The Sonnet and the Lyric Mode." In *The Cambridge Companion to the Sonnet*, edited by A. D. Cousins and Peter Howarth,

25–45. Cambridge: Cambridge University Press, 2011.

Eastman, Max. "Preface about Sonnets." In *Colors of Life*, 71–73. New York: Knopf, 1918.

Edwards, Brent Hayes. *The Practice of Diaspora*. Cambridge, MA: Harvard University Press, 2003.

Hartman, Saidiya V. "The Position of the Unthought: Interview with Frank B. Wilderson III." *Qui Parle* 13, no. 2 (2003): 183–201.

Howarth, Peter. "The Modern Sonnet." In *The Cambridge Companion to the Sonnet*, edited by A.D. Cousins and Peter Howarth, 225–44. Cambridge: Cambridge University Press, 2011.

Hughes, Langston. "Claude McKay: The Best." In vol. 9 of *The Collected Works of Langston Hughes: Essays on Art, Race, Politics and World Affairs*, edited by Christopher C. De Santis, 53–56. Columbia: University of Missouri Press, 2002.

Hughes, Langston. "Negro Art and Claude McKay." In vol. 9 of *The Collected Works of Langston Hughes: Essays on Art, Race, Politics and World Affairs*, edited by Christopher C. De Santis, 46. Columbia: University of Missouri Press, 2002.

James, Winston. *A Fierce Hatred of Injustice*. London: Verso, 2000.

Kent, George E. *A Life of Gwendolyn Brooks*. Lexington: University of Kentucky Press, 1990.

Lewis, David Levering. *W.E.B. Du Bois: The Fight for Equality and the American Century, 1919–1963*. New York: Holt, 2000.

Maxwell, William J. "Notes: 'Cities' circa 1934." In *Complete Poems*, by Claude McKay, 352–53. Urbana: University of Illinois Press, 2004.

McKay, Claude. *Complete Poems*, edited by William J. Maxwell. Urbana: University of Illinois Press, 2004.

McKay, Claude. "Letter to Max Eastman (25 April 1932)." In *The Passion of Claude McKay*, edited by Wayne F. Cooper, 151–55. New York: Schocken, 1973.

McKay, Claude. *A Long Way from Home*. San Diego: Harcourt, Brace and World, 1970.

McKay, Claude. *Negroes in America*, edited by Alan L. McLeod, translated by Robert J. Winter. Port Washington, NY: Kennikat, 1979.

McKay, Claude. *Romance in Marseille*. New York: Penguin, 2020.

McKay, Claude. "Sonnets and Songs." *Liberator* 2, no. 7 (1919): 20–21.

Molesworth, Charles. *And Bid Him Sing: A Biography of Countée Cullen*. Chicago: University of Chicago Press, 2012.

Muldoon, Paul, Meg Tyler, and Jeff Hilson. "Contemporary Poets and the Sonnet: A Trialogue." In *The Cambridge Companion to the Sonnet*, edited by A. D. Cousins and Peter Howarth, 6–24. Cambridge: Cambridge University Press, 2011.

Müller, Timo. *The African American Sonnet: A Literary History*. Jackson: University Press of Mississippi, 2018.

Müller, Timo. "The Vernacular Sonnet and the Resurgence of Afro-modernism in the 1940s." *American Literature* 87, no. 2 (2015): 253–73.

Nealon, Christopher. *The Matter of Capital*. Cambridge, MA: Harvard University Press, 2011.

Nelson, William S. "The French Colonial Exposition at Marseilles." *Crisis* 24, no. 3 (1922): 116–20.

New York Times. "The Problem of Tangier." July 15, 1923.

New York Tribune. "Tangier Suffers and Decays; Status as City Uncertain." July 17, 1921.

Phillips, Caryl. "What Is Africa to Me Now?" *Research in African Literatures* 46, no. 4 (2015): 10–14.

Picker, Giovanni. *Racial Cities*. London: Routledge, 2017.

Posmentier, Sonya. "The Provision Ground in New York: Claude McKay and the Form of Memory." *American Literature* 84, no. 2 (2012): 273–300.

Pound, Ezra. *ABC of Reading*. New York: New Directions, 2010.

Priestly, F. E. L. *Language and Structure in Tennyson's Poetry*. London: Deutsch, 1973.

Rabaka, Reiland. *The Negritude Movement*. Lanham, MD: Lexington, 2015.

Scherle, Nicolai. "Morocco." In *The Sage International Encyclopedia of Travel and Tourism*, edited by Linda L. Lowry, 839–43. Thousand Oaks, CA: Sage, 2017.

Smith, Derek. *Robert Hayden in Verse: New Histories of African American Poetry and the Black Arts Era*. Ann Arbor: University of Michigan Press, 2018.

Spaide, Christopher. "Wallace Stevens and the Generational 'We.'" Panel 482: Wallace Stevens and Lyric Theory, MLA Conference, Chicago, 2019.

Sterner, Lewis G. "The Sonnet in American Literature." PhD diss., University of Pennsylvania, 1930.

Thurman, Wallace. *Infants of the Spring*. Boston: Northeastern University Press, 1992.

Veblen, Thorstein. *The Theory of the Leisure Class*. New York: Macmillan, 1912.

Weber, Max. *The City*, edited and translated by Don Martindale and Gertrud Neuwirth. New York: Free, 1958.

Wharton, Edith. *In Morocco*. Oxford: Beaufoy, 2015.

Afropessimism, Liminal Hotspots, and Claude McKay's Aesthetic of Sovereign Rejection in *Romance in Marseille*

MICHAEL J. COLLINS

Abstract   This article considers Claude McKay's *Romance in Marseille* through two emerging fields of study: "Afropessimism" and anthropological theories of the "liminal hotspot." It suggests that McKay's novel functions as a critique of positive Harlem Renaissance images of diasporic movement by highlighting how racial "Blackness" functions as a system for rejecting people of color from the benefits of modernity and sovereign rights-bearing status in an expanded temporal and spatial frame. To explore this hypothesis, the article turns to new anthropological work on the liminal hotspot as a site of sustained, unresolved transition, reading the affectivity of diaspora as a negative one in McKay's work that places an unsustainable pressure on ritual and performative stylizations and renders them untenable as forms for cultivating a sovereign condition.
Keywords   liminality, Afropessimism, African American modernism, Claude McKay

Lafala had gone on wandering impressionably from change to change like a heedless young pilgrim with nothing but his staff in his hand and playing variations on the march of legs. Come trouble, come worry. . . . Dance away. . . . Think not of age, of accident, the festering and mortification of youth and poisoned worms corroding through the firm young flesh to the sepulchral skeleton. His dancing legs would carry him all over.
—Claude McKay, *Romance in Marseille*

To be black in an antiblack world . . . is to be inundated and under assault at every turn, pushed into an endlessly kinetic movement; which is to say subjected to an open and absolute vulnerability—not so much controlled by the

ENGLISH LANGUAGE NOTES
59:1, April 2021   DOI 10.1215/00138282-8815071
© 2021 Regents of the University of Colorado

transnational channels of "disciplined mobility" as pressed
by the forces of a merciless routing.
—Jared Sexton, "People-of-Color Blindness"

Romance in Marseille is a novel whose main thematic engagements are not with liberation, freedom, and the transformative potential of desire but with the transtemporal persistence of an anti-Blackness that inflicts on the Black subject a condition of "endless kinetic movement" and rejection from sovereignty. The majority of the novel occurs during a period of interregnum while Lafala awaits the arrival of money he has been awarded as a result of his personal injury trial.[1] He lives, therefore, in a state of "credit" in the port of Marseille, which is also (for most of the novel) "debt." Consequently, the novel operates primarily within temporal conditions in relation to capital that permit only a tenuous sense of ownership, and so put pressure on Lockean, liberal categories of self-possession rooted in rights to property that have historically mobilized Euro- and African American emancipatory movements. As Gary Edward Holcomb and William J. Maxwell rightly note in their introduction to the Penguin Classic edition of the novel, this money signifies significantly in terms of African American hopes of reparation, while it also raises the problem of the means by which reparations would be administered and delivered in an anti-Black world: "Can reparations for past centuries of racial slavery and for the ongoing plunder of black working bodies somehow be earned on a case-by-case basis, and, if so, would these reparations implant incurable materialism in those granted them?"[2]

The key surprise of the book is that Lafala actually does receive the cash he is owed, suggesting that McKay's purpose is less to dwell on the hope of reparations than to wonder about the limitations placed on thriving even for those offered the means to thrive. This implies, contrary to McKay's more overtly Marxist works, that anti-Black racism operates as something more than a consequence of economic inequality. It is, instead, a structure that would perpetuate inequality even in the face of transracial economic commonality. Principally, McKay asks how reparations would operate within a global capitalist hegemony underpinned by normative whiteness. Would accepting money in response for past traumas while the world itself is still restrained by the fetters of capitalist control and global anti-Blackness be enough to remedy the effects of history? To explore how McKay reckons with this "anti-Blackness," in direct challenge to Marxist analytic traditions, it is worth turning to new work in the growing field of "Afropessimism." In particular, it is worth beginning with work that attends to the repeated rejection of people of color from a form of the promise of modernity rooted in Lockean categories of sovereignty and self-ownership, theorizing instead with the trauma of facing an ongoing, and mobile, state of exception.

In a 2010 paper titled "People-of-Color Blindness: Notes on the Afterlife of Slavery," Jared Sexton reads Giorgio Agamben's *Means without End: Notes on Politics* to consider the pressure placed on categories of personhood by the "increasing institutionalisation of the state of exception throughout the political-juridical order of modern [twentieth- and twenty-first-century] nation-states." Sexton suggests that for Agamben it is the "refugee"—particularly if contained within the biopolitical nomos of "the camp"—and not the "citizen" in the Romantic fantasy of their natal site, who is the "contemporary political subject par excellence," because the category of the refugee highlights the fictive nature of the sovereign condition on which civil rights discourse has historically relied.[3] In Agamben's formation, the "state of exception," located temporally as a twentieth-century phenomenon whose key nodes are the Holocaust, "ethnic cleansing" in the former Yugoslavia, and the George W. Bush administration's "War on Terror," "becomes the rule" such that there develops a "paradigm of governance by the administration of the absence of order."[4] This is a decentralized "field of obedience in extremis" in which it becomes impossible for the political subject to seek recourse and restitution to grievance within a civil-rights-based, sovereign, or natal model of humanness. This does well as a description of the displaced person, even better as a description of people at Guantánamo Bay or those taken by "extraordinary rendition" to Abu Ghraib. Yet Sexton reveals a certain provincialism in Agamben's foregrounding of the refugee, pointing to how he overlooks that this "state of exception," when configured as the *new normal* of later twentieth-century life, obscures the centrality of Black enslavement and its diasporic logics to the formation of the modern nation-state in the fifteenth century. Essentially, this new normal is very far from new, the state of exception to sovereign humanity and a decentralized field of obedience being a fundamental fact crucial to white modernity's *becoming* off the back of racialized slavery. In fine, the sovereign condition of Western people is reliant on the nonsovereign status of the racialized slave, so "Blackness" comes to serve as a grammar for describing a form of infinitely fungible, mobile, and unprotected labor on which that "white" sovereignty depends.[5]

Romance in Marseille is a meditation on a political ontology of Blackness in the twentieth century that plots the status of the refugee and forced migrant together within and alongside a *longue durée* and global topography of anti-Blackness incorporating the history of slavery and the transatlantic Middle Passage. Turning on the aftereffects of a traumatic transatlantic journey, the novel is McKay's most direct confrontation in fiction with the "afterlife of slavery" and the persistence of anti-Blackness within/alongside modern iterations of "freedom." The novel can be read as the culmination of McKay's meditations on the meaning of "home" as a structure of signification and political meaning in Black history, the conclusion of a "Home Trilogy" that begins with *Home to Harlem* and *Banjo*. Additionally, following the rejection of the manuscript by publishers in the late 1920s and the revisions that followed before McKay himself abandoned it in 1933, it might also be fruitful to see the novel as an expression of a distinctive, specifically pessimistic, phase of McKay's career in which "Home" is dwelled on as a philosophical impossibility; chiming transtemporally with the "Afropessimistic" critical concerns of our own contemporary era in which consideration of the persistence of anti-Blackness emerged as a response to a period occasioning the nominal "defeat" of Progressive social agendas with the rise of Trump, the new Right, and the supposed failures of the Obama era.

In thinking through the categories of home and sovereignty, the novel mobilizes an extended temporality. The port of Marseille (the site in which the African protagonist Lafala finds himself *waiting*, unable to return to Africa after his disablement and deportation from the United States) is rendered as a site of a continual process of becoming ("wandering impressionably from change to change" [4]).[6] Black subjects in Marseille such as Lafala repeatedly fail the ritual test of the bildungsroman in seemingly never being incorporated fully into a recognizable structure of citizenship. Instead, their movement is characterized by its ironic clash between joyous affect and underlying corruption, "the festering and mortification of youth and poisoned worms corroding through the firm young flesh" (*RM*, 4). This implies that the diasporic motion and labor of Lafala in McKay's novel is a condition of celebration only if what motivates it, the social sickness of anti-Blackness, is cheerfully ignored. That is to say, the novel engages with Black exclusion from the promise of a modern liberal subjectivity underpinned by the imaginary of sovereign statehood even as it acknowledges precarious Black labor and status as crucial to the creation of that modern world through a pervasive tone of irony. McKay renders this political ontology as a condition of continuous movement that is also, paradoxically, the condition of being *stuck* in the position of what McKay called, in his previous novel *Banjo*, "trying to live the precarious life of the poisonous orchids of civilization."[7] The "precarious," undomiciled, nonsovereignty of "Blackness" relative to the vaunted benefits of Enlightenment modernity is something that Monica Greco and Paul Stenner would see in antiutopian terms as a "wicked problem," referring to issues that "concern complex open systems" that "resist definitive description, are inherently reflexive, involve moral problems,"[8] and cannot be simply resolved or reformed away without affective or political remainder.

Building on "Afropessimistic" work such as Sexton's, Saidiya Hartman's (though she rejects that term), and Calvin Warren's, it is useful to bring to bear new work in anthropology concerning the phenomenon of the "liminal hotspot" as a site of "troubled becoming" or "sustained liminality,"[9] so as to meditate on the "wicked problem" of the nation-state and global capitalism's dependence on an unstable political ontology of Blackness. This is an ontology that is paradoxically also not an ontology: it is an existence that can inhabit neither ethnographic essence nor the sovereign political condition held as a privilege of "whiteness" but is instead experienced in the realm of affect as unresolved negativity or absence.

For Greco and Stenner, in their contribution to a 2017 special issue of *Theory and Psychology* on the liminal hotspot, certain modern conditions can be defined as "occasion[s] characterised by the experience of being trapped in the interstitial dimension between different forms-of-process, and in the situation of ontological indeterminacy that characterises such a dimension."[10] The liminal hotspot is a condition in which the life of the subject appears to be on a perpetual rolling boil and so has significant value for a Black literary studies seeking to explore the transtemporal effects of the unresolved and continually deferred promise of modernity maintained by the racial category of "Blackness." Seeing McKay through the lens of this ritual theory challenges the assumption that sovereignty can easily be established through performances of "grounding" or "stylizations." In McKay's novel, the vacuum that, according to liminal theorists such as Victor Turner, lies at the center of the ritual process—the moment of nonsovereignty experienced by all liminal subjects—is not overcome performatively, and so "home" is not established as a condition galvanizing the natal, sovereign rights that are associated with modern citizenship. Instead, McKay explores perpetual motion, nonsovereign subjectivity, and failure to achieve rights as a principle of Black modernity through repeated imagery of interrupted, incomplete, or suspended rituals and performances that fail to establish a stable ontological ground for the expression of selfhood.

Historically, anthropologists working in the traditions of Victor Turner and Arnold Van Gennep have rendered "liminality" (the status of being "betwixt and between" that depends on a moment of "antistructure") as a position of *positive* potentiality, and, indeed, for people occupying comparatively high-status positions in the social order, it may be so.[11] Capitalist modernity, after all, celebrates mobility, fungibility, and indeterminacy as the specific forms of Enlightenment freedom's challenge to the static positions of nationalism and feudalism. However, reading through the theory of the liminal hotspot allows us to point to the moments when the condition of mobile and transitional becoming that Gary Edward Holcomb has suggested McKay attributes positively to the Black vagabond of the Marseille docks is felt not as joyous *celebration* but as stasis, frustration, or delay.[12] Or, rather, joyous celebration and affirmation are the feelings that global capital generates to mask an ongoing process of deracination. This sense of impediment is especially significant for the diasporic subalterns of McKay's novel who are living under what Nicholas Bourriaud calls the condition of "altermodernism." For Bourriaud, altermodernism is a state parallel to, yet paradoxically central to, Western modernity, wherein traditional psychological and structural-anthropological concerns with normalized processes of transition and growth cannot hold.[13] This is because the "nation-state with its relatively fixed institutions and disciplines" is not the primary structure in an individual's life. Instead, life is based on "constant flux and interminable transition."[14] This state is partly synonymous with the postmodern condition (in McKay's case it predicts it), but with a tragic or pessimistic inflection.

For Afropessimists, critical celebrations of the subversive potential of symbolic acts that pass under the radar of a master's understanding, and so establish a comparatively stable subjectivity (such as were aimed for in creative works of the mainstream of the Harlem Renaissance), do symbolic violence to oppressed peoples, because "this celebration relies upon an erasure of the structural violence, the hardly discernible terror, of *compelled* performance [my italics]."[15] Or, to take this further, it is to miss the trauma of the sustained diasporic movement that McKay depicts in his novels. In this light, it is worth considering that *Romance in Marseille* is structured around the ironic figure of the disabled dancer (perhaps, after the "free black," the Afropessimistic subject par excellence), who operates as a signifier who is unable to gain from the game of signifying or, rather, gains individually at a material level only when he ceases to signify collectively. This is because there is no easy biopolitical natality, ontology, or root—performative or otherwise—

to which Lafala's signifying may refer back as a basis for making its claim to civil and/or human rights according to the Enlightenment logic of the sovereign subject. Lafala exists, as it were, in a floating state.

Reading in this way renders what Sexton calls out as "uncritical, and ultimately romantic, ethnographic claims . . . about the slave's capacity and capability for 'stylization' as theoretically untenable" when seen in light of the consistent, ambient reign of terror under which postemancipation Black life is lived.[16] For Afropessimists, the political ontology of Blackness does not permit the transformation of Black life into a stable ethnographic condition of subjectivity. It is defined in a white supremacist world by its interstitiality and unresolved negativity more than by its status as Being (in Heideggerian terms). Consequently, the political ontology of Blackness cannot be a basis for emancipatory stylizations and acts that rely on, establish, or refer back to a sovereignty existing outside, or prior to, supranational white hegemony.[17] As Warren expresses this, "Black being, lacking grounding in both ontology and politics/law, moves and floats throughout the world, without a proper place or any geography that could be identified as *home*."[18] Turning to theorizations of the liminal hotspot as a means to describe this condition allows us to despectacularize (perhaps even pessimize) the diaspora and McKay's 1920s to render ethically the affective condition of living "after slavery," but with pervasive, normalized anti-Blackness in a *longue durée* of global capitalism.

At the opening of the novel McKay notes how movement—sometimes joyous yet inextricable from the authoritarian power of white hegemony—is the established pattern of Lafala's youth. For ritual practices of initiation that testify to a sovereign condition that might award rights, Lafala has only the comparatively weak performances of a child's game in which "naked under the moon and stars his playmates trace . . . his image with pieces of crockery" (*RM*, 3). This might pass under the eyes of white power, which would see it only as mere play, and so serves as a ritual marker of his transition to adulthood and his place in the world. However, it is only a temporary outline (literally in chalk) and so also signifies in terms of the outlines drawn around a murder victim that evoke sovereignty's opposite: "social death."[19] By contrast, the "missionaries," whose power is seemingly absolute, impose on him a condition of perpetual motion after they bring "him from the bush to the town" (*RM*, 3) and cultivate him as a figure who can use his legs to travel the world. While this motion nominally appears to be synonymous with the ritualized and performative civilizational practices white society imposes as conditions on the achievement of Black citizenship, McKay ironically nods to their apparently endless recurrence, suggesting that ritual demands operate more cynically as a holding pattern for colonized peoples. Indeed, McKay's word selection in these early scenes is subtle. He talks of how in the "native compounds of the bush with naked black youth, he was *baptized* in a flood of emotion *retasting* the rare delight the members of his tribe felt always by the sight of fine bodies" (*RM*, 3; my italics). *Baptized* evokes a Christian missionary idiom and the forced process to which the tribal people are subject, of course. Yet *retasting* implies something more subversive: the missionaries' hijacking of precolonial cultural practices for the purposes of Christianization and colonialism. Since the "naked black youth" experience their baptism affectively as a "retasting" of the past, the ritual "return" they feel masks their actual defeat at the hands of forces of colonial, white power. Consequently, when describing the childlike game of initiation and grounding Lafala undergoes, McKay has already laid the groundwork for presuming that there is no longer an outside to colonial power and anti-Blackness on which Black subjects can draw to establish the validity of their sovereign condition. It is a groundless, and ultimately frustrated, ritual of grounding.

It is worth turning here to Greco and Stenner on the liminal hotspot's impediment to motion between "potentiality and actuality," since such a trajectory is essential to the establishment of liberal subjectivity through performance and ritual. For Greco and Stenner, within the liminal hotspot, the affectively heightened status of desire (which they call "liminal affectivity") that is felt by the liminar (the "rare delight") is ultimately frustrated and does not resolve into a new phase of being or recognizable ontological condition:[20]

> With respect to the processual dynamic between potentiality and actuality . . .
> we might say that liminal affectivity emerges when potentiality is at a
> maximum and actuality at a minimum. Liminal affectivity in this sense has
> the character of *void* which is both a vacuum (with minimal concrete actuality)
> and a plenum (with all potentialities at play . . .). In ideal-typical ritual
> situations, the liminal phase is designed to maximise the propensity for
> becoming affected, so that old identities may be relinquished and new
> ones acquired.[21]

In an "ideal-typical ritual," the person undergoing the process (the neophyte or liminar) experiences heightened affect in anticipation of transition. Yet in a liminal hotspot this heightened affect remains unresolved. It is a state of suspension loaded with overwhelming affective "charge"—a "romance"—that is also, importantly, a state of absolute vulnerability and precarity relative to power and between two established "forms-of-process." Stuck in this moment of continual unproductive motion (treading water might be an apt metaphor), liminars can neither return to their previous form-of-process (an ostensible, precolonial African "state") nor achieve the anticipated transition into the new one (a modernity coded as "white"). In McKay's novel, the Black children are on the cusp of a new being but are kept from that final status by being subjected to endless motion, implying that anti-Blackness operates within colonialism by suspending the imaginary of precolonial Black sovereignty yet not then incorporating Black being fully into the fold of modern power.

The novel's principal scene of dancing (perhaps the premier system of signification in Afro-diasporic cultures) is remarkable for how McKay renders it as an impeded, frustrated exercise that cannot be conducted freely under the powerful gaze of the white state, and suprastate, apparatus. When two women come into a bar and one says, "Play the phonograph and let's dance," McKay immediately undercuts it by noting, "The proprietor said they couldn't dance for he had no dancing license" (*RM*, 118). Later, when they can resist the music no longer, two primary characters, Big Blonde and Babel, begin "an ungainly shuffle," and Babel remarks that "the police can't interfere for this ain't no dancing. We just swaying to the music of the moon" (*RM*, 119). There is a suspended or gravitationally "weird" quality to the moon, which is associated, of course, with water and so evokes a mood centered in a tidal quality and a peculiar condition of submersion. In the context of Black history, and within a novel whose plot revolves around a damaging transition from Africa to Europe, this also resonates powerfully with the suspended state of the Middle Passage. The song that plays on the phonograph links constant motion with a sense of being infected, overawed, and captivated—speaking to a condition of Blackness as a form of restriction generated by a condition of endless movement:

> I was stricken by the moon,
> I was smitten by the moon,
> Crazy for the fairy moon.
> It lighted my heart and it caused me to roam
> Far away from my loving wife waiting at home. (*RM*, 119)

The "music of the moon" refers to Lafala's childhood "initiation" game, which is played as the children of his village sing "The Moonshine Kid," associating Lafala with a floating, nonsovereign affectivity. Yet, even as Babel's dance might pass the censure of the official channels of state power, other forms of bigotry and anti-Blackness undermine dancing's subversive potential. This half dance is followed by an explosion of violence when an "old woman" peddling a "basket of baubles and dolls" homophobically attacks Petit Frère—a male sex worker—by throwing feces at him. What triggers the homophobic assault is the old woman's disgust at Petit Frère's interracial sex work: "Babel roughly told her that they didn't want anything, she was in the wrong place. . . . 'Indeed I am, there's no doubt I am when you have that thing there between you,' she said, fixing Petit Frère with a malevolent finger" (*RM*, 120). In response, McKay states, "Big Blonde jumped up and knocked her sprawling to the floor"—matching violence with violence.

The woman's use of *thing* and *between* is loaded. Petit Frère's sex work positions him as a figure of transition between distinctly racially demarcated figures, the Black African Babel (whose very name suggests a nonsovereign linguistic subject) and the "Nordic" Big Blonde, making the old woman's violence a simultaneously racist and homophobic assault that points to the ambient terror of Marseille life. Yet *thing* also points to the status of the object or tool that is kept isolated from the ontological condition of the human and so exposes how within the text sovereignty itself is a fiction that can be removed through various acts of bigotry. It is significant that the chapter ends with the Black characters leaving the bar and not the white people with whom they are drinking, including Petit Frère—the erstwhile subject of the attack. The once racially mixed site becomes racially homogeneous through the effects of the old woman's violence. I see this as McKay's recognition of homophobia as commonly bound up in an attempt to police lines of color obliquely by rendering queer sites of interracial mixing unsafe. Nonetheless, it is the Black characters who are deprived of their temporary home by the assault, since they have no recourse to rights either in contacting the police or, as Big Blonde does, in what Richard Slotkin would see as the principal settler-colonial logic of "regeneration through violence," lacking as they do his position of white racial privilege.[22]

Neither the state nor traditions of individual rights stand on their side. The only option available to Lafala, Babel, and St. Dominique is to leave. The "administration of the absence of order" or "state of exception," as Agamben would see it, leads here not to *containment* in the "camp" (a fixed, identifiable site of suspended rights) but to a situation of mobility and indeterminacy. For McKay, Marseille serves as a microcosm of a global system of forced motion that consistently returns the Black characters to a political ontology of nonsovereignty within a regime of global anti-Blackness. Indeed, the novel unfolds through a repeating pattern whereby practically every chapter concludes through some abridgment of full experience. We see this most directly in the final line, when the pimp Titin shoots Aslima while "cursing and calling upon hell to swallow her soul" (*RM*, 130). This is an end that suggests Titin's wish for Aslima to undergo a complete extraction and to be expunged from the world, a hellish reversal of bodily Assumption that would make her ritually unmournable, because invisible, or lost.

I term this pattern McKay's *aesthetic of sovereign rejection*: either an act of violence or a rapid exit (sometimes both). There is a sketchlike quality to the novel that is also repetitious, offering the reader the impression of life being precarious, open, and yet, oddly, predictable. The "openness" of the world is not experienced in the novel as positive potentiality but invites, instead, frustration, violence, even boredom. The aesthetic communicates by evoking a state of heightened affect that lacks futurity: "potentiality" without "actuality." Through this pattern McKay renders the lives of the Black characters as interstitial—marked by a sustained liminality of constant motion that paradoxically *feels*, across time, like political stasis, because it denies access to the completed rituals or stylizations that project into a future of rights-bearing sovereignty.[23]

The opening of the novel describes an adult Lafala, who "as a boy was proud of his legs . . . [and] participat[ed] in all [of] childhood's leg play, running and climbing and jumping, and dancing in the moonlight," who lies now bedridden "in the ward of the great hospital . . . like a sawed-off stump and ponder[ing] the loss of his legs" (*RM*, 3). In rendering Lafala's melancholia temporally in this way (blithe childhood characterized as a joyful use of the legs; adulthood as an incapacitation), McKay calls out *celebration* as insufficiently pessimistic, a sign of incomplete *Bildung* that omits the "hardly-discernible terror" of the real, ongoing, structural violence done to Black bodies in the Atlantic world. McKay's cheerful tone is in clear and ironic contrast to the story of a boy stolen from his home. Consequently, the opening highlights two dominant themes of the novel as a whole—the impossible utopianism of boyish romance (including its ethnographic fantasies of essence) and the condition of endless Black movement that is a paradoxical index of political-ontological stasis: "Legs of ebony, legs of copper, legs of ivory moving pell-mell in columns against his imagination. . . . Dancing on the toes, dancing on the heels, dancing flat-footed. Lafala's dancing legs had carried him from Africa to Europe, from Europe to Africa" (*RM*, 4). What might appear as a condition of comparative freedom of movement built on the basis of Black creativity can equally be read as a sign of that motion's proximity both to the status of the commodity and to that of the refugee—especially in light of the historical centrality of Black performance to the mechanisms of the global culture industry and, consequently, the dominance of a global capitalism rooted in a primal scene of sovereign rejection and the forced movement of racialized peoples. "Legs of ebony, legs of copper, legs of ivory" calls attention to the diverse racializations of the Atlantic world system—there is a clear plurality of oppressed peoples by color here—yet it also renders that racialization synonymous with African resources extracted in free-market circulation: ebony, copper, ivory.

For Holcomb, "Lafala's capacity for movement makes him a kind of . . . desiring machine, to use Deleuze and Guattari, operating between and among. . . . Through his legs Lafala is, or was, able to make such a move both materially and figuratively. . . . Without his legs, he is culturally paralyzed."[24] The "desiring machine" of Deleuze and Guattari's deterritorialized metaphysics describes a status uncoupled from official structures of power, or *nomoi*. Yet a desiring machine can be a dynamo in perpetual motion when it drives nothing forward, and this can lead to despair and exhaustion. Like Turner and Van Gennep's liminal state, Deleuze and Guattari's desiring machine is in a state of distinctly *positive* potentiality: a "void" state that is a "plenum" and blind to dialectical countercharge of the "vacuum." McKay's novel is notable for the bipolar quality of its affective excess. At times the novel is melodramatic and overwrought (including a stagy plotting in the latter sections) and at others cheerfully ironic (as in the opening). This excess dramatizes the affective conditions experienced by the Black liminar trapped in a sustained liminality without futurity.

Sara Ahmed thinks through the affect associated with facing a resisting world as the interruption of what Mihaly Csikszentmihalyi has described as the psychological condition of "flow": a state of transition between "forms-of-process" in which trial and effort are felt as pleasure.[25] For Csikszentmihalyi, "flow" occurs when subjects are sufficiently psychologically adjusted to the demands of the world that even if their labor in it is hard (perhaps even especially), or the world feels like a trial, they feel positive feelings of participation and progress. There is significant benefit for the status quo in keeping individuals committed to the effort of making a life, because under normal conditions "in the long run optimal experiences add up to a sense of mastery—or perhaps better, a sense of *participation* in determining the content of life," such that people become "happy" and unwilling to rebel.[26] However, as Ahmed notes,

> when subjects are not "in flow" they encounter the world as resistant, as
> blocking rather than enabling an action . . . [and so] feel alienated from the
> world as they experience the world as alien. What if to flow into the world is not
> simply understood as a psychological attribute? What if the world "houses"
> some bodies more than others, such that some bodies do not experience that
> world as resistant?[27]

Put another way, the social and political condition of liminality sustained by anti-Blackness can be experienced affectively as an existence lived within the weird gravitational push and pull of an alien world; a site in which one cannot propel oneself forward and where sovereign status cannot hold. Even in moments when individuals may feel progress and "flow," they are in fact blocked, and this is not paradox but an encounter with the sovereign rejection on which "white" modernity depends. Devoid of all recourse to grounded sovereignty and rights, the desiring machine that Deleuze and Guattari celebrate cannot function as it should. Instead, the subject, as Greco and Stenner would express it, experiences a heightened "liminal affectivity" that oscillates almost unbearably between poles of joy and despair but without access to the official forms of process that award rights or protect the individual from state-sanctioned violence.

McKay, I would argue, indicates that Lafala's disablement is to be read not as a process that *interrupts* the subversive power of an individual becoming and unfolding out into the world but as a sign that *interrupted becoming* is the condition of people of color within an Atlantic regime governed by anti-Blackness. Lafala may be "culturally paralyzed" in the sense of the interruption of his own, individual, potentially subversive, bodily gestures of signification, but this is seen by McKay as the central political condition of Blackness in a globalized market. For McKay, dance *is* stasis. It is a floating waltz or, as Babel states, a dancing that "ain't no dancing," just a "swaying to the music of the moon" or, as the narrator shows at the opening of the novel, a pilgrimage-like dance of death: an oftentimes joyous physical movement that nonetheless does not move the subject forward temporally into the recognized condition of full humanity as would "stylization" or a completed ritual process. Moving, desiring, and becoming are, as Hartman notes of the slave's signifying, not resistive power if the desire they dramatize is a means without end. This sustained liminality is of practical use to the status quo because it gives the subject an impression of participation that reduces the threat of rebellion even as it frames that participation in an outer space of effective exclusion. Lafala does not just possess stumps following his amputations; as McKay states emphatically, he *is* a "stump." According to Warren, "Degradation and unfreedom are the manifestations of this nothing [the void that is Blackness], a status within law and politics that is empty—void of the substance of the flesh and any substance of biofuturity."[28] As a "stump," Lafala is such an object without a projective biofuturity.

The liminal hotspot I have described above serves as a direct and unequivocal challenge to the states of joyous play that Deleuze and Guattari attach to the desiring machine uncoupled from the Oedipal structures of capitalist citizenship. Indeed, it highlights the uses that anti-Oedipal desire and free play can be put to by advanced global capital in keeping diasporic Black life in a confused state of utility and action without sovereignty.[29] Considered in view of the theory of the liminal hotspot, in which play ceases its function as a vector within a ritual process or as a system for becoming and is instead an experience that holds progress in suspense and reinforces the status quo, desire and stylization cannot be subversive. Or rather, they are impeded by the dominance of capital from being so. In characterizing Black "play" in the French docklands in these terms in *Romance in Marseille*, McKay performs a critique of the ideology of Harlem "Jazz Age" optimism. Indeed, he points to the speed at which its positive affectivity can curdle into vectors of conservative violence when faced with resistance from the white world. McKay shows how in this state of suspension and heightened desire the liminar can become a harbinger of fascistic fantasies of "return" and/or racial essentialism.

In McKay's novel this lack of futurity forces Lafala into a romantic idealization of the essences of an imagined past, and this, perhaps even more than Lafala's courtship of Aslima, accounts for the novel's title, *Romance in Marseille*. McKay notes that, following Lafala's recognition of his status as a "stump," "more vividly than ever in his life he visualised the glory and joy of having a handsome pair of legs" (*RM*, 3). His mind returns him to Africa and a condition of "handsome" embodiment, placing him in the frame with what the narrator calls "a time of universal excitement after the war . . . [when] among Negroes there were signs of a stirring and from the New World a dark cry of Back to Africa came over the air" (*RM*, 5). This nostalgic "black fascist" fantasy of return (Paul Gilroy) must be read in the context of McKay's own abiding loathing for Garveyism and its regressive mantras, as well as the novel's implication at the outset that "baptism" is felt as a "retasting" of the joy felt at the sight of "fine bodies supported by strong gleaming legs."[30] This fantasy of return "tastes" the same as the primal scene of colonial exploitation because it dramatizes and confirms the establishment of a racial ontology and system of division. For McKay, Lafala's deracination and "endless kinetic movement"[31] are discernible in the pull "Back to Africa" as much as to the New World or France, because following white colonialism's remaking of the world, there is no simple or unadulterated "outside" to white power, even in its evolved form as global capitalism.

Aslima becomes the subject of a similarly alluring but ultimately dangerous fascination with a narrative of racial return. Beginning in chapter 9, a subplot concerning the threat posed to Aslima's body by her pimp, Titin, is shown by McKay to be connected to her attempts to reconnect through Lafala with her nominal "homeland" in Arab North Africa. "Half-jokingly, half-seriously, Lafala had proposed to Aslima that she should return to his tribal Africa with him," only to then take her "to a cinema up in the respectable part of town. It was a romantic sheik picture" (*RM*, 46).[32] McKay implies that their romance depends on Aslima's fascination with the Arab world she left as a child and with Lafala's Africanness. Enraptured in this way, Aslima asks for no money from Lafala for her time and therefore becomes increasingly subject to Titin's aggressions. Immediately following their date, McKay notes, "Titin was waiting for Aslima when she returned to her lair . . . the next morning" (*RM*, 47), after which he becomes an ever-escalating threat and kills her in the novel's final scenes. Just as Lafala's romantic fantasies of return ultimately reconstitute the strong racial ontology on which colonial exploitation depends, Aslima's "romances" erode her independence and power, returning her to a natal state that McKay specifically highlights was one of bondage—a nonsovereign condition: "Aslima was a child of North Africa out of Marrakesh . . . born a slave" (*RM*, 44). She is effectively rejected from her own utopia. Viewed "Afropessimistically," Aslima's racial return or embrace of "Blackness" occasions an inescapable return to slavery—or an acknowledgment that it has never been transcended—and sets her on a path to "social death."[33]

Indeed, Aslima's increasing attraction to the allure of an ontological Blackness that is always already a sovereign rejection is tangled up in complex ways with her tragic demise. McKay notes that her "dominion had been long undisputed until the appearance of La Fleur [Noire]" (*RM*, 29), a competing prostitute described in stereotyped terms as a "brown orchid" (*RM*, 30). La Fleur (whose name resonates significantly with "Lafala") is a hypertrophic embodiment of Black fantasy. Prior to her encounter with Lafala and La Fleur, Aslima is described as "full of an abundance of earthly sap and compact of inexhaustible energy" (*RM*, 29), while at the end of the novel she has become listless and, arguably, suicidally self-destructive. What bridges this character development is an Orientalist dream Aslima has of an African tribal and/or Arabic gathering that turns violent, pointing to a dialectical engagement with the desire and threat that a certain model of "Africanness" poses for her. In the dream a "loving feast" goes sour because "among the multitude . . . one group apart . . . was offering up body and soul as a sacrifice. And in the midst of the group was Aslima divided and struggling against herself" (*RM*, 61, 62). In McKay's "Afropessimistic" vision, this self-divided nature is one in which an ontology of "Africanness" or "Blackness" does not circumvent the effects of slavery and brutality so much as force the individual to confront the dependence of that racial ontology on a history of exploitation and violence. Aslima's vision partakes of the Hollywood fantasies of *The Sheik*, which she saw earlier with Lafala, yet that fantasy does not liberate but ultimately endangers her. The "positive" affectivity she feels when exposed to images of African and Arabian "Blackness" forces her into a liminal hotspot and traps her into treading water, experiencing the outward symbols of modernity but unable to possess them.

This lends potency to McKay's earlier suggestion that Lafala's legs were the vehicles of his motion "from Africa to Europe" *and* "from Europe to Africa": a pattern that occurs within global capitalism and incorporates a history of both Europhile "racial uplift" movements and Black nationalism. Prefiguring this movement is an internalization of Lafala's racial "Blackness" as a condition of inferiority or absence, implied by his reverie of return to precolonial African "handsomeness" and by the imaginary of Harlem as the terminus of a process of transition and uplift. Predating Frantz Fanon's insights into the psychology of the colonial subject by nearly twenty years, McKay's novel focuses on the self-loathing and melancholia inculcated by white colonialism that are the engines of Black deracination *and* romantic fantasies of restorative racial utopia. The rupture of colonial sovereign rejection remains unrepaired by the romance of Black nationalism. For McKay, these "romances" lead to a state of churning desire and despair that often explode into violence. Accounting for the reasons for Lafala's initial attempt to leave Marseille for the United States, McKay writes early on that "on an impulse of *self-disgust* Lafala had stowed away . . . leaving at Quayside pals and wenches, frustrated feelings and dark desire. For there he had met the Negroid wench Aslima, a burning brown mixture of Arab and Negro and other wanton bloods perhaps that had created her a barbaric creature" (*RM*, 5; my italics). Lafala's "self-disgust," as much as the disciplined mobility demanded by nation-states and their biopolitical *nomoi* of control, spurs his attempt to migrate ("An object of ridicule and an object of pity at Quayside, Lafala had no desire to remain there and join the gang of dark drifters until his only suit was worn to rags" [*RM*, 5]). Yet this migration also confirms his "disablement" relative to white power—literally (he loses his legs) and symbolically (in terms of "disenfranchisement")—when he undergoes forced amputation after confinement aboard ship. For Lafala, "Blackness" is felt as falling short of the shore of the sovereign condition and inviolate selfhood. He feels "self-disgust" at his unmixed African "Blackness" and also considers Aslima's "wanton bloods" "barbaric." Consequently, Lafala experiences his color in a white supremacist world as a lack, a void, and an insufficiency. This renders him, as McKay suggests, a "stump." Moreover, because Aslima is described in such overtly bigoted and sexist terms— "barbaric," "wanton bloods," "Negroid wench"—we are privy through McKay's free indirect discourse to Lafala's own internalized racism and expressions of *misogynoir*.[34] Having first described his "self-disgust," McKay indicates that this hostility to Black women expresses the traumatic double consciousness under which he lives his emotional life, wherein Black natality, in the symbolic form of Black womanhood, is a site of desire but also of rejection and despair.

When considered through the theory of the liminal hotspot, McKay's novel implies that to dwell in hope would be to persist interminably in a heightened state of potentiality and liminal affectivity. He intimates that this is a form of "cruel optimism" doing psychological damage to subjects that also threatens to pull them toward fascistic fantasies of essentialism and misogynist cruelty.[35] Since global capitalism depends on an unstable ontology of Blackness and the ongoing process of sovereign rejection to make its world, in *Romance in Marseille* McKay advances a far more radical thesis than hope: a radical condition can emerge only when one dwells in a state of negative dialectical intensity, awakened to the fact that images of positive potentiality can be mobilized by global capital to sustain Black subjects in a suspended rightless state. More so than his other novels, *Romance in Marseille* is oppositional in thesis and tone. It predicts a world, yet to be seen in 1933, when global capital is predominant and immanent in all forms of social interaction. In this way it speaks to the neoliberal moment we now face, in which migrancy, statelessness, and intensifying anti-Black racism globally are calling for a new politics through which to imagine a new world. This is a vision of the political that reaches beyond the vectors of traditional Marxian critique into an engagement with the transtemporalities of ontology and affect. *Romance in Marseille* sees McKay in his most anarchistic mood of theorizing, attempting to cultivate nothing less than a discontent with this world as it stands so as to revivify political leftism. Additionally, in its lament for the absence of ritual practices and forms of performance that can permit a Black subject to experience full participation in modernity, we can see signs of a McKay who is moving intellectually toward the religious visions of the political that characterized his final years of activism following his 1944 conversion to Catholicism.

MICHAEL J. COLLINS is senior lecturer in twentieth-century American literature and culture at King's College, London, specializing in US modernism and the history of anthropology. He is author of *The Drama of the American Short Story* (2016) and *Exoteric Modernisms: Progressive Era Literature and the Aesthetic of Everyday Life* (forthcoming). He is also chair of publications for the British Association for American Studies.

Acknowledgments

A version of this article was presented at MLA 2020 in Seattle on the panel "African American Transnationalism," organized by Laila Amine. I am very grateful to have been asked to participate and for all the comments received.

Notes

1   It is worth thinking through this plot as inspired biographically by Nancy Cunard (the heir to a shipping fortune) refusing to pay McKay for work he had done for her *Negro Anthology* in the late 1920s, as recounted in chapter 29 of his autobiography *A Long Way from Home* (1937). McKay writes: "Meanwhile I had come to the point of breaking down while working on my novel in Morocco; and besides I was in pecuniary difficulties. Nevertheless, I wrote an article for Miss Cunard's anthology and forwarded it to her on her return to France. Miss Cunard extravagantly praised the article and said it was one of the best and also that I was one of the best, whatever that 'best' meant. She said she would use it with a full-page photograph of myself which was done by a friend of ours, the photographer, Berenice Abbot. However, she did not accompany her praise by a check, and I requested payment. I was in need of money" (*A Long Way from Home*, 262).

2   Holcomb and Maxwell, introduction, xiii.

3   Sexton, "People-of-Color Blindness," 31.

4   Sexton, "People-of-Color Blindness," 32.

5   Warren suggests in *Ontological Terror* that "black being" (to use a Heideggerian vocabulary) or "becoming" (to use a Deleuzian formulation) is a philosophical impossibility, because "to *be*, according to Heidegger, is to *become*, to emerge, and to move within Being-as-event. But what happens when such becoming does not occur? When the event of Being does not stimulate a productive anxiety of actualization but gets caught in a repetition of eventless demise and nothingness? To inhabit such a condition is to exist as perpetual falling, without standing-forth, without Being" (13; my italics).

6   McKay, *Romance in Marseille*, 4 (hereafter cited as *RM*).

7   McKay, *Banjo*, 49.

8   Rittell and Webber, quoted in Greco and Stenner, "From Paradox to Pattern Shift," 148.

9   Stenner, "Reflections on the So-Called 'Affective Turn'"; Greco and Stenner, "From Paradox to Pattern Shift," 147; Little et al., "Liminality."

10   Greco and Stenner, "From Paradox to Pattern Shift," 152. *Forms-of-process* is now accepted anthropological language to refer to the condition that was historically called structure. Recognizing that no "structure" is final, *forms-of-process* denotes the "forms" that appear in a life with sufficient stability to be usable by the individual or group. Essentially, they have settled enough to be recognizable as a reproducible form but have not completely ossified into structure.

11   Turner, *Ritual Process*; Van Gennep, *Rites of Passage*.

12   I am here also implicitly drawing on Andrew Culp's recent rewriting of Gilles Deleuze for a radicalized left pessimism. In a world where modern, technological, global capitalism has colonialized the language of playful becoming, and where "escapism has become the great betrayer of escape" (*Dark Deleuze*, 47), Culp proposes a refocused Deleuze that meditates on the world-destroying negativity of "unbecoming" as opposed to a positive vision of eternal play, revision, and refashioning that cannot so easily be co-opted for the project of a static, futureless neoliberalism.

13   Bourriaud, *Altermodernism*.

14   Greco and Stenner, "From Paradox to Pattern Shift," 148.

15   Sexton, "People-of-Color Blindness," 34.

16   Sexton, "People-of-Color Blindness," 35.

17   Thought of in Arendt's terms from *On Revolution* (1963), the political ontology of Blackness exists in the state of "void" precipitated by the revolutionary rupture that birthed capitalist modernity. Arendt notes—contra Marx—that revolution threatens to create conditions in which sufficiently "active" forms

of public that would sustain rights over a long temporal frame cannot thrive. In this sense "anti-Blackness" would be a system of violence that sustains an uncoalesced suspension of the "active" publics that could build new worlds. It is the Enlightenment ever returning to the racialized rupture of slavery that is its origin point and not seeking to establish the futurity of its own promise of universal rights.

18   Warren, *Ontological Terror*, 56.

19   Patterson, *Slavery and Social Death*.

20   Significantly, the case study they use here is the individual suffering with a chronic illness or disability whose effects are unstable and unpredictable.

21   Greco and Stenner, "From Paradox to Pattern Shift," 160.

22   Slotkin, *Regeneration through Violence*.

23   *Sustained* is used here over *perpetual* or *permanent* in reference to liminality to indicate that this effect does not occur without the influence of hegemonic power. It is "sustained" because it is actively willed by white supremacy and global capital. It is not an "ontological" condition in the sense of being in any way "natural" or "biological." This is partly why it is important to highlight that "Blackness" is a status condition not wholly synonymous with phenotype and is also not an "ontology" in the sense of fixity. It is a "political ontology" or a nonontological ontology.

24   Holcomb, *Claude McKay, Code Name Sasha*, 179. See also Deleuze and Guattari, *Anti-Oedipus*; and Deleuze and Guattari, *A Thousand Plateaus*.

25   Ahmed, *Promise of Happiness*. "Flow," of course, also has a distinctly Deleuzian ring to it. In *Anti-Oedipus* Deleuze and Guattari consider the theory of society in terms of the theory of "flows" of desire.

26   Csikszentmihalyi quoted in Ahmed, *Promise of Happiness*, 11.

27   Ahmed, *Promise of Happiness*, 11.

28   Warren, *Ontological Terror*, 59.

29   The right to "play" against a backdrop of a widespread erosion of human rights is a fair description of the form of subjectivity that in the postwar era we have come to define as "neoliberal."

30   See Gilroy, "Black Fascism."

31   Sexton, "People-of-Color Blindness," 44.

32   As Holcomb and Maxwell mention (in *RM*, 152n11), this is most likely the blockbuster romance *The Sheik*, starring Rudolph Valentino, which opened in 1921, or one of the two sequels released later in the 1920s.

33   Patterson, *Slavery and Social Death*.

34   Bailey, "New Terms of Resistance."

35   Berlant, *Cruel Optimism*.

Works Cited

Ahmed, Sara. *The Promise of Happiness*. Durham, NC: Duke University Press, 2006.

Arendt, Hannah. *On Revolution*. London: Penguin, 1990.

Bailey, Moya. "New Terms of Resistance: A Response to Zenzele Isoke." *Souls: A Critical Journal of Black Politics, Culture, and Society* 15, no. 14 (2013): 341–43.

Berlant, Lauren. *Cruel Optimism*. Durham, NC: Duke University Press, 2011.

Bourriaud, Nicholas. *Altermodernism*. London: Tate, 2009.

Culp, Andrew. *Dark Deleuze*. Minneapolis: University of Minnesota Press, 2016.

Deleuze, Gilles, and Félix Guattari. *Anti-Oedipus*, translated by Robert Hurley, Mark Seem, and Helen R. Lane. London: Continuum, 2004.

Deleuze, Gilles, and Félix Guattari. *A Thousand Plateaus*, translated by Brian Massumi. London: Continuum, 2004.

Fanon, Frantz. *Black Skins, White Masks*, translated by Charles Lam Markman. London: Pluto, 1986.

Gilroy, Paul. "Black Fascism." *Transitions*, nos. 81–82 (2000): 70–91.

Greco, Monica, and Paul Stenner. "From Paradox to Pattern Shift: Conceptualising Liminal Hotspots and Their Affective Dynamics." *Theory and Psychology* 27, no. 2 (2017): 147–66.

Hartman, Saidiya. *Scenes of Subjection: Terror, Slavery, and Self-Making in Nineteenth-Century America*. Oxford: Oxford University Press, 1997.

Holcomb, Gary Edward. *Claude McKay, Code Name Sasha: Queer Black Marxism and the Harlem Renaissance*. Gainesville: University Press of Florida, 2007.

Holcomb, Gary Edward, and William J. Maxwell. Introduction to McKay, *Romance in Marseille*, vii–liii.

Little, M., C. F. Jordens, K. Paul, K. Montgomery, and B. Phillipson. "Liminality: A Major Category of the Experience of Cancer Illness." *Social Science and Medicine* 47, no. 10 (1998): 1485–94.

McKay, Claude. *Banjo: A Story without a Plot*. New York: Harcourt Brace, 1957.

McKay, Claude. *A Long Way from Home*, edited by Gene Andrew Jarrett. New Brunswick, NJ: Rutgers University Press, 2007.

McKay, Claude. *Romance in Marseille*, edited by Gary Edward Holcomb and William J. Maxwell. New York: Penguin Classics, 2020.

Patterson, Orlando. *Slavery and Social Death: A Comparative Study, with a New Preface*. Cambridge, MA: Harvard University Press, 2018.

Sexton, Jared. "People-of-Color Blindness: Notes on the Afterlife of Slavery." *Social Text*, no. 103 (2010): 31–56.

Slotkin, Richard. *Regeneration through Violence: The Mythology of the American Frontier, 1600–1860.* Norman: University of Oklahoma Press, 1973.

Stenner, Paul. "Reflections on the So-Called 'Affective Turn.'" Keynote address, V Congreso Internacional de Psicologia Social, Benemérita Universidad Autónoma de Puebla, Puebla, Mexico, 2011.

Turner, Victor. *The Ritual Process.* London: Routledge, 2017.

Van Gennep, Arnold. *The Rites of Passage*, translated by Monika B. Vizedom and Gabrielle L. Caffee. London: Routledge and Kegan Paul, 1960.

Warren, Calvin L. *Ontological Terror: Blackness, Nihilism, and Emancipation.* Durham, NC: Duke University Press, 2018.

Introduction

NAN GOODMAN

"Of Note" continues with four reflections on recent scholarship about slavery and the archive. While the "Of Note" section doesn't always coincide with or complement the special issue topic, this iteration reinforces and enhances the issue's focus on the 2020 posthumous publication of Claude McKay's *Romance in Marseille*, a novel too long missing from the American print archive.

All four contributors, Ariela J. Gross, Stefanie Hunt-Kennedy, Cherene Sherrard-Johnson, and Marisa Fuentes, have written about slavery and the archive and offer invaluable insights into the three articles under examination here. These articles include Saidiya Hartman's "The Dead Book Revisited" (*History of the Present*, Fall 2016), Simon P. Newman's "Freedom-Seeking Slaves in England and Scotland, 1700–1780," *English Historical Review*, Fall 2019), and Stephanie E. Smallwood's "The Politics of the Archive and History's Accountability to the Enslaved" (*History of the Present*, Fall 2016). In different ways, these articles and the "Of Note" pieces they provoked confront the failure of the archive to shed light on the actual lives of the enslaved—their feelings, thoughts, aspirations, and achievements. For these contributors, the archive is "meager," "ghostly," and full of "erasures" and "silences." But the "Of Note" authors also find in the articles the beginnings of alternative approaches to this nonarchival archive. If we listen more carefully and differently, if we treat historical texts as literary opportunities, and if we pay attention to the ways in which we craft an archive about the archive, as these reflections suggest, we may find our way toward a counterhistory that does not place the enslaved, among other voiceless and nonarchived subjects, in a fixed, subaltern position. We hope you find in this "Of Note" section something of a theoretical and practical guide for approaching the archive of slavery in ways that tell us more about the lives of the enslaved than we have heard before.

ENGLISH LANGUAGE NOTES
59:1, April 2021 DOI 10.1215/00138282-8815082
© 2021 Regents of the University of Colorado

Archives of the Dispossessed

Mourning, Memory, and Metahistory

....

ARIELA J. GROSS

Almost two decades ago Saidiya Hartman asked how we can mourn an event that has not yet come to an end.[1] That question, of how to approach the horror of enslavement through a present in which the past lives on, echoes in Stephanie E. Smallwood's meditation, "The Politics of the Archive and History's Accountability to the Enslaved." Smallwood reflects on her own journey in writing *Saltwater Slavery: A Middle Passage from Africa to American Diaspora*: from frustration at the silences of the archive of slavery—the unknowability of the internal experience of enslavement—to a recognition that in fact historical research and writing produce the archive. In approaching the production of archives in a new way, Smallwood explores the possibility of "counterhistories" that could be accountable to the enslaved, doing the work in the present of remembering the past. She questions what it means to read the archive "against the grain," forswearing the metanarrative of a historical search for truth.[2] She gives the example of her own work in *Saltwater Slavery*, reading the marginalia in the numerical ledgers of the slave trade as literary text, to give "interpretive weight to the captives' experience of 'a journey in which some-*one* died fifty-one times.'"[3]

Hartman, in response, extends her own reflection on how to reckon with Black death and the relationship between the then and the now of Black death. However, she continues to express frustration with "slavery's archive, which provides such a meager picture of the life and thought of the enslaved." For Hartman, it appears that literary approaches will always be needed for us to imagine the experience and "apprehend the philosophy" of those who were ensnared in bondage.[4]

How can we read the archives of slavery? As Smallwood shows, an earlier generation answered this question with skepticism and even contempt. Fugitive slave narratives and autobiographies could not be trusted; Works Progress Administration interviews with former slaves were unreliable. When historians and literary scholars began to read these sources carefully in the 1970s, they discovered a treasure trove of personal accounts of the experience of enslavement, at least in the antebellum United States. Yet the archives of the slave trade and the Middle Passage, as Smallwood recounts, remained impervious to efforts to listen for subaltern voices. The ledgers of numbers, the ship manifests, even bills of sale lent them-

ENGLISH LANGUAGE NOTES

59:1, April 2021 DOI 10.1215/00138282-8815093
© 2021 Regents of the University of Colorado

selves to databases, to quantitative approaches to history. The words were the words of the merchants and enslavers, not the enslaved. How to write a history accountable to the enslaved?

More recently, historians have plumbed new archives, especially those of legal records, inspired by the romantic aspiration to hear the voices of those silenced by traditional archives. In legal records, especially suits for freedom, we find fragments of enslaved people's self-presentation. Historians, like Smallwood, have also grown more self-conscious about reading "against the grain" and treating the archive as a self-conscious production, as, for example, Marisa Fuentes's recent *Dispossessed Lives: Enslaved Women, Violence, and the Archive.*

Simon P. Newman's article "Freedom-Seeking Slaves in England and Scotland, 1700–1780" presents one example of self-consciously reading the archive against the grain. He reads advertisements for fugitives from bondage as well as advertisements for "Negro" women, boys, girls or "Servants" for sale, documents written by slave owners, for the mundane and cruel purpose of recapturing freedom-seekers to enslavement or selling them in the marketplace. While these advertisements are among the more traditional white-authored texts in the slavery archive, Newman examines them with an eye toward their eventual disappearance, asking implicitly what their presence for a time in a changing archive might suggest. Newman uses these ephemera to illuminate racial slavery in Britain, an institution about which most Britons have almost total amnesia, showing that "many enslaved Africans and their descendants who were brought to Britain as domestic servants, craftsmen and sailors remained bound by and vulnerable to the conditions of New World slavery."[5] Despite legal precedents regarding the "free soil" of Britain,[6] it would be more accurate to consider Britain, to invert the Rupert Brooks poem, as a corner of a foreign field forever America.

Mindful of the meagerness of these ads, Newman applies quantitative techniques to them, not only reading the descriptions but counting the racial descriptors, skills, languages, and other attributes by which enslaved people were identified and also counting the number of advertisements over time. He parses the legal status of individuals named as both "slaves" and "servants" for a period of years. Finally, he speculates on the motivations of those who ran away, based on their choices, and on the few accounts we have from fugitives themselves. In this, however, he seems not to seek the "truth" of the subjective experiences of the enslaved but to repopulate the landscape that was eighteenth-century Britain with the fact of the many enslaved individuals who are so often absent from the literary and visual representations of that time. Thus, like Smallwood and Hartman, Newman helps us construct new archives and imagine new counterhistories.

ARIELA J. GROSS is John B. and Alice R. Sharp Professor of Law and History at the University of Southern California; codirector of the USC Center for Law, History, and Culture; and author of *Becoming Free, Becoming Black: Race, Freedom, and Law in Cuba, Virginia, and Louisiana,* with Alejandro de la Fuente (2020). Her book *What Blood Won't Tell: A History of Race on Trial in America* (2008) was cowinner of the James Willard Hurst

Prize from the Law and Society Association; winner of the Lillian Smith Award for the best book on the US South and the struggle for racial justice; the American Political Science Association's Best Book on Race, Ethnicity, and Politics; and a Choice Outstanding Academic Title. She is also author of *Double Character: Slavery and Mastery in the Antebellum Southern Courtroom* (2000).

Notes

1 Hartman, "The Time of Slavery."
2 Smallwood, "Politics of the Archive," 128.
3 Smallwood, "Politics of the Archive," 126.
4 Hartman, "The Dead Book Revisited," 213.
5 Newman, "Freedom-Seeking Slaves," 1139.
6 Newman, "Freedom-Seeking Slaves," 1146.

Works Cited

Hartman, Saidiya. "The Dead Book Revisited." *History of the Present* 6, no. 2 (2016): 208–15.

Hartman, Saidiya. "The Time of Slavery." *South Atlantic Quarterly* 101, no. 4 (2002): 757–77.

Newman, Simon P. "Freedom-Seeking Slaves in England and Scotland, 1700–1780." *English Historical Review*, no. 570 (2019): 1136–68.

Smallwood, Stephanie E. "The Politics of the Archive and History's Accountability to the Enslaved." *History of the Present* 6, no. 2 (2016): 117–32.

Silence and Violence in the Archive of Slavery

STEFANIE HUNT-KENNEDY

I n his classic text, *Silencing the Past: Power and the Production of History*, Michel-Rolph Trouillot asked of the Haitian Revolution: "How does one write a history of the impossible?"[1] Planters and colonial powers represented the thirteen-year event that resulted in the enslaved overthrow of colonial power and the independent state of Haiti (the first black republic of the Atlantic World) as an "unthinkable history," "a non-event," even as it was happening. Although Trouillot wrote specifically of Haiti, his work on how social and political inequalities of the past shape the ways historical events are recorded in their moment and then archived, retrieved, and written about in the present is widely applicable to historians of slavery.

The archive of slavery is steeped in silences. This is true especially for the colonial Caribbean, where enslaved individuals left few if any sources of their own and often appear in the archives as voiceless and fleeting figures. In this way, to write a history that recognizes the complex personhood of the enslaved, while adhering to traditional disciplinary methodologies, appears to be nearly impossible. How do historians of slavery, faced with a disruptive, fragmented, and contested archive, re-create the lifeworlds of enslaved individuals who appear as fleeting moments in the archives?[2] How do we engage with an archive and a discipline very much tied to imperialism and colonial violence? How do historians make space for a cultural and social history of the enslaved while recognizing the condition of slavery, which betokens alienation, abjection, and social death? While Trouillot acknowledged that "history is the fruit of power," it is for this reason that we must study its production: "Power itself is never so transparent that its analysis becomes superfluous." Indeed, Trouillot argued that "the ultimate mark of power may be its invisibility; the ultimate challenge, the exposition of its roots."[3] The three articles under consideration here reveal the fraught relationship historians have with the archive of slavery and the ways in which we might address the silences that abound in it.

One of the fundamental challenges historians of slavery face is how to exhume the lives of the enslaved from the archive of slavery. Saidiya Hartman begins "The Dead Book Revisited" by asking: "How do we attend to black death? How do we find life where only traces of destructions remain?"[4] Reflecting on two of her previous

ENGLISH LANGUAGE NOTES

59:1, April 2021 DOI 10.1215/00138282-8815104
© 2021 Regents of the University of Colorado

works, *Lose Your Mother* (2006) and "Venus in Two Acts" (2008), Hartman raises questions about the silences and violence of the colonial archive, in particular how historians can create space for thinking about possibilities of life, grief, and mourning in the "ever growing archive of black death."[5] For Hartman, the dearth of empirical evidence about the lived experiences of enslaved individuals called her to explore "a series of speculative arguments . . . the what might have been."[6] Hartman's work challenges disciplinary methodologies in allowing space for imagining and responsibly speculating on the lives of enslaved individuals from archival fragments.

Responding to Hartman's work, Stephanie E. Smallwood exposes the methodological limits of the discipline of history in "The Politics of the Archive and History's Accountability to the Enslaved." She traces a historiography of scholars who have pressed against the limits of the archive and written the enslaved into history. For Smallwood, slavery's archive always seeks to conceal. It provides empirical evidence and quantitative information for histories of slavery and the slave trade, but these numbers deny the human experience, allow us to take comfort in abstraction, and reveal themselves "for the fictions that they were—false representations meant to make a stark political contest over the commodification of a human life as a natural and foregone conclusion."[7] The archive seeks to disavow, however, that there is always an impermeable counterhistory bubbling at the surface. This counterhistory is accountable to the enslaved, and it requires historians to imagine and reveal what cannot be verified by the archive.

Whereas Smallwood's work focuses on methodological approaches to deal with the archive's silences, Simon P. Newman's work illustrates how the archive both obscures and reveals. In "Freedom-Seeking Slaves in England and Scotland, 1700–1780," Newman begins his analysis of a runaway advertisement with a series of questions about the fugitive's life that may always allude us. Based on an analysis of more than eight hundred runaway advertisements in England and Scotland, Newman reveals an often-silenced history of metropolitan slavery. His work includes a number of statistics about these advertisements and fugitive bondspeople in the metropole. Despite the detailed information advertisements provide, however, Newman is left to ponder "what might have been."[8] Runaway advertisements embody the tension between enslaved people being everywhere in the archive yet conspicuously silent. Often written by slave owners or overseers, they were meant to help identify and apprehend the runaway. Runaway advertisements give detailed descriptions of enslaved people's bodies, speculate on their whereabouts, and reveal kin relations on neighboring plantations. Despite all the information the advertisements glean, the enslaved individual's personhood is almost absent. It is here that we see the effect of white colonial power on the archive, where enslaved people are visible on the outside, yet their experiences remain unknown.

The different approaches to and meditations on slavery's archive that these articles analyze speak to the reverberations of violence and silence that continue to attend black life in the Americas. Hartman speaks of the renewed visibility of state violence against black people in North America and connects this to its early modern legacies. Slavery still haunts the Americas—in the US prison system, in the killing of black individuals by police, and in the Caribbean, where social and political disablement prevents equitable access to health care, causing high rates of illness and impairment in already marginalized (i.e., racialized, poor, indigenous) communities. The epistemic violence that makes black death a "non-event" in the archives of slavery structures black dispossession even today. We must never ignore that the living and the dead are intimately connected. As Trouillot reminds us: "We are never as steeped in history as when we pretend not to be, but if we stop pretending we may gain in understanding what we lose in false innocence. Naiveté is often an excuse for those who exercise power. For those upon whom that power is exercised, naiveté is always a mistake."[9]

STEFANIE HUNT-KENNEDY is a historian of the Caribbean and the Atlantic world and of disability history at the University of New Brunswick. She is author of *Between Fitness and Death: Disability and Slavery in the Caribbean* (2020), which explores the constitutive relationship between disability, antiblack racism, and slavery in the Caribbean from the sixteenth to the nineteenth centuries.

Notes

1   Trouillot, *Silencing the Past*, 73.
2   This question is inspired by the work of Marisa J. Fuentes, who challenges us to rethink the way the historical discipline deals with archival absence (*Dispossessed Lives*).
3   Trouillot, *Silencing the Past*, xix.
4   Hartman, "The Dead Book Revisited," 208.
5   Hartman, "The Dead Book Revisited," 212.
6   Hartman, "The Dead Book Revisited," 210.
7   Smallwood, "Politics of the Archive," 126.
8   Quotation from Hartman, "The Dead Book Revisited," 210. Examples of this kind of speculation are found in Newman, "Freedom-Seeking Slaves," 1140–41, 1145, 1156, 1158.
9   Trouillot, *Silencing the Past*, xix.

Works Cited

Fuentes, Marisa J. *Dispossessed Lives: Enslaved Women, Violence, and the Archive.* Philadelphia: University of Pennsylvania Press, 2016.

Hartman, Saidiya. "The Dead Book Revisited." *History of the Present* 6, no. 2 (2016): 208–15.

Newman, Simon P. "Freedom-Seeking Slaves in England and Scotland, 1700–1780." *English Historical Review*, no. 570 (2019): 1136–68.

Smallwood, Stephanie E. "The Politics of the Archive and History's Accountability to the Enslaved." *History of the Present* 6, no. 2 (2016): 117–32.

Trouillot, Michel-Rolph. *Silencing the Past: Power and the Production of History.* Boston: Beacon, 1995.

Ghostly Outlines

CHERENE SHERRARD-JOHNSON

W hy acknowledge the non-event of black death?" asks Saidiya Hartman.[1] In light of protests incited by the murders of George Floyd in Minneapolis; Ahmaud Arbery in Glynn County, Georgia; and Breonna Taylor in Louisville, this question resonates with urgent frequency. The events of spring 2020 throughout the United States underscored that the political platform of Black Indigenous People of Color has not changed in four hundred years. Hartman summates this platform beautifully: "the abolition of the carceral world, the abolition of capitalism . . . [and] a remaking of the social order."[2] Police brutality, strategic disenfranchisement, and state and intimate violence are all outgrowths of racial capitalism. As long as these systems persist, we remained trapped in a fatal loop that keeps us entangled with our past and continues to produce a scholarship of recovery and longing in the face of an "ever growing archive of black death."[3]

Three recent essays, Simon P. Newman's "Freedom-Seeking Slaves in England and Scotland, 1700–1780," Saidiya Hartman's "The Dead Book Revisited," and Stephanie E. Smallwood's "The Politics of the Archive and History's Accountability to the Enslaved," offer distinct but convergent takes on these recovery efforts in the face of the elusiveness of the archive. They raise the problems of what to do with the documentary fragment (Smallwood), the asterisk (Hartman), and the runaway advertisement (Newman). However meaningfully scholars engage these tantalizing object lessons in counterhistory, they rarely produce the longed-for authenticity of the unmediated subaltern voice.

Demanding that documents do more than speak, Smallwood craves to know her subjects' interiors. Can we achieve intimate access by "asking different questions and seeking different answers"?[4] Is emotional revelation found only in the realm of the imagination, through poetry, visual art, or fiction? Smallwood argues that sustained attentiveness reveals what the official archive suppresses: the counterfacts in the ledgers' margins. Her "longing for stories the archive disavows" undergirds her metacommentary on the "documentary fragment."[5] In her desire for more than a "ghostly outline," she aligns herself with Hartman's intent to put flesh on numbers.[6] Smallwood urges historians to follow Hartman's lead with regard to narrative experimentation. The ghostly outline she references isn't the longed-for voice; it's a metahistorical method that works to dismantle the structures of power that

ENGLISH LANGUAGE NOTES

59:1, April 2021 DOI 10.1215/00138282-8815115
© 2021 Regents of the University of Colorado

produced subaltern subjects. Smallwood stays in close conversation with Hartman around the "ethics of historical representation." Where she sets herself apart is in her understanding that such considerations do not "re-violate the enslaved but rather [disrupt] the archive's naturalization of the violence it narrates."[7]

Hartman urges us to forge new pathways and undertake writing practices that redress slavery's violations. To this end, she revisits her essay "Venus in Two Acts" not with new evidentiary material but with a bifocal lens that allows her to inhabit "the entanglement of that time with our own, by thinking inside the circle of slavery" and also potentially to capture and celebrate some of the beauty borne in the terror of the hold.[8] Faced with "stark outlines" (Hartman) and "ghostly" "fragments" (Smallwood), scholars must invent imaginative toolkits, such as Hartman's critical fabulation or the alternative narrative forms Smallwood hopes will result in a more rigorous and reflective reading against the grain. One such example is Cheryl Finley's tracing of the evolution and persistence of the eighteenth-century engraving of a slave ship as an icon that retains purchase into the twenty-first century through visual artists' reiterations. As scholars continue to plumb the archive and theorize the ethics of retrieval, it's imperative that they work in tandem with artists aiming to repossess the past symbolically through what Finley calls "mnemonic aesthetics": a "ritualized politics of remembering."[9]

Simon P. Newman's exegesis of early eighteenth-century fugitive notices challenges notions of archival silence and deceptive sentiment that the air in England was too pure for any slave to breathe. Through careful collation he reveals the contours and constraints of enslaved life in London. Responsible speculation and expert inference are the only ways to glean what might motivate an enslaved servant to run. A number of those who absconded worked as domestic servants, grooms, or skilled artisans. Newman notes that the postings often described their wardrobes, identifying fancy waistcoats and other ornaments as well as any scarification (rare) or iron/collars.[10] He reads advertisements such as "handsome Negro Boy" for sale alongside popular commissioned paintings of elites attended by young, liveried Black servants.[11] These youths served as status symbols, which added to their cachet. Newman surmises that some slaves ran when threatened with return to the colonies and plantation slavery, which gives us some sense of how the enslaved understood the varying severity of bondage. Careful, cross-disciplinary scrutiny of runaway ads can serve as an alternative to, or augmentation of, the slave-ship manifest. Collating the advertisements provides a sense of sociality absent from numerical data.

Newman's microhistories stand alongside Erica Armstrong Dunbar's *Never Caught*: a book-length exegesis of a runaway ad tracing the enslavement and liberty of Ona Judge, who absconded from the household of President George Washington.[12] Dunbar relies on the written documentation of the Washington family's pursuit as well as Judge's dictated testimony. Dunbar lets the documents speak but provides a textured, critical account of Judge's motivation that "fulfills our yearning for romance" for the "heroic actor whose agency triumphs over the forces of oppression."[13] Of course, we would be hard-pressed to call Judge's story a romance. A free life in eighteenth-century Maine was still a life beset by hardship, loss, and persecution. While the depth of records that Dunbar mines is not available to New-man, he offers a glimpse into the complexity of urban servitude in eighteenth-century London by weaving together documentary fragments. His acknowledgment of his positionality and the limits of his archive lead him to engage performance artists to respond to the advertisements; this is the type of creative act against the grain of historiography that Smallwood encourages.

Scholars like Stephen Best have begun to ask what happens if we channel in a different direction the energy Black studies has invested in taking down Hegel's infamous pronouncement that Africans are unhistorical. Best is concerned that responding to irrecoverable traumas and archival fixation on the "abject sublime" (Hartman) may occlude our understandings of Blackness and foreclose other ave-nues for belonging and community. He wants to draw limits around the "impera-tive towards melancholy in the historiography of slavery."[14] Almost in anticipation of Best, Hartman offers waywardness as a "disruptive poetics" to the overdeter-mined shadow of the hold.[15]

As a scholar and writer who has also been seduced by the archival turn, I appreciate Smallwood's advocacy of attentive listening, a slow interpretive process that enfleshes the ghostly outline, whether it is in the visual artists' continued inter-rogation of the slave-ship icon or in Hartman's practice of waywardness that cele-brates without sensation enslaved women's fugitive arc. Together, these essays advo-cate for and enact various forms of scholarly inhabitation that serve as an anodyne to a melancholy preoccupation with the irretrievable. By thoughtfully probing the dark recesses of the archive, they illuminate how "unaccountable" acts of resistance, from a slave-ship uprising to small, daily acts of refusal, can yield sustaining mod-els of resilience.

....

CHERENE SHERRARD-JOHNSON is Sally Mead Hands-Bascom Professor of English at the University of Wisconsin–Madison, where she teaches African American and Caribbean literature, visual culture, and feminist theory. She is author of *Portraits of the New Negro Woman: Visual and Literary Culture in the Harlem Renaissance* (2007), *Dorothy West's Paradise: A Biography of Class and Color* (2012), and two poetry collections: *Vixen* (2017) and *Grimoire* (2020).

Notes

1   Hartman, "The Dead Book Revisited," 209.

2   Hartman, interview.

3   Hartman, "The Dead Book Revisited," 212.

4   Smallwood, "Politics of the Archive," 124.

5   Smallwood, "Politics of the Archive," 119.

6   Smallwood, "Politics of the Archive," 128; Hartman, "The Dead Book Revisited," 211.

7   Smallwood, "Politics of the Archive," 120, 129.

8   Hartman, "The Dead Book Revisited," 212.

9   Finley, *Committed to Memory*, 9.

10   Newman, "Freedom-Seeking Slaves," 1161.

11   Newman, "Freedom-Seeking Slaves," 1150.

12   Dunbar, *Never Caught*.

13   Smallwood, "Politics of the Archive," 128.

14   Best, *None Like Us*, 22.

15   Hartman, "The Dead Book Revisited," 210.

Works Cited

Best, Stephen. *None Like Us: Blackness, Belonging, Aesthetic Life*. Durham, NC: Duke University Press, 2018.

Dunbar, Erica Armstrong. *Never Caught: The Washingtons' Relentless Pursuit of Their Runaway Slave, Ona Judge*. New York: Atria, 2017.

Finley, Cheryl. *Committed to Memory: The Art of the Slave Ship Icon*. Princeton, NJ: Princeton University Press, 2018.

Hartman, Saidiya. "The Dead Book Revisited." *History of the Present* 6, no. 2 (2016): 208–15.

Hartman, Saidiya. Interview with Catherine Damman on insurgent histories and the abolitionist imaginary. *Artforum*, July 14, 2020. www.artforum.com/interviews/saidiya -hartman-83579.

Newman, Simon P. "Freedom-Seeking Slaves in England and Scotland, 1700–1780." *English Historical Review*, no. 570 (2019): 1136–68.

Smallwood, Stephanie E. "The Politics of the Archive and History's Accountability to the Enslaved." *History of the Present* 6, no. 2 (2016): 117–32.

Slavery's Archive and the Matter of Black Atlantic Lives

MARISA J. FUENTES

How do we redress the ongoing violence of slavery's archive and its effects on our present? Thinking with three recent articles that address the history of slavery and the slave trade in the Atlantic world, the following short reflection considers different approaches to contextualizing Black lives in the past and present.[1] Two of the three articles, by Stephanie E. Smallwood and Saidiya Hartman, critically engage Hartman's 2008 essay "Venus in Two Acts."[2] The third article, Simon P. Newman's "Freedom-Seeking Slaves in England and Scotland, 1700–1780," explores hundreds of eighteenth-century newspaper advertisements for runaway enslaved (and "servant") men and women in England and Scotland. For vastly different audiences and to different ends, Hartman, Smallwood, and Newman contend with the erasures of enslaved people from the archives and national or imperial historiographies. Seemingly disconnected by geographies, methods, and fields, these articles, brought together in conversation, invite us to consider the state of historical research on Black lives and how to approach their erasure in the field of history.

In the wake of her previous work and a summer of intense police brutality, Hartman writes about the stakes of engaging slavery's archive in the enduring context of Black death, the seemingly unchanged patterns of anti-Black violence, and how we must make room for the ways in which Black people live, mourn, and steal away to grieve in the midst of this ongoing terror.[3] Smallwood, in revisiting "Venus in Two Acts," reassesses her own book, *Saltwater Slavery*, to demonstrate the method of exploring the "counter-factual"—what is in the archive but is denied—as the starting point to writing histories of slavery (or the slave trade). Smallwood also offers us an incredibly thorough historiography of the uses of slavery's archive from the early twentieth century—when the planter's perspective prevailed in authority and objectivity—to the 1970s, when social historians shifted their method to "bottom up" by using an "abundance" of archival material to tell the enslaved story. What Smallwood points out, important to us for this short reflection, is the move to quantitative methods—the counting and tallying and charting of bodies, demographics, and geographies that gave historians "evidence" that enslaved people shaped

ENGLISH LANGUAGE NOTES

59:1, April 2021 DOI 10.1215/00138282-8815140
© 2021 Regents of the University of Colorado

their environments and families and enacted resistance. However, these data did little to elaborate the social and intimate lives of enslaved people. Smallwood explains, "What is lost in uncritical celebration of the new approach is attention to how it also helped to sediment a theory of historical knowledge production that figured the archive as merely a repository of free-floating empirical facts to be lifted off the page by the researcher."[4] This critique provides the entry point for a closer look at Newman's article.

Newman uses quantitative methods to examine eighteenth-century newspapers from Scotland and England for evidence that legal slavery existed and persisted in the United Kingdom despite the absence of explicit laws. With hundreds of runaway ads (and others for sale) attempting to reclaim people in the language of "property," Newman argues that slavery existed in the United Kingdom for people of African descent and was distinct from other forms of servitude in the region. More than this, he asserts that the threat of New World slavery—of being sent to the Caribbean plantation system—was ever present, making servitude for Africans and their descendants in the United Kingdom unique among the servant classes. Newman convincingly makes the case that slavery was pervasive in the eighteenth-century United Kingdom. The corpus of runaway ads exposes the violence and surveillance against enslaved people in the region. But we must still ask: What are the consequences of reproducing archival representations of enslaved people as "quantitative data" to prove these points? This method raises larger questions about the disavowal of slavery's existence in the UK historical guild and the demands for a particular kind of empiricism required to make Black lives visible.

Both Hartman and Smallwood call for a crucial encounter with the broader structures of knowledge production and the effects that histories of racial subjugation have on our present. Therefore, why does the historiography deny the existence of slavery in the United Kingdom? Is it because it threatens the "mystique of British anti-racism" that represents Britain as the bastion of abolition activism, liberalism, and multiculturalism?[5] Or perhaps it would force a reckoning with the continued marginalization and underrepresentation of Black British scholars in the UK academy?[6] In what ways does the disavowal of slavery's legality in the United Kingdom help the continued denial of the responsibility of the UK to its Black subjects and citizens, many of whom have been part of the state/empire since the time Newman explores if not well before? What would it mean to acknowledge this history? Is there a fear of being made fiscally responsible for its harm and violence?[7] Hartman makes plain the unequivocal links between the past and our present conditions— the precarity, incarceration, early death—that make imperative the need to ask questions of the historical guild and society that go beyond the empirical.[8] For it matters little what "evidence" one marshals to prove Black existence when Black people have been demanding recognition since their arrival in the western Atlantic world. Following Smallwood, "We might say . . . that what is at issue in the writing of histories of modern racial slavery is not the archive per se, but rather the critical philosophical assumptions that shape and structure our understandings of history."[9]

MARISA J. FUENTES is Presidential Term Chair in African American History and associate professor of history and of women's and gender studies at Rutgers University. She is author of *Dispossessed Lives: Enslaved Women, Violence, and the Archive* (2016); coeditor of *Scarlet and Black: Slavery and Dispossession in Rutgers History*, volumes 1–3 (2016, 2020, 2021); and the "Slavery and the Archive" special issue of *History of the Present* (2016).

Notes

1   I want to be very specific here to qualify the records under discussion. All three articles I address are engaged with records of slavery from the seventeenth and eighteenth centuries that are generated primarily by the slave-trading and slave-holding classes of the United Kingdom and the Caribbean. These records from the UK colonial archive are qualitatively distinct from records of the nineteenth-century antebellum-era United States, from postbellum interviews with formerly enslaved people, and from the surviving "slave narratives" of those eras.

2   Hartman, "Venus in Two Acts."

3   Hartman, "The Dead Book Revisited." In the summer of 2016, Black communities throughout the United States reeled from the shootings by police officers of Alton Sterling in Baton Rouge, Louisiana; Philando Castile, outside St. Paul, Minnesota; and Delrawn Small of Brooklyn, New York. These killings initiated an intense backlash of protest across the country and a continued sense of unease in Black communities (Bellafante, "Road Rage, Then a Shot").

4   Smallwood, "Politics of the Archive," 124.

5   Perry, *London Is the Place for Me*, 100–101.

6   Andrews and Palmer, "Why Black Studies Matter."

7   See Beckles, *Britain's Black Debt*; and Hall et al., *Legacies of British Slave-Ownership*.

8   Hartman, "The Dead Book Revisited," 208.

9   Smallwood, "The Politics of the Archive," 126–27.

Works Cited

Andrews, Kehinde, and Lisa Palmer. "Why Black Studies Matter." *Discovery Society*, no. 2 (2013): 1–4.

Beckles, Hilary M. *Britain's Black Debt: Reparations for Caribbean Slavery and Native Genocide*. Kingston: University of the West Indies Press, 2013.

Bellafante, Ginia. "Road Rage, Then a Shot. For a Police Officer, It Is Called Self-Defense." *New York Times*, November 9, 2017. www.nytimes .com/2017/11/09/nyregion/wayne-isaacs -acquittal-police-shooting-.html.

Hall, Catherine, Nicholas Draper, Keith McClelland, Katie Donington, and Rachel Lang. *Legacies of British Slave-Ownership: Colonial Slavery and the Formation of Victorian Britain*. Cambridge: Cambridge University Press, 2014.

Hartman, Saidiya. "The Dead Book Revisited." *History of the Present* 6, no. 2 (2016): 208–15.

Hartman, Saidiya. "Venus in Two Acts." *Small Axe*, no. 26 (2008): 1–14.

Newman, Simon P. "Freedom-Seeking Slaves in England and Scotland, 1700–1780." *English Historical Review*, no. 570 (2019): 1136–68.

Perry, Kennetta. *London Is the Place for Me: Black Britons, Citizenship, and the Politics of Race*. New York: Oxford University Press, 2016.

Smallwood, Stephanie E. "The Politics of the Archive and History's Accountability to the Enslaved." *History of the Present* 6, no. 2 (2016): 117–32.

Keep up to date on new scholarship

Issue alerts are a great way to stay current on all the cutting-edge scholarship from your favorite Duke University Press journals. This free service delivers tables of contents directly to your inbox, informing you of the latest groundbreaking work as soon as it is published.

To sign up for issue alerts:

1. Visit **dukeu.press/register** and register for an account. You do not need to provide a customer number.

2. After registering, visit **dukeu.press/alerts**.

3. Go to "Latest Issue Alerts" and click on "Add Alerts."

4. Select as many publications as you would like from the pop-up window and click "Add Alerts."

read.dukeupress.edu/journals　　

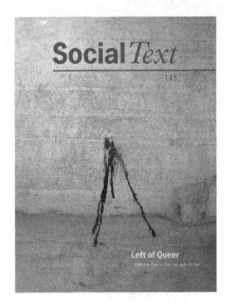